I0641274

Hands and Hearts

HANDS AND HEARTS

A History of Courtship in America

ELLEN K. ROTHMAN

Basic Books, Inc., Publishers

NEW YORK

Library of Congress Cataloging in Publication Data

Rothman, Ellen K., 1950–
  Hands and hearts.

  Includes bibliographical references and index.
  1. Courtship—United States—History. 2. United
States—Social life and customs. I. Title.
HQ801.R85 1984   306.7′34′0973   83-45261
ISBN 0-465-02880-2

Copyright © 1984 by Ellen K. Rothman
Printed in the United States of America
Designed by Vincent Torre
10 9 8 7 6 5 4 3 2 1

For Davey,

olov ha-shalom

CONTENTS

Contents

PART III / 1870–1920

ACKNOWLEDGMENTS

I F I HAD KNOWN at the beginning of this project how difficult and lonely it would at times be, I might not have undertaken it. That I had so few moments of regret is due in large part to the kindness and generosity of the people thanked here.

The search for sources led me to the archives and libraries listed at the front of the notes. I am grateful for all the help I received there. I spent many months at the Schlesinger Library at Radcliffe and accumulated a large debt to Kathy Kraft, Eva Moseley, and Karen Morgan for their interest, patience, and good humor. When I became an itinerant researcher, I enjoyed the warm hospitality of Barry and Kristin O'Connell in Amherst, Ruth and Alan Shwartzman in New York, Marjorie Waxman and Charles Bosk in Philadelphia, Susan Schreiber in Washington, Kay Huggins in Pittsburgh, Bea and Irv Fink in Indianapolis, Seth and Franny Taft in Cleveland, Marcia Baum and Frank Untermyer in Chicago, Daniel Strouse in Madison, Joan Seidl in St. Paul, Abigail Ginzberg, Catherine Lewis and Andrew Leavitt in San Francisco, and Barbara Evans in Pasadena.

This book grew out of a dissertation, work on which was generously supported by a Crown Fellowship at Brandeis University. Nancy F. Cott and David Hackett Fischer were constructive critics of that earlier version. Their enthusiasm and confidence were important ingredients in my decision to make the thesis into something more. I only hope they are not disappointed.

ix

Acknowledgments

John Demos provided excellent direction for the dissertation and something less tangible, and even more valuable, for the book: he was a sympathetic listener, an unfailing source of encouragement, and a warm friend. The extent of my scholarly debt to Tony Rotundo will be evident in the notes; my personal debt to him, for being such a good critic, colleague, and friend, is greater still. Three people whom I was lucky enough to have as my teachers at an earlier time in my life also deserve thanks: Sarah L. Cooper, Barry O'Connell, and Gail Thain Parker Wickes.

Susan Bolotin, Ellen Fitzpatrick, Elaine Tyler May, Joan Seidl, and Michael Wheeler took time from their own work to give careful readings to earlier drafts of the book. Somehow each of them knew exactly the right recipe for mixing reassurance and criticism; the effect on my spirits, if not always on my prose, was wonderfully therapeutic. I am deeply grateful to them all.

My research assistant Dana Snyder, my typists Dianne Saran and Terry Kovich, my agent Raphael Sagalyn, my legal adviser Thomas Rothman, my editor Phoebe Hoss, and the staff of the Henry A. Murray Center at Radcliffe all did their parts to see the project through to completion. The Andrew W. Mellon Foundation provided financial support during my year as a Radcliffe Research Scholar.

The contributions of my friends were largely invisible, but I cannot imagine the book without them. In spite of being thousands of miles away, Abby Ginzberg, Cathy Lewis, and Joan Seidl managed to keep close tabs on the state of the book and its author. Nearer to home, Steve Cohen, John Englund, Lisa Gelfand, Jim Glickman, Barbara, Steve, Michael, and Rebecca Neel, Peter and Trudy O'Connell, and Cindy Taft made sure that I was well taken care of. During the final stage of the project, an errant ball put my eyes out of commission, and I have Michael, Candace, and Katrin Wheeler and Dr. Frederic Breed to thank for making that ordeal into an adventure. Holly Sidford has been lightening my burdens for the past ten years. I have relied on her understanding and love, and she has never let me down.

Acknowledgments

Thanks to the generosity of my family, I was able to do much of the writing in one of my favorite and the world's most beautiful places. My parents have shown their love and support in so many ways over the years that I cannot even begin to express my gratitude to them here.

This book is dedicated to the memory of my grandfather, who lived almost long enough to see it completed. I like to think that if he had, he would have found in these pages some of the great pleasure his stories of the past gave me.

Hands and Hearts

Introduction

O N THE AFTERNOON of December 30, 1852, Lucy Webb
and Rutherford Hayes were married at Lucy's home in Cincinnati. Three months later, the newlyweds had a daguerreotype
taken so that, as twenty-one-year-old Lucy explained, "as old age
draws on we might see what we once were."[1] What *we* see today
in the image that survives is a young couple seated side by side:
The man, in a black suit and starched white collar, appears
handsome, self-possessed, and serious. The woman, in a silk
dress with full sleeves and a brooch at the throat, is smiling
slightly; her dark hair is parted in the middle and drawn back
at the neck.

What Lucy Webb Hayes saw was a look of "love, happiness,
and a tinge of pride" in her new mate. "He seems to have just
said, 'This is my wife,'" she wrote. Her own expression also
pleased her: "It has rather a meek, subdued air, clinging to its
only support—remove that and it will droop." Rutherford did

not record his reactions to the portrait, but he did reveal his feelings about the union it commemorated. Two weeks before the trip to the photographer's studio, the future president of the United States had noted in his diary: "Almost two months married. . . . This is indeed life. The love of wedded wife!"[2]

Rutherford and Lucy Hayes, gazing intently into the camera, were just beginning a marriage that would last nearly forty years, but already they had shared a world of experience. Their relationship had grown from acquaintance to intimacy, from interest to commitment; they had courted, fallen in love, become pledged, and been married. Together they had taken what Rutherford Hayes called "the step of life which makes or mars the whole after journey."[3] In this book, we will explore what it was like to take that step and the ones leading up to it during two hundred years of American history.

Marriage may no longer appear to make or mar "the whole after journey," but it remains one of the most significant and universal life events. Most of us subscribe to Rutherford Hayes's belief that there is no "source or truer, purer happiness" than marriage.[4] Even at a time when record numbers of Americans are delaying marriage, remaining single, or filing for divorce, marriage continues to represent the ideal expression of romantic love and sexual fidelity. As men and women come together and begin, even if they do not complete, the transition to marriage, they reveal a great deal about what they expect of themselves, of each other, and of marriage.

Although the search for someone to love—and ultimately to marry—takes place today in different settings from those of a century, or even a decade, ago, it has not lost its urgency. Few individuals come to maturity without experiencing the delight, pain, confusion, excitement that accompanies the choice of a mate. Now we talk about "relationships," not courtships; about boyfriends and roommates, not suitors and beaux. Still, we easily understand and share many of the feelings expressed by people who made the transition to marriage in another time and place. We recognize in them our own desire for the intimacy, security, and companionship that marriage promises, and our

Introduction

own fear of disappointment. We, too, know the vulnerability and the strength that come with love. And yet our connection to these people is no less real for being distant. We see ourselves in them the way we might find a family resemblance in a photograph of an ancestor who died long before we were born.

This book, in a sense, is an album of old photographs. If one views them quickly, the result is a primitive moving picture; if one examines each carefully, a sequence of distinct images emerges. The images are created much the way an archaeologist assembles the material remains of a lost culture. Sometimes, like the archaeologist, we find only shards and fragments; other times, we come upon pieces of evidence that scarcely show the mark of time. All are useful to us: the elliptical reference to a call paid or received, a caress exchanged, or a promise made; the daily diarist's account of a suit pursued or an offer spurned; the long letters written in anger, hope, or uncertainty. Taken together, they allow us to reconstruct the "life cycle" of courtship, from casual social visiting to betrothal, from flirtation to sexual intimacy, from the decision to marry to the exchange of vows.

While the concept of life cycle sets the general direction of our course, it does not provide specific coordinates for every step along the way. Courtship was not a linear progression but an amalgam of expectation, experience, and convention. In surveying this familiar but largely uncharted territory, we will explore more than the outward features of the landscape. The transition to marriage was both a private journey and a public rite of passage. The nature of courtship defies precise explanations. The vicissitudes of love, the selection of a mate, the decisions people make as they approach marriage are always somewhat mysterious to an outsider. When the outsider is not a contemporary but a historian, the element of the unknowable increases. Even if we can never re-create completely the experience of courtship in the past, we can uncover, examine closely, and try to make sense out of whatever clues have been left behind.

It is in personal documents, far more than in vital statistics, sermon literature, or sentimental novels, that such clues are

Introduction

found. Unfortunately, while this approach has the power to illuminate a world that is otherwise lost to us, it leaves whole regions entirely in the dark. Large segments of the population—blacks, immigrants, the poor—lie beyond the reach of research that relies on the written record of the past. It is not that no one in these groups wrote letters or kept diaries, but that those who did were such a small minority that they cannot be used as the basis for historical generalization. The relative scarcity of documents generated by working-class, immigrant, and black Americans also reflects the biases of most historical societies and libraries which have, until recently, limited their collecting to the papers of those families who belonged to the white, native-born, Protestant middle and upper classes.

The evidence in this study is drawn from the reminiscences, diaries, and letters of 350 American women and men who reached adulthood in the years between 1770 and 1920.* As members of the white, Protestant middle class living in the settled areas of the North, they were the kind of people who produced, and whose descendants preserved, personal documents.[5]

The locale of this book is Main Street, not Hester Street. The dramatis personae lived in boardinghouses, not crowded tenements; in modern suburban cottages, not tarpaper shacks. They were more likely to spend their youth in a schoolroom than in a sweatshop. They made their living as teachers, ministers, and lawyers, rather than as laborers, field hands, or mill operatives. These men and women enjoyed a higher educational and occupational status than their working-class contemporaries, but few possessed the wealth or social position of the nation's élite. They took a two-week summer holiday in the White Mountains rather than a grand tour of Europe; they were more comfortable saving than spending money, more likely to borrow than lend. Some went on to careers in public life, a few to fame and fortune; but at the time of courtship, such distinctions lay in the future. They were middle-class youths without the disadvantages of the poor or the advantages of the rich.

*See Note on Sources, pages 312–15 for a discussion of how the individuals were selected.

6

Introduction

Especially in the earlier period, many of these young people were raised on farms, but few chose to devote themselves to farming. The men preferred to pursue careers in law, medicine, business, or the ministry. Many of them spent some time as teachers, but for most, teaching was a short-term arrangement, an interim measure until they were able to take up other work. However, with the rapid growth of high schools, colleges, and universities in the second half of the nineteenth century, ever more men made teaching a career. College professors are well represented among the couples who appear in the later chapters of the book.

There were other changes in the occupations followed by the men. After 1830, the proportion of the nation's college graduates who joined the ministry declined; and at the end of the nineteenth century, an educated young man was more likely to become an engineer, a politician, or a journalist than a minister. Thus, among the men whose courtships are considered in the earlier chapters, the ministry and the law were the most common careers; the men who courted in the late nineteenth and early twentieth centuries were aspiring architects, professors, and scientists as well as doctors and lawyers.*

The women these men wooed were, on the whole, better educated than their contemporaries. In the early nineteenth century, the norm was a term or two's attendance at a ladies' seminary or academy after completing the course at the local school. By the end of the century, public high schools, women's colleges, and coeducational universities were widening women's educational horizons. In 1870, more than half of the country's sixteen thousand high school graduates were female. Thirty years later, six times as many Americans completed high school, and 60 per-

---

*It is difficult to give a precise occupational breakdown of the men in the group, since many young men pursued several careers, in sequence or simultaneously. According to Burton Bledstein, "career patterns in the mid-nineteenth century were still uncertain as men jumped from profession to profession. . . . Lax entrance requirements facilitated occupational fluidity even in the established professions."[6] Levi Coman is a good example of this phenomenon. His wife described his career this way: "He came to Newark [Ohio] to teach the select school for boys. Later he organized and was superintendant of the union schools. At the time of our marriage [1848] he became a partner of my father in the store. After a few years he closed that business and read law."[7]

cent of them were women. By 1910, nearly one quarter of all eighteen-year-old women were enrolled in school.[8] While the middle-class woman of the 1890s was better educated than her grandmother before the Civil War, she followed a similar career pattern. If teaching was no longer the only, it remained the leading, profession for middle-class women. Many of the women whose courtships are studied here worked before marriage, all but a few of them as teachers.

Americans coming of age around the turn of the century lived in a wider world than their parents and grandparents had known. One consequence of the improvements in transportation, the spread of higher education and paid employment for women, and the growth of cities was the shrinking place of personal writing in the lives of middle-class people. While young men and women did not entirely abandon diary keeping and letter writing, they were less committed, perhaps because less dependent on, written forms of communication than earlier generations had been. Since the interpretations developed in this book are based on evidence uncovered in such personal writing, it deserves a short history of its own.

Even though it was an unusual man, and still more unusual woman, who paused in later life to transcribe his or her recollections, a substantial number of autobiographical works were written and many published in the nineteenth century. Most of them, however, pay little heed to the transition to marriage, and those that do, reveal more about the external circumstances, than the subjective experience, of courtship. Diaries and journals represent a more immediate, if not always more illuminating, record of everyday life. Especially before the Civil War, diary keeping was an established part of many people's routine. Thirteen-year-old Louisa Jane Trumbull explained, "In Keeping a journal I at first did it because my sisters kept one—afterwards I wrote because it was the wish of my mother and now it is done not only to serve as means of being employed about something useful and proper but because it is a source of pleasure to me."[9] Louisa was an unusual diarist; she attended to what was going on within as well as around her. Most nine-

Introduction

teenth-century journals were more reportorial than reflective. They chronicled the cheese made, the yarn spun, the hay cut, the potatoes dug; they commented on the weather, the preacher's sermon, or the new dancing master. More introspective diarists usually took the soul for their subject and were more likely to record the search for salvation than for a mate. Thus many diaries contain only an entry or two about courtship. Fortunately, there are others that provide a vivid, day-by-day picture of the outward life, and occasionally the feelings, of a young person approaching marriage. Diary writing persisted into the early twentieth century, especially among women, but more as a means of record keeping than of self-expression.

Correspondence was by far the most common form of personal writing, and letters exchanged between young women and men during courtship provide a remarkably full record of the ideas and experiences surrounding the transition to marriage. These letters are more than the artifacts of a relationship; in many cases they were, for a time, the relationship itself. They were as different as the people who wrote them: Some overflow with ideas about politics, religion, literature; others narrate the events of daily life—pies baked, shirts mended, fields plowed. Some shine with wit; others ache with awkwardness.

In this book, the emphasis is on the *content* of courtship correspondence, but the *form* also rewards careful study. There are important, if subtle, differences between correspondence characteristic of the half-century after Independence and that typical a hundred years later. These differences reflect the gradual erosion of a traditional part of early nineteenth century social life: correspondence as courtship. In 1786, a young Connecticut lawyer, writing to a young woman in the stilted language of his time, captured the spirit of the suitor as correspondent:

I am not so much a trespasser now even as you think of me—ten o'clock on Sabbath eve is frequently employed in less noble purposes than those which enrapture the friend or the Lover. . . . What untutored savage would have thought . . . that the feelings of the Heart can inspire the Head . . . give Expression to the Pen—and a voice to Letters

9

which the greatest Distance could not weaken—and that thus the interval of Absence, which separates friends may be happily filled up, by a frequent & mutual interchange of their friendly Communications.[10]

The "frequent & mutual interchange" of written communication was a new phenomenon when this letter was written. Mail service in the colonies was irregular, inconvenient, and costly. Many letters were sent by "personal conveyance" rather than by the "infrequent and cruelly expensive pre-Revolutionary mails." At the beginning of the war with Great Britain, America had only twenty-eight post offices. By 1789, there were a mere seventy-five to serve three million people. After 1800, the situation improved rapidly; and by the 1820s, people in the settled areas of the North could rely on fairly regular, if still costly, service.[11]

Between 1815 and 1840, a "transportation" revolution transformed the loosely connected colonies into a nation linked by roads, turnpikes, canals, and, by the 1840s, railroads. Mail traveled more easily and carried news between families and friends separated by ever-greater distances. In the 1790s, migrants from southern New England poured into the newly settled areas of Vermont, Maine, and New Hampshire. After 1810, the shift of population westward began, as the rich farming lands of the Genesee and Ohio countries were claimed. By the 1830s, the Old Northwest was filling up with the sons and daughters of the Middle States and New England. At the same time, migration from countryside to city swelled the urban population of the nation. All of this movement stretched old ties of consanguinity and affection and made possible the establishment of new ones. Letters were lifelines across time and space.

Not just the quantity but the quality of correspondence changed after 1800. Eighteenth-century letters fulfilled the obligation of family members to keep one another informed of their whereabouts, health, and prospects. In the 1780s and 1790s, letters were valued above all as evidence of the writer's well-being. A failure to appear "on schedule" was a sign that something was amiss. Epistles in this period invariably opened with a report on the writer's health and closed with a formal expression of his or her "duty."

Beginning in the early 1800s, the emphasis shifted. Correspondents were less likely to make health their primary concern—many mention it only in passing—or to write from a sense of obligation. Where the state of one's body and, to a lesser extent, of one's soul dominated eighteenth-century correspondence, the state of one's heart became a central theme in the nineteenth. This change is evident in letters exchanged between family members, but it is more conspicuous in the correspondence of friends and lovers. Increasingly after 1800, letters both demonstrated and deepened commitment between people who believed in the power of the written word. Although most of the letters cited here were written during periods of separation, it was not uncommon for a couple to correspond when apart only for a few hours. Many people shared the sentiments of the woman who observed that "a correspondence sometimes brings out more of the inner soul than long converse together."[12]

A pattern emerges in the correspondence of young women and men who courted in the first half of the nineteenth century: Men were more likely than women to complain that letters were answered too slowly or too cursorily. Both men and women were concerned about the appearance of their letters; but while men labored over elaborate, self-conscious expositions on romantic love, women's responses tended to be apologetic, brief, at times almost impersonal in tone. Few women presumed to give the "mountain-pile of information and advice on pretty much every topic within the range of philosophy or belles-lettres" with which more than one suitor filled his "love letters."[13] The fact that males were more expansive correspondents in this period reflects the prevailing stereotypes of men and women. Women's role was to embody rather than articulate the sentimental ideal. They were not expected to analyze or elaborate on what was theirs by nature; men, on the other hand, felt free to offer "learned and loving counsel on all possible subjects of womanly culture, physical, mental, and moral" in letters to their fiancées.[14]

Even as they eschewed the abstract discussions of which men

were so fond, women shared the conviction that letters were invaluable as a means to know, and be known by, a prospective mate. Couples could and did use correspondence to unburden their hearts, to confess their worst fears and their highest hopes, to share past mistakes and dreams for the future. Letters were a safe and, in some cases, the only way for men and women to get to know each other. The knowledge shared was emotional as well as biographical: "I think we ought to understand each other's love for each other," one midwesterner told her fiancé in 1866, "and we can do it no other way than by writing."[15]

By the last quarter of the nineteenth century, there were other ways. A man whose grandfather might have devoted his Sabbath leisure to letter writing would instead make weekly visits by train to a woman he was courting. During the week, he had time only for one or two quick notes, dashed off before leaving the office or after an evening out. Young women, who in an earlier period were overwhelmed by steady streams of long, intimate letters from suitors, now lamented that men were too busy to write. Reversing the pattern in which it was men who clamored for more and longer letters, a woman might have cause to object that her fiancé was "so hurried with business, [he] scarce had time for other thoughts."[16]

But young women were busy, too. By the 1880s and 1890s, they were occupied with high school or college, with jobs in classrooms, offices and shops, with charity work, music, and parties. The regular exchange of long letters between couples, a mainstay of courtship for over a century, became the exception where it had been the rule. Unless they were facing long-term, long-distance separations, men and women had little need—and little time—to maintain a serious correspondence. Improved transportation allowed couples greater face-to-face contact. The expansion of coeducational schools, the presence of single women in the workforce, the growth of cities and suburbs, all had the effect of increasing opportunities for young women and men to meet, and to court, without ever exchanging a single letter.

When they did write, their correspondence tended to be su-

Introduction

perficial, more a matter of good manners than the joint venture
in self-discovery that it had been for earlier generations. Fortunately for the historian, there are exceptions. Although the practice of keeping diaries and writing letters declined after 1900,
it persisted long enough for us to follow the story of
middle-class courtship into the first decades of the twentieth
century.

This book traces that story as it unfolded in the 150 years between the Treaty of Paris and the Treaty of Versailles. An epilogue presents an overview of the 1920 to 1980 period, drawn
from published literature on the attitudes, dating patterns, and
sexual behavior of recent generations of Americans. The organization of the study into three parts—1770–1840, 1830–1880, and
1870–1920—represents a narrative device rather than an analytic
scheme and is meant to help keep the reader oriented in time
rather than to delineate distinctive epochs. The dividing lines
are to a certain extent arbitrary. All three periods encompass
change; all could fairly be termed transitional. So as to explore
courtship on three levels at once—thought, affect, and behavior—I shall move forward and backward within each period.

The pattern, then, is not a simple one. We are probing several
layers of tissue: the ideas, feelings, and behavior of people in the
past. We are charting the stages of courtship, through attraction,
avowal, commitment, and the decision to marry. And we are
covering a wide span of historical time. The design of this pattern reflects my interpretation of the evidence, but whenever
possible, it is described in the participants' own words. One is
hard put to match the eloquence with which young men and
women offered each other their hands and hearts.

PART I
1770–1840

Linda Raymond's short, carefully phrased letter to Benjamin Ward is typical of the 1780 to 1840 period, a time when men were often more expansive correspondents than the women they courted. (Linda Raymond to Benjamin Ward, 4 July 1818, Gertrude Foster Brown Papers, SL.)

CHAPTER 1

"A Connection
of Hands"

IN THE SPRING of 1808, Eliphalet Pearson, professor of theology and acting president of Harvard College, prepared to move his family from Cambridge to the village of Andover, twenty miles north of Boston. His wife and four children would accompany him when he left Harvard, now the domain of the Unitarians, to take up the first professorship of natural theology at the new seminary being founded to train Orthodox clergymen for the Congregational churches of New England. Among the young men who planned to enter the school when it opened in September was twenty-nine-year-old Ephraim Abbott. Preceptor of the Charlestown Academy near Boston, Ephraim Abbott had graduated from Harvard in 1806. Andover and Harvard were not all these two men had in common. In May 1808, Ephraim Abbott began secretly courting Pearson's daughter Mary.*

Twenty-six-year-old Mary Holyoke Pearson was the only child of Eliphalet Pearson and his first wife, Priscilla Holyoke, who died in 1782. The oldest of a Maine farmer's nine children, Ephraim Abbott had attended Exeter Academy as a "charity student," before entering Harvard at the age of twenty-three. During his years in Cambridge, he supported himself doing odd jobs around the college and teaching school. In 1808, Ephraim had "no property, except a few books and clothes with some trifling articles of personal property." Although he was in no position to marry, he could not conceal that he felt "the most ardent yet the most honorable passion" for Mary Pearson. "Excepting my obligation to [God]," he told her in May, "my heart, my affections, my undivided and unreserved love are yours."[1]

At first, Mary Pearson encouraged Ephraim's suit; but in June, she asked for her letters back. She explained that "a step, so important as that of forming a connexion for life, requires great deliberation"; she worried that they had been "too hasty." Ephraim insisted that he had not meant to suggest their "entering into any engagement that . . . should be binding . . . at this time." All he wanted, he wrote in December, was the assurance, "If I am ever in circumstances to make honorable provision for a family, you will then become my companion, my consort." He considered his own tie to her "binding," but he understood and shared her reluctance to become formally pledged. "As much as I love you," he explained, "I cannot think of your ever giving yourself to me, unless you can rationally promise yourself that you shall by such a step increase your own felicity."[2]

Mary relented and the relationship resumed, but it was hardly

*For the first year of the relationship, Mary's half-sister Margaret acted as go-between. It is unclear why secrecy was necessary. Certainly Mary Pearson was old enough for a serious courtship; and as a Harvard graduate and prospective Andover student, Ephraim Abbott would have seemed an acceptable suitor. Perhaps his precarious financial situation was the problem, or perhaps Mary and Ephraim were anticipating the intrusiveness her father later displayed.

felicitous. She considered herself unworthy of the affection Ephraim offered her and undeserving of his praise. Her suitor was confident: "If I am deceived it is sweet deception. I hope never to be undeceived. I see benevolence, sensibility, sincerity, candor, prudence, good sense, sweet disposition. Where," he asked, "is my blindness? or if I am blind, what should I see were I not blind?" Mary's answer does not survive; it seems likely that where Ephraim saw "all that [his] imagination ever suggested as contributing to constitute a woman who could make [him] happy," *she* saw only an ordinary woman full of self-doubt and insecurity. Because she feared she "could not make [Ephraim] happy," she was herself "unhappy in being the object of [his] love." The idea that Mary might not return his love made Ephraim cry out: "You have seen my very soul, do not I interest you? Do not ever again suggest the painful thought. You have searched my heart. You know it yours."[3]

At times, Mary was both overwhelmed by Ephraim's love and mistrustful of it; his fear was that he loved her too much—more than he loved God. From the beginning, the young seminarian made it clear: "I would love my Creator supremely for without his love I know nothing can make me happy," and asked "that nothing may alienate my affections from him." Throughout the courtship, Ephraim perceived his love for Mary as a model for his love of God as well as a threat to it. "Our love for each other," he instructed her in the spring of 1810, "shows us how we ought to love Christ." But Ephraim worried that they would allow their love for each other to outstrip their love of God, and Mary shared his anxiety. "Daily you occupy a portion of my thoughts," she wrote in June 1812, "too large a share, I fear. Could I love my Creator in proportion to the creature, I should be happier."[4]

Mary Pearson's unhappiness had another side as well: she was afraid that what she gave Ephraim was not enough. The feelings of unworthiness that had troubled her in the early days of the courtship never left her. "Alas, how far short do I fall in every duty," she lamented in 1812 and then asked Ephraim, "Forgive me for intruding on you my secret thoughts and reflections."

19

No doubt he welcomed the "intrusion"; he had all along sought to express his thoughts "candidly and without reserve."[5]

In the years after his graduation from Andover, Ephraim Abbott's thoughts—and his letters to Mary—were filled with his prospects for a pastorate and for the marriage that would follow. He spent the summer of 1811 traveling in eastern Maine as a missionary. The town of Robinson invited him to stay through the winter, and in September, Bowdoin College offered him a position as tutor. He presented his view of the matter to Mary, at home in Andover: "I am almost 32 years old and if I accept the tutorship I deduct a year from a life already far [illegible]. . . . I need knowledge and skill in preaching more than in college lore. Therefore I think it is my duty to stay [in Robinson]." But his duty conflicted with desire. He pointed out to Mary, "Were I to go to [Bowdoin], I might see you sooner than spring, but if I stay here I shall be more worthy of you."[6]

Although at such times, he sought her counsel, Mary was ambivalent about her role in these decisions. When a church in Coventry, Connecticut, called him in 1812, Mary wrote to Ephraim, who was preaching in Rhode Island, "It seems to me you would be more useful in a place like Smithfield [Rhode Island] than in so small a place as Coventry & as happy." But having given her opinion, she was quick to disqualify it: "I am glad I have not to decide so important a question—I don't wish a voice in it—nor to be considered at any time. The duty which becomes me is submission. My happiness is centered* in my immediate family, *place* is of small moment."[7]†

Ephraim Abbott maintained ties with most of the members of Mary's immediate family. Her sister Margaret and her brother Edward all carried on their own correspondences with Ephraim. Many of his letters to Mary include requests for mending, or refer to purchases he was making for the Pearsons, or even, in August 1812, discuss his instructions for bringing the younger Pearson son home from Yale. No wonder that he reported to Mary, "I have dreamed of your family and of you sev-

*In the original, Mary crossed out "confined" and wrote "centered."
†In all quotes, italics are the respective letter writers', unless I indicate otherwise.

eral times lately," and that by the spring of 1813, Mary was asking Ephraim to write "for my *dear self only*—it is an age since I had one that was not designed for the family."[8]

But of all Mary's relations, Ephraim was closest to her father. Eliphalet Pearson was deeply involved in Ephraim's career planning. The young man repeatedly expressed his desire for Reverend Pearson's approval and made frequent references to the older man's authority and wisdom. "I wish you and your Papa would give me your advice as soon as possible," he wrote Mary from Maine in 1811; "I have never wanted to consult you & your Papa more than at the present time." When he was finally settled in Greenland, New Hampshire, in 1813, it was Eliphalet Pearson—without his daughter Mary—who came from Massachusetts to preach the ordination sermon. But on this occasion, Ephraim found himself in conflict with his mentor. "He thinks we ought to wait for decency," he reported to Mary. "He says also that your health is not good enough to be married. If it could be mended by delay I should *gladly* wait as long as you think proper. But I do not think your Father views the subject of decency as he would do, if it were his own case." A month later, Ephraim was importuning Mary to set an early date: "I hope that you and your father will be willing to agree on a time for making us one in name as well as affection."[9]

In spite of Eliphalet Pearson's urging that Mary and Ephraim "wait for decency," the wedding was set for January 1814. But Mary, who had alternatively welcomed and resented the delay, made one last retreat from the decision. On December 20, she warned Ephraim, "I have found more to be done than I expected—& may not be ready at the time set as I told you might be the case." It was more than the details of setting up a household, although those were burdensome enough, that constrained Mary. "I assure you *this marrying is a very troublesome sort of business*," she told him. Again, she stated her willingness—and revealed her struggle—"to leave the event to the Great & good Being who has preserved us in life, & to each other & brought us so near the consummation of our wishes tho' *I greatly feel my incapacity for a situation which affords much room for usefulness.*"[10]

21

For five years, Mary Pearson's ambivalence about her relationship with Ephraim Abbott had been mediated by circumstances; now that the long delay was over, she was almost overwhelmed by fears. She was still unworthy and unready, and she was alone. She believed that Ephraim had never fully appreciated the inadequacy she had felt throughout their courtship and felt so intensely even now at its end. "It is vain to write or speak to you, *for you do not enter into my views & feelings on this subject—at all times they are so keen, as to lead me to wish I had never consented to an union.*"[11] But there was no going back, and in January 1814, Ephraim Abbott and Mary Holyoke Pearson became husband and wife.

"All the young people were there"

In the fall of 1812, four years after they exchanged their first letter, Mary Pearson expressed her hope that she and Ephraim Abbott would "not live another year separated—It is really troublesome writing so much," she complained. After Ephraim left Andover Seminary in 1810, he and Mary were forced to rely on letters and occasional visits. Because many of these letters survive, we are able to document the ideas and feelings with which this couple approached marriage.[12] But Ephraim and Mary were apart so much of the time that their correspondence reveals more about the inward than the outward transition to marriage. For a more holistic picture of courtship, we must turn to sources that illuminate how men and women behaved when they were together as well as how they felt when they were apart.

More than a year before they were finally married, Mary Pearson observed to Ephraim Abbott that they were both the "wrong side of 30."[13] Indeed, most of their contemporaries were wed on the "right side" of thirty. The average young man of the early republic married in his middle to late twenties and was a few years older than his bride. Young people began as teenagers to participate in the social rituals and activities that led to courtship;* thus they devoted the better part of a decade to the process of finding, knowing, and choosing a "partner for life." Girls and boys met on the lanes and commons of the village and in the houses of their neighbors and kinfolk; they encountered each other in church, schoolroom, and shop. Sitting side by side in the meetinghouse week after week and in the one-room school year after year, boys and girls could not be strangers to one another. Their daily lives and future prospects were closely tied to the land. Even when going about their separate tasks, men and women moved within the same small world. The boy cutting hay in the fields, hauling logs in the woods, or carting grain to the mill was never far from the young woman milking cows in the barn, making cheese in the buttery, or baking bread in the kitchen.

When young women and men ventured away from home, it was often in mixed company. They went berrying, riding, picnicking; they sang and danced together at parties and balls and at the singing and dancing schools that were popular in small towns and country villages. One historian of the period observed that "boys took girls for walks, escorted them to college debates and lectures, congregated at young ladies' homes to chat, eat apples, and cakes, and gather round the piano to sing." Male-female socializing did not depend on special occasions but was integrated into the routine of everyday life. In the 1830s, a young woman in Plymouth Notch, Vermont, Pamela Brown, recounted a typical Sunday at her house:

Elmina [her friend] and I laid abed very late. We had hardly got the [house] work done before James Merrill, Joel Slack and Thomas Fletcher came in. They staid and talked and sang an hour or two. Then

*The word *courtship* applied to situations where the intention to marry was explicit (if not formally—and mutually—stated). *Courting* was the broader term used to describe socializing between unmarried men and women. Courting sometimes but not always led to courtship; few courtships began without a period of courting.

we all walked down to the "Five Corners" where we met Solomon Carlisle, H. Willis, the two Briggs and Charlotte Duncan. Staid there and sang a few tunes and then walked up to Mr. Pinney's.[14]

At twenty-one, Pamela's life was full of such spontaneous meetings with young men; more formal social occasions occurred regularly as well. Many young people attended balls and dances almost as often as they did church. On Town Meeting Day in 1836, Pamela Brown went to a ball with thirty-five couples in attendance. She reported in her diary: "We staid until about day. I danced until I was about tired of it." The next day, she noted: "I kept school and was so sleepy and dull I had a very hard time of it, to keep the scholars in order." On the Fourth of July, there was another celebration. "All the young people were there from this part of town and none from our neighborhood but Thomas [her brother]. He carried Euridice Boynton." Dances—and the traveling they entailed—gave men and women the opportunity to pair off, but they were not limited to couples. It was the custom in many places for a small group of single men to take responsibility for organizing the dance and transporting the women. A young lawyer described the practice for celebrating Washington's birthday in Worcester, Massachusetts, in 1830:

The music generally consists of two fiddles, a clarionet or bugle and base viol. The entertainer furnishes this under direction of the managers, and also carriages to collect & distribute the ladies. Two coaches are employed with a manager in each, who commence soon after sunset to carry the ladies to the hall, and it is a part of their duties to wait upon them home in the same way.[15]

While the occasions which brought men and women together on a regular basis were usually group affairs, twosomes were not discouraged. A young woman and man who were interested in each other could spend time alone as well as in the company of friends and relations. They were free to go off walking or riding together, to sit alone in the parlor late at night, and to make unchaperoned visits to family and friends. David Shepard, Jr., for example, was living on his parents' farm in western Massachusetts in 1798, the year he turned twenty-one. His affections belonged to Ellen Savage, a young woman whom he favored with invitations to balls, poetic verses, and stolen looks in church. Even though David had never declared an intention to marry Ellen, he regularly exchanged letters, thoughts, and caresses with "his girl." A sample from David's journal reveals the freedom and privacy he and Ellen enjoyed:

Sunday 27 May . . . proceeded on down to Capt. Plum's where I found my girl—passed the time here till about two . . . then walked home with my Ellen, where I found the little bed room empty and a good fire, by which I spent the evening sweetly with my little girl—gave her the fictitious letter I wrote.
Wednesday 4 July . . . In the course of the P.M. & evening had opportunity & danced several times with my little Ellen . . . between one & two sat out to see my little partner home. We both being well mounted on one horse as I had purposely started before the others, that I might have the company of my little girl to myself.[16]

The lack of parental surveillance over David and Ellen's conduct is not unusual. In the half-century after Independence, middle-class youths expected and experienced considerable autonomy in courtship. Parents who tried to supervise their childrens' social activities might have as little success as Lucy Harris's father, who insisted his daughters "ask his permission to go [out], and promise to come home early." But Lucy and her sister Lorena, who "began to go in company pretty young . . . to balls, and quiltings, and applebees," did not always comply. At least once they returned from a dance at five A.M. Although their father "woke up, and asked [their] stepmother what time the girls came home," no punishment was forthcoming. More commonly, parents made little or no effort to oversee their children's courting behavior, and some families took active steps to give a young couple privacy: family members might go out for a walk or early to bed when a suitor came to call. This was often the only way a couple could visit alone without leaving the house themselves, since the parlor was generally the only domestic space considered appropriate for courting activities. Twenty-five year-old Mary Guion described a typical visit from her suitor Samuel Brown: "After tea Samuel came here we were all reading in the Parlor when he came but they [her family] soon all took a walk but him who chose to stay with me, we read, sung, and discoursed . . . till they returned."[17]

On occasion, it was the couple rather than the family who left the room, but doing so might raise questions of propriety. Mary described her discomfort during another evening visit from Samuel:

I was showing him some things and as I went to put them in the bead-room [sic], he followed me in and we sat there by the window by the light only of the full moon, but that act I very much disapprove. When he first went in he asked me how long he [might] stay not more than tenn minutes said I. Ah ten o'clock said he, that will do very well and I am almost ashamed to own we sat there til twelve and there was company in the Parlour all the time.[18]

Mary "disapproved" and was "almost ashamed" of Samuel's actions and her response to them, but there is no evidence that her parents condemned, or even commented on, the couple's behavior. It was Mary who would accept or reject Samuel's suit, and it was Mary who must draw the limits for their behavior.

"A right to be consulted"

Just as young people were on their own when courting, they made their own decisions when serious courtships developed. By the last quarter of the eighteenth century, middle-class Americans enjoyed considerable autonomy when it came to choosing their future mates. Legal requirements for parental consent were being steadily eroded. In Puritan New England, the law had given parents "the care and power . . . for the disposing their Children in Marriage," but few matches were made by parental fiat or arranged by family councils. In most colonial families, parents exercised control indirectly, more in the matter of *when* than of *whom* their children would marry.[19] Before a man could marry, he had to possess the means to support a wife and children, and for this was dependent on his parents. His marriage "portion"—the land he would farm, the house in which he and his bride would live—came from a share of his father's property. A man could marry only when his father was willing to divide the family's lands and to forego the son's labor on the farm.

If parents thus controlled the timing of marriage, they permitted their children a great deal of latitude when it came to choosing a mate. Even in wealthy families, where parents might promote a match they thought desirable, children always had the right of "veto." Ministers forbade parents "to put a force on their children," something "neither Reason nor Religion" allowed. Fitz John Winthrop noted in 1707, "it has been the way and custome of the country for young folkes to choose, and where there is noe visible exception everybody approves it."[20]

By the end of the eighteenth century, "the way and custome of the country" was to leave marriage making to young people. The scarcity of land in the older towns and the geographic dispersal that resulted, the growth of business and commerce, all had the effect of loosening parents' control over their young-adult offspring. By the time a young man was in his late teens, he had reached a state of "semidependence" on his parents. He remained financially tied to his family, giving and receiving assistance according to his circumstances and theirs, while he learned a craft, completed his studies, or got a start in trade. If his father was a farmer who needed his labor, a young man might spend part of the year at home, but he had already attained a large measure of freedom from parental authority.[21]

Young women were less likely than their brothers to leave home, but they, too, experienced a period of "semidependence." By the time they were teenagers, most middle-class girls in the North had served an informal apprenticeship in frugal housewifery and learned the basic skills of reading, writing, and ciphering in the town schools. A young woman could earn small sums at home, by braiding palm-leaf hats, stitching shoes, or producing surplus textiles for sale in the cities or the West. During the summer and winter months, she might teach in the one-room school that she herself had attended. A woman who was more venturesome—or more needy—might seek employment as an operative in a textile mill, as a milliner or dressmaker in a small town, or as a domestic servant in another family. None of these situations offered her full autonomy, but each allowed her a degree of independence.[22]

Thus, it is not surprising that parents exercised little control over their children's courtships. "Upon changes so great and so interesting" as the marriage of a daughter, one young man observed, parents had "a right to be consulted"; but parents and children alike understood "consultation" to mean *post facto* consent. Parental consent was usually a formality, but if a woman received a proposal while away from home, she might hesitate to accept it without first getting her parents' approval. Eliza Southgate, for example, was on a visit to Saratoga in 1802 when she met Henry Bowne. Although she was "deeply interested" in him, she would only go "so far as to tell him I approved him as far as I knew him, but the decision must rest with my Parents, their wishes were my law."[23] Distressed because her fiancé had not obtained his guardian's approval, a Connecticut woman explained: "I only wish to have our attachment sanctioned by parental wisdom." Lewis Morris, Jr., hoped his father would not think him disrespectful for his silence concerning his "attachment" to a woman he met while serving with the Continental Army in Virginia. "My hopes and wishes would only have served to increase your anxiety," he wrote after Nancy Elliott had agreed to be his wife. "I take it for granted that such a connection will meet with your cordial approbation and that of my good mother and all my friends."[24]

Lewis Morris's confidence that his parents would approve was well founded. Much as they expected to be consulted, middle-class parents in the new nation regarded the choice of a mate as rightly belonging to their children. One father told his son:

"A Connection of Hands"

"Your solicitude for my consent to the connection you propose to form shows something more of a dependance on my opinion than I require, and a new instance of your regard to the very appearance of duty." Young women enjoyed the same freedom of action as their brothers. When Lois Freeman and Daniel Davis became engaged in the summer of 1785, Lois's father wrote the young man he had never met: "My daughter's happiness is one of the great objects I have in view, and I have so high an opinion of her good sence that I think she would not make a bad choice in a partner for life." Even when parents had reservations, they were unlikely to do more than simply express them. "My parents have not interposed with any substantial objections," Harriet Porter assured Lyman Beecher in 1817. "They think I am not aware of the difficulties & that I should have taken more time for deliberation but they have not made me unhappy."[25]

The relative rarity and gentleness of parental interference in marriage making does not mean that children were indifferent to their parents' views. Although most couples were prepared to marry without their parents' blessing, they much preferred to marry with it. The abolitionist William Lloyd Garrison expressed the common feeling of his contemporaries when he told Helen Benson that receiving her parents' approval consummated his happiness. "The obtainment of your own consent was indeed of primary importance, but the sanction of your parents was essential to the quietude and full enjoyment of my mind," he wrote.[26]

When parents sought to impose their will, as a small minority did, their children often subverted or resisted their control.[27] Secret courtships, conditional engagements, clandestine marriages were the result; and public opinion was inclined to hold parents responsible for such undesirable situations. A young Maine lawyer stated the general principle: "No good comes from opposition. In affairs of love, young peoples hearts are generally much wiser than old peoples heads."[28]

Parents themselves subscribed to this proposition. It was generally agreed that "in a matter of such importance," a woman "ought to be left intirely to herself." In fact, it was not uncommon for a young woman, or occasionally a young man, to find that parents were unwilling to intercede, even when they were asked to. Women who faced a major move if they married were often in this difficult position. A proposal of marriage from Samuel Newell, who was soon to go to India as a missionary, threw Harriet Atwood into turmoil. "My heart aches—I know not *what* to do!" she told her diary. "Perhaps my dear Mother will *immediately* say, *Harriet shall never go*. Well, if this should be the case, my duty would be plain." But Mrs. Atwood raised no obstacles and "cheerfully left [Harriet] to act according to her conviction of duty." Mary Carter's experience was similar. In 1831, her suitor received a call to do missionary work in the West; although Mrs. Carter was sad to see her daughter go, Mary told Edmund Hovey that "she makes no objections but wishes me to act my own pleasure entirely."[29]

Harriet Atwood and Mary Carter were to follow their own inclinations, rather than the dictates of their parents. In the inner recesses of the heart, parental preferences and material considerations could provide only the most basic signposts. Young women and men looked for a mate whom they loved and who loved them, rather than for one with the right family connections, financial prospects, or religious affiliation. The veto power that children had exercised in the seventeenth century was based on the Puritan belief in the importance of affection in marriage; but in the eighteenth century, love was becoming an essential ingredient in the marital equation. In 1782, a New Englander reminded his sister "that disappointment attends all those who are joined together upon any other motives than pure affection." This rule had all the power of a natural force: "Nature always revenges herself upon those who violate her laws," he warned. One woman described the "poor souls, who drag through life a galling chain; *souls* must be kindred to make the bands silken, all others I call unions of hands not *hearts*." Parents agreed. In 1792, a Massachusetts mother told her daughter "she should not wish any friend of hers to give their hand where they could not give their heart."[30]

"A Connection of Hands"

"Struck with love"

In her words, we hear an echo of the Puritan insistence on children choosing mates whom they *could* love, but by the end of the eighteenth century, more was required. Americans were beginning to make love between men and women a necessary rather than a desirable precondition for marriage. A content analysis of magazines published from 1741 to 1794 has shown that the concept of romantic love was well known in the colonies and "may have been a common pattern among large sections of the upper status groups." Especially after 1777, the poetry, fiction, and essays read by the American gentry made frequent references to aspects of romantic love. Other evidence indicates that these ideas were being internalized, even when the reality fell short. In the second half of the eighteenth century, parties in Massachusetts divorce cases "more frequently manifested awareness of and hope for romantic love." Between 1736 and 1765, none of the fifty-eight petitioners "named loss of conjugal affection among their grievances." By contrast, more than 10 percent of the suits brought over the next twenty years included such complaints as "He lost all affection for her," he "ceased to cherish her," and she had "almost broken his heart."[31] As both a cultural ideal and an individual expectation, romantic love was taking hold in late eighteenth century America.

While a system of mate choice based on love increased young people's autonomy from their parents, it imposed its own set of limitations. A man might find preparation helpful in the search for a woman to love and marry, but the result was ultimately beyond his control. According to advice books, the selection of a wife required as much discipline, frugality, and study as the choice of a career, but young men realized that courtship was one area of life where assertiveness and planning could not ensure success. A man could not arrange to fall in love. "I now wait to be impelled by some [irresistible] impulse," a young minister told a friend in 1797.[32]

31

For a woman, it was not enough to be "struck with love," in the phrase of the day; she must await a lover. While a man might have the illusion of control, a woman knew that her role in the early stages of courtship was a reactive one: she might accept, defer, or decline a suitor's offer. Men might claim it was "ladies to whom all matrimonial causes are ultimately referred," but an observant young woman like Eliza Southgate could see that "the inequality of privilege between the sexes is . . . in no instance . . . greater than in the liberty of choosing a partner in marriage; true, we have the liberty of refusing those we don't like, but not of selecting those we do." Eliza considered herself "at liberty to refuse" those she did not like; and two years before she met Henry Bowne at Saratoga, she congratulated herself on having "firmness enough to brave the sneers of the world and live an old maid," if the right man never came along. Twenty years later, in 1824, Georgina Amory told her fiancé John Lowell, Jr., that before she met him, she knew no one who appeared to be worthy of her love:

When I looked round and saw how very few young men there were who were not influenced by the principles of false honour, how much fewer still who thought not if they forbore to speak lightly of those subjects which I considered the most important . . . whose motives likewise in selecting me I should be perfectly convinced were disinterested, I saw no other prospect than remaining in my present condition.[33]

Both Eliza Southgate and Georgina Amory were better situated than most women to contemplate a single life. They came from families whose resources were sufficient to ensure that they would at least be comfortable, if not fruitful. Early nineteenth century women who did not marry—and of these, in spite of the unfavorable sex ratio in the eastern states, there were very few—could generally look forward to a life of dependency and perhaps poverty. Still, the Salem schoolteacher Eliza Chaplin spoke for many when she expressed her preference "ever [to] remain in 'single blessedness' than to enter those sacred indissoluble bonds [of marriage] from mere motives of interest."[34]*

---

*Although she was "enamored of the object [her] imagination had created," Eliza Chaplin in fact had a modest standard by which she judged her suitors: "Never have

A woman was better off single than married to a man she did not love.

Since love was the determining as well as the motivating factor in mate choice, disappointment and personal rejection were always possibilities. Obviously, the longer a couple's acquaintance, the more likely they were to know whether their affections were reciprocated. The more intimately a man knew the hand he sought—and the more time he had spent holding it—the better his chances of acceptance. (Surely the two young men who wrote to propose marriage to Linda Raymond—one whom she had not seen for four years, the other who had spent a single evening at her father's house—could not have been surprised when she declined their offers.)[36]

Since it was risky for a woman to express her feelings before she had an offer of marriage, a man could not be sure until he asked. Some young men shielded themselves from the pain a negative answer would cause them. When James Barnard, a young Massachusetts seaman, sought to discover "how the affair stood" between himself and the woman he had long been courting, he "got no satisfaction except she told [him] she did not intend to marry." This statement had the same impact as an outright refusal (especially since James knew her to have another suitor), but James concealed his disappointment. "She did not know the strength of my feelings, she could not. I had guarded myself with the utmost care—too *proud* to let anyone know he or she had the power to mar my peace one moment," he later recalled. James might have "guarded" himself, but his proposal of marriage was evidence of "the strength of [his] feelings." Because men were the initiators of the transaction, they were more at risk than women and could protect themselves only so much. Women were reminded of the need to preserve the dignity of the men who courted them. A typical advice book instructed a woman who received a proposal to make it "a subject of immediate consideration." If she wished to decline a man's offer, she should "inform him in a manner which will least wound his sensibility, and let the secret of his having addressed [her] never pass [her] lips."[37]

I rejected an individual, whose presence gave me equal pleasure to that of his absence," she explained.[35]

When a man declared himself, a woman was to treat him with utmost candor and kindness; until his avowal, she must exercise restraint. Men were thus in the uncomfortable position of having to gauge sentiments that women sought to conceal. Mary Guion admitted that she had "disguised [her] feelings and every emotion of [her] heart" when she was with Samuel Brown, up to the time she was certain they would marry. The "disguise" was for Samuel's benefit, but it also served to keep Mary at a safe distance from her true feelings. In 1800, Eliza Southgate asserted that no woman "suffers herself to think she could love any one before she has discovered an affection for her."[38] A woman would wait to be sure that her feelings were reciprocated before admitting them even to herself.

Such self-deception was not always possible, but it was imperative that a woman avoid being the first to show her heart. Helen Benson considered it indisputable that "in every instance professions of love should be made by [men] to [women], and not *vice versa.*" She told William Lloyd Garrison after their engagement, "However strong might have been your attachment for me, I would never have revealed it to you had you not first offered yourself to me." Garrison wondered whether there were not "cases in which it would be no real breach of modesty, or the rules of decorum, for a lady to reveal the love which she cherished towards him who had captivated her heart."[39] Perhaps Garrison was hoping to reduce the risks men faced when the "rules of decorum" compelled them to put their feelings on the line first, but it was a rare woman who was willing to expose herself to rejection by a lover. She needed all the safety her "modesty" could provide.

Because a woman had to protect herself not only against disappointment but also indiscretion, she waited for evidence of her suitor's intentions as well as of his affections. In "The Spinning Wheel," a ballad popular in the 1790s, a woman continues to turn her wheel while a young "jockey" woos her. "Unusual joy [her] heart did feel," and her fondness she "could scarce conceal," as the man praised and embraced her, but she spun on. Only when "He swore he meant [her] for his bride" did she interrupt her work. " 'Twas then my love I did reveal,/ And flung away my spinning wheel."[40]

If the ardent lover in this song was like most of his contemporaries, he would have spent little time building a case for himself. The nineteenth-century suitor expected that where there was mutual love, there would, once his circumstances allowed, be marriage. It was his affection, rather than anything else about him—his social or professional position, for example—that justified his proposal. Even when a man alluded to the benefits a woman would enjoy if she agreed to become his wife, they were all secondary to the love she would receive. Zadoc Long, a twenty-four-year-old storekeeper in Buckfield, Maine, provided an illustration when he proposed to Julia Davis after a year's courtship:

I feel sad when I don't see you. Be married, why won't you? And come to live with me. I will make you as happy as I can. You shall not be obliged to work hard; and when you are tired, you may lie in my lap, and I will sing you to rest. . . . I will play you a tune upon the violin as often as you ask and as well as I can; and leave off smoking, if you say so. . . . I would be always very kind to you, I think, because I love you so well. I will not make you bring in wood and water, or feed the pig, or milk the cow, or go to the neighbors to borrow milk. Will you be married?[41]

Indeed, she would, and in the summer of 1824, Julia Davis and Zadoc Long were wed.

"What the feeling of love is"

When a man proposed marriage, love was his most important qualification; when a woman responded, love was her first consideration. But while all couples ended their courtships in love, few began that way. Men and women knew that to find a mate they must first find love, but love did not always elicit a shock of recognition. People might have feelings for one another that could be mistaken for love. Efforts to measure love involved a series of negative calculations: it must be more compelling than friendship, more lasting than passion, more serious than romance.

When Zadoc Long first became acquainted with Julia Davis, he confided to his brother, "I have never seen a girl so much to my liking." But he was not at all sure that he was in love. "I am not ready to sink into despair if my regards should not be reciprocal," he assured her. If what he felt was love, "I am your lover; if it be friendship, I am your friend," he wrote to Julia. When Zadoc gallantly asked if he could "aspire to so high a seat as that of friend in [her] regard," he was being cautious.[42] Friendship was the halfway station, not the ultimate destination he hoped to reach. By the 1820s, friendship was clearly demarcated from, and given less value than, love. This distinction had not always been made.

In the colonial period, *friend* was commonly used to refer to kin; in the years after Independence, "language released 'friendship' from blood ties so that it existed purely in elective relationships."[43] One's mate was one's "nearest" or "best friend," but in spite of their close identification, friendship and love were not interchangeable. When Esther DeBerdt and Joseph Reed encountered obstacles to their courtship in the 1760s, Esther was "sure Providence will point out some way to hinder the painfull taske of breaking the tye of Friendship so firm, so sincere as ours but why do I say Friendship for I believe that will ever last, tho' time should force us to forswear our love." As early as 1764, Esther perceived a difference between friendship and love. She looked for both in marriage. "All I desire," she told Joseph, "is a companion who would make it his endeavor to be both a friend & lover to me whom he chose for life." Friendship was still an essential element in conjugal love. A popular 1779 treatise described the ideal marriage as "a union of mind and a sympathy of mutual esteem and friendship for each other," but friendship was increasingly valued as a steppingstone to love. One young wife told her husband in 1791, "Friendship was the basis of our more Ardent Regard which when disjoined from those feelings which ought to unite married persons is like a plant when the fibers are cut."[44]

After 1800, references to the even greater felicity—and intimacy—promised by romantic love gradually reduced the value placed on friendship. As American society experienced a shift away from the communal values of its past toward the individualism that would shape its future, friendship became less and less a matter of circumstance and more and more a matter of choice. Yet for young men and women, it was not the *first* choice. From its earliest beginnings, the ideology of romantic love made friendship between men and women into a consolation prize of sorts. Although *friend* continued to be used to refer to a mate, friendship was increasingly defined in terms of its distinction from—and implied inferiority to—love.

Friendship alone was not a sufficient basis for marriage. When Elizabeth Sherman declined an offer of marriage in 1786, she explained to her suitor, "Your friendship Sir, I shall ever wish for & mine you have most sincerely—But that particular kind which wishes a connection of hands I am necessitated to withhold & hope that you will not censure me for it since the sensations of the heart in these respects are not Controulable." She reminded him that he had once agreed to the proposition that a woman who was uncertain about a "Gentlemen who felt a particular attachment for her [should] cultivate a friendship until she could be well satisfied in her own mind—& then she ought explicitly & speedily to make it known to him."[45]

Friendship provided boundaries within which men and women could test themselves and each other. A young New Yorker confided to her cousin in 1792: "There is a certain person that I will not drive very soon from my memory not as a friend I own but as for a lover I will deny until I see that his affection is fixed on me and me alone." In the late eighteenth century, friendship served to contain and distinguish feelings that had not yet, or would not ever, lead to conjugal love. After the turn of the century, it became an increasingly distinctive relationship, marked off from both kinship and love.

By 1835, Mary Peabody could tell her sister that the friendship she felt for a recently widowed friend had nothing to do with love: "I know what the feeling of love is for I have been sought and all but won—and this knowledge has always given me assurance that, strong as my friendship is . . . it is a totally different feeling."[46]

If the "feeling of love" was not friendship, neither was it passion. As they sought to comprehend love, men and women remained wary of passion. They did not expect the earth to move; in fact, they believed they were in danger if it did. Dwight Foster's perspective is typical. In 1780, the young New Englander wrote in his journal: "There is something heavenly in the Passion of Love—but the Misfortune of it often makes a Man act in a very ridiculous Manner—even a Man of Sense is frequently unable to command himself when his heart is affected by this Passion." In Foster's world, a man could and must exercise reason to control his passions—anger, greed, envy, as well as love. The threat came not so much from passion itself as from the failure to contain it. Love was "an inherent principle & ought to be indulged, in the bounds of moderation and prudence," as one Salem man noted in his diary.[47]

If the bounds were exceeded, unhappiness was the inevitable result. "Into what a deplorable condition are ardent lovers sometimes plunged by giving an unrestrained look to their passions," observed a young man who was determined to avoid "the combustible materials of enflamed passions." A man's task was to convince a woman—and himself—that he could be both ardent and rational. To achieve this, he might construct elaborate assurances such as the one Theodore Dwight offered Abigail Alsop in 1792: "My reason and my judgment led me to the indulgence of the passion which gains new strength from every step it advances, and in the extremest pitch of affectionate enthusiasm . . ., reason adds her sacred sanction to the feelings of the heart & stamps the love it inspires, rational, real, virtuous, & devine."[48]

Women were even more wary of "the extremest pitch" than were men. The female sex was believed to lack the male ability to cultivate reason and to be therefore more easily led astray by feelings. To reject passion in favor of less volatile and absorbing emotions was an act of self-preservation. Hannah Huntington did "not express passion" for her fiancé, but she assured him: "I feel that steady attachment that you will at some future point descend to." As another Connecticut woman saw it, when passion was "the substance of the love which is to unite husband and wife," it was not likely to lead to a "steady attachment." Instead, there was "a great danger of its proving like a fire of dry stubble, which though it may burn to the skies for the present moment, soon dies away, to be enkindled no more." This did not mean that she was an "advocate for cold esteem only between those who are to live together," but she foresaw trouble when "the understanding and judgment condemn what the passions only approve." Mary Guion agreed; she might refer to love as "the tender passion," but the young New Yorker believed, "we must not let our passions lead the way but have reason for our guide."[49] Passion posed a grave threat to love.

An equally dangerous counterfeit was romance. Recognition of the limits of friendship and the risks of passion did not mean the celebration of romantic love. Romance required caution: it was fertile soil for a flower that could all too easily overrun the garden. Both women and men used *romantic* to describe feelings that were childish, uncontrolled, and unreliable. Margaret Bayard remembered herself as a "wild and romantick" teenager in the 1790s; she had indulged in "all the romantick extravagancies, which [her] situation and age allowed." Such "extravagancies" need not do lasting damage, but in serious courtship, romance was suspect. Sarah Connell's feelings for her fiancé Samuel Ayer sound romantic, but she hoped they were not:

Absent from the *Man* who possesses my undivided heart, nothing interests me. I am alone in a crowd. I pass through life in a kind of stupid indifference to all around me. It is not a momentary romantic attachment I feel for Mr. Ayer. No, "It has severest virture for its basis, and such a friendship ends not but with life."

In 1810, Sarah still considered friendship preferable to romantic love.[50]

The connotations of *romantic* and *romance* were decidedly negative; thus, the appearance of words such as *ridicule, wild, extravagancies,* and *momentary* in connection with romantic love. The Salem lawyer Daniel White spoke for many suitors when he declared in 1807: "I am not romantic; I am solemnly serious." *Romantic* connoted a lack not merely of seriousness but of maturity. One had to be careful that romantic diversions did not interfere with one's adult responsibilities. On his twenty-first birthday in 1814, a young schoolteacher expressed his disgust at the wastefulness of romance and his determination to reform:

I should seek to drive away the wish always to wander by the moonlight of romantic happiness when I could toil to some purpose in the sunshine of real utility. . . . On this day I arrive at the age in which by the laws of my country I am left to the control of myself. . . . I am now a man and the "childish things" of romance and love should be flung aside.[51]

Chief among the "childish things" to be renounced was novel reading. "I must . . . shun vain conversation and books which are ushered into the world under the titles of novels," one self-critical bride resolved in 1802. She complained, "They cheat us of tears for fictitious sorrow." For Margaret Bayard, the "extravagant and false views of life" she had held as a teenager were the unfortunate result of the novels she read. A well-off and well-educated young woman, Margaret had the leisure to read widely. When she met a young man to whom she was attracted, her "strong inclination, cooperating with a tender heart, gave birth to a sentiment, which occupied every thought & every hour." A few years later she recalled: "In all the novels I read, his idea accompanied me & I did little else from morning to night but read novels."[52]

Novel reading was more harmful for women than for men, not only because women had more time to read but because what they read had special significance for their sex. The danger went beyond filling women's heads with romantic fantasies or encouraging female idleness. Much of the fiction published in the late eighteenth and early nineteenth centuries had an implicit message for women: it taught them to act on their feelings. One woman reproached herself for shedding "tears for Clementina's or Clarissa's woes." Novels, she charged, "are calculated to soften, but not correct the heart." They took advantage of the weakness of female rationality to show women the strength of their emotions. While the ministerial and didactic literature was promoting a view of women as sexually passionless and morally pure, romantic novels were glorifying passion. The romantic heroine—even if her fate was a sad one—was a woman of passion and experience. She hearkened back to Eve, whose sexuality was powerful enough to lead her and her mate astray.[53]

Under the spell of novels and the romantic ideas they inspired, women might be moved to exercise their power over men, and thus men must be on their guard. Young men who courted in the early nineteenth century felt themselves vulnerable to female ensnarement, deception, and insincerity. When the widely read author and reformer Lydia Maria Child decried the American tendency to make "the education of girls a series of 'man traps,'" she expressed a complaint often heard from young men. They issued dire warnings to each other: "All I have to say is beware lest the little d---ls with their laughing, swearing eyes, their passions [sic] brow, their damask cheeks bedevil your heart, and lampoon you as they do most men." So Adriel Ely wrote to his classmate Aaron Olmstead."[54]

To Adriel Ely, women were "little devils"; to Aaron Olmstead, women were "angels" and "heavenly spirits." Indeed, two conflicting images of woman coexisted in the first century after Independence: the traditional image of woman as sexually predatory and irrational, who appeared in the guise of the "coquette"; and the newer image of woman as morally pure and sexually passionless—the idealized Republican Mother or True Woman. The coquette used her sexuality to manipulate men; the True Woman improved and instructed them, but in each of these roles, woman posed a threat to man. Both the coquette and the moral guardian might seem to exult in having power over men. While a man could not openly question the moral superiority of a True Woman (or reject the influence of his mother), he could safely condemn the woman who practiced what one man called "the witching art [of] coquetting."[55]

A woman who encouraged a man skillfully, even if sincerely, was suspect. "You cannot put confidence in such a person," Lucien Boynton wrote, "because she has become so accustomed to practice this art on others, you may not be sure she will entirely cease for you." Furthermore, the young lawyer continued, "there is reason to expect, that such a person has not strict and well-established moral principles." Young women were required to be sincere; they must communicate their sincerity without any sign of calculation. They must never appear "studious to be attractive" or adept at receiving suitors; experience was a liability to a woman. An Indiana man resolved to "be the first courtier of [his] intended wife, who must not be "hackneyed in the way of coquetry." Women were also expected to avoid any suggestion of coquetry in the way they discouraged a man's attentions. Hannah Huntington explained that, because she had a "fear of being thought capricious," she had allowed a man to court her long after she knew that she would not marry him. When the man she did choose to marry questioned her sincerity, she was mortified. She conceded, "I am perhaps Capricious, inconsistent and flighty," but she begged him to believe, "I would not deceive you—neither would I be willing you should ever have it in your power to say 'I did not think things were so & so.' "[56]

Women were also vulnerable to deception. A woman who was misled in courtship might find herself married to a man whose affections were not genuine, or—worse still—pregnant by a man who would not marry her. Men understood this danger and filled their letters with frequent, almost ritualized, incantations of sincerity, such as "no man ever loved with more sincerity," "my love for you is sincere, real and unaffected," and "do not doubt the Sincerity of him who does adore you." Lewis Morris, Jr., for example, signed most of his letters to Nancy Elliott, "your sincere and affectionate friend"; he was constantly declaring not only his love but his honesty. "Think not that I speak a language I do not mean," he wrote in 1782, as though Nancy would think he was dissembling.[57]

For both men and women, the best defense against deception was openness. People who devalued friendship, were wary of passion, and distrustful of romance made candor the basis for intimacy.* If sincerity was the foundation of a relationship, candor was the mortar that held it together. "Let confidence and explicitness banish all distrust and suspicion," intoned a New Jersey woman who shared the common belief that "for the security of matrimonial felicity, no quality is more necessary than candour."[59] After the turn of the century, openness became almost an obsession for courting couples. The eighteenth century had demanded frankness on certain subjects: Men were required to present themselves and their intentions without pretense; women, to respond honestly to a man's advances. It was expected that lovers would not deceive each other, but it was not necessary that one expose one's whole self. In the nineteenth century, it was no longer enough to be sincere in one's affections; lovers were urged to be frank and open about everything.

In the 1807 courtship of Mary Wilder and the young Massachusetts lawyer Daniel White, openness was all. Mary told Daniel: "I know not how to unfold to you less than my whole heart. . . . I know that in your character candor and constancy are not less conspicuous than tenderness." For his part, Daniel promised her, "I feel no more a wish than I have the power, to conceal anything from my dearest friend." He observed, "We can ever converse together without reserve or restraint and give to each other our first thoughts as they arise."[60] At a time when young people were following their own inclinations rather than their parents' direction in the choice of mates, candor served as a compass for charting open seas. Suitors who adopted the formal

---

*In the seventeenth and eighteenth centuries, candor was associated with fairness and impartiality or with kindliness and sweetness of temper. When John Adams first met Abigail Smith in 1759, he decided she was "not candid." Candor, he told his diary, "is a Disposition to palliate faults and Mistakes, to put the best Construction upon Words and Actions, and to forgive Injuries."[58] But by the end of the colonial period, the word had begun to acquire the meaning it has today: "freedom from reserve."

mode of discourse fashionable in genteel circles created an impression of insincerity, and insincerity posed as great a threat as intimacy. Candor emerged to minimize the danger.[61]

The first generation of Americans to emphasize the importance of candor in courtship was raised in a society where relationships were duty-bound; obligation was a diminishing but still powerful element in the social fabric of the new republic. So it is not surprising that lovers defined candor as an obligation they owed to each other, although for many it was an obligation not easily fulfilled. Women, especially, found it a struggle to be free of reserve; they were more at risk than men. If a woman was too free, she might appear immodest; if she was too reserved, she might appear cold. Eliza Southgate resolved "to steer between the rocks of prudery and coquetry"—a demanding course indeed. Hannah Huntington expected that it would be her "duty, pleasure & happiness to love" her husband—an expectation that meant a commitment to candor. "I have not a thought I am unwilling you should know," she told her fiancé. After one visit when she had "too much [to say] and could say nothing," she was afraid he might see "prudery . . . affectation [or] coldness" in her behavior. She assured him: "I am not more reserved with you than with others—I am less so than I ever was with any one besides." Her reticence, she believed, was "partly owing to nature & partly to education," and she labored to convince her fiancé that it did not signal any lack of affection for him.[62]

"All the walks and kisses"

Words were one measure of a couple's freedom from reserve; their behavior was another. As they courted, young men and women had the privacy to develop and express their feelings for one another; thus, inevitably, they would either act on or suppress their sexual impulses.* The proportion of couples whose first child was born less than eight and a half months after marriage—nearly 30 percent in the 1780s, more than 20 percent by the 1830s—is one indication that the conflict was not always resolved in favor of self-control.[63] But there is more to sex than coitus; and while the trend in prenuptial conception is significant, the percentage of pregnant brides does not tell us how many couples engaged in sexually expressive behavior before marriage.

Not surprisingly, it is possible to reconstruct the sexual histories of only a handful of relationships. Of the men and women who kept journals and wrote letters, most left no record of the joys, fears, and fantasies surrounding sex. They were too self-conscious (or perhaps not self-conscious enough) to refer in writing to their sexual encounters. For some writers, sexual matters required an intentional exercise of self-censorship; for others, sex was so much a part of daily life that it rarely merited comment. From our vantage point, the results are indistinguishable. Here, even more than in other areas of life, we cannot equate a paucity of evidence with an absence of experience.†

*Defining the term *sexual* is difficult but important. Certain behavior would have been considered sexual in the nineteenth century and is easily categorized as such today. However, many other acts, and many of the images associated with romantic love, would have had a different meaning for the men and women recording them than they do for us reading those records. They were not sexual in the sense that they led to intercourse (although sometimes they did), but they involved the physical expression of affection. In this book, *sexual* refers to any physical intimacy between a man and a woman and to the feelings and fantasies aroused by that intimacy.

†Compared with men and women who courted after the 1820s, couples in the earlier cohorts were relatively silent on sexual matters. This difference reflects a combination of factors. First is the changing nature of correspondence itself. Late eighteenth and early nineteenth century letters had a more formal, less personal cast than those written later, during the middle decades of the nineteenth century, and were therefore less likely to expose the most intimate aspects of courtship. There is also a collecting bias to be taken into account. Historical societies and libraries with strong colonial holdings tend to focus on the careers of men in politics, the ministry, or law and to be weak in the kinds of personal document where sexual references are most likely to be found. However, it is also possible that a disparity in the socioeconomic status of the pre- and post-1820 samples is involved. The earlier data were generated by a more élite group (in education, family background, and wealth); and the sons and daughters of the wealthy may have observed conventions that inhibited the discussion of sexual feelings or behavior, or may have actually been more restrained in their premarital sexual conduct. Both of these conjectures are supported by other studies. The first is consistent with Herman Lantz

We know from the analysis of bridal pregnancy ratios that the last quarter of the eighteenth century marked a low point in premarital sexual restraint.[65] This was the heyday of bundling, the custom that allowed courting couples to sleep together without undressing. Unfortunately, while we can measure ratios of prenuptial conception fairly precisely, the evidence on bundling is mostly anecdotal and often unreliable. The only study of the subject was made by Henry Stiles in 1871. He concluded that bundling "came nearest to being a universal custom from 1750 to 1780."[66] Neither the chronology nor the prevalence of the practice has been well documented, but the association of bundling with the generation responsible for the boom in premarital pregnancy is worth exploring.

Premarital pregnancy was relatively rare in the seventeenth and early eighteenth centuries. If early American couples engaged in bundling, they appear not to have used it as an opportunity for sexual intercourse. Perhaps "the mutual understanding that innocent endearments should not be exceeded" had more force in the carefully regulated Puritan communities than it would a century later? The question remains, for the present, unanswerable. In his *History of Matrimonial Institutions*, George Elliott Howard stated that "a search in the manuscript court records reveals not a single clear case of bundling," but we do know that it was well enough established to be attacked from the pulpit by Jonathan Edwards during the Great Awakening, and that by the 1760s, it was being reported by foreign travelers. Whether it was a new practice or an old one with new rules, bundling seems to have been an accepted part of northern courtship in the middle of the eighteenth century.[67]

In the view of some historians, bundling emerged as "an eighteenth-century compromise between persistent parental control and the pressures of the young to subvert traditional family authority."[68] But how "subversive" was bundling when parents

et al.'s finding of "sexual conservatism" in the magazines read by upper status groups between 1776 and 1794. The second fits with Daniel Scott Smith and Michael Hindus's argument that there was "a sexually permissive subculture in eighteenth-century Hingham," the continuity of which "depended on the female line and on the less wealthy section of the population."[64]

widely sanctioned it? The young Englishman who published an account of his travels in New England in 1759–60 described how it worked:

When a man is enamoured of a young woman and wishes to marry her, he proposes that affair to her parents. . . . If they have no objection, they allow him to tarry with her one night, in order to make his court to her. At their usual time the old couple retire to bed, leaving the young ones to settle matters as they can.[69]

While in this scene, both parents were implicated, critics of bundling often singled out mothers for special opprobrium. A 1785 anti-bundling broadside, which Stiles credited with hastening the decline of the practice, was subtitled: "A reproof to those Young Country Women, who follow that reproachful Practice, and to their Mothers for upholding them herein." The author censured mothers for their complicity in their daughters' behavior:

> Some maidens say, if through the nation,
> Bundling should quite go out of fashion,
> Courtship would lose its sweets; and they
> Could have no fun till wedding day.
> It shant be so, they rage and storm,
> And country girls in clusters swarm,
> And fly and buz, like angry bees,
> And vow they'll bundle when they please.
> Some mothers too, will plead their cause
> And give their daughters great applause,
> And tell them, 'tis no sin nor shame,
> For we, your mothers, did the same.

The songster recognized that it was difficult to change the practice "when mothers herein bear a sway, and daughters joyfully obey."[70]

Perhaps mothers and daughters favored bundling because it was a ritual over which their sex had control. It was the young woman who permitted or denied access to the bundling bed. A Connecticut man remembered that it was "not the fashion to bundle with any chap who might call on a girl, but that it was a special favor, granted only to a favorite lover . . . only after long continued urging in most cases." Bundling with a suitor in her parents' house gave a woman a way to hold a man accountable for his actions; the situation offered protection and independence in equal measure. This was the reason John Adams gave for supporting the practice. In an unpublished essay written in 1761, early on in his courtship of Abigail Smith, he advised young women of the importance of getting to know their suitors. "You must therefore associate yourselves in some good Degree, and under certain Guards and Restraints, even privately with young fellows," he wrote. "And, tho Discretion must be used, and Caution, yet on [considering] the whole of the Arguments on each side," he concluded, "I cannot wholly disapprove of Bundling."[71]

If the 1785 broadside is to be believed, young women used cunning as well as "Discretion . . . and Caution" when they bundled. The song presents a series of short vignettes in which couples break one or another of the rules for bundling. In each case, it is the maid rather than the man who takes the initiative, who engineers and excuses what happens. For example, there is the maid who would not "be quite naked found, With spark in bed, for thousand pound." But petticoats, she said, "Were never made to wear to bed / I'll take them off, keep on my gown / And then I dare defy the town / To charge me with immodesty / While I so ever cautious be." The young man, of course, "was pleased with his maid, . . . Her witty scheme was keen he swore / Lying in gown open before."[72]

This woman and the others in the song were active participants in bundling; but the "pretty lass . . . that loves to bundle with a man" belonged to a world that, in the late eighteenth century, was slipping away. "The traditionally dominant Anglo-American definition of women as *especially* sexual" was being transformed "into the view that women . . . were *less* carnal and lustful than men." The redefinition of woman as chaste, pure, and sexually passionless by *nature* had no room for the bundling maids and their "sparks courting in a bed of love." As woman's image was recast in the mold of moral purity, standards for female behavior were tightened. Women formed, as one minister put it, "for exalted purity, felicity, and glory" would surely not engage in bundling. This new definition of womanhood, which would have much influence in the nineteenth century, was only beginning to emerge in the last years of the eighteenth. By itself, it does not provide a sufficient explanation for the disappearance of bundling around 1800, but it does suggest the climate of ideas in which the custom fell into disuse.[73] While bundling was in decline, sexual boundaries between unmarried women and men were still loosely drawn and crossed with relative ease. This was the period when a young man like David Shepard, Jr., thought nothing of going into a bedroom where his cousin and confidante Polly Austin was asleep, and "spending a few minutes in hugging and kissing" her. Nor was he shy about "hugging, talking to, and sometimes kissing [his] sweet girl" during walks with Ellen Savage.[74]

Transgressions often met with little more than a scolding. One evening in 1807, Samuel Brown arrived early to escort Mary Guion to a dance, and entered the room where she was dressing. She recorded the incident in her diary:

"Polly," said he, advancing towards me, "Don't you want me to help you dress?" I felt rather confused, and gave him a very abrupt answer. "No," said I, "and you may just march out." He stood and laughed at me some time and then went into the Parlour.

Confronted with a more flagrant offense, a couple might exchange harsher words. During a visit in 1785, a young man she called "Philamon" put his hand on Patty Rogers's breast; afterward she reported:

In the course of the evening he took some liberties that would not have been *strictly* decent had they come to light—It gave me *pain*—Surely thought I he must have mistaken my Character—Don't you *hate* me said I? I hate you? . . . no indeed—why—what made you ask that? Because you treated me Ill ass if you thot me a bad girl.[75]

Patty Rogers worried that her suitor would think her "a bad girl." She directed her disapproval not at him but inward at herself and was not so much outraged by his behavior as ashamed of her own. At a time when the rate of premarital pregnancy was at its peak in New England, Patty Rogers was aware of a conflict between ideal female behavior and her responsiveness to Philamon's caress. As a woman, she held herself responsible for maintaining the sexual boundaries in a relationship with a man. She was more vulnerable than he to the consequences of sexual exploration, more likely to be stranded outside the pale of propriety. There was nothing new about Patty's situation; it expressed the age-old "double standard." What was new in the late eighteenth century was the proposition that women had the inclination as well as the obligation to control sexuality. By the time Patty Rogers reached courting age in the 1780s, the first stage in the establishment of female passionlessness as "the central tenet of Victorian sexual ideology" was under way. A literate and lonely young woman, Patty might have read English etiquette and advice books, such as John Gregory's *A Father's Legacy to His Daughters,* first published in the colonies in 1775. Gregory advised women to behave with restraint and affectation, while remaining modest and demure. If Patty was "a bad girl," it was because she had been immodest; she had failed to show the "superior delicacy" such writers expected from women.[76]

It remained for the conservative reformers of the next decade to emphasize woman's moral potential and her virtuous—because passionless—nature. Evangelical writers of the 1790s attributed to women "quick feelings of native delicacy and a stronger sense of shame" than men and argued that the female sex was "naturally attached to purity." The message of the evangelical clergy, who after 1790 preached to an increasingly female audience, was that women could, through obedience to God, replace their traditional sexual power with moral influence over men and male society. Joseph Buckminster's 1810 sermon to the members of the Boston Female Asylum called upon them "to raise the standard of character" of the male sex: "We look to you, to guard and fortify those barriers, which still exist in society, against the encroachments of impudence and licentiousness." In statements such as this, the clergy "renewed and generalized the idea that women under God's grace were more pure than men, and they expected," concludes historian Nancy Cott, "not merely the souls but the bodies of women to corroborate that claim."[77]

For their part, men were assumed to be carnal creatures. The late eighteenth century made moderation as central to male virtue as modesty was to female, and disapproved of sexual (and all other kinds of) excess; but sexual activity itself appeared to be normal and necessary for adult males. The authors of etiquette manuals circulated in the second half of the eighteenth century expected men to behave in a licentious manner. They simply urged women to take precautions, since, as one writer advised, men "will always be ready to take more than you ought to allow them." After the turn of the century, as the evangelical view of female sexuality spread through middle-class culture, the traditional good man who moderated his passions would be supplanted by what one historian has called the "Christian gentleman" who was "continually testing his manliness in the fire of self-denial." And the etiquette works of the antebellum period condemned as deviant male salacity which their eighteenth-century predecessors had considered merely unfortunate.[78]

These, then, were the new gender ideals in the 1820s and 1830s: the "True Woman" who was above sexual passion, and the "Christian gentleman" who was ever in control of it. Of course, ideals influence but do not describe behavior, and the behavior of young women and men in the second quarter of the nineteenth century suggests that the new sexual ideology had limited effect. While the trend in premarital pregnancy continued the decline begun in 1780, couples courting in the 1820s and 1830s were comfortable with a wide range of sexually expressive behavior. Coquetry and seduction were condemned, but flirtation and sexual playfulness remained common features of male-female social life.

In 1834, Elias Nason reviewed "all the *walks* and *kisses* and *larks*

and *sings* and *thoughts* and *meetings* and *partings* and *clingings*"
he and his sweetheart had shared. When he encouraged his
friend Charles Everett to "let the girls alone," Charles assured
him, "I have done so, as yet that is. I have not shocked their modesty by putting my hands where they should not be, but once
this vacation or rather twice." Of the first time, on an overnight
visit to Pawtucket, Rhode Island, he reported: "I felt *of a leg there*,
a most glorious pretty girl. She was an old acquaintance but
some parts of her were new to me." His second lapse occurred
in—of all places—church: "Sitting beside a young lady . . . I
passed my hand through the armholes of her and my cloak and
had a very interesting meeting, but she, owing to my *feeling so
affectionately,* told me to take it out, but I consoled her and *felt
on* til meeting was done." Although Charles instructed Elias
Nason to return the letter if it was illegible or burn it if it was
not, his embarrassment was mixed with a large measure of male
pride in his accomplishments. George Cutler, who was studying
law in Litchfield, Connecticut, in the 1820s, was less boastful of
his conquests, but his diary presents a similar picture. He reported regularly on girls who looked "kissable," or came "near
being swallowed at the kissing bout," or were "all but kissed
to death" at a party.[79]

These kisses were clearly not extorted, but were the interest
and the initiative all on the man's side? Some women merely
allowed themselves to be kissed. Catherine Joss remembered
that when a suitor kissed her, she "did not kiss him, as [she] had
never kissed a young man, though had often been kissed." When
she bowed her head to be kissed, the man complained, "That
is only obedience. I want a token of your love." There is ample
evidence that other young women gave such tokens without
being asked and were active participants in the sexual play that
was included in courting. Charles Everett reported to Elias
Nason that the young woman he had "fondled" on his visit to
Pawtucket "told me that she should know I was a collegian, because I took such measures to please her."[80]

In more serious relationships, a woman's sexual responsiveness could cause conflict. Mira Bigelow, the young woman in

"A Connection of Hands"

Elias Nason's life, expressed her sexual feelings openly. "I sincerely regret not kissing you more that day I came down," she wrote at the beginning of one separation. She and Elias were often apart, and Mira looked forward to their reunions:

O! I do really want to kiss you. . . . How I should like to be in that old parlor with you. . . . I hope there will be a carpet on the floor for it seems you intend to act worse than you ever did before by your letter . . . but I shall humbly submit to my fate and willingly too, to speak candidly.

Mira was "willing," but she was given to second thoughts. Elias described her ambivalence on one occasion:

My how you did act when I was at home. to say you "don't care" [illegible] that's the rub—Why, Mi, what a girl you are! I can't but laugh to think how perfectly indifferent you would be and in a moment clinging around me would say "Oh do do"—For *shame* of you Mira Ann Bigelow—And then to say I never will again and the very next night. . . .

Elias was teasing in his judgment of Mira's behavior; he found her inconsistency more amusing than incriminating. He was less sure about his own conduct. He made no secret of his desire for Mira: "Oh Mi how intensely do I long to see you—to *feel* you—to put these hands that hold his pen upon you. Yes in your bosom—that soft delicious bosom. . . . I shall tear you to pieces." He was not afraid to admit, "I cannot restrain my passions when I see my own loved girl," but he believed that they *should* be restrained. "How is it, Mi, that you can bear so much from me? How can you *love* me after *all?*" In the absence of his own powers of self-control, he relied on her: "My passions are terrible and none but you could master them. And you forgive me all and love me still."[81] Both Mira and Elias expected that Mira would restrain her own feelings as well as her suitor's, but neither made an effort to deny those feelings.

For Mira Bigelow and Elias Nason, sexual restraint was difficult precisely because they had both the desire and the opportu-

53

nity to express their feelings. Early nineteenth century couples responded to this difficulty by defining romantic love so that it included sexual attraction and gratification but excluded coitus. What happened might be called the "invention of petting," or the removal of intercourse from the range of premarital sexual behavior. Coitus was placed on its own continuum rather than at the far end of one that began with hand holding in church. Thus, intercourse was posted as not only "off limits" but as an altogether separate territory, accessible only to married people. Courtship did not lose its erotic elements, but boundaries were drawn so as to contain sexual expressiveness and minimize its consequences. Unlike the restraints of the seventeenth century, which were enforced by community and familial authorities, these boundaries functioned to make safe a *self-guided* transition to marriage. Both women and men sought to preserve—and enjoy—the sexual freedom of eighteenth-century courtship by exercising a new level of self-control.

Self-control was a distinct advantage for men involved in a world that demanded constant balancing between deferred gratification and risk taking, between saving and spending.[82] For women, who were now defined by their role as the morally superior sex, self-control was an instrument of domestic and, by extension, social power. Premarital pregnancy was no longer a sign of natural weakness and sinfulness but rather a dramatic and irrefutable statement that a woman lacked the purity with which she was believed to be endowed "by nature" and on which the future of the republic rested. As the early stages of industrial capitalism and urbanization moved productive work from the home into the office, shop, and factory, men spent more and more time physically separate from their wives and children. Maternal affection replaced paternal authority as the guiding principal of middle-class child rearing, and women assumed greater responsibility for what went on at home as well as in schools and churches. Women thus increased their leverage—and their need—to promote a mating system that maximized their sexual control and minimized their vulnerability; that is, that limited coitus to marriage. What emerged was a system that depended on *self*-control.

54

"A Connection of Hands"

In general, couples became involved in sexual "boundary disputes" only when they were well on their way toward marriage. The course they followed was like a footpath through a familiar wood: the markings were informal, but everyone knew the route. Places on this road were out of public view, and travelers were often alone, yet they were never far from home. In a climate that fostered self-determination in mate selection, self-regulation of behavior, and self-control of sexuality, men and women took the steps that brought them closer to each other and to marriage.

CHAPTER 2

"The Scene Is About to Be Changed"

ONCE a young person had succeeded in finding a mate who would be friend and lover, sincere and candid, trustworthy and affectionate, a new and sometimes difficult phase of the transition to marriage began. The timing of marriage generated far more conflict than did the choice of a mate. A man had to acquire the means to support not only himself but a wife and children. A woman had material preparations to complete, but compared with the emotional obstacles she faced, the piles of sewing were easily surmounted. Women and men saw marriage as their destiny, but they recognized that it could bring grief as well as joy. Women were especially attuned to the somber side. Because marriage meant the first break from home and the assumption of new duties and obligations, women were in general less eager than men to change their station in life. Conventions and rituals developed to give women companionship, confidence, and courage as they made the transition to marriage.

"Considering my circumstances"

"Marriage," Timothy Pickering declared in 1799, "is a goal which every man, for his own happiness and honor and the good of society cannot reach too soon."[1] Young men took this admonition to heart. Once they completed their schooling, established themselves in business, acquired a farm, or simply passed into their middle twenties, they began to ready themselves for marriage.

Men hesitated to commit themselves to marry—even at some date in the indefinite future—until they felt emotionally ready and could be sure of acquiring the necessary financial resources. Emotional preparedness for marriage was simply defined: If a young man fell in love with a woman, he wanted—some day—to marry her. Marriage was the natural and Christian response to heterosexual love. Few people questioned that love was required for marriage, and even fewer entertained the truly radical notion that marriage might not necessarily follow from love. A young man who found himself in love turned his thoughts toward marriage, but he could not ask for a woman's hand if all he could offer was his heart. With the decline of farming, especially in the long-settled areas of the Northeast, a young man could no longer rely on his father to furnish him with a "portion" of land, but had to make his own way in the world. Before he could marry, a man had to assure himself, as well as his prospective bride and her family, that he had the means to provide the necessities of domestic life. Thus, the failure of a young man's resources to grow as quickly as his attachment could lead to a painful crisis in a relationship.

Take the case of Silas Felton, the son of a Massachusetts farmer. Silas began his "address" to Lucretia Fay in 1794, when he was about eighteen. At first he had "no intention of Marrying her but merely [wished] to spend a few evenings in a social and agreeable way." At the time, he was teaching district school and helping support himself by itinerant farm work. When in 1795, his father agreed to allow him to attend an academy for a term, Silas sought to end his relationship with Lucretia Fay.

Considering my circumstances and knowing that I was not in any condition to marry, and that if I attended school, it was necessary to have my mind fix'd there, that if I followed the same course much longer it would be difficult to part with each other. Considering all these I finally drew up a resolution in my own mind to bid her farewell.

Silas acted on his resolution, but a few months later, he found himself at Lucretia's house. In the course of his visit, his resolution crumbled, and the relationship resumed.[2]

Two years later, another crisis developed when Lucretia's family decided to move to Vermont. Silas was teaching school, surveying roads, and cutting hay during the summer months; his future was still uncertain.

I now began seriously to consider what I could do with a family, that if I did not intend to marry it was time our courtship ended. My fortune was small and my prospects of gaining it, to any considerable amount, was also gloomy; so that it appeared best to end our Courtship.

Time and again, "when going in the evening to visit" Lucretia, Silas would resolve "that this should be the last," but it was not until July of 1798 that the couple "mutually agreed to part with each other, after a considerable conversation." Silas set himself a new course:

I can live without troubling myself about the means of providing for a family at present. That I will enjoy myself as easy as possibly, visit some of the Misses now and then; but declared to myself that I would not court any one steadily.[3]

Thus Silas passed the summer, but at night he lay awake "meditating . . . what step to take." He surmised that Lucretia "was not altogether easy, for I had reason to believe her mind was not more calm than my own." After spending so much time together "without ever having the least difference," Silas concluded that it "was very hard for any young Couple to part with each other." Finally, in September, he wrote Lucretia "the theme of [his] thoughts for some time past":

Every project, which could be devised, has not escaped the strict scrutiny of my mind. I have ransacked and ransacked the different occupations, which are followed in the world until I have almost distracted my brain; yet I know not what to do.

What Silas resolved was to recommence his visits to Lucretia Fay, and four months later, they were married.[4]

This account of the courtship of Silas Felton and Lucretia Fay reveals the seriousness with which young men took their responsibilities in forming a marriage. When Silas's interest in Lucretia ripened into love—a feeling he described (modestly, by the standards of the next generation) as "something implanted in my breast, which seems to say that your company is of much more satisfaction to me than your absence"—marriage was not automatically at hand. However strong his feelings for Lucretia, and they were strong enough to make it almost impossible for him to stay away from her, those feelings did not justify marriage so long as his future prospects were uncertain. It is significant that Silas, rather than Lucretia or any member of either family, imposed this requirement; it was he who decided, finally, to wait no longer but to take the leap. At twenty-two, his chances of financial security were better than they had been at eighteen. If inner doubts had moved him to prolong his courtship of Lucretia Fay, these were no longer enough to keep the couple apart.[5]*

*Immediately following their marriage, Silas and Lucretia lived with his parents while he taught school, but soon he entered into a business partnership and began keep-

"Very happy or very miserable"

When Silas Felton was struggling to decide whether to break off with Lucretia Fay or to marry her, his sleepless nights were filled with thoughts of marriage: It was "the most important step of Life; and ought to be entered upon as such." Like most of his contemporaries, he had concluded, "by viewing other people and contemplating on their Lives," that marriage was the best and worst of what was possible in life. The Massachusetts woman who declared, "There can be no medium in the wedded state. It must either be happy or miserable," expressed an idea that appears with striking regularity in the writings of early nineteenth century men and women. In 1810, a nineteen-year-old girl thought of marriage as a "state which must be very happy or very miserable." Ten years later, a middle-aged matron agreed that "no state can admit of a greater or purer degree of happiness . . . and there is none, where a dissimilarity of sentiment & feeling exist, that is admissible of greater misery." To the itinerant preacher Lorenzo Dow, "an unhappy marriage was the greatest curse which is endured this side of hell, next to the horrors of a guilty conscience." To the college student Enoch Lincoln, a "conjugal connection" with the right woman, "would be Heaven itself."[7]

The belief that marriage brought extremes of both pleasure and pain followed from the common perception that marriage as an institution was perfect but individual marriages were much less so. Marriage was not merely a way to organize society's daily life and to ensure its future, but was the primary source of nurturance, intimacy, and security available to individual adults. Yet observation revealed that most *marriages* failed to fulfill the expectations of *marriage*. Many less radical observers echoed the abolitionist Theodore Weld's judgment: Of all the people he knew, there was "not one husband or wife who . . . embody in their example an illustration of what married

---

ing a store. "With a family to provide for, [he] therefore thought it necessary to follow some other occupation."[6]

life was designed to be"; and his fiancée Angelina Grimké's assessment of "the almost universal unhappiness of married persons" was widely shared by her more conventional female contemporaries.[8]

In his 1833 work, *The Young Wife*, William Alcott observed that there was "a very general opinion abroad, that the love of husband and wife must, after marriage, necessarily begin to decline." Benjamin Ward pointed to the "melancholy truth" that many who "fancied a world of bliss before them on tying the nuptial knot" found matrimony a bitter disappointment.[9] One way to resolve the conflict between the reality of married life and the ideals of domesticity—between the "melancholy truth" and "fancied . . . bliss"—was to define marriage as having the potential for both. If marriage was the best in life, then the risks involved were warranted; but those risks remained and were reflected in the conception of marriage as the worst that fate could bring.

Men and women concurred in this two-sided view, but their attitudes toward marriage reflected the difference in what each sex stood to gain (and lose) at the altar. In general men were more likely to emphasize the positive and women the negative aspects. Men could adopt a jesting tone about a matter that to women had the awful seriousness of life and death. When Thomas Merrill wondered if his friend Daniel Webster was "about to be caught in the toils of wedlock," the young Webster replied, "This said wed-lock is a very dangerous sort of a lock. Once fastened, it is fastened forever. It is a lock that one can't unlock; you can't break it, you can't pick it." The future senator had imagined himself "a king . . . a priest . . . a doctor, a lawyer, and a thousand other things," but, he claimed, "in the most wayward frolic of fancy, I never dreamed myself to be a husband. A husband!" Webster himself admitted that this outburst was "all nonsense." At age twenty-three he was regrettably "making no progress towards matrimony," and he was quick to defend himself against the unspoken charge that he had "a stony heart, unpenetrated and impenetrable." In fact, like most young men, Daniel Webster was anxious to find a woman who would "participate in his joys as well as troubles—by making his every sorrow—his every *care*— or happiness [her] own." Another young man confided to a friend, "One thing is as true as that two halves are equal to a whole, that is I am tired of being a bachelor, and of being such an isolated being."[10]

For men, marriage meant an end to isolation, but it also brought a lifetime of heavy responsibility. A man's failures were no longer his own alone. "If I should sink in my professional efforts . . . how would that friend be wounded, how would her days be embittered. . . . If I were wholly independent, . . . my fear of . . . defeat would be far less terrible," Benjamin Ward reflected in 1822 as his marriage approached. Men must shoulder the financial burdens attendant upon marriage, and the anticipation of carrying that weight through life could make a young man doubt his strength. In 1795, Jesse Appleton wrote to his school friend Ebenezer Adams:

Matrimony appears . . . like a great house, seen at a distance. You give it a general glance, and it appears well. You have no objection to live in such a one thro' life—But if you think seriously of purchasing it, a thousand considerations will influence the bargain which never entered your mind when you took a general view. . . . 'To wed nor not to wed'—that's the question.

One young man who admitted he had "entertained some wild notions respecting the question" had at last been "fully persuaded that the greatest share of happiness of which humanity is susceptible is derived from the conjugal connection."[11]

Perhaps he had been convinced by the arguments of a newly wedded friend, who had discovered that marriage was not so onerous as he had been led to believe. At least one young husband concluded that the "cares that one imagines this state brings with it, arise more from the false representation of people that are discontented without any real cause to be so, than from what is actually the truth." He had formed his "Ideas of the wants and perplexities that a man with a family is constantly involved in, from the groundless representations of the world." He insisted to a bachelor friend, "The moment you taste the happiness of the marriage union, you will curse yourself for a fool, that you have lived so long without it," and urged him to "become a *steady man* . . . be married." Another newly married man wrote in a similar vein to his friend Henry Channing: "Marry & be happy," he advised. But Henry wanted to "think coolly." He had "already had a large portion of happiness" in his courtship, and—looking ahead to marriage—sought "to be prepared for the reverse, not by anticipating evil but by moderating [his] expectations."[12]

In thinking about marriage, the young women of the early republic seemed unable not to anticipate evil—or at least unhappiness. When Erastus Smith told Sarah Williams of the pleasure he foresaw in their impending union, she replied that her feelings were "rather depressed than elevated." "I would not by any means presage misfortune neither dare I anticipate uninterrupted tranquility," she wrote in 1806. The fear that "fate may heave her quiver filled with poison'd darts to deaden every pure domestic joy" was, she believed, known to "every woman who contemplates a marriage connection . . . as happiness or misery, the most complete misery in this world, may enter the list with them."[13] Sarah Williams's concern was widely shared in early nineteenth century America. While men were inclined to dwell on the pleasure marriage could bring, women pointed to its potential for grief. One woman told her cousin that she did not "expect any bright reverse of the common course of things" in her married life. Like many of her contemporaries, she looked upon it "as an untried scene of care and temptation." Images of confinement, struggle, and loss dominate women's descriptions of matrimony; it was "a sad, sour, sober beverage" that brought "some joys, but many crosses." Marriage was woman's destiny, but it appeared a dreadful one. The Massachusetts woman who had "always anticipated the event with a degree of solemnity almost equal to that which [would] terminate [her] present existence," was not alone in her cataclysmic view of marriage.[14]*

---

*At least one young man shared this sense of the terrible finality of marriage. When William Edmond Curtis learned that his childhood friend Elizabeth Prince was to be

In a sense, marriage did bring a young woman's "present exis-tence" to an end. It redefined woman's routine and her role so completely that girlhood seemed to disappear overnight; becom-ing a wife altered a woman's approach to life as well as her way of life. Alexis de Tocqueville's observation that "the amuse-ments of the girl cannot become the recreations of the wife" ac-curately reflected a popular sentiment among early nineteenth century Americans. Marriage meant the end of a woman's "sea-son for gaiety." Any woman "on the road to matrimony" would have "too much good sense to approve the same conduct in a wife, which is allowable in a gay girl," one recent bride declared. Lydia Maria Child objected to the conception of marriage that lay behind this sentiment. Observing that it was often said about a young woman, "Let her enjoy herself all she can, while she is single," the author of *The Frugal Housewife* protested in 1832:

Instead of representing domestic life as the gathering place of the deepest and purest affections; as the sphere of woman's *enjoyments* as well as of her *duties*, . . . that one pernicious sentence teaches a girl that [marriage] is a necessary sacrifice of her freedom and gayety.[16]

However much Mrs. Child might have wished to brighten the somber light in which marriage appeared to women, she could not change the fact that it represented a dramatic coming of age for them. Especially in the first half of the century, marriage was both the biggest and the first step a woman took away from her family. When Mary Brown heard that her sister Eunice had been married, she wrote, "I could not realize the alterations that have taken place since I parted with you. . . . It seemed like a dream—a little girl when you left our paternal home, now grown to a woman—married & entering into all the cares and pleasures of that important station." Mary, who had herself been married less than two years, confessed: "I could hardly help feeling something like regret at the thought that I should no more see you as I wos won't [*sic*] to do a little lively playmate participating in every amusement which a childish fancy could

---

married, he wrote in his diary: "The idea of her being married seems to me much the same as her being buried."[15]

suggest." Girlhood gave way, a Connecticut woman explained, to "the many hours of confinement and other necessary duties that deprive the married woman of a thousand innocent girlish enjoyments." Married women appeared not merely to have grown up but to have grown old. When twenty-one-year-old Abigail May met an old friend, now married, she reported in her journal:

The lady was Mrs. Poor—Meriam Fullerton—that gay sprightly Meriam Fullerton that was—but oh! how alter'd—she looks dull, dejected, in short, like a *married woman. I'll say* with Solus—"oh! I'll never be married" if such sower [*sic*] looks comes of matrimony.[17]

The giving up of girlish pleasures was only part of the trouble; even more fearsome was the taking on of "great and responsible duties which such a connection inevitably brings with it." When Mary Winsor agreed to marry the minister Henry Ware, she told a friend, "It is true, dreadfully true, I have taken upon myself great and unknown duties for which I feel incompetent." Women pledged to clergymen were especially susceptible to such self-doubts, but they were not alone in their suffering. Many women questioned their ability to fulfill "the responsibility of the station." One woman facing marriage confessed, "I can not contemplate . . . its total dissimilarity to that to which I have been accustomed, and the arduous duties resulting from it, together with my own inability to perform them as I ought, without feeling a degree of anxiety lest I shall be found wholly unqualified for the situation." All of this language—the loss of "innocent girlish enjoyments," the evoking of things inevitable and dreadful—resonates with the sexual transformation that marriage represented. Of the many "great and unknown duties" women assumed at marriage, sex (and its consequences) must have seemed the most awesome. When a woman steeled herself "to encounter difficulties and to meet with disappointments," she foresaw the poor harvests, ill health, or financial troubles that might afflict her future family, but she must also have thought of the marriage bed and the risks of disease and death to which it exposed her. Surely this is what would come to mind when young women read William Alcott's discussion of the "concession and submission" required of them when they left home to marry. "In addition to the physical comforts of which she voluntarily deprives herself, does she not subject herself to numerous cares and responsibilities, and trials?" he asked. "Does she not submit, at least prospectively, to a long train of circumstances and consequences which, in her father's house, she would be able to escape?"[18]

In addition to the tangible responsibilities a woman took on when she married, there were equally weighty spiritual obligations. A middle-class wife's charge involved more than the physical care of her family; she was also entrusted with their moral health and happiness. In the aftermath of the Revolution, the ideal of Republican Motherhood had emerged to preserve patriarchal authority while assigning to women the all-important task of rearing patriotic citizens. The affectionate nurture of children was the best means to ensure their future success and the safety of the republic. American women were to mold their sons into men who combined industry, loyalty, and virtue, and their daughters into pure, pious, submissive, and domestic exemplars of True Womanhood; and they were to fortify their husbands against the temptations and dangers of the world beyond the home. As a New York minister sermonized, "interesting and important . . . duties devolved on females as WIVES." The wife, "by her pious, assiduous, and attractive deportment, constantly endeavors to render [her husband] more virtuous, more useful, more honourable, and more happy." Margaret Bayard set herself on this difficult course. Shortly before her marriage in 1800, she wrote in her diary: "To perform these duties, various in their objects, & important in their nature, is to be the future object of my life. . . . The happiness & the virtue of others is committed to my charge."[19]

But what vexed women about marriage was the double burden it imposed. Not only was a woman accountable for "the happiness & virtue of others," but she was completely dependent on the man she married for her own and her children's well-being. The ever-insightful de Tocqueville noted the "extreme dependence" of American women, in spite of the lofty position they occupied. It was this relationship that so troubled Hannah Huntington. "Every joy in anticipation depends on you," she wrote her fiancé, "and from you must I derive every pleasure." Margaret Bayard assured Samuel Smith, "to be dependent on you, for all the comforts of life is far from irksome," but she did not want to be "indulged like a child." Mary Winsor realized that her "happiness [was] intimately dependent" upon Henry Ware, but she lacked Margaret Bayard's self-confidence. "A feeling of distrust and fearfulness" affected Mary. "O, it is solemn, it is awful, thus to bind one's self for life!" she wrote to a friend.[20]

Even if they were "made silken" by love, the bonds that a woman accepted when she married tied her to a lifelong role. Her husband and children would look to her for the purity, piety, submissiveness, and domesticity that were expected of a True Woman; yet the source of all her authority, influence, and material welfare was her mate. At least one young man recognized this special burden borne by women. "The contract is so much more important in its consequences to females than to males," George Cutler pointed out in 1820, "for besides leaving everything else to unite themselves to one man they subject themselves to his authority—they depend more upon their husband than he does upon the wife for society and for the happiness & enjoyment of their lives—he is their all—their only relative—their only hope."[21]

George Cutler's conclusion that a woman's husband was her "only relative" reflected his assumption that marriage separated a woman from her own family. Women regularly made—and were distressed by—the same assumption. "There has always been something unpleasant in my idea of a married state, when I consider it as connected with the relinquishment of those nameless ties which render *home* so delightful in early years," one Maine woman wrote. "It must be a strong attachment that can attract a young female from her father's house, and from the companions of her juvenile days," she thought.[22]* Even

*When Anne Robbins became engaged in 1811, her sister Sally was "angry that she should allow this prepossession apparently to occupy every feeling of her heart, and

when a "strong attachment" existed, the prospect of marriage could be fearful. Although Catharine Beecher was strongly attracted to the young mathematics professor Alexander Fisher, she told a friend, "I never could give up such a father and such a home and friends as mine for one who after the first novelty of wedded life had worn away would be so engrossed in science and study as to forget I existed." In the Reverend Lyman Beecher, Catharine had an unusually attentive father, but her view of marriage as the "giving up" of family and home was widely shared. It was a painful exchange. A young Pennsylvanian told her fiancé that the "ties of so many years would not be sundered without doing violence in some degree to the heart." While she regarded separation from her family as a "severe trial," she asked him, "Can I not bear to be separated from them better than from you?"[24] For many women, that question was not easily answered.

Women often talked about the pain of giving up their home in terms of its association with childhood. Childhood may have stood for the close connection with parents, for safety and familiarity, all of which were at risk in marriage. It may also be that what was most frightening on an unconscious level about the transition to marriage was the motherhood it would almost certainly—and almost immediately—bring. Motherhood not only meant a loss of sexual control but the demands of True Womanhood in its highest form. The emphasis on the loss of childhood associations may have been the only safe expression of the fear women felt at taking on their "natural" responsibilities.

"The scene is about to be changed"

By the time they could afford to marry, middle-class men were likely to be living away from home—in rooms at college, with

---

so entirely to engross and swallow up every other, as never to have named as a privation that she has to remove a hundred miles from all she has formerly known and loved."[23] This may be one exception that proves the rule.

another family, in a boardinghouse. Many of them had experienced difficulty in leaving home, but the break was behind them. For their sisters, however, it lay ahead, inextricably linked to the transition to marriage. Many girls went away to work or study for a time or for extended visits to friends or kinfolk, but most lived at home for at least part of the year. While young men could look forward to marriage as their chance to *have* a home, young women saw it as a *separation from* home. When two friends became engaged, Persis Sibley thought both had made "good matches" but did not envy either one. In her journal, the Maine schoolmistress wrote, "I had rather go to my school, much as I dread it, but it isn't leaving home for life." Only marriage required that sacrifice.[25]

Even if little physical distance was involved, marriage still meant, in the words of one amateur poet, "Leaving the place of our childhood mirth/Seeking a home by another hearth." A bride whose new hearth was near her old could be grateful, as Jerusha Kellogg was, for "the consolation of living in sight of home." Young women without such consolation suffered the most intense anxiety about separation from home. Two weeks before her marriage to Samuel Smith, whom she was to accompany to Washington, D.C., Margaret Bayard expressed to him her fears:

Until this moment, I never fully realized the separation that was to take place; I did not *feel* that I was to leave my friends, . . . The scene is about to be changed. I am going I was about to say to the land of strangers, but it is not so, for where you are, must be a home to me.

Margaret Bayard was unusually sanguine. She was confident of Samuel's ability to take the place "of an indulgent parent, fond sister, & most tender & attentive friends," and assured him, "Your affection, your society will be an all-sufficient compensation for their loss." Men understood that they were expected to provide such compensation. A woman who told her fiancé, "I know you will supply the place of all I leave," was giving him both a vote of confidence and a difficult charge. At least one man wondered out loud if he was worthy. "Can I fill that void in your heart which a separation from your beautiful home—your father, mother, brothers, and sisters—is to create?" William Lloyd Garrison asked Helen Benson. The young reformer promised, "I will try to do so," but he admitted to Helen, "I am almost afraid to receive you, lest I shall fail in making you happy."[26]*

Garrison set himself the task of making his wife happy, a more intangible goal than the one commonly assigned to men. Women were to make their mates happy; men were to make their wives comfortable. After all, it was the female sex that, as one suitor put it, was "calculated to happify" the male. Material welfare was far easier to measure than happiness. It is not surprising, then, that William Lloyd Garrison, who took on the traditionally female responsibility for his mate's emotional well-being, suffered from a lack of self-confidence that more commonly afflicted women. It was usually women who voiced the concern Margaret Bayard expressed to Samuel Smith shortly before their wedding: "If I can but make *you* happy. . . . I fear sometimes I shall not be all you wish."[28] Garrison's direct statement of self-doubt was unusual. If men were frightened at the prospect of having to compensate women for the loss suffered at marriage, they did not respond by hesitating when the time neared. Once a man had made his choice and prepared himself for marriage, he showed little ambivalence in the pursuit of his goal. Women, on the other hand, vacillated and wavered as they took the last steps to the altar.

A man who had found, wooed, and won the woman he wanted for his wife, and obtained the approval of her parents, could relax. "The most embarrassing part of the affair" was behind him, but for his future bride, it was yet to come.[29] Except when marriage would be followed immediately by a long-distance move, women generally made the decision to marry with far less conflict than the decision of *when* to marry. It was the timing of marriage that created the most ambivalence, distress, and self-doubt in women. If a young woman loved and

---

*It may be that men who, like Garrison, were involved in abolition, woman's rights, and other reform causes were more prone than other men to worry about their ability to "fill the void" created when a woman left her family. A man who held critical views of marriage might fear that he, too, would somehow oppress his wife.[27]

trusted a man, she could agree to an engagement without raising the issues—of loss, separation, vulnerability—that were the source of so much distress when marriage itself approached. But as it came time to bring the period of betrothal to a close, all of those issues emerged in force.

An occasional man might assure his fiancée that he was in "no haste" for their wedding; but most suitors echoed John March, who told Alice Hale he hoped "there was no sin in declaring that I am *extremely* anxious for our union." John was chagrined that Alice expressed no disappointment when their wedding was delayed a week; "even that . . . would afford me some consolation," he told her.[30] This was the common pattern in the early republic: a young man eager to hurdle any obstacles; a young woman whose instinct was to shy at the gate. Because men expected marriage to enrich rather than restrict their daily lives, they were more eager than women to have the wedding take place. By the time a young man's circumstances enabled him to support a wife, any ambivalence he may have felt about the responsibilities and intimacies of married life receded, leaving him unconflicted about his desire for a speedy marriage. He could, however, expect resistance and procrastination on his fiancée's part.

It is hardly surprising that anyone who thought of marriage in terms of a "catastrophe" should have been reluctant to rush into it. It seemed obvious to Hannah Huntington that she would not "wish to hasten those days that will bring more cares than the present."[31] Young women were caught between their desire for the benefits of marriage and their perception of its costs. They wanted—they *had*—to be married to assume the role that they had been raised to play; and perhaps as a result, they believed that a happy marriage was the ideal state in which to live. Hence, the relative ease with which most of them handled proposals of marriage. But, when the time came to *get married*, many women responded by staging a holding action.*

Since it was the woman's prerogative to set the wedding date,

---

*The fact that these women had little hope of delaying conception once they were married may have intensified their need to postpone the wedding as long as possible; after marriage, motherhood was imminent and almost inevitable.

71

engagements often stretched out past the time when men were ready to marry. Many weddings were timed to meet external demands: the outcome of a business deal, the exigencies of travel, the imperatives of the agricultural calendar, even the lyceum schedule.[32] But whenever possible, the woman chose the wedding date, and very few selected the earliest possible one. They cited financial constraints, age, personal or family health, even the weather to explain and justify their desire to delay marriage. They often added a disclaimer that they were seeking "to prolong the period of their power," or a declaration that they were acting "on the grounds of duty rather than personal preference." Women consistently sought longer, and men shorter, engagements. Georgina Amory tried to explain to John Lowell that "tho two years were a long courtship, it was not too long to be courted."[33]

When the courtship drew to a close, even the most confident women were gripped by intense anxiety. Perhaps this was nothing more than last-minute jitters, but it was taken—and stated—with deadly seriousness. From the 1780s to the 1830s, diaries and correspondence are full of women who "trembled" at the approach of their wedding day; who were "anxious," "mortified," "fretful"; whose minds were "loaded with doubts and fears"; or whose "spirits were much depressed" as the day drew near.[34] Like Margaret Bayard, they wondered whether "it was possible, in the contemplation of such an object, that the mind can be free from apprehension?" "Where there is so much to lose, must we not fear?" she asked her fiancé two weeks before their wedding. To some women the prospect was so frightening that they experienced a kind of paralysis. A young Quaker woman was so overwhelmed by last-minute doubts that she was "almost ready to get up [in meeting] and say she would not proceed." Those women for whom it had been a trial just to *set* a wedding date were subject to especially painful sensations when the date approached.[35]

Some women tried to comfort and calm themselves with a form of positive thinking, although at times it seemed forced. A Loyalist bride-to-be wrote her mother in 1783, shortly before her wedding, "What a change will it make! Yet if I am to be un-happy I console myself with reflecting on the shortness of life, and that at the end of it the enquiry will not be if it was passed pleasantly, but well." Thirty years later Mary Pearson told her fiancé, "I am willing to leave the Event to that great & good Being who has preserved us in life, & to each other." In 1824, another New Englander explained that her willingness to be married soon was not because she expected to be happier than she had been. "I am afraid I shall not," she wrote her future husband, "but as the die is cast, & there is nothing but death to separate us, I may as well look upon the bright side of the question."[36]

One can easily imagine that the closer a young woman came to marriage, the more she would have felt—and feared—the dis-parity between the ideal and the reality. In the "fearful ex-change" that would take place on her wedding day, she would give up courtship for the demands of True Womanhood made by marriage. A woman would be both more isolated from the world and more exposed to its dangers as a wife than as a daugh-ter in her parents' house. She would no longer be free to come and go from the domestic circle; she would be enclosed within and defined by it. The transition to marriage, then, appeared to women to have freedom and security at one end and confine-ment and risk at the other.

De Tocqueville saw this predicament with remarkable clari-ty. Observing that "in America, the independence of woman is irrecoverably lost in the bonds of matrimony," the perceptive Frenchman drew a contrast between the unmarried woman, who "makes her father's house an abode of freedom and of plea-sure," and the married woman, who "lives in the home of her husband as if it were a cloister." Although the middle-class home might seem as confining as a cloister, it did not promise the safety and tranquillity (or, of course, the celibacy) of a clois-tered life. De Tocqueville realized that, in the United States, for-tunes were as easily lost as made; and he lauded American women for having the strength of character to "support these vicissitudes with calm and unquenchable energy." However, in his admiration, he failed to see (perhaps because it was endemic?) that women were far from calm as marriage approached. Rather than surrendering their independence "without a struggle and without a murmur when the time comes for making the sacrifice," as de Tocqueville thought, many prospective brides experienced—and expressed—intense conflict.[37]

Marriage might be a woman's destiny, even her heart's desire, but in the new nation, it appeared to be a cataclysmic event. This had not always been the case. In early America, the transition to marriage was a smooth seam in the fabric of everyday life; a wedding meant a brief pause, not a disruption, in the daily routine. The colonial couple whose guests danced ninety-two jigs, fifty contras, fifty-three minuets, and seventeen hornpipes until one o'clock in the morning were no doubt weary as they went about their chores the next day, but the rhythm of life in this rural society was not broken by a trip to the altar.[38] The demands of an agricultural existence provided continuity. A young woman served a long apprenticeship in "huswifery"; once wed, she would do the milking in her husband's barn rather than her father's, but the tasks and setting were unchanged. Having been bound always by the ties that knit these communities together, a bride would not have found her new position confining. If anything, she would have enjoyed increased authority as the manager of her own household and the helpmeet and sometimes stand-in for her husband.[39] In the colonies, marriage was not a leap from one life to another but was one of many steps marked out by God and watched over by kin and community.

By the end of the eighteenth century, middle-class Americans in the settled areas of the country had already begun to move away from subsistence farming toward a more commercial, urban, modern way of life. The traditional division of labor was fast becoming a separation of "spheres." Where once women reigned in the dairy and men in the fields, now True Women protected the Home, while men tested themselves in the World. But even as these gender roles sharpened, young unmarried women and men remained relatively unconstrained by them.

"The Scene Is About to Be Changed"

It was the "Home" and the "World" that defined the proper spheres for women and men; and most single women were not yet responsible for a home, nor most young men completely on their own in the world. It was marriage that empowered a woman to fulfill the ideals of Republican Motherhood and True Womanhood. In increasing both the dependence and the responsibilities of middle-class women, these ideals contributed to their anxiety about marriage.

There is another complementary explanation for why so many women shied at the gate. The prospect of relinquishing their independence may have caused women to delay marriage as long as possible, but a loss of intimacy was also at stake. Although a woman was dependent on her husband for her livelihood and social position, and a man was dependent on his wife to provide a well-ordered and virtuous home, marriage might appear to require less emotional interdependence than courtship offered. The shared world of the courting couple, with its mutual exploration, its common activities and joint planning, and its aura of romantic love, fostered a closeness that marriage might appear to threaten. Marriage brought to an end the stage of the life cycle in which middle-class men and women interacted in relative freedom from the restrictions of their separate spheres. For the bride, it meant accepting the limits of domesticity. The ambivalence many women felt—after all, those limits offered protection as well—was compounded by a fear that the separation of spheres would destroy the intimacy of courtship. The intimacy that developed on the road to marriage, and that made the road safe for traveling, might be difficult to sustain once the destination was reached.

"These last weeks"

Many women found both justification for delay and distraction from their gloomy thoughts in the preparations required for a wedding and the new life it celebrated. One bride-to-be confessed to her sister, "I do not dare to think of leaving home. I try not to realize it & hope thus to lighten the parting—I am perfectly thankful that these last weeks will be very busy ones to all of us." Harriet Porter was so busy that she was moved to wish "not only that the days may be longer but that there might be *more* of *them*" before her marriage to Lyman Beecher.[40]

It was the tasks to be accomplished, rather than any predetermined sequence of activities, that set the pace for the last stage of the transition to marriage. Both men and women devoted themselves to preparing for the wedding and for the home to which they would go as newlyweds. While men generally took responsibility for providing the house and women for the furnishings, many brides contributed only clothing, linens, and other items a woman could produce at home or buy with her limited funds.* Parents helped with their daughter's share of the costs if they could, but through teaching, sewing, or mill work, many women were able to earn some or all of the money themselves. Gifts of cash or property from close relatives might ease the initial financial burdens; before the Civil War, these were the only gifts a middle-class couple was likely to receive. One New Englander remembered that when he was married in 1833, he and his bride did not receive "a single present, except some money from the father. It was not the custom then."[42]

Prospective brides were often involved in selecting and readying the house or rooms they would occupy as newlyweds. They issued feminine reminders "that closets are *very convenient* though not absolutely indispensable; a painted kitchen floor is much preferable to an unpainted . . . a good well, accommodations for wood may be considered." Cost and comfort were the key factors. Sarah Chester Williams worried that her fiancé had "expended more upon the house than [he] proposed merely to gratify [her] feelings." "The shades for windows is quite beyond

---

*Zadoc Long sent Julia Davis a list of the articles he purchased for her in Boston; they included silk stockings, a shell hair comb, a bonnet and trimmings, silverware, carpeting, bed and table linens, and silver thimble. Since Zadoc sent along a bill, it appears that he was merely acting as Julia's agent.[41]

my expectations," she told him, although she admitted, "I think them very convenient."[43] The biggest decision concerned whether the couple would set up housekeeping or board in another household. Many couples chose the latter as a financial expediency, but most preferred to have their own home, however simply furnished it was. Living with the family of the bride or the groom was also unpopular—although, once again, it was sometimes unavoidable. Mary Guion felt "strangely melancholy" whenever her fiancé pressed her for a wedding date. Finally, she "with frankness told him that it was owing to the thot of our living in the same house with his family and that if we was going to live by ourselves my fealings would be very different." Catherine Joss was less reticent. When she married the son of Swiss immigrants to the Ohio Territory in 1839, her husband's family wanted the newlyweds to come and live with them. "I did not intend to do so, else I should have stayed at home," she later wrote.[44]

Setting up a new household occupied the prospective bride and groom and their families for weeks and sometimes months before the wedding. Men looked at rooms or houses to rent or buy; women stitched table and bed linens. Alone and together, they shopped for bedsteads, tables, chairs, and other objects necessary for domestic life. As these tasks neared completion—as the rooms were papered, the carpets laid, the sewing finished—the wedding itself became the center of attention. Early nineteenth century weddings were generally simple, almost informal affairs, which required little planning and advance preparation. Arrangements for the wedding were not made until shortly before the appointed day.[45] A week appears to have been the average length of time between the issuing of invitations and the wedding; invitations were often even less formal than weddings. Sometimes couples had cards printed, but usually they simply sent notes or oral messages to friends and relatives about a week ahead of time. Especially when the couple's families lived far apart, it was not uncommon for members of the groom's immediate family to be absent from the wedding. Ira Miltimore's kin lived in the Western Reserve; when he was married in New

York in 1839, he "did not expect many of [his] relatives present on that occasion although it would be very gratifying to have them there."[46] While guests did not gather from far and wide, life was still unscheduled enough for people to travel short distances, with little notice, for the wedding of a friend or relation.

The great majority of northern weddings took place at the home of the bride, although the popularity of church weddings was growing, especially among the urban élite. Because the Puritans regarded marriage not as a sacrament but as "a civil thing," they at first prohibited ministers from officiating at weddings. Even after clergymen were legally empowered to perform marriages, colonial couples continued to prefer a magistrate or justice of the peace. However, by the early 1800s, civil marriages were on the wane. Couples who chose the civil service usually did so as a matter of necessity. Thomas Whittemore, himself a Universalist minister, remembered, "I would not call on the orthodox clergyman to marry me, for he had treated me with neglect, and . . . there was no Universalist clergyman sufficiently near." When Sarah Connell married Charles Ayer in 1810, there was no clergyman of any kind near her home in New Hampshire, so she turned reluctantly to the justice of the peace. "I do not approve of this being married by a justice, notwithstanding it has of late become fashionable," she noted in her diary.[47] The "fashion" that Sarah Connell so deplored was in fact a dying tradition; by the end of the nineteenth century, church weddings would be the norm among middle-class Americans.

Most couples were married by a minister, at the bride's home, in the presence of a small group of friends and relatives, but wedding ritual was showing signs of elaboration. Bridal attendants were not unheard of in the eighteenth century; by the second quarter of the nineteenth, they had become *de rigueur*. In 1828, a young New Bedford woman asked her more worldly Boston cousin, "Must people have bride-maids & groom's men, whether they want them or not?" A likely reply was that one *could* be married without attendants, but few respectable couples chose to do so. In 1839, the young lawyer Henry Poor reported from Bangor, Maine, "We have adopted the good Massa-

chusetts faction [*sic*] of having bridesmaids and groomsmen."
The usual practice was to have one or two of each, although
some bridal parties were as large as twelve.[48]

Ties of friendship and kinship determined the selection.*
Typically, a prospective groom asked a brother. Roger Baldwin,
for example, wrote his brother Ebenezer two weeks before his
wedding to "express a hope that you will come without fail, and
do me the favor to officiate as Groomsman on the occasion."
Young women turned to sisters or close female friends. Ordinar-
ily, the prospective bride chose the female, and the groom the
male, members of the wedding party, but when a young man
was married at a distance from his own home, he had to forego
groomsmen or rely on his bride's male connections. Albert Bledsoe was traveling from Ohio to New Jersey for his wedding to
Harriet Coxe; she wrote to him, "I fear you will find some difficulty . . . in supplying yourself with the important article of
groomsmen. . . . You must import some of your friends for the
occasion, or else make use of mine, whichever you please." Albert responded, "It is customary, I believe, to have groomsmen,
and I would not deviate from custom in such matters . . . but
they must be chosen from the circle of your friends, since I cannot import any of mine."[50]

By the 1830s, there were other new developments as well. The
simple celebrations that prevailed in the first decades after Independence were still common but no longer universal. Mary
Guion's diary for February 1803 records a wedding week typical
of the 1770–1820 period:

Feb. 1 [Tuesday] Mr. Sarles came to ask consent of my father for a connection in the family by marrying my sister to which he acquiesced
& the nuptials is to be celebrated at our house on Tuesday of this week.
Mon. [7 February] All day engaged making preparations for the wedding.
Feb. 8 [Tuesday] About 1 o'clock the company came: [groom's father,
mother, siblings, and eight others]. Ceremony was performed about
2 o'clock before we dined—in the evening we got Tea.

*However, for some people, the choice of attendants was simply a matter of appear-
ance. One young man reported, "I could not act as groomsman to Bro. A there being
so much difference in our sizes and looks."[49]

The following day a "party and dance" were held at the Guion home.[51] Over the next two decades, this basic sequence would be extended, the steps elaborated, and greater formality and regularity imposed.

Weddings first became gala social affairs among the élite. When Elizabeth Margaret Carter, the daughter of a Newburyport, Massachusetts, merchant, married William Reynolds in 1821, her wedding anticipated much of what would soon be standard practice among less well-to-do families. The bride's sister recorded it in great detail:

At 7 o'clock precisely, Mr. Reynolds led Miss Carter, Mr. Andrews led Miss Reynolds, Mr. Smith, Miss Lamb and Mr. Marquant Miss C. Carter in to their places which was in front of the couch . . . & the Bride Maids arranged themselves on one side, the groomsmen on the other & the ceremony began. . . . The benediction was pronounced & Mrs. Reynolds was seated, with her Bride Maids on each side.

The dozen or so family members present for this service enjoyed "cake, wine & lemonade" before being joined by a much larger crowd of friends and neighbors. At eight o'clock, "the thundering knocker announced a crowded levee"; fashionable Newburyport "sent forth [its] inhabitants decorated in all the ornamentals their wardrobes could possibly furnish." The groomsmen cut, and the bridesmaids distributed, a wedding cake "purely white . . . studded with gilded almonds. In the centre towered a beautiful collection of artificial flowers and round its body was a wreath of laurel."[52] Such elaborate rituals did not take hold in middle-class circles overnight, but the direction was clear—and irreversible.

Lucy Harris was married the same year as Elizabeth Carter; her wedding in upstate New York was a simpler version of the Newburyport affair: there were thirty guests; cake and wine were served. Although many brides in the early republic appeared at the altar in gowns of gray, brown, or other colors, Lucy was in style in her white-embroidered mull.[53] She was married on a Friday.* Because the groom was a hatter who "did

---

*Friday was unusual: most weddings seem to have taken place on Tuesday, Wednesday, or Thursday, for reasons that are not entirely clear. It may have been that ministers' schedules tended to be freer during the middle of the week.

not want to be away from his shop any longer than necessary," the newlyweds took up residence at once in the small town where they would live. In the early 1800s, the custom was for newly married couples to proceed directly from the wedding to their new household and then to receive visits from family, friends, and neighbors. After Albert Poor's evening wedding, there was "a most merry time until 10 o'clock when the party broke up and the new married couple *moved home.*" Sometimes the party went home along with the bride and groom. When George Moore's cousin was married to "a worthy farmer, . . . the wedding was attended by about forty, and [they] all accompanied the bride home and took tea with her."[54]

Where longer distances were involved, the newlyweds often spent several days "visiting round" before leaving the area. Other couples moved first and then received company. For example, Elizabeth Carter and William Reynolds moved to Boston the day after their Newburyport wedding. Her sister reported that the next day "the connections generally called to see the bride . . . and to look at her in her rocking chair, you would imagine her an old housekeeper. She has placed all things in order & will for the coming fortnight remain stationary at home to receive visitors." While Elizabeth Carter had helped set up her new household, Eliza Rotch was "going to a house where there has been no lady to arrange anything." Eliza felt that she could "not possibly be ready to see company directly." Her novel solution was "to be a week incog & . . . after that see company for a week."[55]

One of Eliza's friends was to "be married on the 15th see company on the 16 and set off on a journey on the 17 and be gone two weeks." Such post-wedding trips were still relatively uncommon in the 1820s, but they were beginning to grow in popularity. Newlywed travel took two forms: one organized around a move; the other around visits to significant people or interesting places. Moves were often arranged to allow the couple to visit families and friends en route. When William Watson Andrews was married in 1833, he and his bride "at once set out for [their] home in Cornwall [Connecticut], making a three days journey . . . loitering of course with friends by the way." Just as common were journeys of a week or two taken to see friends or kinfolk who had not attended the wedding.[56]

Increasingly after 1820, bridal trips were planned around places as well as people. The couple who "went off immediately on a journey [with] Lake George as their object" represented a new phenomenon in 1821, but by 1840, such "wedding tours" were becoming common practice in middle-class circles. Destinations ranged from New York City to the Green Mountains, from Cincinnati—especially popular among midwesterners—to Niagara Falls. In 1836, one young woman reminded her fiancé of his promise to take her "by way of Niagara, to see the most wonderful and grand of the works of God—a spot [she] had always longed to behold."[57] Many couples were accompanied on their travels by friends or close relatives. The bridal trip or nuptial journey—two terms that were more widely used than *honeymoon*—began as an extension of the visiting ritual; it offered another way of affirming connections between newlyweds and their family and community networks.

The changes in post-wedding practices after 1820 reflect changes in how work and family life were organized in the North. In the first decades after the Revolution, the agricultural character of American society severely limited the ability of most people to travel for pleasure. If a farmer was married in winter and the sleighing was fine, he might ask a neighbor to do his chores for two or three days so that he could take his bride on a short round of visiting. Few young men were in a position, physically or financially, to interrupt their work for much longer than it took to get married and settled. The custom of "seeing company" ensured that newlyweds would feel part of, rather than cut off from, the community by virtue of their altered status. But in the 1820s and 1830s, developments on several fronts began to affect post-wedding rituals. First, of course, was the "transportation revolution" that made travel easier and more affordable for ordinary Americans. Second, the growth of the non-agricultural sectors of the economy meant that ever more young men could arrange to be away from their work. A lawyer, a banker, a clerk, a salesman, or a mechanic would have found it easier to leave his work for a week than would even a well-to-do farmer or rural craftsman.

But if changes in economic conditions made the wedding tour possible, changes in emotional needs made it necessary. Women's association of marriage with the pain of separation from their families and the fear of the confinement and responsibilities of domesticity rendered the last steps in the transition to marriage especially difficult. The friends and relatives who went along on the trip, or who were visited along the way, served to minimize the couple's feelings of isolation, feelings that intensified as the isolation of the middle-class home increased. With leaving home at the root of so many women's anxieties as they approached marriage, the wedding tour had special appeal. It seems likely that a woman found it less stressful to go from single daughter to traveling companion to housewife, than directly from her parents' home to her husband's. The journey could provide a sort of buffer state that prolonged the closeness of courtship and delayed the assumption of the heavy responsibilities of married life.[58]

After the festivities, married life began. The husband went back to work in his office, shop, or study and looked to his wife for love, of course, but also now for clean linen, punctual meals, and a tidy sitting room. Men reported on the change with great satisfaction. William Lloyd Garrison told his brother-in-law how pleased he was to have "sunk the character of a bachelor in that of husband." A week after his marriage to Helen Benson, he had already "settled down into domestic quietude, and . . . found that which [he had] long been yearning to find, a home, a wife, and a beautiful retreat from a turbulent city." For the woman, whose job it was to create that "beautiful retreat," both her work and her home—the warp and woof of her daily life—had changed. One young bride remembered that when she and her husband returned from their wedding trip, "an entirely new life opened for [her] . . . duties, interests, associations hitherto unknown forcibly presented themselves; new cares & anxieties replaced the old ones, & life altogether assumed a more serious aspect."[59]

The increased responsibilities a woman faced after marriage—to embody the ideals of domesticity and to meet its concrete demands—contributed to women's ambivalence about marriage; but in the first weeks of wedlock, they could help a woman to regain her emotional balance and guide her behavior. Reflecting on her life before marriage, one bride of three weeks could "still recollect the companions of those early, happy days, which are never to return. The sensations which accompanied [her] separation from them were such as can never be described." She reported, however, "I was not long the victim of them. New duties offered themselves to my recollection, and new pleasures promised to repay me for every privation. I recovered the tone of my mind sooner than I expected." Another bride who entered her new home "under all the interesting circumstances of grateful joy and fearful responsibilities" appreciated the latter for a different reason: "I feel it happy for me that with all these blessings and pleasant circumstances, I have so much of responsibility and anxiety as will effectually prevent my head being turned by it."[60] The "new duties . . . and new pleasures," the "grateful joy and fearful responsibilities" were the two sides of the bargain women struck when they married.

A married woman carried a heavier burden than her single sister, but its weight could be measured in terms of companionship and comfort as well as of confinement and danger. Many new wives were happier than they had expected to be; first reports on conjugal life were generally optimistic.[61] It may be that—having shied at the gate—once she was through it, a woman experienced relief and satisfaction, not only at finally entering the course but at the discovery that she had not lost herself along the way.

PART II
1830 – 1880

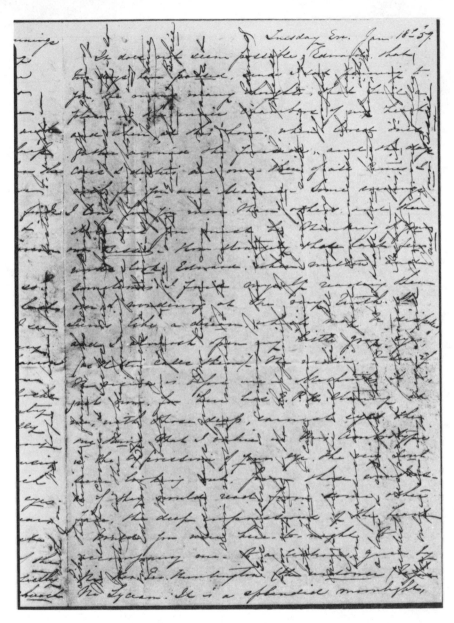

Bessie Huntting poured out her heart to her fiancé in long letters that filled at least four sides of paper on which she often resorted to "cross-hatching." Like many women courting in the 1830-to-1880 period, she regularly pleaded with her intended to respond in kind. (Bessie Huntting to Edward Rudd, 18 January 1859, Huntting-Rudd Papers, SL.)

CHAPTER 3

"*We* Are Not Like Most People"

I N JUNE of 1857, eighteen year-old Mary Ballard arrived in the small Illinois town of Pittsfield to spend the summer with her married sister. In the fall she would return to Oxford, Ohio, for her second year at the Western Female Seminary, an institution recently founded to advance the proposition that "the intellectual privileges of young ladies should be much greater than are commonly afforded them."[1] The death of her mother in 1852 and her father in 1856 had left Mary Ballard "to think and act for [her]self." When a summer friendship with the town's young banker, William Ross, ripened into love, Mary faced a difficult decision. "It was my Father's wish that I should pursue the course at Oxford or some other institution equally as good," she explained; "I love and cherish the memory of my Parents and under *no* consideration would pursue a different course from what they would have me were they living." She concluded, "That I should return and finish the course of study seems clearly to be my duty." Declining William's proposal, Mary asked him to think of her "in no other light than that of a friend."[2]

William Ross did not give up hope. If Mary Ballard did not "yet cherish those feelings kindred to [his]," he would be patient until she did. He did not have to wait long. In October he visited Mary in Oxford; and in "the cheerless parlor of the 'Great Western' where . . . the teachers keep an ever watchful eye on those that have company," he renewed his suit. This time, Mary agreed to become his wife, and William returned home an engaged man.[3]

He hoped they could be married the following fall, but to Mary that seemed much too soon. "I feel . . . that I am too young and have not a sufficient knowledge of domestic affairs to assume the responsibility that you would next Fall have me. Besides," she added, "I am very anxious to continue my music and one year will be a short time to learn what I hope to." Mary Ballard had another reason for wishing to delay her marriage. In spite of attending a school that required three years of Latin study, she worried about how she would "appear in the presence of the intelligent and learned." William reminded her that at Oxford—as opposed to provincial Pittsfield—she was "among the very elements of Intellectuality," and assured her that she was "prepared to grace any walk of life, and have been for years." He was "willing to sacrifice all the pleasure of [her] company during another long year if it is for the best," but did not believe Mary was "too young & giddy" for marriage. As to her lack of domestic experience, he promised that she would not "be required . . . to go immediately into domestic departments after marriage. I had not thought of such a thing," he wrote. Mary seemed to William no less accomplished than other women he knew: "If I am not mistaken the greater number of young ladies who marry have but little idea of such matters at first."[4]

But the underlying cause of Mary's trepidation was not so easily allayed. She confided to William her fear that if they were to "assume the new relations in life so soon [he] would discover too late [her] imperfections." The "imperfection" of which she was most ashamed was not intellectual or domestic but spiritual: her failure to "sympathize with [William] on religious subjects. I can not for I am not a christian and have not for several years thought I was one," she told him. The daughter of devout Presbyterians, Mary Ballard had joined the church as a child, but she now saw herself as "past hope." Instead of helping William in his "Christian course," she would be a "draw back"—and a disappointment to him. Mary offered William his liberty, but he had no wish to dissolve the engagement. He and Mary were "too much *endeared* to each other to allow the difference of religious sentiment [to] separate" them. He trusted that in time he would "be the means of influencing [her] favorably on that subject."[5]

So they would marry—but when? The question was still unresolved at the end of December 1857, but Mary was leaning toward leaving the seminary for good the following June. "I would not have you do it unless you felt it was your duty and that it would be pleasant for you," William wrote, in a letter that made it clear he, his parents, and her sister were all in favor of the plan. Spring came, and Mary had still not made up her mind. "I do not think I am very young but *feel* young when I think of taking such a responsibility upon my self in so short a time," she explained. William had already assured Mary that his parents approved an early marriage; now he suggested that they *actively desired* it: "My parents feel an anxiety in the matter. My father is approaching the close of life & he feels that it would be gratifying to him if we would be united while he is living." When, three months later, Mary was still unwilling to give a "decided answer," she cited her own family pressures. She had disregarded her brother John's advice when she became engaged to William Ross. John Ballard was "determined that [Mary] should have a thorough education and when he found that his long cherished hopes were to be dashed to the ground he was very angry." Mary wondered if it were not her "duty to return and graduate if he would be reconciled in *no* other way."[6]

Finally, the term was over, and Mary returned to her sister's home in Pittsfield. Whether by proximity or sheer persuasiveness, William Ross overcame her reservations and an early October date was set. Mary spent the summer days improving her domestic skills and many of her evenings alone with William. After one such visit, she thanked her fiancé for "curing" her headache. "I should not have much faith in the remedy should other hands than yours administer it," she told him a few days later. This episode made Mary question if she was perhaps "too free and familiar" with William. "It is because I feel so well acquainted with you," she explained, but added, "I will endeavor to be more guarded in future." Still, the letter closed with a wish that she could give him a " 'goodnight' kiss." For his part, William Ross celebrated their growing closeness and looked forward to the day when they would "enjoy each other's society more intimately."[7]

That day was fast approaching. At the end of September, William reported that at his house "the folks are beginning to talk of making Cake, etc." Mary was occupied with her sewing. William offered his counsel on local dressmakers—"Don't *risk* Mrs. Harris," he wrote—and advised his future wife, "If you don't get all done do not care. You can finish them afterwards. Just see that the Bridal & travelling dresses are completed."[8] Mary and William were to be married on the same day as William's sister Anna, so that neither couple would miss a wedding while away on a bridal journey. On October 6, 1858—almost exactly one year from the day they became engaged—Mary Ballard and William Ross were married.

"The spheres of action"

When Mary Ballard married William Ross, she had behind her two years at a school dedicated, in the words of its founders, to "drawing forth the mental energies," rather than "ornamenting the surface," of its students.[9] The Western Female Seminary was one of dozens of institutions founded in the second quarter of the nineteenth century to give girls some of the same intellectual discipline available to boys in their academies and colleges. And yet even as the female seminaries moved closer to the curriculum of their male models, with physiology and astronomy supplanting embroidery and painting, a fundamental difference persisted. Young men pursued higher education as preparation for the ministry, law, medicine. Even as they studied moral philosophy and Latin, young women were in training for the one career open to them—as wives to men and as mothers (or, at least, teachers) to children.

This state of affairs had profound implications for—and roots in—the world beyond the classroom. The eighteenth century had recognized differences between men and women, but the nineteenth century made distinctions based on gender in every aspect of life, from the most mundane to the most metaphysical. On his visit to America in 1831, Alexis de Tocqueville was struck by the "constant care" taken to "trace two clearly distinct lines of action for the two sexes . . . in two pathways that are always different."[10] In the 1830s, these lines were relatively new features of American social geography; but in the next fifty years, they would dominate the landscape, demarcating clear roles for—and boundaries between—people in the family, in the community, and in the world of work. The definition of gender differences provided the context for courtship and had important consequences for how young men and women experienced the transition to marriage. It created separate spheres and the need to bridge them; it impelled young people to balance idealization against the fear of disappointment; and it made romance and self-revelation essential accomplishments for any couple en route to marriage.

By the time they reached courting age, young men and women looked at the world—and each other—through a lens that magnified the "natural," as well as the circumstantial, differences between men and women. A Harvard divinity student reported approvingly on Ralph Waldo Emerson's "remarks upon marriage, in which he gave the characteristic differences of the sexes." The father of New England Transcendentalism was hardly breaking new ground here: "Man's sphere is out of doors and among men—woman's is in the house—Man seeks for power and influence—woman for order and beauty—Man is just—Woman is kind." Emerson's view was echoed in every corner of the land; ministers, reformers, pedagogues portrayed male and female in sharp contrast to each other. An 1854 volume on *The Sphere and Duties of Woman* declared, "Woman despises in man everything like herself except a tender heart"; and man presumably felt the same disgust for any sign of masculine qualities in a woman.[11]

Ordinary men and women shared this view. Like John Patch, a struggling editor and poet, they believed that "the spheres of action are different" for men and women. "Where courage, activity and endurance are required, there is the place for man—where cleanliness, order, affection and all the finer sensibilities of the heart and soul are needed for comfort and consolation in the difficulties and trials of life, there should bloom the never fading rose of woman's constancy and affection," he wrote in 1848. Woman did more than comfort and console man; she improved him as well. As a young midwesterner told his fiancée, "The true female character was perfectly adapted and designed by its influence often exerted to soften and beautify the wild rough and turbulent spirit of man." William Lloyd Garrison II put it more simply: "Men would be much better if they acted always as if [woman] were looking at them."[12]

This expectation shaped individual relationships as much as it did general views of "female character." Every woman was empowered by reason of her sex. Twenty-three-year-old Ulysses S. Grant was a junior officer with the Fourth Infantry in Louisiana when he wrote to Julia Dent at home in St. Louis:

You can have but little idea of the influance you have over me, even while so far away. If I feel tempted to do anything that I now think is not right I am shure to think, "Well now if Julia saw me would I do so" and thus it is, absent or present, I am more or less governed by what I think is your will.

A woman could, by her very existence, help a man keep to the path of virtue. A Wisconsin lawyer told his intended, "I expect you to infuse strength into all my intellectual and moral powers."[13]

It was the latter that women were especially well equipped to enhance. Harry Pierce credited his fiancée with reconciling him to the church and improving him "in the moral sphere." The Indianapolis attorney told Libbie Vinton: "Your presence drew me to church after I had neglected every thought not worldly for years," and he believed that her love was "a greater mainspring to excellence and the magnet to draw [him] nearer the better locality" of her views. Women, it was believed, had an innate sense of direction that enabled them to find "the better locality," while men wandered in darkness. The Protestant clergy looked out from their pulpits at a flock in which women outnumbered men, and conceded that woman was naturally more religious than man. Medical authorities agreed. As one physician explained in 1847, woman's was "a pious mind. Her confiding nature leads her more readily than man to accept the proffered graces of the Gospel."[14]*

While women may have shared the culture's obeisance to the moral superiority of the female sex, they were uncomfortable with its implications for their own behavior. In the face of regular pleas from the pulpit, the popular press, and the men they knew to uphold and embody the peculiar virtues of True Womanhood, some women asserted their common humanity instead. "*I am not an angel,*" Mollie Clark declared in a letter to her suitor, a man who was only looking "to find . . . a Woman noble & true." Another New Yorker objected to her fiancé, "As to my being your superior in every respect and my mind's being of a more lofty order than yours—*I don't believe one word of it.* . . . Our minds may be different but that don't go to show that either is of a higher order than the other." Some women simply declined to accept responsibility for the moral uplift of the men who loved them. Winan Allen, a student at the University of Michi-

*One man went so far as to tell his fiancée, "If you were not better than I—pardon me—what would you be good for to make me better?"[15]

gan in the 1860s, wrote Annie Cox, "I constitute you, if you'll accept so burdensome a charge, my spiritual doctor exclusively and unreservedly." But Annie insisted that she herself was "but an abcedarian in the spiritual school. . . . We may council together," she concluded.[16]

If a man and woman were to "council together"—if a woman was to exercise the influence that was hers by birth—she had to have access to the men in her life, but the prevailing definition of the male role made such access problematical. The assumption that men were preoccupied and absorbed by worldly matters was as pervasive at midcentury as the expectation that women were naturally inclined toward moral virtue. In the course of the nineteenth century, middle-class men became increasingly defined by their involvement in the world. In this era of the "self-made" man, ideals of manhood all emphasized man's pursuit of worldly—if not purely material—success. "Man is made for action, and the bustling scenes of moving life," wrote one youth just starting out on his own.[17]

Those "bustling scenes" had no room for women—as girls, even in adolescence, understood. "A young man can occupy himself with his business and look forward to his life and prospects, but all we [young women] have to do is to pass our time agreeably to ourselves," one Boston girl observed in 1838. Thirty years later, Mollie Clarke reflected to a suitor, "I often think it is so different from men from what it is with us women. Love is our life our reality, business yours. We stake our all and if it is lost our all is gone." A young Ohio woman had a similar sense of the risks involved; she believed that "a lady could not shape the future . . . she went down or up as her husband did . . . he led the way, made the reputation, the fortune of both." Men perceived this situation too, of course. In 1820, George Cutler had observed that a wife was more dependent on marriage than was her husband, whose "business leads him out of doors." By midcentury, more men were working away from home, and the distance between married men and women had widened. It seemed obvious to the young Bangor, Maine, lawyer Henry Poor that "a gentleman's happiness is not so entirely confined in the domestic circle as a lady's. If he cannot be happy at home, he can go into the world where in the business and bustle of life, he can forget his troubles."[18]

The fact that middle-class women were dependent on and excluded from the world in which "the business and bustle of life" took place could create tension in a relationship. Without the freedom to enter that world herself, a woman might resent the claims it made on the men in her life. Mary Butterfield, a nineteen-year-old graduate of the Troy Female Seminary in New York, observed in 1846 that "it is a common & a great fault with young men when they enter upon active life to become entirely absorbed by business." Men so absorbed might come into conflict with their mates. The midwestern bride who complained in 1858 that it was "not right" that her storekeeper husband "don't come home nights until it is very late" would have received much sympathy from her sisters, but men would have understood why her husband felt strongly "that he was right to be there."[19] Men had to keep their balance on a narrow beam: a man who was not involved *enough* in business was a threat to the economic security of his family; one who was "entirely absorbed" was a threat to the emotional cohesiveness of the home.

Many middle-class men began practicing this "balancing act" during courtship. Men could—and, to the dismay of their women, often did—fulfill the stereotype of the work-oriented male while still single, and when they did, they jeopardized the closeness of courtship. Horace Allen was a lawyer in Boston when he became engaged to Daisy Chamberlain. If he stayed late in his office, he was likely to receive a note from Daisy: "I know you are doing [it] for me, but . . . I don't *want you to work so hard.*" Even more disturbing than his evenings at the office were the Sundays he spent there. Daisy pleaded with him to try and "not let business creep into [his] bachelor Sundays for then it will be hard to change the habit." Like Horace Allen, Harry Pierce was an energetic young attorney who was in the habit of working hard. When a riding accident kept him at home, he realized how thoroughly he was identified with—and dependent on—his work in the world. His fiancée was also ailing and confined at home, but that was where she spent her time anyway. "If you were well," he reminded her, "you would still be mostly with your Mother & Sue & Tom [her sister and brother]." His situation was different and more difficult. "If I were well I would be in the whirl of business—I am out of my world entirely," he concluded miserably.[20] Even before marriage, Harry Pierce's world was "the world"; at home, he felt displaced, resentful, unmanned.

For most couples, the identification of men and maleness with the world and of women and femaleness with the home was largely a theoretical issue during courtship. In the middle decades of the nineteenth century, especially after the 1848 Woman's Rights Convention in Seneca Falls, New York, it was an issue many couples found worthy of serious debate. Cast in terms of what one young man called "this fermented question" of woman's rights, sex roles became a favorite topic of discussion among middle-class men and women.[21]

George Wright and Serena Ames are a good example. New England-born midwesterners, with little formal education, George and Serena both supported woman's rights but neither questioned the accepted sexual stereotypes. Serena told George that she wished "God speed to those women who feel it *duty* to labor *publicly* for the good of the world," although she had to confess that it seemed to her "an unwomanly thing . . . to leave home, . . . to renounce what to every woman is natural." George was relieved; he admitted his fear that in her heart Serena might have had "a lurking determination (latent perhaps as yet) to become a *lecturer*, and to try to do for the world, what [he] believed women may best accomplish in another way."[22]

George Wright considered himself a liberal on woman's rights. He objected to the fact that women did not get equal pay for equal work, that they were barred from "many trades and professions for which women are better qualified than men," and from colleges and schools. "This is wrong. Their natural rights are the same as those of *men*," he declared. He assured Serena, "I care not how 'Strong Minded' women are for every advance I know helps *us* too"; but with reasoning that serves as a testament to the power of traditional views of gender, George Wright revealed his unshaken allegiance to the status quo:

I do not think that the "Good Time Coming" would be at all hastened by having one half of the learned professions and of the Offices of State filled by women, for though perhaps they could do as well *there* as men, their time is worth *more* elsewhere. . . . If a woman had the strength and Eloquence that *Webster* had, I still think it would be better & nobler in her & better for the world if she would teach half a dozen of her *boys* to be Websters, instead of being one herself, and *would it not be* more agreeable & natural for her to do so? Women can never attain to that eminence in scientific pursuits that men can—as a primary reason, they *haven't the time* and with that lack is the lack of inclination to do so, and all the cultivation & crowding* in the world couldn't overcome it. It is a part of their nature & I believe it is right that it *should* be so.[23]

With her belief that marriage was "usually fatal to a woman's hopes of attaining to anything like full growth of mind," Serena Ames had the makings of a feminist, yet she settled for George Wright's expression of support for economic and educational "equality" and overlooked—or perhaps agreed with—his traditional view of woman's nature. Except for a handful of utopians and radicals, mid-nineteenth-century Americans accepted the conventional definition of sex roles and looked only for superficial changes. They agreed with the young New York State woman who confided to her diary in 1860: "I do not ask for woman a higher sphere than home, a more noble position than wife and mother, though I sometimes ask that she may have the privilege of varying her duties more than she does now."[24]

When women like Serena Ames accepted the sexual stereotypes even as they opposed the sexual inequalities those stereotypes produced, they were following the common path. They

*This apparent malapropism may provide a clue to Wright's self-contradictory desire to keep women in their place, "out of the way" of striving young men who may have felt threatened enough by competition with each other not to want women on the scene.

97

were also assuming that they and the men they loved could deviate from prescribed sex roles. In individual relationships, men and women suspended many of the rules laid down as part of their culture's definition of gender: they made exceptions for themselves. "*We* are not like most people—at least *you* are not & so *I* am not," George Wright told his fiancée. For her part, Serena Ames felt sure she "should not know what to do were [George] like other men."[25] The more intimate the relationship, the more a person tended to see his or her mate as an exception to the negative and an embodiment of the positive aspects of the sexual stereotype.

This process had its cost, however. As they acquired immunity to the infirmities of their sex, lovers were left exposed to the risks of idealization. Intimacy between men and women rested on the belief that one's prospective mate did not carry the liabilities attributed to his or her sex; on the other hand, young lovers went to great pains to set themselves apart from idealized versions of manhood and womanhood. Mollie Clarke spoke for many of her contemporaries when she asked her suitor, "Did you ever think that we may be . . . placing each other as our *Ideal* and that sometime we might awake from our dreams to find that we were not what we have thought we were?"[26] Both men and women were anxious to avoid the pain of that awakening.

As the more idealized sex, women were more likely than men to fear that their lovers pictured them too highly. A Long Island teacher pleaded with her fiancé, "While you think of me, so far superior to what I am, I would have you know me, just as I am; weak, frail, impetuous & wayward." After her engagement to Albert Bledsoe, Harriet Coxe had similar feelings, but she kept them to herself. In a "private letter," she wrote, "The depth and fervour of his affection for me, should not excite my vanity for I know that he greatly over-rates me in every way." A New York woman hoped her suitor would not make that mistake: "Do not look upon me as without faults for no doubt you will find many. I should not wish you to be disappointed by thinking me faultless," she wrote her admirer. In Maine, Persis Sibley believed she had failed to convince her fiancé that she was "not faultless." She imagined the "severe trial" she would face when, after marriage, she would "see the scales falling from *his* eyes who has been blindly worshipping me as perfection. . . . 'Tis injurious to anyone to be overrated."[27]

Indeed, men also suffered from the fear of being overrated. When Mary Ballard told William Ross that he "might discover too late [her] imperfections," he responded, "Ah, Mary, I feel that it is the reverse. That I am unworthy to claim so large an interest for you, that my imperfections would more than cancel all of yours." After three years of courtship, George Wright worried out loud to Serena Ames, "You do not know me as I am. . . . *You will be so disappointed—I am not what you think me.*" And two years into their relationship, Winan Allen gave Annie Cox "a word of caution. . . . I would not for my own sake have the reality fall below your expectations. . . . I would not have you color your pictures too highly."[28]

Although both women and men expressed fear that they would prove a disappointment to a future mate, they may have done so from different underlying causes. A woman worried that she would not fulfill the ideal of womanhood which men were taught to revere. A generalized expectation of female superiority together with the "blindness" of a fond lover might create a conceit she could not match, a pedestal she could not reach. If a woman worried that she would not be *enough* like the image of womankind, a man was more likely to fear that he would be *too much* like the image of his sex. A man might prove all too manly, thus disappointing the woman who thought she had found a man who was not "like other men."

There may have been another dimension to male fears of disappointment as well. The Connecticut mechanic Samuel Clayton Kingman had noticed that when he anticipated "a great deal of pleasure [he] was generally disappointed," and he advised his fiancée Emily Brooks to "look on the dark side." This was Joseph Taylor's approach, not just to marriage but to life itself: "Persons should expect little or nothing or at most but very little and then disappointments will not follow." Joseph's reasoning—"the future is, at least, very uncertain and of course is not to be relied on"—suggests that men's fear of disappointment in

99

courtship may have reflected the climate of high expectation, unpredictability, and frequent failure in which middle-class men functioned.[29]

People could find reassurance in the advice books' dictum that "true love . . . will not be destroyed by evidence of imperfection not before seen," and some couples recognized that the reality must *inevitably* "fall below . . . expectations." "No matter how sensible we are," an Indianapolis girl observed in her diary, "somehow we are always a little disappointed in each other afterwards." She and her fiancé were prepared, however: "He knows I am far from being perfect, and I know that he is ditto, so I hope we will not expect too much of each other." Clayton Kingman believed that both he and Emily Brooks had their faults, but, he supposed, "we *cannot* know each other until we are bound together."[30]

Even if he was right, there could be no doubt that the better acquainted a couple were, the less likely they were to be disappointed. Knowledge depended on contact, not only with each other but with members of the opposite sex in general. As they grew up, people learned that women and men did not always behave according to their prescribed roles. The more experience men and women had with each other, the better able they were to reconcile ideals with reality. Joseph Griffin, a New England seaman, remembered that he once "had a notion that girls were angels or just one step removed from them, but [he] got rather rudely awakened to the fact that girls could do as rough things in a gentle way as boys." Likewise, Annie Cox discovered that some men were not "up to" their roles as providers and protectors:

I think a woman's place is in home's quiet retreat. She may sympathize, encourage, make home a green pasture . . . but 'tis his place to meet the storm of outside care, and yet there is this to consider. All men are not fit to take that responsibility. I know that from observation.[31]

The way gender ideals were being defined in the mid-nineteenth century—women "in home's quiet retreat"; men meeting "the storm of outside care"—limited the opportunities men and women had to observe and understand each other.

Augusta Hubbard, a New York State schoolgirl, recognized and regretted the restrictions on male-female interaction. After reading T. S. Arthur's popular *Advice to Ladies,* which urged women to be "modest, retiring, and have a very great sense of propriety," she admitted that there was "much truth in what he says," but complained:

It makes our intercourse with the gentlemen very artificial. I cannot endure to feel restrained and guarded. I had much rather treat the other sex naturally—fairly—with as much respect as I feel and no more—more as I treat my lady friends.

In Augusta's mind, the problem was the limit imposed on friendship between men and women. "I will *not* be insincere and society allows no sincere hearty friendship" between men and women, she observed in 1860.[32] Some couples tried, but friendship was too fragile a vessel to contain the powerful feelings and expectations stimulated by male-female intimacy in a romantic age. By the 1840s, the process that had begun at the end of the eighteenth century was complete: friendship had been thoroughly devalued and demarcated from love. Phrases such as "mere friendship," "common friends," and "ordinary friendship" appeared—clear evidence that friendship was less intimate, and less desirable, than love.[33]

How much less was sometimes hard to tell; friendship implied a limited commitment, but the precise boundaries were often unclear. In Indiana, Will Adkinson asked Lu Burlingame, "Should any young man or woman be so totally unguarded about their correspondence as we if they are simply friends as the term is used?" Mary Butterfield made just that error when she put "too great confidence in [the] professions of mere friendship" of a male acquaintance. J. M. More was more honest with Cornelia Curtis; he sensed that his affection for her had "probably [been] mistaken for that of mere friendship," which he declared it was not. It differed "from that of mere Friendship in the . . . ardour of its nature."[34]

101

J. M. More knew that what he felt for Cornelia Curtis was more than friendship, but was it love? As couples struggled to find their bearings beyond the narrow confines of friendship, many of them relied on a familial compass. Men and women who felt or sought more than "mere" friendship could regard each other as siblings and still respect the exclusiveness and uniqueness of romantic love. By using a familial model, a couple could be sure that, without an explicit and mutual reassessment, their relationship would remain distinct from romantic love.

Sometimes, however, reassessment was wished for all along. For the first six months of Annie Cox and Winan Allen's correspondence in the 1860s, their letters were addressed, "My dearest sister" or "My dearest brother." In response to the news that her family was planning a move to California, Winan wrote Annie, "When we meet again we will talk of California, *til then*, you will be my sister, my best, my dearest sister." Nineteenth-century evangelicals often addressed each other as "Brother" and "Sister," but Winan and Annie's language signified something more. After they were engaged, Annie looked back on this time and admitted, "I read the name of sister with aching fear that I might never be more to you." In other cases, the redrawing of boundaries was cause for alarm. Will Adkinson and Lu Burlingame promised each other a brother's and a sister's love, but Will worried that she would "crave more from [him] and be clamorous for it." He was ready to be a *friend, a brother at least*" but feared "that a brother's love though deep, though boundless, though lasting, though sacred [would] not satisfy" Lu.[35]

"The life of the whole thing"

What *would* satisfy Lu Burlingame? What lay beyond friendship, beyond the deep feeling brothers and sisters had for each other? Men and women courting at midcentury believed that love was, in the words of one Indiana girl, "the first thing, the beginning and the end, the life of the whole thing." "Marriage without love," a Pennsylvania man declared, "cannot fail to be a source of perpetual unhappiness." Even a conservative minister admitted, "This question must finally have the utmost prominence. Do you love the man?"[36] With marriage so dependent on and identified with love, the ability to recognize and experience "true love" became all important.

Fifty years before, Americans had been wary of romantic love. They had associated it with immaturity, self-indulgence, and impermanence. The romance of novels was not the stuff of which good marriages were made. But their children took a more positive view both of novels and of the romances they brought to life: "The elaboration of the mysteries of heterosexual love" was the novelists' favorite subject. As early as the 1840s, books and magazines were preoccupied with romantic love, and in the fiction of the 1850s, "romantic expectations were vindicated by the heroine who overcame great obstacles to secure a perfect mate and domestic bliss."[37] Henry Poor read Dickens's *Nicholas Nickleby* and was delighted with it. "I never was so carried away with any book in my life," he reported to his fiancée. He concluded that "Dickens must sometime in his life have been thoroughly in love, to have painted the passion so well as he has done it." Henry found it "very pleasant to compare another's history with your own experience, provided it has been an agreeable one," and added gallantly, "I therefore feel great interest in the love part of every novel."[38]

In the middle decades of the century, romance was fast losing its negative connotations and emerging as the only acceptable basis for intimacy between women and men. It was no longer associated with wildness and youthful passion; it was made safe. Romance was redefined as the key to domestic harmony rather than as a threat to it. As romantic love became something to celebrate rather than mistrust, "falling in love" would become an increasingly normative part of middle-class courtship. The acceptance of romantic passion did not happen all at once. Even in the 1840s and 1850s, when one was more likely to hear apologies for "unromantic objections" than for "romantick extravagancies," young people were not likely to perceive themselves as "falling" in love.[39] They might respond to powerful feelings, but men especially sought to preserve a measure of control.

In 1844, Alexander Rice, a student at Union College in Schnectady, described his first meeting with Augusta McKim: "I felt . . . as I never felt in the presence of a lady before and there seemed to be a kind of [direction?] saying to me that I was now meeting her whom it was appointed should be my special object of affection and love." But he hastened to assure Augusta that this was not all, "nor would it have led me blindly forward had not I discovered in you those elements of character and those qualities of mind which my judgment approved." The attraction came first, but it was followed by a reassertion of rationality. Henry Poor had his own analysis of what happened when young people were "first in love":

They always feel within themselves two impulses or sentiments, one of attraction toward the beloved object, the other of repulsion, which last impulse is at first always the strongest, and is only overcome by time, by a gradual knowledge and conviction of the real nature of that sentiment which excites such a tumult in our hearts and such overpowering sensations through our whole frames, and by a more familiar acquaintance with the object of our affection.[40]

Some people anticipated those "overpowering sensations" with pleasure. Elizabeth Prentiss mused in 1842, "If I ever fall in love I dare say I shall do it so madly and absorbingly as to become in a measure and for a season forgetful of everything and everybody else." Other people were more guarded. Winan Allen told Annie Cox, "I always liked you . . . but it was a long time before I *loved* you. It was never my disposition to *fall* in love." Not so with Annie, who, he thought, "must have fallen in and couldn't get out." Annie professed to welcome her lover's caution. "I am glad you did not *fall* in love with me," she wrote him, "for such love is not based on any knowledge of the object and when the knowledge is gained the love is often lost."[41]

Women were assumed to be the more emotional, less rational sex. The poet Lydia Sigourney expressed the conventional wisdom: "A woman's nature feeds on love. Love is its life." But while women seem to have allowed themselves to fall in love more readily than men, they too understood the danger. A young Indiana woman reflected in 1871, "Of all the foolish things under the sun, the most foolish and saddest is for very young and ignorant people to rush into marriage under the impression that they are 'in love.' 'In love' they are crazy, and they make themselves miserable for life, for want of a little sense." The solution was not to avoid falling in love but to beware of the consequences. "If I had married the first time I thought I was in love, where would I have been now?" wondered Mary Ann Smith at twenty-two.[42]

Falling in love was risky; but after about 1860, it was increasingly regarded as desirable, even compulsory. Augusta Hubbard doubted whether her heart "was capable of an orthodox love experience." "I guess my head is stronger than my heart," she wrote sadly—and prematurely, as it turned out. Augusta did not approve of her friend Lucy, who would never "advise any one else to let their hearts get the mastery over their heads or allow it in herself." Lucy had "so many *sensible* ideas on the subject of marriage and is not a bit romantic. I don't think she ever *fell* in love but calmly and dispassionately made up her mind that he would or would not *do*. . . . *Can* we not have more romance than *that?*" Augusta asked.[43]

For young Americans at midcentury, the answer was not only "we can" but "we must." Everyone wanted to fall in love, and men especially seemed to feel a sense of obligation, even of desperation about it. That bachelors were marginal figures no doubt contributed to male anxiety, but women were even more dependent on marriage than were men. A more likely explanation is the responsibility that men bore to be the initiators of intimate relationships. Women were expected to *receive* offers of marriage (although their role in courtship was far from passive). They tended to look at falling in love as something that would or would not happen to them, while men conveyed a sense that they could, or should, *make* it happen.

Aurora Koehler was a single woman living at home in Indiana. In her 1871 journal, she wondered:

Suppose I should meet a man who came up to my standard of man-hood. Would I, could I, *love* that man well enough to marry him? I cannot tell, my heart cannot tell me for it has not been tried. They tell us that once in every one's lifetime that strange spell is thrown over us that passion called love is awakened.

Aurora waited patiently for "that passion called love" to be awakened in her. Her contemporary Susan Winchester took a similarly passive, although less serious, position. She told a suitor that "she had always expected to marry some romantic scamp, and to feel swallowed up in the passion of love for him, and that the want of this absorbing passion had made her hesitate a good deal." But for Simeon Baldwin, the New Haven lawyer who courted Susan Winchester, "the want of this absorbing passion" was deeply disturbing. "I have little doubt," he confided in his diary, "but that she would marry me, if I gave her the offer. I think it likely that if I pursued the acquaintance, I should fall in love with her." A few months later, he wrote, "I am really inclined to believe that I am actually in love. I have been hoping for it; yes, and praying for it, to act as the solution of my doubts."[44]

Simeon Baldwin's anxiety was desperation in Wilson Carpenter. At twenty-two, the Pittsburgh clerk believed that there were "not many men who have not fallen in love at least once or twice," but *he* was still "free from anything more than a fleeting fancy for any of the female sex." While Wilson had "loved four of [his] male friends passionately," what he wanted, at least consciously, was to fall in love with a woman.[45] Four years later, in January 1872, he wrote that he longed "to be out of these fleetings from certainty to doubt. I *hope* I am in love now."* But once again he was disappointed. "Not being in love I am not blind. T'were much better to be in love and therefore blind than to be tossed about, as I am, by every idle wind that blows. Poor old bachelor."[47] Wilson Carpenter's intense need to fall in love with a woman must have been in large part an expression of his

*One telling reason was to test his love for his closest male friend Ed: "I am anxious to fall in love to see whether I would love Ed as much then as now."[46]

desire to resolve his sexual identity in a socially acceptable way, but it also reflects the common pattern of a young man's pushing himself to fall in love. If he failed, then perhaps he would not fall in love and would be forever excluded from the most sought-after circle of middle-class life: the home.

"Such entire sympathy and confidence"

For this generation, romantic love was the only means to the end for which both men and women assumed they were destined: marriage. Marriage, they believed, must be based not on transient passions but on sympathy and shared interests. The vision of romantic love that prevailed in the mid-1800s stressed mutuality, commonality, and sympathy between man and woman—precisely those qualities most likely to bridge the widening gap between home and world. The increasing isolation of married women in the home and the involvement of married men in the world made it imperative that lovers sympathize with each other; they must have a mutuality of tastes and interests because they might have little else to share.

Alexander Rice anticipated this possibility when he proposed that he and his fiancée commit themselves to some common course of study. "I daily think how happy we could be in married life," he wrote Augusta McKim, "provided our tastes correspond in one respect, if in addition to our love we should strike out some common pursuit in which we should sit and sport (for it would be sport) together." Alexander's plan would have pleased the writers of the day's domestic advice literature. They stressed the idea that proper contrasts between husband and wife in temperament but similarity in background and interests were essential for the "marriage of companionship" idealized by middle-class Americans. George Wright's 1860 statement to

Serena Ames, "We *must* be alike," sums up the imperative of couples at midcentury.[48]

What these lovers expected from romance was not emotional abandon but "the appreciation of each others character & the strong sympathy & similitude of thought & feeling." Henry Poor, who looked forward to his marriage with "emotions paramount to all others," described the love he and Mary Pierce had for each other as "the kind that seeks its gratification in mutual sympathy." In Vermont, Eliza Pattee rejoiced that in William Onion she had at last found someone who could sympathize with her: "My frail spirit hails with sweet delight every glimpse of hope that promises succor and protection, or in other words, *sympathy.*" When Clayton Kingman thought about marriage to Emily Brooks, he expected simply that they would "sympathize and contrive together & be so happy." A chaplain in the Union Army observed to his fiancée that "few couples . . . attain such *entire sympathy and confidence* as without effort we have already glided into."[49]

Indeed, many couples found that creating bonds of sympathy and confidence did require concerted effort. The abolitionist Henry Blackwell considered it a "practical fiction . . . that any two human beings are constituted *peculiarly* & *in all respects* fitted for each other—perfect counterparts, capable of a mystical & absolute union." The truth was more complex and demanded a plan of action. Clayton Kingman outlined his strategy to Emily Brooks: "Let us be more like one, let us communicate our ideas, our notions to each other." Early on in their relationship, he told her, "I want you to be as open & confiding *to me,* as to *any one,* and I will be *to you.*" When their marriage approached, he restated his wish: "May we be frank & open, and with all, kind and forbearing, then we can be happy."[50]

Clayton Kingman's faith in candor as the key to a successful courtship and a happy marriage was widely shared by men and women at midcentury. Antoinette Brown made a common request when she urged Henry's brother Sam, "You must always say everything to me, darling. Nothing but the utmost confidence can make us quite happy and nothing but the want of it can destroy happiness."[51] The men and women who courted at midcentury did not invent this formula; they inherited it from middle-class Americans who came of age in the first quarter of the century. The earlier generation had valued candor for the protection it offered against insincerity and misplaced affections. Their children and grandchildren feared disappointment in love more than they did deception. In an age that embraced romance wholeheartedly, the great virtue of candor was the counterweight it provided to the idealization inherent in romantic love. Openness would ensure that a lover was loved for himself or herself.

The ethic of openness both relied on and helped develop a high level of trust between future mates. Questions about fidelity disturbed some relationships, but explicit discussions of sexual faithfulness were unusual. An Indiana farmer's postscript to his fiancée suggests the straightforward nature of most of them: "I have bin true to my promise I have not bin to see a girl since I have bin here neither do I expect [to] till I see you I want you to do the same as I am doing." Where there was sufficient trust to support a serious courtship or formal engagement, doubts about fidelity were rarely expressed.[52] What was more important was establishing the trustworthiness of oneself and one's affections.

In the nineteenth century, people believed that confidence was as essential to happiness in love as candor; it was the end to which sincerity and candor were the means. "The best way is to begin right on the broadest platform of mutual confidence," a Union soldier told his sweetheart. Only on this ground was it safe to be as open as lovers were required to be. "You see how I am telling my heart out to you, trusting you implicitly, I do not want to hide from you any feeling," the New Yorker Katherine Smith wrote Walter Hill. She credited Walter's trust to their knowledge of one another: "You know me and yet you love me. . . . There is one who loves me just for myself—no earthly reason for it but because he does and he trusts and depends upon me." Without trust, the dependency and closeness of serious courtship could be dangerous. Mary Butterfield told Champion Chase, "To regard you with less confidence than now would be *dreadful*. . . . It would frighten me to know that my happiness was intwined with anothers, did I not trust your love so entirely."[53] Confidence was the foundation on which relationships were built, and confidence was impossible without candor.

But there was another reason that candor was the dominant value in mid-nineteenth-century courtship: it offered a link between people who inhabited the ever more disparate worlds of men and women. Candor involved communication, and communication—then as now—created a way to narrow the gap between ideals and reality and between husband and wife. By feeling at liberty—indeed, under obligation—to share their inner selves, young men and women could lessen the distance that divided them. After a visit that both agreed was "nicer and brighter" than others, Katherine Smith suggested to Walter Hill that it was because they "talked more naturally and easily to each other so that each began to feel that the other's life belonged to us."[54] Like the association of romantic love with sympathy and mutuality, the commitment to candor reflected the need to foster closeness in a world where idealization and domesticity daily distanced men and women from each other.

But candor did not come easily, precisely because males and females were raised to embrace separate spheres. The more closely an individual conformed to his or her gender ideal, the more conflict he or she could expect in fulfilling the expectation for candor in courtship. At the same time, deviations from role could be seen as evidence of unwillingness or inability to be the "true man" or "true woman" middle-class marriage required. When they heeded the call for candor, both men and women had to balance the demands of one ideal against another. The problem was especially acute for men. Candor demanded openness about feelings, but manliness was associated with emotional restraint and self-control. For many middle-class men, courtship was the setting for a struggle between the self-exposure expected in intimate relationships and the self-control men were called upon to show in society. "The expression of tender feeling was a special threat" to what one historian has called the ideal of the Manly Achiever. It "could interfere with a man's competitive impulses, and . . . might prevent him from going out in the world to seek his fortune."[55]

The threat was contained by collective disapproval and internalized sanctions. J. M. More believed that "among a certain class of men, . . . that man who cannot easily banish from his heart a feeling . . . of deep love . . . is thought to be weak," and objected that "a wrong view has been taken of the man of strong feelings." The young New Bedford businessman, W. C. Whitridge, believed he was the victim of just such a wrong view. He anticipated that most people would be surprised at the pain he suffered when his proposal of marriage was rejected. His description of how he thought he was misperceived suggests how little room there was for men to express their feelings:

They would not expect it to make me miserable . . . but why not? Because he is cold and phlegmatic in his temperament they would say . . . it will be viewed by him with no deeper feeling than he would experience by adding up an account on his ledger—finding he had lost $100 when he expected to make that amount. To the eyes of the world it is even so and I am glad that it is. . . . I do not wish their sympathy.[56]

Exposure to "the eyes of the world" for Whitridge clearly meant his fellow men. It was especially awkward for men to share their feelings with each other. When Serena Ames's father and her fiancé attempted to "construct a friendship" the way they would a house, Serena was amused by their efforts; but she could appreciate "the difficulty men have in showing another man their heart." Her fiancé agreed that he could talk more freely with her mother than her father: "It is very true as you say, because . . . *Men* are not the natural confidantes of men."[57]

If men had "natural confidantes," presumably these were female; but even in their relationships with women, men often found it embarrassing to express their feelings. One man who suffered for his reticence was George Moore, a Harvard student whose fiancée broke their engagement because she "felt there was a reserve in [his] nature," which in spite of her hopes, had not "upon intimate acquaintance become the more open & frank." Mary Butterfield had a similar complaint about Champion Chase. Realizing that she "at times thought [him] too cold and reserved at heart," he explained, "I have endeavored to govern my feelings in all circumstances." To do so was the manly thing. When a midwestern professor revealed his "unsettled spirits" in a letter to the woman he loved, he thought that a "determined effort to recover self-control and self-regard" was in order. "A man should not feel as I do; nor above all give utterance to such emotion," he declared.[58]

The implication that *women* might have—and express—such emotion was stated explicitly elsewhere. Many men agreed with George Wright's observation:

Even at the moment when uncovering the deepest sacredest secret of their whole lives, [people] are most afraid of showing themselves in their true color & as *they are.* I do not speak of women, as they have a great advantage over us at such a time.[59]

Women did, indeed, have a certain advantage here. They might be thought the weaker sex in intellect, but they were stronger in sensibility. They did not generally see emotional reserve as part of their nature as many men did; nor was it written into the role society prescribed for women. For them, the risk lay, as it always had, in too open an expression of feeling. No one questioned the axiom that a woman could be "too ready to tell [a man] of her love." The result could be betrayal and humiliation. The Vermont teacher who feared that she "may have been to unfeminine in . . . openly avowing [her] *love,* " believed in the dictum that "woman should never confess her love lest the object of it . . . take advantage of the same." Perhaps she had consulted the Reverend Jesse Pleck's chapter "How to Get a Good Husband." "Be sure that your gentleman friend is in advance of you in manifestations," he told his readers.[60]

Even when a woman was formally bound to the "object" of

her love, she might struggle with the expression of her feelings. A young mill worker told her fiancé, "I just begin to know what it is to love with my whole heart. I have not dared to love [too] much for fear that you would find somebody else that you would like better." Perhaps that was what held back Blanche Butler, who admitted to her fiancé, the young congressman Adelbert Ames, "I always shrink a little from telling you how much I care for you." She explained, "It is only when driven to desperation by seeing you unhappy . . . that I can rid myself of the feeling & show you my heart." When she did thus expose herself, Blanche was likely to regret that she had not "been quite subdued enough." Likewise, Katherine Smith worried that she might overwhelm her fiancé with the strength of her feelings. She was willing "to take the consequences of being natural and as I am." After one especially intense letter to Walter Hill, she asked him, "Now what do you think of this expression of feeling? Are you frightened?" She wondered if she did not "seem more quiet" than she really was. "What quiet and self restraint I have comes from hard work," she explained.[61] While "manly" men might have to work to express their feelings openly enough to meet the shared goal of candor, women had to work to restrain their feelings as fully as the ideal of True Womanhood required. True Women were pure, and "perfect openness and frankness" might reveal impurities; True Women were submissive, and a declaration of feeling might be mistaken for assertiveness.

When they overcame these obstacles, couples often found that candor produced an intimacy unequaled elsewhere in their lives. Mary Butterfield assured Champion Chase, "However many may claim a place in the *outer* chamber, you dwell alone in the inner sanctuary." Two years later, she told him, "I can love you better from the fact that to no one have I made myself known as to you, to no one have I given such confidences." When Augusta McKim gave "such confidences" to Alexander Rice, he considered it "a sacred . . . trust"; she had shown him the "secret, unobserved emotions of [her] heart," what he knew she "would not reveal to the eye of any other being upon earth."

To another woman, it seemed "right" that her fiancé was willing to tell her what he "could not tell to anyone else."[62]

For many men and women, the sharing of themselves that occurred in courtship stood in direct contrast to the reserve they felt with other people. Although there were women who found openness and intimacy only with female friends, there were many others whose relationships with lovers and future husbands provided their first experience with closeness.[63] Before she fell in love with Henry Poor, Mary Pierce had "never had an intimate friend." Her openness with Henry caught her by surprise. "I have sometimes wondered at myself that I had told you some thoughts and feelings of mine or something about myself," she wrote to him, adding: "It is so new to me to *confide* in *any one.* There always appeared to me to be two distinct sets of thought, the upper currents of my heart and the inner life that nobody knew about." Serena Ames had a similar experience; she eloquently described what made her bond with George Wright unique:

My heart is a castle with most obstinate doors that I myself can scarcely throw open when once closed. Walls of impenetrable reserve are selfbuilt between my soul and other souls. Into the fields and garden and even into the front yard into the very threshold many may come, but . . . even as they stumble at the door way, or turn away chilled by my inhospitality. . . . *you* have a right to enter in, explore and know all the recesses of my heart.

George replied, "You are the only one that I *can* give free access to. . . . We will be near, and never distant."[64]

George Wright and Serena Ames lived in a world that demanded distance, even while it valued closeness, between men and women. The fact that they would occupy separate spheres did not mean that they were content to know and love each other from a distance. On the contrary, young men and women sought, through the medium of romance and the commitment to candor, to remain near to one another as they approached marriage, and as they assumed its roles.

114

"Sacrifice of feelings"

The closeness of courtship forced young women and men to reconcile the demands of their new ties with the claims of the old. Mid-nineteenth-century courtships took place in a climate of heightened expectations for the parent-child, especially the mother-child, relationship. By the 1840s and 1850s, the members of a middle-class family were emotionally as well as economically interdependent. The domestic educator Samuel Goodrich observed in 1838: "With the advance of refinement and knowledge the family circle is drawn closer together, and the solicitude of parents for their children and their influence over them are proportionately increased."[65] The drawing together of the family affected both parents; but as men spent more of their time outside the circle, women dominated more of what went on within it. Father was still a powerful figure in his children's lives, but he exercised his authority from the sidelines. It was mother who stood at—indeed, defined—the center of family life.

The Republican Mother had replaced the eighteenth-century patriarch as the primary molder of the next generation. Where ministers and educators had once urged women not to "spoil their children," they now advocated maternal affection and sympathy as the best means to ensure the piety, patriotism, and industriousness of the young. "Mothers," a typical advice book declared, "have as powerful an influence over the welfare of future generations as all other earthly causes combined." The continuing decline in fertility (the average for white women fell from 7.04 in 1800 to 5.21 in 1860) allowed women to concentrate their influence on, and develop more intimate relationships with, their individual offspring.[66]

When the time came to make the transition to marriage, young people found their mother more affected by, or at least expressive of, the impending loss than was their father. This difference was especially true for a man, who could expect his father to remain aloof from the unfolding drama of courtship. Fathers may have been less authoritarian, but they were also less involved with their sons in this period than fifty years before. Diffidence, even distance, characterized relationships between fathers and sons at midcentury. Victorian men evidenced willingness to show love and tenderness for their sons, but their concern focused on worldly and therefore "manly" issues. Few men confided in their father during courtship; those who did *"unveil*... some of [their] heart's secrets" could expect to receive counsel on the practical, especially pecuniary, aspects of the matter. Questions of finance or career were proper subjects for male counsel; emotions were the province of women.[67]

It was his relationship with his mother that carried the emotional current in a young man's life. Other than Mary Pierce, there was only one person in Henry Poor's life who was privy to his secrets: his mother. "Next to yourself," he told Mary, shortly after his mother's death in 1841, "she seemed nearer to me than any one else, and I felt myself on such terms of familiarity and sympathy with her, that I could pour out to her my whole heart without reserve." The special closeness Henry Poor felt with his mother was not unusual. Young men who came of age in the middle decades of the nineteenth century were bound to their mother more closely and to a later age than earlier generations had been. The Union soldier who described his mother as his "most confidential and intimate friend" reveals the emotional dependence of many men on their mothers. Seventeenth- and eighteenth-century boys had moved at an earlier age out of their mother's domain and into their father's. Now women retained control over, and responsibility for, their sons until the latter were young adults, and consequently the ties of mutual dependence remained strong.[68] Thus it is not surprising that men who were closely tied to their mothers did not necessarily communicate the feelings aroused by courtship and the transition to marriage. In fact, as middle-class mothers moved closer to the emotional center of their son's lives—and stayed there longer—one finds no diminution in the distance young men kept from their mothers during courtship. Even men who were close to their mothers were seldom forthcoming about courtship; a strong mother-son bond did not translate into openness on this highly charged subject. A man whose mother felt that she was "losing her boy—her 'baby'" when he became engaged, may have preferred to present his mother with a *fait accompli.*[69]

The changes in child-rearing and gender roles that brought mothers and sons closer together also affected daughters. As middle-class families became comfortable with, even devoted to, the expression of affection between parents and children, the marriage of a daughter meant a "sacrifice of feelings" for both mother and father. Although fathers were less involved than mothers in the business of child rearing, many men faced with the loss of a daughter at marriage also experienced what one parent called a "struggle between love & duty."[70] Blanche Butler's father, a Massachusetts congressman, approved of her engagement to Adelbert Ames, a native New Englander who represented Mississippi in the Senate, but could not conceal his mixed feelings. "In a letter to Mother," Blanche reported to her fiancé in 1870, "Father says he thinks I have more than my 'share of love and attention.' He, I fear is growing *jealous.*" Del told Blanche he had come to the same conclusion after a conversation with Benjamin Butler in Washington:

Just as I left your Father, after dinner, I said "I shall probably leave here next Friday evening [for Massachusetts] adding "unless you have objections." I had told him some time ago, before he left here . . . that I would soon go there, when he said "You had better remain here and attend to your duties" or words to that effect. So last evening I said "unless you object." His reply was "I don't captain this business—someone else is responsible for your visits and not I."

Butler's resistance to the plan was due, he said, to his wife: "She claims you take away her friend and companion," he explained to Del.[71] It was safer to project these painful feelings onto the mother who was expected to feel keenly a daughter's loss.

The mother-daughter relationship was the traditional focus for the fear of separation that marriage aroused. A mother was more closely connected to and dependent on her daughters than a father was. She had more to lose when a daughter left home and, as a woman, was allowed to feel and express the pain of that loss. But however strong the bond between mothers and daughters, and however great the pain of loosening it, before 1860, women rarely became involved in their daughters' courtships. Although young women were linked to their mothers by a variety of female experiences—years of domestic apprenticeship, long hours of bedside care during childbirth and illness, and shared social activities—there is little evidence of ante-bellum mothers serving as confidantes, advisers, or companions during a daughter's courtship. Mary Pierce was not unusual. In the weekly letters she wrote home during her year in Bangor, she made only passing reference to Henry Poor. Even when Mrs. Pierce came to spend a few weeks in Bangor, Henry was introduced to her merely as a neighbor of her daughter's. Mary Pierce had an affectionate relationship with her parents, but their closeness did not require the giving of confidences during courtship.[72]

As the century progressed, and women had ever fewer children who remained dependent on them longer, middle-class mothers drew closer to their adolescent offspring. One result was that daughters were more likely to make their mothers privy to the inner workings of courtship. One young woman explained, "A mother seems more intimately connected with our home life than a father, and we are so much more accustomed to confide in her than in him." The custom involved a sense of obligation. After telling her mother about her romance with a fellow student, a Massachusetts woman reported, "I feel very much better for it was not right for me to conceal anything from her who is my best friend." Augusta Hubbard, an upstate New York schoolgirl, did not view her mother as her "best friend," but she did take her into her confidence. Near the beginning of her relationship with Frank Blakeslee in 1867, she noted in her diary, "I told Ma *some* about Frank."[73] The mixture of distance and closeness, of autonomy and dependence, that marked young people's relationships with their parents would be very much in evidence when it came to sexual intimacy, the most private part of courtship.

CHAPTER 4

"Such a Loving, Joyous Time"

WHEN they began the serious game of courting and seeking a mate, young women and men found themselves on a field
where definite rules were in force and penalties applied but
where parents could be counted on to remain on the sidelines.
People who allowed their parents to influence the course of
their courtship were weak and irresponsible. "A man that is not
capable of managing his love affairs without the assistance of
friends," one midwesterner declared, "is not fit to be married
at all, and he who will permit himself to be *dictated* [to] is worse
yet." Parents who tried to influence their children's choice were
considered to be at best misguided and at worst malicious. Nineteen-year-old Augusta Hubbard declared that "lovers more than

all others . . . ought not to be opposed in such a way as parents often treat their children, if they wish to have them act with any moderation."[1]

Augusta was thankful she possessed the complete trust of her parents. "I know if they were in the habit of acting as if they suspected me," she wrote in her diary, "I should be sly, deceitful and very obstinate." She had observed such suspicious behavior in parents and its effect on their children: "I think if my father was like some . . . I should be as wild as their daughters are," she concluded.[2] Clearly, there were parents who sought to control their children's courtship behavior, but they were greatly outnumbered by people like the Hubbards who gave their children a large measure of freedom.* Augusta's diary for the summer of 1867 records many occasions on which she and her suitor Frank Blakeslee were on their own. For example:

June 30 Sunday We all (the young folks) went to shaker meeting at Mount Morriss—had a pleasant ride. F[rank] and I spent a pleasant afternoon in the orchard & we sat on the steps to visit during the eve except when we went upstairs to pray.
July 15 Monday . . . Frank came this eve. We spent the evening in the graveyard alone.[4]

This may not have the playful feeling of David Shepard's visits to Ellen Savage in the 1790s or of Elias Nason's trysts with Mira Bigelow in the 1830s, but the restraint was self-imposed rather than the result of parental oversight.

Couples courting at midcentury were accustomed to regulating their own behavior; even when they did not, their parents might be slow to intervene. The diary of Lester Frank Ward, who would some day play a vital role in the development of American sociology, furnishes a case in point. At seventeen, Illinois-born Lester came to Bradford County, Pennsylvania, to

---

*The freedom does not reflect a lack of parental attentiveness. When Augusta was eighteen, she was courted by a young man who showered her with letters. She thought it best to wait to answer them until after she had gone back to school, lest her mother "think [she was] too affectionate."[3] Mrs. Hubbard was aware of what was going on in her daughter's life, and Augusta cared what her mother thought, but the interference was minimal.

work for his brother who was manufacturing wagon hubs in Myersburg. Two years later, in 1860, he began courting a young woman whom he referred to simply as "the girl." (Only after their marriage does she begin to appear in his diary as "Lizzie.") On the first Sunday in November 1860—two days before Lincoln was elected President—Lester paid a visit to Lizzie Vought at her family's house in Towanda, the county seat:

I found the family as usual seated around the warm and crackling fire with every indication of comfort and relief. Sarah [Lizzie's sister] did not go to bed until ten o'clock, after which my beloved and I went down, made a fire, and sat down to talk and kiss and embrace and bathe in love.[5]

In 1861, Lester enrolled at the Susquehanna Collegiate Institute in Towanda. His visits to Lizzie—and their sexual relationship—continued. By the summer Mrs. Vought's opposition was aroused. Lester reported a confrontation that took place after he and Lizzie had watched together at a dead neighbor's bedside:

I accompanied the girl home, and she insisted on my staying there and getting a little sleep, but she came into my room to give me my socks and to kiss me a little, and her mother found her there and she said several things concerning us which made me angry and I got up and soon left the house. I shall never spend another night there.

This episode did not, however, mark the end of Lester and Lizzie's nighttime intimacies, nor was it the last time Mrs. Vought intervened. In April 1862, Lester reported: "Her mother gave me an invitation to discontinue my visits but I do not know that I shall accept. She is angry with the girl, and with me also, I think." A week later, he believed "the affair with her mother is cleared up"; but shortly thereafter, when Lizzie was ill, he noted in his diary, "Her mother was very angry with me because I sat down on the girl's bed yesterday. That made me miserable."[6]

Mrs. Vought's anger in this situation is striking for two reasons: first, because parents rarely became so directly involved in a child's courtship; and second, because the extraordinary intimacy between Lizzie and Lester apparently developed unchecked for two years before engendering any parental opposition. It is difficult to believe that Lizzie's parents were completely unaware of what was going on in their own house.* When Lester Ward was first courting Lizzie, he was disturbed by rumors about her sister Sarah's moral character, so it is possible that the Voughts' standards were looser than most of their neighbors'. However, given Mrs. Vought's eventual disapproval, it is clear that she did have standards for her daughter's behavior. The laxity and inconsistency with which she enforced them reflects a strong bias in the culture against parental interference in courtship. Young people had the autonomy and privacy to develop relationships that were sexually and emotionally intimate, and they did.

"These loving impulses *of ours"*

Mid-nineteenth century courtship had room for erotic play, both in fantasy and in reality. Separated lovers evoked the past and anticipated the future with images of sexual intimacy. The Union College student Alexander Hamilton Rice looked forward to his reunion with Augusta McKim this way:

O happy hours when I may *once more* encircle within these arms the dearest object of my love—when I shall again feel the pressure of that "aching head" which will delight to recline upon my bosom, when I

---

*The only indication we have of Lizzie's father's reaction is this entry in Lester's diary for 24 February 1861: "Her father growled a little, and I am determined not to go back before the end of two weeks."[7] There is other evidence to suggest that on the rare occasions when parental sanctions were imposed, mothers were more watchful disciplinarians than were fathers. Lucy Harris, for example, remembered that during her courtship in the 1850s, she and her suitor shared the sitting room with her father while he read his newspaper. At ten o'clock, her father said good night and left the room, and she and her suitor exchanged pledges and kisses. When Lucy "went into the sitting room to make ready for bed," her mother "sputtered out, 'If *I'd* been in there as your father was, I guess I wouldn't a come out.'"[8]

may *again* press to my heart which palpitates with the purest affection the loved one who has so long shared its undivided devotion.[9]

Sometimes the fantasies were more explicit. Lawrence Chamberlain was a divinity student when he became engaged to Fannie Adams in 1852. In a letter to his fiancée, who was teaching school in Georgia, he recounted a dream that he himself understood to be about the dangers of sexual intimacy:

I dreamed last night that my F—— had a little "gold.——" tossing him up in her arms and playing with him. I was very jealous, for she would not let me take him at all and I was so unreasonable as to imagine that I had as much right to him as she. But there wasn't any *quarrel*. I wish I could tell you my feelings when I looked upon those two. . . . Only I remember my starting when I thought that my F—— was not F—****[Chamberlain] yet. After that I dreamed something else, which if it had been carried much farther, I am afraid would have made the two dreams come in rather an inverted order.[10]

Men were not the only ones to record erotic fantasies. Mary Butterfield told Champion Chase, "In fancy my arms have been around you & myself clasped to that dear 'home' of mine your own loving heart & I have kissed you again & again & felt your cheek resting against mine & your fond embrace so vividly that I could scarce believe it was not real." Couples remembered partings in terms of the kisses exchanged and envisioned meetings that would allow unembarrassed embraces. Elizabeth Prentiss hoped there would "be nobody within two miles" of her rendezvous with her returning suitor. "Suppose you stop in some out of the way place just out of town, and let me trot out there to see you?" she playfully proposed.[11]

If women and men permitted themselves fantasies of sexual union and reunion when separated, their behavior when together might well have been more restrained and controlled. Fantasies of sexual expression do not necessarily reflect sexual freedom in reality. For couples courting at midcentury, the picture was mixed: while the process of tightening standards for premarital conduct, begun in the early republic, continued, physical demonstrativeness remained an accepted and expected part of both casual courting and serious courtship. Well into the 1860s, young men and women did not shy away from physical expressions of affection. In New Jersey in 1861, John Henry Smith noted in his diary: "Came up with Lizzie Green. I don't know how many kisses I had that evening, was almost smothered with the sweet things." Lizzie Green was far from unique; two days later, Smith and a classmate " 'escourted' two girls to a Mrs. Norwood's where they played cards and ate chestnuts. Miss Albert gave me a sweet kiss before I was aware of the fact; went home with my lady. She too gave me a farewell salute."[12]

Such physical contact between young people was not limited to the citified eastern seaboard. In Ohio, for example, John Ballard teased his sixteen-year-old sister Mary because she "was so obstinate and unyielding to the oft-repeated efforts of the young men to get a *sweet kiss* from [her] lips." Mary replied, "I look with contempt on such things and especially on little girls having beaux." In Indiana, a young Quaker was more regretful than contemptuous. Emma Hadley told her cousin: "I have no 'Beau' to while away the Sabbath eve or I would not be writing to thee." Emma had mixed feelings about what she was missing, described in this verse:

> The boys they go courting they dress very fine
> To keep the girls up 'tis all their design
> They will hug them & kiss them & flatter & lie
> And keep the girls up till they are ready to die.

She added: "Isn't that nearly true? I don't want thee to think I have lost confidence in all the young gents."[13]

Although Mary Ballard and Emma Hadley viewed men as sexual aggressors, there is ample evidence that women were often willing participants in the sexual play that was common in courting. When Mary Ballard was no longer a little girl but a woman about to be married, she was hardly "obstinate and unyielding." After what he considered the "happiest night of [his] life," William Ross wrote to her, "We were too happy last night to part. You came very near persuading me to stay all night." And John Henry Smith hardly had to extort kisses from the young women he encountered in the 1860s.[14]

A few women took the initiative from the very outset. An Illinois Quaker reported being approached after meeting by "a real nice looking young lady [who] rode up . . . and said . . . 'Why won't you go out & take dinner with me?' " And in 1865, an Indiana woman asked a friend to bring along her cousin so she "could find out wheather [sic] he would be worth going after or not." Women who "went after" men were undoubtedly in the minority, but those who encouraged a suitor's sexual advances were not. A young Philadelphian found that his "regular system of *proposing* and making love" did not work with Charlotte Willcocks, who "kept [her] gloves on & kept him at bay." Charlotte's view that she was "strange and different from other women" suggests that midcentury standards for sexual conduct were still relatively lax.[15]

Many couples engaged freely in a kind of sexual banter. A New Hampshire clerk wrote his sweetheart, "You need not be alarmed about your daguerreotype fading but *you would fade* if you had had the kissing that your picture has. . . . I wish I could see you this very moment I would make you think I have not done all my busing on your picture." An Illinois schoolteacher warned James Bell, "I mean to bite your neck if I have to get false [teeth] to do it." Kisses were used as rewards—Annie Cox told Winan Allen that if he wished to chew tobacco, he would "forfeit the privilege" of kissing her—and to keep score in relationships. The Pennsylvanian Mary Thorn teased her fiancé James White, "Don't you dare to say one word about the debt I owe you for in the way you calculate I *will never repay* it. . . . I have been entirely too liberal in time past but I don't intend my kisses to diminish in value by their frequent repetition." He was undaunted and, a month later, told her, "Would that I could *now* throw my arm again around your neck and steal another of those burning kisses!"[16]

The images Mary and James used—of debt, repayment, even theft—give a hint of the issues raised by their sexual attraction.

Kisses were something Mary "owed" James, but it was up to her to determine the schedule of "repayment." "Burning kisses," on the other hand, were for James to "steal" from Mary. In this case, the images are our only clue; but other couples left behind revealing evidence of the process by which sexual limits were drawn, enforced, and on occasion violated.

Like James White, Champion Chase was a lawyer, struggling to make his way in the Midwest. He was twenty-five and clerking in a law office in Buffalo, New York, when he met Mary Butterfield. The Butterfields were soon to move to Wisconsin, and in the summer of 1846, Champion visited them there. In August, he and Mary became engaged. During the next two years, Mary lived with her family in Racine, while her fiancé moved from one part of Wisconsin to another, giving lectures on phrenology and getting established in business. From the beginning, their relationship involved those forms of touching and kissing common to mid-nineteenth-century courtship. Then, during a visit together in January 1848, they seem to have ventured into new—and perhaps forbidden—sexual territory. The next morning, "after sleeping three or four hours" in the Racine Hotel, Champion exclaimed that he "never had such a loving joyous time before." For Mary, it was not so simple. In a painfully honest letter, she described her feelings:

I did not feel so quiet a part of the time last night as I appeared & you supposed. Although I love you dearly & trust you so perfectly that I am perfectly willing & glad to make you happy by those favors which no one else in the wide world could obtain, yet even towards you I can not at once resign all the feelings which nature & education have fixed in my mind—I *was glad* afterwards when you seemed so sincerely pleased & happy—so *satisfied* with *me*.

Mary was anxious that Champion not misunderstand her:

I did not feel unpleasantly or unwilling. No, it was a *pleasure* and yet women so naturally guard such treasures with jealousy & care, that it seems very "strange" to yield them even to the "best loved one" who has a claim to such kindnesses. So of course it seemed very "strange" to me.[17]

"Such a Loving, Joyous Time"

For a week or two after this episode, Champion addressed his letters to Mary "Dear Wife." Only one of Mary's letters, two months later, began "My Dear Husband"; but much of her correspondence after the January visit dealt with the question of how soon they could marry. It is tempting to conclude from all this that Mary Butterfield and Champion Chase had intercourse on that night in Racine, but the correspondence offers no direct evidence. It seems clear, however, that their behavior that night was more intimate than any they had engaged in before, and, in their own minds, brought them much closer to marriage.

During the next months, there was no retreat from whatever had taken place in January. Champion's letters closed with statements such as "Ah, if I could get at you just now there would be some aching lips I guess before I should get through," and Mary's fantasies were equally erotic:

When I get to *housekeeping* . . . if I make any blunders I fancy all that will be necessary to make you think your food is all right will be to give you that magic touch—hey? . . . It will save sugar in your cake, coffee, & so forth—I can sweeten them with kisses? . . . I always laugh when I think of those kisses upon your neck, they used to amuse me so. It was half mischief that prompted them but I loved them because they were half denied. My lips are growing too heavy there are so many kisses accumulated there—[18]

If either had doubts, they did not admit them. In March, Champion told Mary:

How I love to have you write me so frankly about your feelings and reflections upon our *late intimacy*. . . . I am so [illegible] to find that opportunity for reflection is satisfying you more and more that we were right. You have reason to put confidence in these loving *impulses* of ours dearest. . . . They are our best indices surely and I am perfectly satisfied that, however intimate we might permit ourselves to be, *they* would not permit us to be too much so.

For her part, Mary celebrated what she had learned: that she was "endowed with every womanly attribute in perfectness & beauty." Her passion unsettled her but did not un-sex her. She assured her fiancé, "the knowledge has no base effect upon me. I am . . . *proud* that I can give myself to you as I am. . . . I *am* a woman now." Mary Butterfield's affirmation of her woman-hood through her sexuality suggests that although "nature and education" might point to female passionlessness, experience could tell a different tale. "You have lifted a veil which concealed from me many beautiful paths of happiness & taught me joys & blessings I had never dreamed of," she told Champion.[19]

Mary Butterfield's first response, however, had been less positive. She confessed to Champion that, during their January encounter in Racine, she had "felt very strongly inclined to turn or fly away and hide [her] face in some corner." But she did not. "*I shut my eyes* and was a good, quiet little Fron [her nickname], was I not?" Other women were more active participants. Lizzie Vought, for example, was apparently as interested as Lester Ward in the sexual explorations that characterized their courtship. In his diary, Lester recorded a Sunday morning he spent with "the girl":

I did not plan to remain more than two hours, but O, the charms of love! She had never before been so sweet. She looked at me so gently and spoke so tenderly. "I love you," she said, kissing me on the mouth, "I love this mouth, I love these dear eyes, I love this head" and a thousand other little caressing pet-names. At about three o'clock we were sleepy. Arranging three chairs and the old shoemaker's bench in a line, she sat down in the middle chair. I sat in the chair near the end of the bench, and stretching myself on the bench put my head in her gentle lap. . . . We lay with out faces together. I unfastened my shirt and put her tender little hands on my bare breast, and . . . she gave me her heart and her body, asking nothing more in exchange than my own.[20]

In the spring of 1861, when they were often separated, Lizzie did her part to see that their sexual explorations could continue. After one Saturday spent in the company of friends, Lizzie and Lester conspired to be alone. Lester reported:

I was certain that I should accompany my brother to his house, and in that case I should not kiss my darling at all and how I should feel it before the end of another long week! I could not tolerate the thought.

Accordingly I wrote a note and gave it to the girl [that is, Lizzie]. She felt as I did and told me to let him return alone, because she wanted to kiss me. I did it, and O what a happy night. . . . Closely held in loving arms we lay, embraced, and kissed all night (not going to bed until five in the morning). We have never acted in such a way before. All that we did I shall not tell here, but it was all very sweet and loving and nothing infamous.

Six months later, in the fall of 1861, Lester Ward and Lizzie Vought "tasted the joys of love and happiness which only belong to a married life." In August 1862, two days after enlisting in the Union Army, Lester Ward was married to the woman he had "loved so long, so constantly, so frantically." In his diary, he exclaimed, "How sweet it is to sleep with her."[21]

Since we must rely on Lester Ward for our picture of Lizzie Vought, we cannot know for certain whether she was indeed as sexually free and unconflicted as she appears in her lover's account. Perhaps Lester failed to record her protestations or self-doubts, or perhaps she hesitated to express them, but the diary suggests otherwise. On the one occasion when Lizzie admitted, "I am afraid I am doing something I shouldn't in putting my hand on your bare breast," Lester found the "tenderness and humility" of her remark endearing. It apparently generated little guilt or conflict in either of them.[22]

Things were less harmonious between another couple courting in the 1860s, Annie Cox and Gideon Winan Allen. They met in 1861, when twenty-six-year-old Winan was studying law at the University of Wisconsin in Madison. Annie Cox, five years his junior, lived in Madison with her mother and stepfather. Unhappy at home, Annie spent her time teaching school and painting, while she waited for Winan to finish his education and set up a law practice. Winan Allen was a Copperhead Democrat whose opposition to the war and desire to evade the draft led him to leave Wisconsin in 1862.* A committed Republican, Annie tried to persuade Winan that the war was justified, but

---

*The circumstances under which Winan Allen left the University of Wisconsin for the University of Michigan are unclear from the extant correspondence. Apparently, his politics made him unpopular with both students and faculty at Wisconsin.

their political differences did not interfere with the intimacy that developed between them. In the summer of 1863, they became formally engaged.

Winan spent part of that summer doing agricultural day labor, the rest of it living with the Coxes in Madison. It appears that, at least once during that extended visit, Annie and Winan also "tasted the joys of love and happiness which only belong to a married life." But for Annie, the taste was bitter. In response to a letter that does not survive, she explained how she viewed their actions:

When temptation to wrong suggested itself from natural passions and opportunity, 'twas my mission to have been *fine,* giving you a kind refusal and leading your mind away and beyond. In the first instance, I failed in the full possession of my reason & judgments thus giving strength to your desire and weakening my better nature. We made firm resolves and the next opportunity showed how they were kept.

Winan's passions were "natural"—for a man; as a woman, Annie's "reason and judgment" were weak. When she "reviewed [her] conduct," she concluded, "God only knows how I detested myself. You meanwhile," she told her fiancé, "kept your old standing place in my estimation."[23]

Annie did not absolve Winan of all responsibility: "I own I think you to blame in some degree. That is, for not accepting my first denial"; but in a postscript the next day, she added, "We have both done wrong. I having done much the greater because I should have acted the part of a true, noble, Christian woman." Although hers was the greater wrong, his was the greater loss. "If I have not injured you dear one, fear not for me," she wrote. "Tis only for you I weep for the sorrow I have caused when you . think of me." She herself did "not feel, strange as it may seem, any the less pure *now.*" She declared to Winan, "I shall stand at the altar with you, only humble and for that reason better. . . . I know this experience will be for my good, though it would have been better if it could never happen [*sic*]."[24]

But it *had* happened, and Annie's ultimate response was to retreat sexually. "Let it all pass," she told Winan; and on subsequent visits, they apparently did not repeat their indiscretions of the summer of 1863. Only in the months before their marriage did they return to the subject. Then Winan wondered if Annie did "not judge a little harshly of the past? *Whom* could you have confided in more securely than me?" he asked. "Do you know of any with whom judgment would have had greater control?"[25] Winan Allen was willing to admit that self-control cost him an effort. He could compare himself with other members of his sex, among whom sexual discipline was assumed to be lacking, and earn credit for his own attempt—regardless of the results. It was an occasion for self-congratulation.

Annie, on the other hand, expected self-control of herself. "I should have made my Christian principles guide and restrain me in all things," she said.[26] His role was to accept; hers, to enforce restraint. But was this the restraining influence of propriety—as in Lizzie Vought's case—or of female passionlessness? More than Mira Bigelow, Mary Butterfield, or Lizzie Vought, Annie Cox can be said to have denied her sexual feelings; yet she did not use passionlessness to assert control of her relationship with Winan Allen. The issue was her failure to restrain *his* sexual feelings, rather than the absence of her own. Her implicit message of reproof to Winan was, "You are too passionate"—not, "I have no passion."

"The highest appreciation of man and woman"

Winan Allen gave himself credit for having as much (or more), self-mastery as other men, but did he view Annie as an exception to her sex? If he was *more* in control of himself than most men, was she *less* in control of herself than most women? Was her disclaimer of pleasure in their sexual activities what he expected of a woman? The Cox-Allen manuscripts leave these questions unanswered, but we do know that other men of

Winan Allen's generation expected and encouraged the women in their lives to express their affection sexually. They ignored or internalized incompletely the authoritative view that "women lacked carnal motivation." A New England mechanic wrote his absent fiancée in 1853, "No doubt you often think it would be pleasant to have a young man by your side, with your hand in his; or perhaps with his arm twined fondly around your neck. . . . I presume that you have the same feelings that I often have." Lawrence Chamberlain was more insistent:

It might make a person a little angry for a woman to *try* to ignore the fact that she was not above human passion & susceptibilities . . . a warm blooded girl come & lie in a warm blooded man's bosom & think that he will not "touch" her ever? Why, leave a girl to her own way about it & my word for it, she wouldn't lie very still a great while without *extending* her *acquaintance,* I know that.[27]

Lawrence was prepared to defer to his fiancée on sexual matters. *"Your will shall be my law,"* he told Fannie Adams, but he wanted her to admit that "it was a matter requiring as much self-denial on [her] part as on [his]." Will Adkinson, an Indiana lawyer, took a similar stand, telling Lu Burlingame that he thought of her "not as an angel but as a woman . . . [his] equal with flesh and blood, with magnetism, electricity, passion." But what about the women themselves? Did they, as historian Nancy Cott suggests, use "passionlessness as a way to assert control in the sexual arena?"[28] Were Lawrence Chamberlain and Will Adkinson responding to—and assailing—a position of self-conscious female passionlessness? Both of them were involved with women for whom sexual ideology was a powerful force, shaping self-image if not always behavior. By reconstructing Lawrence's relationship with Fannie Adams and, in greater detail, Will's with Lu Burlingame, we can see how acts of passion could throw the ideal of passionlessness into grave doubt.

Lawrence Chamberlain and Fannie Adams had a troubled courtship. Their relationship was sexually intimate and may have been consummated before marriage. In 1852, there is a mysterious admonition from Lawrence to "remember the jar in the cellar way. He would have been three weeks old today"; and two years later, this plaintive letter from Fannie to her fiancé:

You know dear Lawrence that I may breathe to you, even as to my own heart, in all innocence and perfect trustfulness, those things which would ever sink me in the estimation and respect of any third person; for no other being can know what we are to each other.

Fannie's reference to Lawrence as "my own husband to whom I have pledged my very being" suggests that whatever they were—or had once been—to each other, she saw them as husband and wife.[29]

Fannie Adams's views of love and marriage were highly unconventional. According to Lawrence, she believed "marriage has no proper reference to children" and deemed "a man unreasonable who presumes to think of children as a *natural* offspring of marriage." What Lawrence found difficult to accept was Fannie's claim that she had no desire for him as a man:

If you said nothing about the *general principle,* but merely that for some particular reasons you would shrink very much from the peril & pain of motherhood & that you did not (although you loved me as a *man* & a *husband*) you did not dare to pass so great a hazard . . . that your love for me was to some extent a love in which difference of sex was quite an interesting & important feature . . . why then Fan I would not have one word of objection to make—I would agree with you fully.

Lawrence was willing to do all he "could to find a sure safeguard," and even agreed that "on the whole for the best preservation of chastity a man & woman would do well not to sleep together," but he could not bear the idea that Fannie felt no sexual desire for him. "Let me only beg of you not to pretend that you have no passionate feelings," he entreated; "I do not like to contemplate you as a *fossil remain.*"[30] Unfortunately, Fannie Adams's answer to this remarkable letter does not survive. We are left to speculate that for her a profession of passionlessness may have been a way to resolve the conflict created by failure to control her sexual feelings. Another couple, whose courtship followed Fannie and Lawrence's by fifteen years, left behind a much fuller record of a strikingly similar experience.

The story of Lu Burlingame and Will Adkinson begins in 1867 when they were students at Moore's Hill College, a "one horse institution" in the small Indiana town where both grew up. After two years of college, Lu left school to earn a living as a magazine writer and lecturer while caring for her widowed father and younger brother. Will set out to establish himself, first teaching, then lawyering in small Indiana towns. For two years, their relationship was defined explicitly as a brother's and sister's love—"deep and pure and unselfish." In 1869, when they were twenty-two, Lu assured Will, "A brother's love from you satisfies me now, whether it will always satisfy or not is more than I can tell." She worried that "away down in [his] heart, carefully guarded, [Will] had a dream of a closer relation." Indeed, within a year, Will proposed marriage and Lu accepted, telling him that she felt "a new value in [herself], a new motive to be a pure, true woman." She reminded Will, "The man to whom I give my life must always be brave, true and pure." "I want you to be as pure as I am *trying* to be," she wrote soon after their engagement.[31]

Lu's emphasis on trying suggests that she did not find it easy to remain pure in the face of her feelings for Will. That these feelings had a physical dimension seems clear. "Cheek and soul and brain are aflame at thought of you," she told him; "every fiber of my being trembles with passionate, weakening thrills." Will had "awakened the slumbering nature of a woman, roused her to the realization of depths and heights before undreamed of." Lu admitted to struggling for the purity she valued; but in Will's eyes, she was a "model of purity." He had long since told her, "I love you because you are pure," and now he added, "You set a standard of purity which I have never been able to reach." He confessed to being troubled by the feeling that she was "purer, nobler, more refined."[32] Will did not make explicit his standard of comparison. Was Lu "purer, nobler, more refined" than other women? than he? than he wished she were? The crisis that rocked their relationship in the summer of 1871 reveals the affirmative answers—and the deep ambivalence—behind all three questions.

In 1871, Will was practicing law in North Vernon, twenty miles from Moore's Hill. On Saturdays, he came by train to visit Lu. They referred to these visits as their "talks," but they seem to have involved something more intimate than conversation. The evidence is fragmentary but it strongly suggests that Lu and Will were engaging in sexual activity, perhaps even coitus. Their sexual contact produced enough conflict for Lu to want to break their engagement. The resolution of that conflict offers an unusual opportunity to observe at close hand the interaction between ideology and behavior.

To Will, Lu's "perfect" purity did not preclude passion. "You have never pretended to be an Angel," he told her. In his most pedantic tone, he reminded her, "There is a physical nature to be regarded in love, . . . let me love you for your beautiful body, your looks, hand pressure, and heart throb all these are a part of the highest appreciation of man and woman." Will refused to accept the possibility that he had "no attraction" for Lu. "I don't believe there has been or is or will be a time when you are folded in my arms and caressed . . . when . . . you can be cold indifferent negative toward me." There had been a time when he had seen his "power to awaken . . . emotion" within Lu, but he had also experienced her resistance to that power.[33]

He knew that she was "purer in every sense" than he was. He was "stronger physically, more passionate," but he felt she "would be drawn out. . . . I tried to draw from you passionate love not sensuality," he told her. Lu's mind was "too strong for [her] body," and so he sought "to cause [her] to grow, to expand, to develop." In doing so, he was looking ahead to married life. "I studied how to draw out this part of your nature," he explained, "so that . . . I would not have should not [sic] go hungering." But he admitted, "In the effort to tempt you and draw out this part of your nature . . . I was excited beyond my control."[34]

His efforts had not been in vain. Although Lu was "so self-possessed, . . . so determined that [Will] made but little progress," he believed that she "did develop. You know how you grew toward me, one trust after another asked for and . . . granted." Perhaps remembering the time she had told him, "Willie, put your hand where you wish to," Lu conceded that she had been "drawn toward" him:

True, . . . I learned to hunger for your tender words & caresses, the shelter of your arms & the pressure of your lips, but I never wanted extremes. When your magnetism tempted me into a responsive condition there was no real sweetnes in it (except that *you* were *more tender* afterwards.)[35]

She was angry about the "promises of abstinence given, but never kept," and resentful that Will had "resolved on self-discipline & self-control, then pursued a method of 'development' of [her] which invariably ended in self-gratification or a quarrel." Will had, she admitted, developed her "moral and emotional natures & [her] sensibilities, but not [her] passional nature." In fact, "during the last three years, *especially* during the *last* year, a change had been going on within [her], a refining, a spiritualizing"; as a result, "the animal part of [her] passional nature had grown less." It seems that the more sexually intimate Lu's relationship with Will became, the more she defined herself as asexual. "There has been a purifying of my whole nature," she concluded without irony. It was because of "a spiritualizing force at work" in her—not her sexual activities—that she felt "more liable to be injured by circumstances & by mental & emotional conditions."[36]

Still, it was the "circumstances" and "conditions" of sexual intimacy that threatened injury. Even within marriage, sex brought risks and dangers. Will and Lu discussed at length their anxieties about "the mountain weight of care" that came with children, a weight Lu was not prepared to carry. Her ideal woman was "strong, & perfectly developed in body, brain & heart, & crowns her womanhood with capable, healthy, glad wifehood & motherhood," but she was adamant that "all women were not intended to be mothers." Lu claimed that if she "were a wife, & *fully* competent and *wanted* to be a mother," the sex act would be "the most sacred & perfect expression of love possible." However, in her case there was a "physical derangement" ("explained verbally" to Will and therefore a mystery to us) that would "preclude the exercise of passionate love except through suffering."[37]

Will's failure to control himself produced in Lu a *"morbid, abnormal* feeling of repulsion, amounting almost to abhorrence in regard to the passional element in as far as it concerns me." In her assertion of passionlessness, Lu Burlingame presented herself as an exception. *She* may have felt repulsion, but the feeling was "morbid" and "abnormal." For other women, sex was a "sacred & perfect expression of love." She told Will, "If I become as well and as strong as my organization and temperament will allow, I will not *even then* have as much strength for passion and results as many, perhaps most women." Passionlessness might be a common complaint, but it was not an inherent trait of the female sex. Lu was "not to be blamed for being afflicted." It was because she was "not fully competent . . . to be a mother" that her sexual passions were weak.[38]

Clearly, Lu Burlingame made the connection that gave the ideology of passionlessness its appeal to women: the control of sex was the key to the control of reproduction. Her assertion of "passional weakness" was indeed an effort to preserve her autonomy; it was when Will "interfered with [her] personal liberty & ownership" that she recoiled, offering "pleas of physical weakness & suffering." But Lu considered passionlessness a weakness of her own constitution rather than a strength of her sex, the result of an "affliction" rather than of woman's moral superiority. It may be that Lu felt too guilty about her own complicity—her failure to *be* passionless—to assume the mantle of moral superiority. Instead, she focused on a physical condition that disabled her from participating in sexual activity and maternity. Or it may have been that female passionlessness was simply too bitter a pill for women to ask men to swallow. If Lu's passionlessness was an affliction, there was always the hope that it could be cured. Lu held out to Will the possibility that she might "grow stronger & more as you wish"—which obviously meant more sexually passionate.[39]

Even if Lu's passionlessness reflected a personal problem rather than a sexual characteristic, the implications for Will were the same: he must control himself. "I doubt whether my nature would give as much as your nature *uncontrolled* would demand," Lu wrote; "If you are unwilling to hold your nature in check, I doubt there being harmony." Few middle-class men were likely to admit an inability or unwillingness to "hold . . . in check" their sexual impulses. Will Adkinson was more direct than most in expressing his self-doubts; he did not know whether he "could be tuned up to a passionless nature or not." He agreed on the importance of self-control; he was "willing to discipline" himself but not to deny his sexuality. "I want to purify my nature, keep the mastery of my passions and will, but if you ask or expect me to be entirely negative, free from all passion, . . . I fear you will never realize it." And he believed Lu did not really even desire him to be so. Although she might think she would love him more if he "had not these qualities . . . , in the end," he told her, "you would have a contempt for me which you could not control."[40]

Will Adkinson was ambivalent about his failure to exercise self-control, and he did not claim to value self-denial. Lu Burlingame may have denied her sexuality, perhaps in response to her failure to control it; but she denied it for herself and not for her sex. However attractive as an ideology, in practice passionlessness created more problems than it solved.[41] After fifty years as the "central tenet of Victorian sexual ideology," passionlessness still failed to describe behavior. A significant number of medical experts rejected it; ordinary men and women who resisted it could find their position affirmed in the medical literature.[42] The alternative was not, of course, a world in which sexuality was unleashed. Indeed, the recognition of female sexual passion made self-control all the more important. Couples who did not deny the existence of powerful sexual feelings might have had a greater need for self-control than those who subscribed to passionlessness. Sexual passion might be natural, but excess was still dangerous.

"Perpetual fear of consequences"

Completing the passage from courtship to marriage required a couple to navigate perilous sexual waters. They must avoid the shoals on which Will and Lu almost foundered, and stay safely inside the channel marked by convention and illuminated by caution. Once they were married, they would move into more open seas, which were dangerous in a different way.

Men and women took for granted and, in some cases, celebrated the fact that marriage created a sexual union between man and wife. The expectation of sexual intimacy was implicit in the way young people, especially young men, talked about marriage. When Augusta McKim suggested that she and Alexander Hamilton Rice be married as soon as his term at college was over, Alexander was delighted. *"We can then enjoy ourselves as much as we please and as we please while we are together and no harm done,"* he wrote her. The next two lines of his letter were crossed out, but Augusta could see what he had in mind: "We should have to spend one night in Providence and there would be fun there I fancy—what say you? Mercy, what have I written—Keep this out of sight." A midwestern farmer with a fondness for words told his fiancée, "I look forward with much more pleasing anticipation when we may be united and enjoy all the pleasure of two loving soles joined in one and engulphed in each others arms and swim in a sea of pleasure though our fortunes are small."[43]

Women understood that the sexual consummation of marriage did not mean the end of balancing desire and caution, instinct and training. What worried women, as they approached marriage, was less the abstract threat sex presented to the ideal

139

of female passionlessness and more the all-too-concrete dangers
to which marriage exposed them. A woman's failure to restrain
her feelings might keep her from fulfilling the culture's ideal
of womanhood, but something much greater was at stake: she
might lose control of her life. She would be at the mercy of
biology.

Where women of an earlier generation had expressed their
sexual anxiety obliquely, and to a great extent unconsciously,
nineteenth-century women were more direct. The terms they
used sound old-fashioned, perhaps even coy, to our ears, but
their correspondents understood perfectly. Men used the same
code to reassure women that they need not dread the sexual demands of marriage. Emily Smith thanked her fiancé "for that
assurance which you give of your desire to save me from too
much of the same sort of care" which he believed had ruined
the health of his prolific mother. When Champion Chase "promised to do so much that is kind & careful for the one who gives
her all into [his] keeping," he allayed "the fears which formerly
marred" Mary Butterfield's hopes.[44]

A small minority of couples were more explicit about the nature of their concern: pregnancy created what one young
woman called a "perpetual fear of consequences." William
Lloyd Garrison II told his fiancée Ellen Wright, "One moment,
in which mutual passion overcomes reason may make years of
sadness and self reproach. . . . An 'accident' is a sad confession."
Young Garrison and his fiancée clearly intended to have children, but he believed they should "do it consciously & only
when [their] bodily condition will warrant it." Other couples
were concerned to avoid pregnancy altogether. Lawrence
Chamberlain could understand that Fannie Adams might
"shrink very much from the perils and pain of motherhood."
He pledged, "If we are ever married (as Heaven grant that
we may be) we will not subject ourselves to any fears of this
nature."[45]

Will Adkinson and Lu Burlingame were equally anxious to
avoid "the results of matrimony." Will told Lu, "I am resolved
to be just to you and very careful of you. . . . I dread marriage

for this and for nothing else." He asked her, "Help me think," since he believed she had "more opportunity to be educated." Her answer was "either continence—or moderate passion with efficient means for avoiding risk. . . . As to means, drugs & instruments used by many are not healthful ways. . . . In regard to the healthfulness & varieties of other efficient means, I have not sufficient light."[46]

For "light," couples could turn to one of many popular treatises on sex, and there is evidence that both women and men were anxious to consult them.[47] In Pennsylvania in 1861, Lester Ward procured a copy of Frederick Hollick's popular marriage manual.* The day after they had "lay, embraced, and kissed all night," the couple went out for a walk together. He claimed that he had forgotten and brought Hollick along by mistake. When he refused to let Lizzie open the book, she suspected what it was; Lester had "informed her that [he] had such a book in [his] letters." While they were sitting in the woods talking "of love and future happiness," Lizzie asked Lester to read to her from Hollick. "I tried, but failed entirely," Lester related. "I could not either give it nor read it to her. I wished to show it to her, and accordingly I went into the woods to cut canes for us, and left the book with her." He did not know how much of it she read but reported, "She liked it. . . . She told me she was ignorant like myself, and she wished to have the book but had not the place to hide it."[49]

Hollick may have been among the authors Annie Cox and Winan Allen consulted "to discover the means by which [Annie] might avoid the dreaded maelstrom." Winan assured her, "I know the consequences now and hereafter, on us and others, of

---

*According to *Young Ward's Diary*, the book was Hollick's *Phisiology*, but either Ward or the editor of his diary must have been mistaken. Hollick's manual, first published in 1850, was called *The Marriage Guide: or, Natural History of Generation: A Private Instructor for Married Persons and Those About to Marry Both Male and Female*. *Sexual Phisiology* was the title of a book by R. T. Trall, not published until 1866. If it was, in fact, the *Marriage Guide* that Lester and Lizzie were reading, they would have been informed of the merits of various methods of birth control, including douching, condoms, and the safe period. Frederick Hollick was a strong advocate of birth control. He objected that it showed "a very low and degrading opinion of young persons, especially of females, to suppose that they are only kept from indulgence by fear of the consequences."[48]

the realization of your fears. . . . You must escape that too common fate of [woman?] at all events." They discussed the merits of Dr. R. T. Trall's *Pathology of the Reproductives* (1861) and other authorities. Annie wondered whether she was "wise in speaking thus plainly by letter," but told Winan, "I feel very seriously the great responsibility before me and my own lack of education in this direction. Yet I will best improve the remaining time for I think modesty as the world terms it is false." William Lloyd Garrison II agreed and urged his fiancée, "Come to me frankly with your doubts & questions, I will do the same to you. Truth only can make us really happy. May no false delicacy prevent our speaking it to each other."[50]

It may have been "false," but modesty of discourse about sexual matters was a rule rarely broken by couples during courtship. While the expectation of sexual union as a consequence of marriage was universal, it went largely unspoken. When it was named, it was as a problem for those couples who wished to control their fertility. Will Adkinson's candid admission, "I would like the married state if I could spend it with the one entering upon it with me—her and her alone," was unique; but it is revealing that in men's and women's fantasies of married life, the "home circle" was composed only of husband and wife—no children.[51] While men married to have a home, which presumably would include children, there may have been many men who shared, perhaps unconsciously, Will Adkinson's desire for an exclusive—that is to say, childless—marriage. Children could pose a threat to the intimacy and nurturance that men sought in marriage, and they certainly increased the pressure on a man to succeed in the world. Motherhood was the basis for the middle-class woman's authority at home and influence in the world; it was her natural vocation, her Christian calling, and her patriotic duty, but on some level, children may have represented the most fearful and dangerous aspect of marriage—sexuality.

The historian catches only the most fleeting glimpses of such deeply hidden feelings. If young women and men associated the sexual side of marriage with a loss of innocence, control, and exclusiveness, they rarely betrayed those fears in their writing. It was the domestic rather than the sexual demands and rewards of marriage that captured their imagination. The middle-class portrait of marriage was invariably set in the home. The home had a bedroom, of course, but it occupied little or no space in the plans which young lovers laid as they neared the close of courtship. Their hopes and hesitations centered on the hearth—the home.

CHAPTER 5

"This Waiting & Hoping & Planning"

HOME! Blessed bride, thou art about to enter this sanctuary, and to become a priestess at its altar!" So wrote the sentimental poet Lydia Sigourney in her 1850 collection, *Whisper to a Bride.* Mrs. Sigourney hardly needed to whisper; the message she addressed to "many a fair young creature as she left the paternal hearthstone" was as familiar to her readers as the Lord's prayer.[1] From the pulpit and in the pages of magazines and novels, came fervent paeans to the home and woman's place in it.

Home was far more than the setting for middle-class marriage. It was a sacred shrine, where women were isolated but powerful; a realm where they bore heavy responsibilities but enjoyed great privilege. Men were not excluded from this tem-

144

ple. Indeed, it existed primarily for their benefit; but they were free—in fact, they were required—to come and go. Middle-class men and women shared a strong allegiance to the home, men supporting it from without and women from within. This combination of common devotion and divided duties profoundly shaped the way men and women thought about marriage, and determined the steps and the pace with which they approached it.

"A safe refuge"

If Alexis de Tocqueville had returned to America in the 1850s, he would have had little reason to alter his view that "the inexorable opinion of the public carefully circumscribes woman within the narrow circle of domestic interests and duties and forbids her to step beyond it." In spite of the fact that the mid-nineteenth century exalted "the idea of a loving, companionate, egalitarian marriage" and paid homage to "the doctrine of companionship and collaboration," husbands and wives carried separate, and unequal, burdens. A young man might declare that "the only true rule of life calculated to ensure mutual peace and happiness in the married state, is that of *reciprocal self-sacrifice, generosity and forbearance*, the only true relation between husband and wife that of equality"; in reality, women remained subordinate.[2]

The proposition that "in a true marriage duties & sacrifices are about equally divided between the wife and husband" was widely accepted in theory but rarely put into practice. Twenty-two-year-old Mary Ann Smith believed that " 'Bear and Forbear' ought to be the motto of all husbands and wives"; but when she described the difficulty she would have in realizing this ideal, it was clear she understood that a wife must bear and forbear *more*. She asked herself:

If somebody should not feel like petting you all the time, should come home tired and cross, should order you around, tell you you ought to do this when you want to do that, should not feel able to afford you a new dress when you wanted it, should do the thousand and one things that people always do sometimes in their lives; are you Mary, then going to remember your motto "Bear and Forbear," going to keep your heart and face pleasant, be patient until the petting humor comes, be cheerful and bright when he is cross, do what he thinks is best, if it is right, go without the new dress contentedly, and fix up your old one?[3]

Growing up in the 1870s, Mary Ann Smith might not question the wife's subordinate position in marriage, but she was likely to reject as old-fashioned the sentiments expressed by Georgina Amory fifty years before: "I do not wish to govern myself, so long as I conceive I can be better governed by another," Georgina wrote in 1824. To her fiancé, she had declared, "May I ever follow what I feel to be the duty of a wife, in every thing the will & inclination of her husband, when it is consonant with the higher duties which she owes to her creator."[4] From the elevated position afforded her by the cult of domesticity, the mid-nineteenth-century woman redefined "the duty of a wife." There were now areas of life in which she would lead, rather than follow, her husband. She would direct the spiritual progress of her family, tenderly guide her children to a virtuous maturity, and preside over the home circle.

But if a woman could no longer be asked to make all the sacrifices in marriage, the definition of her sphere meant that her sacrifices were in many ways greater than ever. Domesticity increased her autonomy in the home but heightened her isolation from the world. Like de Tocqueville in the 1830s, Clayton Kingman realized what marriage required of a woman and, in 1853, asked his fiancée, "Have you thought that you must leave all: home friends & every acquaintance & share you know not what, have you thought of the misery that the married woman may endure, her confinement to the house & her duties &c?" Doubtless Emily had thought about it, for she looked "to the future with a mingled feeling of hope and fear," and added, somewhat plaintively, "I hope we shall have a happy home and it will be my fault if we do not." Clayton disagreed, "No! It will be *our* fault, yes *our* fault, perhaps all mine." Henry Blackwell, a more critical observer, understood that men and women were hampered in different ways by the roles assigned them in marriage: "All the arrangments of Society . . . fetter a woman with household cares & ties, while they impose on a man the whole burden of acquiring subsistence."[5] Thus Emily Brooks and Clayton Kingman might each feel that she or he would be to blame if their home—and with it their marriage—were not happy. Clayton recognized the "fetters" that would confine Emily to the home, but he felt bound by "cares and ties" of his own: he was responsible for making sure Emily *had* a home.

"A home is the work of husband and wife," wrote a young college professor in 1875, "but the unequal position of women and men make the husband responsible for the support of this home."[6] The professor meant support in a financial sense, for it was as the breadwinner that the middle-class man sustained the home. His role was to supply the matériel with which his wife would construct the domestic shrine; hers was to tend that shrine and protect it from the harshness of the world. Woman's role as homemaker and man's as provider were not new; what had changed in the nineteenth century was the context and significance of these roles.

In early America, women were charged with the care of home and family. They performed the same tasks—the preparation of food and clothing, the rearing of children, the nursing of the sick—that fell to their daughters and granddaughters in the mid-nineteenth century. The chief difference was that the sexual division of labor was far less complete. Eighteenth-century women and men were engaged jointly—if not equally—in the productive work of the household. Men sheared the sheep, women spun the wool; men harvested the grain, women baked the bread. The home, and woman's place in it, were not yet enveloped in the shrouds of domesticity.[7] But by the mid-1800s, there had emerged a new meaning for home and new expectations of marriage. Home was no longer a place to return to after a day in the fields, a trip to the village store, or a morning in church; it was now "a nucleus around which all that is desirable in life centers." It was, as one minister intoned in a wedding sermon, "the dearest spot on earth, always operating with a powerfully attractive force to draw back the absent one."[8]

It went without saying that the "absent one" was male. Ever more middle-class men left the home every day to work in offices, mills, and shops, while their wives managed the household, nurtured the children, and created a refuge to which men could retreat from the world. That a man needed a retreat seemed obvious. The world was a harsh place where men gave vent to the aggressiveness that was required for success. William Lloyd Garrison II observed that "few men would care to have their wives know them as they are away from home." Home was now the antithesis of (and antidote for) the world. To couples in the late stages of courtship, it might appear that marriage would separate even as it united them. No wonder Katherine Smith looked with "sad amazement" at married people: "They seem so separate in their lives—their interests so little dependent upon each other."[9] The shared interests, the interdependence of courtship would be difficult to sustain after marriage.

While half of the dichotomy that divided married men and women, home was at the same time their most important common endeavor. Married women moved into "the world" only to extend their domestic influence through the traditional channels of female benevolence.[10] Men, on the other hand, moved back and forth between the home and the world every day. The boundaries around the home were permeable to men in a way that they were not to women. Men belonged in the world but, like women, they also belonged at home. Husbands and wives may not have been *equal* participants in the home, but both had a place there. Thus, it is not surprising that home was so closely identified with marriage in the minds of both men and women. Home was not just one of many consequences of marriage; it was *the* result to which marriage invariably (and, in most cases, immediately) led. A week before her marriage in 1851, Caroline Barrett felt herself to be "on the eve of some great change.

. . . It is to be the formation of a new circle—*a new home*—May it be all a *home* should be."[11]

What should a home be? In language that evokes perfectly the mid-nineteenth century's idealized view, the writer Abigail Dodge told her brother:

When weary of the troubles and turmoils of the day, you will return to your home, and there in the bosom of your family, with a wife who will be the delight of your eyes, though the clouds of adversity should lower around, you will find a safe refuge from the "peltings of the pitiless storm."

Mary Butterfield held out a similar promise to Champion Chase. Their marriage would provide him with a home and dispel his "blues" even if, she wrote, "it is only a little, quiet comfortable room sacred to 'you & I' into which you can enter and shut out the world with its strife and care, even if we have to deny ourselves many gratifications & indulgences which wealth could insure."[12]

The link between marriage and home was as solid as the connection between love and marriage. Will Adkinson's feelings were typical. In 1872, the struggling young lawyer told Lu Burlingame, "I could say let us marry and risk it but I cannot ask you to be mine when I have no home for you." In a standard letter of congratulation to a recently engaged young man, an old friend "rejoiced that you are going to have a home of your own." This was more than a figure of speech. Both women and men regarded their *own* home as one of the chief benefits of marriage. Women did not expect to begin married life in luxury or even in comfort, but they did want a home, however simple its furnishings or inconvenient its location. Although boarding was sometimes unavoidable, it was regarded as a last resort. "Let us keep house no matter how little we have to begin on," Lu Burlingame entreated Will Adkinson. "There is too much of the quiet, the closeness, the nearness to be given up in boarding," she concluded.[13]

Men agreed. A newly married friend's plan to board at a local hotel confounded Henry Poor. He believed that "one great advantage of getting married, to Gentlemen at least, is having a *home* which an hotel can never furnish." Echoing Henry Poor's thought, Winan Allen told Annie Cox, "I don't want to board. We might as well not be married. I want a *home.* "[14]* Home offered a man refuge from, but also justification for, worldly strivings. Home sheltered and solaced a man but did not restrain him; like a safe harbor, it left him free to sail the high seas.

At midcentury, the ability to support a home remained the single most important determinant of a man's readiness to marry. Many a young man must have repeated Winan Allen's words to Annie Cox: "I can't convince myself that it would be right to take upon myself the responsibility of a married man without first having a home." Writers of prescriptive literature, the occasional parent who offered advice, and young men in their own statements agreed that a man must be able to support a home before he could marry. The paternal warning that "love . . . will achieve a great many things but there are somethings it cannot do; it cannot pay your rent Bill nor your Board Bill," sounded in the thoughts of young men who believed that "a man ought to do more than love a woman; he ought to prove to her that he can provide as well as love." It seemed self-evident that no woman would question these priorities: "Would it be showing any affection to take you from your present comfortable home to a situation of less comfort and one of privation and anxiety to us both?" a collegian asked his fiancée, without any doubt of her answer.[16]

The men of the nineteenth century were no more willing than their fathers and grandfathers to embark on marriage without first having at least a modest competence. However, the definition of what constituted a competence had changed. Where the eighteenth-century man had looked to provide a simply furnished house for his family, men who married in the increas-

*Sometimes men felt even more strongly about boarding than women did. Kate French, for example, wrote to her fiancé: "As you express such a decided aversion to boarding and I share it *to some extent,* perhaps we'd better try to wait contentedly for a while longer." Some reformers opposed this insistence on individual homes for married couples.[15]

ingly industrialized, market-oriented middle years of the nineteenth century set higher standards for themselves. They aspired to equip their households with cook stoves, pianos, Irish servant girls, indoor plumbing, or whatever they and their families needed to enjoy and demonstrate their middle-class status. Still, one wonders if the allegiance, and adherence, to the canon linking home and marriage may reflect underlying male ambivalence toward marriage as much as it does these new economic realities. Were young men who insisted on the necessity of putting off marriage until they could make a home of their own, responding to economic pressures or to an unconscious fear of marriage?

The evidence suggests that, although there were men who set a standard for home so high that they were forced to postpone marriage longer than may have been necessary, they were far less common than men who based career decisions at least in part on the desire to minimize the delay before they could provide a home. Whether giving up schoolteaching, a "secret desire" to be a physician, or a career in the ministry, many men made occupational choices that improved their prospects for marriage. Some, like Ulysses S. Grant, who offered to resign his army commission to win Julia Dent, did not actually make such a change; but the willingness to alter career plans to hasten marriage was sincere and widespread.

I do not mean to say that men were entirely unconflicted as they approached marriage and a home of their own. While explicit references to anxiety are rare, young men must have worried about their ability to provide for a wife and the children who would almost certainly follow. Joseph Taylor expressed his uneasiness in terms of what he thought his bride would demand. He was so afraid she might expect more than he could afford that, even as he pushed for an early wedding date, he painted a grim picture of what married life would be like in his home town in Ohio, "living in this old brick house . . . waiting until it is patched up, a piece at a time." He declared, "I would rather live as a [bachelor] than to marry a lady who would expect a thousand luxuries and comforts that I could not furnish, who would look at neighbor 'B' and talk about all the nice things he has, and where he goes and what he does and how he lives etc." For Will Adkinson, it was the prospect of children rather than an acquisitive wife that made marriage seem like "a mountain weight of care . . . a terrible responsibility." Yet both of these men pressured their fiancées for early wedding dates.[17]

If a man failed, he endangered more than his livelihood. Men understood that "to share in the embarrassment of failure . . . there is to be another—and that very fact, no matter how cheerfully her loving heart may sympathize with you, will only make the burden to be borne the more crushing."[18] A man who failed in the world could not escape homeward, for home depended on his worldly competence; it was both a refuge from, and a spur to, worldly efforts. At the same time, and in a way that rarely appeared in conscious thought, home could be a threat to masculine achievement. Middle-class men were raised to associate home with warmth and safety; even when they had—often with great difficulty—broken their ties with their childhood homes, they continued to feel a "backward pull." If the pull was too strong, they might not exhibit the competitive and aggressive behavior required for success in the world.

Serena Ames sensed this danger when she asked George Wright, "[Do you] sometimes have uneasy feelings about a time to come when a weak, childish woman will cling too closely, impeding your progress, and by too much coaxing, thwart your desires, making you less free to go your way in the full liberty of manhood?"[19] Serena was not a "weak, childish woman"; but George may have been uneasy anyway, for the "full liberty of manhood" was to be enjoyed only in the world outside the home. "Too much coaxing"—precisely what home offered—could indeed be a hindrance. Thus, the security of the home could be undermined as much if a man's ties to it were too strong as if they were not strong enough. The relationship between home and world, then, was complex and interdependent: Home, and the woman who presided over it, were completely dependent on the world, and on the man who ventured into it, for the means with which to counter and control its influence. A man had to leave—and, in some sense, reject—home in order to achieve the success on which it—and his manhood—depended.

Men married in order to have a home where they could re-create the comfort, sympathy, and nurturance they had known in childhood. Many found it easier to own their desire for these qualities than their wish for worldly success. There was a common belief that, in Winan Allen's words, "family is, and should be, the center of all personal ambition, the altar on which its fires are kindled. . . . If this motive is not sufficient to urge one to success, none other will be." Across a range of occupations, young men declared their preference for home life over fame and fortune. A New England mechanic explained:

I do not desire to aspire to the high places of the Land, or to receive the praise of my fellow men . . . I would much prefer to be an humble citizen, in my own humble home. . . . Then, I should escape many cares & troubles, and enjoy myself at home.

Three decades later, a midwestern professor expressed similar feelings: "My ideal of a home has been a lofty one, and the love and companionship of the woman I love is more essential to my happiness than fame, and riches and honor combined."[20]

Men made these statements voluntarily—and sincerely; but, given the intensity with which men immersed themselves in work, one must see their words as reflections of a world in which ambition was both rewarded and feared. Nineteenth-century males were, after all, socialized to achieve but suspect worldly success. When Augusta McKim wrote Alexander Rice that he was "too ambitious of worldly distinction," the young collegian examined his motives and concluded that he was not "ambitious to a fault." As he readied himself to go out into the world, Alexander revealed his ambivalence:

I am now on the verge of the arena in which I have all the while in view with my armor on and my powers disciplined for the test. . . . Would my friends have me now lay down my armor and in mortification decline a contest in which I voluntarily enlisted . . . ? It is so unmanly so unnatural to spend a lifetime in the pursuit of nothing or of something which is as nothing . . . I do not feel proud of my literary and scientific attainments . . . yet I should not like . . . to enter some subordinate field.[21]

Young men had to struggle to make their ambition acceptable to themselves and to the women in their lives. Seeing home and wife as its true beneficiaries helped a man own his ambition. Charles VanHise told Alice Ring about an academic honor he had received and then explained:

It would be untrue for me to say that I do not care for honors. . . . I think desire to be noted for intellectual attainment is not ignoble. But above all else I am glad to prove to my Alice, my wife to be, that she may be proud of her boy's record here. To me the thought that any wealth or honor I may gain is not only for myself but "Agnes" [his nickname for her] is a never ending stimulus.

Charles could be ambitious as long as he was ambitious on behalf of Alice and not of himself. A man who seemed to be putting his career before his marriage could justify his actions by making them serve a woman's needs rather than his own. One young man who stayed home to prepare for his medical studies instead of visiting his fiancée, assured her, "It is not from an over anxiety about my future prospects because they are *mine* that I place so much stress upon them; *mine* are *yours.*"[22]

Identifying his interest with that of the woman he was to marry could help a man resolve his ambivalence about ambition. For women, on the other hand, sanctions against ambition were not revoked by the reality of the work world; they were as clear as the dividing line between the home and the world. Thus it struck Mary Butterfield as "unnatural and almost revolting to see a *lady* contending for fame and the applause of the world." The *only* appropriate sphere for her ambition was the home, since it was conceded that men and women might "each . . . be suitably ambitious in their spheres of action." The popular writer T. S. Arthur reminded the American woman of her "mission: Let her not look away from her own little family circle for the means of producing moral and social reforms, but begin at home."[23]

In spite of this allowance for female ambition at home, women recognized that the pursuit of excellence in household management, in motherhood, or even in community benevolence was a completely different thing from the drive for success and achievement in the outside world. Woman's options were hardly interchangeable; in fact, one required the denial of the other. Even at sixteen, Augusta Hubbard struggled with this hard fact of female existence. At an exhibition at the local boys' academy, she had all her "old restless ambition roused by those miniature orators." That ambition threatened her submission to domesticity:

I had gradually come to look upon my future life as partaking considerably of a domestic character. But tonight I feel I must be [original erased]. . . . Does God want me to be ever a wife—Does not nature teach us to marry & yet what is the voice that leads me away from such a course?[24]

A young woman like Augusta Hubbard might acceptably pursue the rewards and distinctions offered at school or college; but when she returned home, and especially when she approached marriage, she was expected to confine her aspirations to the domestic arena. Champion Chase told Mary Butterfield, "I hope ambition does not influence you so much now that your school days are over." She assured him, "As to my 'ambition' I believe I left it all behind me."[25]

Annie Cox was not so sure. She desperately wanted to continue her education, to fit herself "for that position in social and intellectual life which [she was] determined to occupy," but she knew her ambition was an anomaly. "If I were a man, action would settle the question," she observed, "but a woman must not step over the threshold of the parlor door to accomplish an object."[26]* While Annie knew that she should "settle down and

*Although Annie approved of the conventional belief that women should be "keepers at home, darners of stockings," she was willing "to transgress upon Adam's domain

find enjoyment in home pleasures and duties, and never look beyond," she was affected by "a controlling restlessness." Even an 1842 treatise on *Woman in Her Social and Domestic Character,* which declared that "St. Paul knew what was best for women when he advised them to be domestic," allowed that there was "something sedative in the duties which home involves." Domesticity offered fulfillment but also confinement—even a kind of extinction. There was a serious concern behind the fanciful scenario Blanche Butler imagined for herself after marriage: "If worse comes to worse, I will just . . . screw up the corners of my mouth, devote myself to household duties, & vanish."[28]

The transition to marriage exacted a different price from women and men: in order to assume her position in the home, a woman relinquished her ambition for worldly achievement; while a man had to loosen—without ever cutting—his ties to home in order to succeed in the world. This process of renunciation and redirection was rarely acknowledged, but it had a noticeable effect. "Marriage does so change people; they never do seam the same," a midwestern woman observed to a male friend in 1861. Her contemporary Ada Jefferson agreed: "There is and must be a change in the relations, even if as dear." She recognized that marriage worked its greatest changes on women: "When a friend marries she has so many new thoughts, feelings, and aims that I may sympathize with and appreciate, yet not wholly understand."[29] To a young schoolteacher in Ohio, marriage appeared to be "the final separation for it certainly separates the parties, the woman especially from all friends." In upstate New York, Mollie Clarke lamented that, "when one marries they are so lost to their friends, as if they were miles away and we know they are gone."[30]

---

a little" in order to try and persuade Winan to abandon his opposition to the Union war effort. When he persisted in his support of the Copperhead Democrats, Annie, a faithful Republican, announced a truce: "You and I shall have to agree to disagree," she wrote. As a woman, she felt unqualified for sustained political debate. "I do not think it well for women to meddle in politics anyway, for they are more [ten]acious, more excitable & more governed in their conduct by their opinions, therefore they could not meet an opponent as the men do after a hot argument as pleasantly as before. They would carry the matter into their social relations," she concluded.[27]

"This Waiting & Hoping & Planning"

"A kind of interregnum"

Given that women saw marriage in these terms, it is not surprising that they, like their mothers and grandmothers, were not eager to rush into it. Although the terrible anxiety that afflicted many early nineteenth century brides was less evident among their midcentury descendants, the old pattern persisted: A man could expect to be ready for marriage before his bride. The preliminaries were likely to seem drawn out to men and abbreviated to women. Men tended to see engagement as the time before they *could* marry, while women viewed it as the time before they *would* marry. Annie Wilson was typical. She wanted to wait to marry Frank Fiske "on many accounts," but after a long courtship, she finally acceded to his wishes. "The ostensible reason is that there is no necessity for waiting—the real reason [is] that Frank *won't* wait . . . so I in the most dutiful manner consented to put him out of his misery," she explained with good humor.[31]

Frank Fiske had plenty of company in his misery. Like their predecessors in the early republic, most midcentury suitors found themselves pressing their fiancées to name the wedding day. They agreed with James White, who believed his intended must set the date but whose "own feelings and inclinations would say, the sooner the better." Women, on the other hand, remained far less eager to bring courtship to a close. Joseph Taylor and Elizabeth Hill are a good example. The young Ohio lawyer lobbied hard for an early wedding date but conceded that such "things should be determined by the lady . . . as she knows better than a gentleman how much time she wants to get ready." What worried Joseph was that his fiancée appeared to be in no hurry at all for marriage. "You seemed so inclined to put the consummation of the matter so far off that I felt you less interested in it sometimes than I would rather have seen you," he lamented at one point.[32]

But at midcentury, a new wrinkle appeared in this familiar

157

pattern. A small but growing minority of women expressed the traditional male eagerness to embark on married life. They tended to be women who had joined the work force, particularly the growing ranks of schoolteachers. Like Annie Cox, they sounded a note previously heard only from men: "I would make any sacrifice to begin life with you soon," she told Winan Allen, and asked him, "Please forgive me for pleading this against your judgment but I cannot tell why I dread this delay."[33]* Some women knew precisely why they opposed a delay. Fannie Adams had left her native New England to take a teaching position in the South. From Georgia, she wrote to Lawrence Chamberlain, "I am afraid that if your poor little girl stays here toiling on . . . she will indeed have no youth left for you. . . . I would rather help you to struggle on at first, than wait until all my bloom had vanished." She reiterated her offer to "help along by teaching, at first at any rate." That idea had no appeal to Lucy Harris, who admitted that she had "looked at marriage as an escape from drudgery (poor girl)," and resented her brother's suggestions that she continue to teach after her marriage to a poor young lawyer.[35]

Many middle-class women counted on marriage to free them from the burdens of paid employment. Elizabeth and Anna Blackwell were teaching school in Cincinnati when Elizabeth noted in her diary, "Anna and I had a great deal of matrimonial talk we are so sick of school keeping." Certainly, this connection existed in Mary Butterfield's mind. She was giving music lessons to support herself until she and Champion Chase could be married. She made plain why she favored the earliest possible date:

I have just returned from giving my lessons & an unpleasant time I have had of it getting through the drifts. I thought to myself that another winter would hardly find me going about in the cold & snow to give lessons—But I might be much worse off & I am thankful that

*In an earlier letter, she had half-teasingly suggested, "Perhaps you think my haste to be married is to be accounted for on the principle that I cannot trust you. I'm in fun now, Winan," she added.[34]

I have the ability to maintain myself although I would so gladly be in my own quiet home.[36]

In her automatic association of marriage and home, and in her eagerness to have both, Mary Butterfield resembled young men who also had to contend with the elements of the world. Like them, young women who labored in mills, schoolrooms, or shops often looked longingly at "home" as something missing from their lives that only marriage could provide. Thus the teacher Katherine Smith assured Walter Hill that they had made the right decision not to wait another year before marrying. "You need a wife," she told him, adding: "I feel my need of you—I need too the home that you will give me—the quiet home & rest that will come with home."[37] Working women perceived marriage not in terms of separation from home but as the opportunity to *have* a home. In that respect, they had more in common with their brothers than with their more leisured sisters.

Women who lived at home under emotional or economic stress also seem to have been less interested in prolonging engagement than women whose home lives were happy and comfortable. "I shall welcome the time when I shall leave home," wrote one woman who was constantly at odds with her mother. Another midwesterner who lived with her mother and stepfather hoped her fiancé would come soon to claim her: "The quicker I get out of this *shanty* . . . the better I shall like it," she declared. She was willing, she told him, "to put what I have along with what you have so that we can have a *home of our own*."[38]* Women had long shared with men a commitment to that goal, but now some of them were taking more aggressive steps in pursuit of it. If her parents' home failed to provide the financial and emotional support she needed, a

---

*The lack of a pleasant home could make a woman *too* eager to marry. A young man whose sisters had left home to work observed that young women "when away from home . . . have plenty of inconveniences and there is many an unhappy match brought about from these circumstances." He felt certain that had his family been "in more agreeable circumstances [his sister] would never have made her unhappy marriage."[39]

woman might perceive marriage in terms of the gains it offered rather than the losses it entailed.

Except in this indirect way, parents had little influence over
the timing of their children's marriages. I do not mean to say
that young people failed to take their parents into account. Remember how William Ross argued his case for an early wedding
date: "My father is approaching the close of life and he feels that
it would be gratifying to him if we would be united while he
is living." Katherine Smith's concern was more specific: "Whenever I am married it will cost my family some money," she reminded her fiancé.[40] But parents were almost always considered
after the fact. A woman's parents were asked, and a man's parents were told (usually in that order); but in both cases, the process was little more than a formality. The ritual required a man
to make the request, but it was not unheard of for women to
deal directly with their parents.* Those who did experienced
firsthand the distressing sensations of which men had long complained. Mary Thorn admitted to James White, "I found it a
more difficult task than I imagined to speak to my parents on
the subject about which we conversed so I put if off day after
day." For a woman, broaching the issue of her wedding day
meant raising the specter of separation from her parents, and
for many women this was still an unsettling prospect. Persis
Sibley noted in her diary that her fiancé had had "a long talk
. . . with [her] parents," and added: "(This talking with them
about leaving home forever is too tender a subject for me.)"[42]

This affecting conversation took place a week after she had
agreed to marry Charles Andrews, an impecunious member of
the Maine legislature. A few days before, the couple had paid
a call on one of the Sibleys' neighbors. "I thought that I should
acknowledge my engagement but *positively I could not*," Persis
wrote in her diary. "It is so new. I felt an excessive modesty

*At least one woman was outraged when her fiancé followed the conventional prac-
tice of asking for her father's permission. Lu Burlingame berated Will Adkinson: "I
knew that Pa's consent did not make one hair's difference to you, he knew that we would
marry despite his consent, we both knew it was hypocritical asking & we are neither
favorably impressed with *sham* courtesies, especially when they involve the observance
of an old barbarous relic & recognize woman as property."[41]

about it. . . . No one knows it yet out of the family." She had a sense that her engagement should be known "out of the family," but it turned out to be "a delicate business . . . much more difficult than [she] expected to communicate the information."[43] Community surveillance of the transition to marriage was declining, but engagement remained a subject for public disclosure. It was a personal event, which retained vestiges of its public significance.

New rituals emerged to communicate the news of a couple's intentions beyond the family circle. Mary Pierce reported from Brookline, Massachusetts, in 1841: "When people are engaged here they have a singular custom, the way they make it public is the gentleman instead of sitting in his own pew with his family sits in that of his lady love." Over the next forty years, announcement of engagements became both more formal and more personal. The New England woman who explained after the Civil War that "the conventional method of procedure" was to "get 'betrothed' . . . and publish the fact," might have used the language of the early republic, but the rituals she described were products of the midcentury.[44] Once an act required by church doctrine and state law, betrothal had, by 1880, become a quaint word in need of quotation marks; and "publishing the fact" no longer meant posting a notice on the meetinghouse door. Intentions to marry were made public not from the pulpit, as they had been in the eighteenth and early nineteenth centuries, but in writing. Although newspapers began to carry news of local families' engagements, most people spread the word by writing personally to their friends. Relatives and close friends received the news first; then more casual acquaintances. The prospective bride and groom and their parents each took responsibility for informing the individuals nearest to them.

At midcentury, making an engagement known was not yet the exclusive prerogative of the bride and her family. Engagement was still something that happened to both men and women. Even rings, which were associated with engagement beginning in the 1840s, were at first presented to men as well as women. When Harry McCall and Charlotte Willcocks became secretly pledged to each other in 1842, they gave each other rings. Nearly thirty years later, Blanche Butler had trouble finding a ring she liked for her fiancé; she was determined, she told him, "You shall have my mark upon you, . . . & if it could not be done by a ring, some other method should be devised." She finally settled for a miniature of herself.[45] The exchange of tokens served as a statement of a couple's commitment to each other. As such, it was a new—and very personal—form of publicity.

But an engagement ring signified more than an intention to wed. As Blanche Butler recognized, it left a "mark upon" one's future mate, declaring him or her "taken." At midcentury, the engaged couple were clearly perceived to be bound by an exclusive tie, but it was not one that isolated them from others. Engaged people continued to take part in the social life of the community. Even when separated, they encouraged each other to attend parties, balls, and other social events. A Wisconsin woman wrote her absent fiancé, "If you would rather I would not go out with any one I wont do it and if you dont care why I will go sometimes it is so nice to take a ride once in a while." Men rarely objected to this kind of activity; in fact, they often encouraged it. In 1842, Anna Sitwell asked her fiancé George Tucker if she should "accept the invitations of other gentlemen" while he was away on his travels for the American Foreign and Bible Society. He responded, "Certainly I would say where you can derive pleasure or profit or both yes! Go and my soul shall go with you." Two decades later, in Michigan, William Mason assured Harriet Chamberlain, "I always want you to have a good time when you can. You needn't think that I'm agoing to be jealous while I am away from you."[46]

It was understood that sexual faithfulness did not require social restrictiveness. When she was in Wisconsin and he was in New York, Mary Butterfield assured Champion Chase that she "esteemed" rather than faulted him for "seeking the acquaintance of those ladies whose characters you admire." She did the same thing herself: "I certainly enjoy some gentlemanly society and particularly when I regard them as personal friends and I know you do the same and hope you ever will." In fact, Mary found that being engaged made friendship with men easier: "I like gentlemen's society when I know they have no *designs* upon my heart and when I know any cordiality of mine will not be misinterpreted."[47]* In New York, Emily Smith had a similar experience. She reported that, since she had become engaged, her feelings toward young men had changed: "All desire to be agreeable to them for my own pleasure in their society, or care for their good opinion, has vanished so that I am quite at ease."[49]

A woman who felt more "at ease" with men after her engagement might "rejoice in its length as a period of freedom," but to other women, engagement appeared to be the relinquishment of freedom. When Anna Webb declined Thomas Farris's proposal in 1844, she explained, "I am not quite ready and willing to . . . say that I will be *yours alone,* no, I cannot give up this delightful freedom yet."[50] Both Emily Smith and Anna Webb were right: an engaged woman was more *and* less free than her unpledged sister. She might feel less constrained with men, once she was clearly out of the marriage "market," but she might also feel the loss of the freedom to choose her future. Women, after all, made only one truly fateful choice in their lives. A man was not born to assume any preordained occupational role; he made a series of decisions—whether to keep a store, go to sea, study law—any one of which could alter the future course of his life. A woman, on the other hand, knew that whether she went to work in a mill, taught school, or sewed for the deserving poor, she was preparing for the one career open to her: to be a man's wife and mother to his children. Once she made her choice, her options were suddenly, irrevocably gone.

Engagement was a mixed condition in another sense as well: a woman retained a large measure of autonomy while readying herself to surrender it. Consciousness of this could make a woman restless. Elizabeth Cady Stanton remembered her en-

---

*Mary hastened to assure Champion that the sexual intimacy between them was not replicated in other relationships: "As to your having kissed me so much making me more willing or desirous to be kissed by others, it is quite the contrary. . . . I have many ways of amusing and interesting myself as you say during your absence so you need not fear I shall have to resort to flirtation or excitement to keep up my spirits."[48]

gagement as "a season of doubt and conflict—doubt as to the
wisdom of changing a girlhood of freedom and enjoyment for
I knew not what."[51] Marriage might bring a woman confinement and hardship, or it might bring her security and fulfillment. The engaged woman thus stood between the familiarity
and freedom of her single life and the greater restrictions—and
greater risks—of marriage. What lay ahead was hardly uncharted territory, but it was, ultimately, unknown. Most women
approached it expectantly, cautiously. They used engagement
as a time to rehearse the role until they felt ready to play the
part.

As engagement had fewer benefits for men, they were more
impatient with it. William Edmond Curtis was "so anxious to
. . . wear the silken fetters" that he was yearning to see "the last
days of [his] liberty . . . hasten away." A man thought of engagement primarily in terms of when it would be over: how could
he exert himself—and persuade his fiancée—to bring about the
earliest possible wedding day? Many men found engagement a
stressful time. A New Hampshire man declared that he could
"do no work and [was] good for nothing." From Ohio, Joseph
Taylor wrote to Elizabeth Hill in Maine:

I do not feel that I will do one bit of good at any kind of business until
we are married. One would think that this should stimulate me to a
greater effort, but it don't. . . . It is a kind of suspense, a kind of inter-
regnum, a kind of preparatory state that forbids all solid thinking and
all real business-like employments.[52]

In New York, Katherine Smith could see that engagement
was the cause of "strain & anxiety" for the young engineer she
was to wed. "This waiting & hoping & planning being succeeded by certainty . . . will make you attend to ordinary work
with more singlemindedness," she told him.[53] While engagement interfered with a man's work, it *was* a woman's work.
Finding a house or boarding place, laying carpets, having a new
suit made, all kept a man from his "ordinary work"; shopping
for furniture, bedding, and kitchen utensils, sewing on dresses,

bonnets, and linens were, on the other hand, already an important part of a woman's "ordinary work."

"In the New-Fashioned Way"

As they applied themselves to the traditional tasks assigned to prospective brides and grooms, couples marrying at midcentury faced demands and received assistance from new quarters. Setting up a household and arranging a wedding both required more extensive preparation than they had in the past, and the added burden fell on both men and women. Men continued to be responsible for acquiring the house (or rooms), and women the household furnishings. Parents did as much as they could for their children, but many couples had already received as much help as their parents could offer in the form of formal education. Middle-class parents recognized the value of prolonged schooling for their sons and did what they could to give them the competitive advantage an education represented. Because the "opportunity costs" of keeping daughters in school were lower than for sons, girls made up the majority of students in the public high schools which were opening around the country in the middle decades of the century. Many of these well-educated young women joined the labor force and were thus in a position to contribute their earnings toward the establishment of a home.

Women who were not in a position to help were likely to feel embarrassment. One Wisconsin woman who had "no way . . . to earn the means" felt it was "mortifying . . . to a young lady" to ask her fiancé for money to buy what was needed to set up house. Emily Brooks, who had worked as a mill hand and schoolteacher, preferred to delay her marriage rather than take money from her future mate. "I should not care if I did not have any thing new only you will be ashamed of me, but [I] shall not feel very proud to be dressed up with your money," she told

Clayton Kingman. "I should rather buy every thing with my own if I had it," she declared and asked, "Dont you think we had better wait till Spring now, and I can go into the mill and you can earn a good bunch of Money?"[54]

Not all of what a woman needed to equip herself for marriage could be bought, even if she had the funds. In the weeks and months before her wedding, a young middle-class woman "had not a moment to spare in idleness—being in the last stages of courtship—when 'fixing' is so urgently necessary." Women shopped, and sewed, and packed, and sewed, and cleaned house, and sewed some more. Assembling the clothing and linens for her trousseau was a woman's most time-consuming task. When Lucy Harris was getting ready to marry in the 1850s, she remembered "seeing sewing machines, operated by girls, in some window on Broadway, and crowds of people stood about the window"; but a sewing machine was beyond her means. She did all her finish sewing by hand and hired a dressmaker to help her make up the three silks, one crimson merino house dress trimmed with velvet, another brown wool traveling dress trimmed with silk, a French organdie, and the white Swiss muslin in which she was married. The dresses, bonnets, gloves, shoes, and other "knicknacks" cost Lucy the considerable sum of "a little over $200, which was what [she] had put in the Savings Bank from time to time." As a music teacher, Lucy Harris was able to indulge herself in "all the fancies which [she] had had in mind for years." Aurelia Porter was less fortunate. When she married an Indiana farmer in the 1860s, she was able to buy only "a 50 cent alpaca besides [her] silk and did not get any fancy things."[55]* By the 1860s, Aurelia Porter was unusual; most middle-class brides were well provided with "fancy things," whether they were the fruit of their own labors or the largesse of family and friends.

The elaboration of the wedding trousseau was not an isolated

*In her 1912 tract, *Why Women Are So*, Dr. Mary Roberts Coolidge observed that the mid-nineteenth-century "trousseau was as essential to the prospective bride as an outfit to the explorer of arctic or tropical wilds; or, rather, it was like the equipment of a traveler who sets out for an unknown Oriental country—for who knew what might be needed and yet unattainable in the great adventure upon which she was about to embark!"[56]

development. As standards for furnishing and managing a middle-class household rose, young couples turned to friends and family for assistance. Couples marrying at midcentury could count on bridal gifts to help them meet the rising standards for middle-class domesticity. The whitewashed walls, straw floor coverings, and country furniture with which middle-class people had begun married life in the early 1800s were no longer sufficient; the material culture of domesticity generated new demands. Brussels carpeting, carved sideboards, matching parlor sets, framed chromos for the walls were now necessary accouterments for the middle-class home. As domesticity became the central value of middle-class culture, young couples "needed" more to fulfill its requirements. Wedding gifts were the community's way of helping newly wedded members acquire the emblems of their class.

Late eighteenth and early nineteenth century gift giving had been confined to near relations; after about 1830, it spread to other family members and friends. By the last quarter of the century, distant relatives, acquaintances, even co-workers were expected to participate in the ritual of bridal gift giving. In addition to cash, couples now received silver cake baskets, sugar bowls, ice cream knives, napkin rings, and the like—sometimes in triplicate—from friends and relatives. The people who bestowed these gifts were not just demonstrating the sufficiency of their means; they were expressing their stake in the ideal of domesticity.[57]

As bridal gift giving spread from the élite downward, it expanded to include useful as well as luxury items. Even in middle-class circles, however, real necessities did not appear on the lists of wedding presents. Bridal gifts might decorate the newlyweds' home but not furnish its basic necessities; the gifts attested to the means of both the giver, who could afford "the fancy silver things" brides increasingly received, and the recipient, whose parents or prospective husband could provide the elementals of married life. Wedding gifts were almost always directed to the bride, and with the exception of books and pictures, they pertained to the feminine realms of kitchen and dining room. Thorstein Veblen's observation that the middle-class wife became "the ceremonial consumer of goods which [the man] produces" explains why gift giving developed its orientation toward the woman: in their association with luxury and leisure, wedding presents properly belonged in the female domain. The giving of purely useful objects would have raised doubts about the ability of the father and the future husband to supply them and might have suggested that the bride was destined to be a "lady who does her own work." In a related way, the giving of objects used by men would have been inappropriate in a society in which, as Veblen put it, "the duties of vicarious leisure and consumption devolve upon the wife."[58] Furthermore, the woman was the embodiment of domesticity, and it was domesticity that the gifts were meant to celebrate. They were artifacts of a middle-class ideal, on display for all to see. By the 1870s, exhibiting presents "for the public gaze" was a common—if not universally approved—feature of middle-class weddings.* Descriptions of tables "covered with beautiful and valuable gifts" and "presents handsome and expensive" begin to appear in wedding accounts.[60] Conspicuous consumption and domesticity were were served equally well by the array of bridal gifts.

"A nice time among ourselves"

Weddings, as well as the gifts given to commemorate them, grew steadily more formal and public. By midcentury, elaborate wedding rituals had become widespread, and more extensive preparations were required. As the routines of daily life and the rituals of marriage making became more complex, it became

---

*The popular magazine *Godey's Lady's Book* objected not just to wedding presents being displayed, but to their being given at all. In March 1870, the editors lauded couples who had "No Presents Received" engraved on their wedding cards, although three years later, they were forced to report that cards had appeared with "No Plate Ware" printed in the corner.[59]

common for printed invitations to be sent several weeks in advance, sometimes to as many as two hundred guests. Many couples were still married in simple ceremonies, attended only by family and a few friends, but there were more and more whose weddings were crowded and formal affairs. A Long Island schoolteacher told her fiancé a few weeks before their 1859 wedding, "I agree with you . . . that our marriage be simple and quick. I do not intend any parade whatever." Yet she felt it necessary "to give about one hundred invitations to the wedding." She concluded her discussion of the invitations this way: "I do not care for outsiders. I only desire a nice time among ourselves, friends we value." Even when the gathering was small, printed invitations had become the rule. In Wisconsin, Charles Van Hise and Alice Ring sent out engraved invitations only to their "most intimate friends . . . less than thirty [were] invited."[61]

The tradition of small weddings followed by bigger, more festive celebrations continued after the middle of the century, but both the ceremonies and the receptions became larger, more public events. By 1880, the distinction between private ceremony and public celebration had almost disappeared. The presence of large numbers of people at the wedding and related festivities reveals a growing need for public display and validation. The same forces that made wedding presents *de rigueur* generated a demand for lavish wedding celebrations; conspicuous consumption was well satisfied by the gathering—and feeding—of a hundred wedding guests.

The elegantly dressed guests not only attested to the wealth and status of their hosts; their attendance was a recognition of the significance to the community of the nuptial vow. Although the couple had made their own match, the community had a stake in its success. While nineteenth-century marriage was indeed between individuals, once joined in wedlock, those individuals had social roles to perform that were essential to the stability and continuity of middle-class life. In an earlier time, when the community—clergy, kin, neighbors—was more involved in the marriage making of its members, there was no need for its presence at the ceremony; thus, the small numbers gathered at colonial weddings. By the middle of the nineteenth century, with the community largely excluded from courtship and the decision to marry, its attendance at the wedding testified to the fact that it had not relinquished all ties to the event. Just as wedding gifts expressed a collective investment in the success of a new marriage, so the presence of many people demonstrated their interest in the union they witnessed.

By the 1840s, elaborate wedding rituals—from printed invitations to costumed attendants dispensing slices of white wedding cake—were no longer the province of élite merchant families. Mary Pierce described the wedding of her cousin Arthur in Boston in the fall of 1840:

At half past seven we repaired to Cousin Charles' [the groom's father] where we found quite a collection of relations. . . . These were all collected in the front parlour where they remained until eight o'clock when the folding doors were thrown open and the bridal party appeared all ready for the ceremony. They stood in the new-fashioned way each gentleman by his lady (there were two groomsmen and bridesmaids). . . . At the close of the whole, [the minister] requested Arthur to present his bride with the wedding ring as a token of the sincerity of his intentions, etc. Soon after the levee commenced and the rooms were crowded with [the bride's] friends. . . . After all had left, but those who were at the wedding, supper was announced which was got up in first rate style.[62]*

In less urban settings, especially in the Midwest, weddings were likely to be simpler and to have more in common with those of the early nineteenth century. For example, in 1842 a young Ohioan "was married to Miss Nancy Maria Currier in the presence of her sisters, [his] Bro. William and a few friends at her residence at 7 o'clock P.M. Mr. H. Blodgett pastor of the Presbyterian Church in Euclid performed the ceremony."[64]

But even the Western Reserve was within reach of the advice

*I cannot say whether the presentation of the ring was standard practice. I encountered only four references to wedding rings in my research: two from 1840, both in New England; one in 1865, in the Midwest; another in 1895. An 1846 etiquette book advised: "If a ring is to be used, the bridegroom procures a plain gold one previously."[63]

offered by the authors of such works as *A Complete Guide for Ladies and Gentlemen Particularly Those Who Have Not Enjoyed the Advantages of Fashionable Life,* published in 1846. These books instructed readers on the attire, refreshments, choice and arrangement of attendants, and behavior appropriate at weddings. Dress and deportment were increasingly matters of protocol rather than of individual discretion or local custom. Thanks to etiquette books and "guides to polite society," customs could become fashions, and fashions could be carried from one region and one class to another. An occasional midcentury bride wore "dark chocolate silk" or "brown silk," but most conformed to the "white rule" stated and restated by the etiquette books and magazine writers. They agreed that the bride was "usually dressed in pure white" with a white veil, and her head "crowned with a wreath of white flowers, usually artificial orange blossoms are preferred."[65] Veils became popular in the 1840s and remained a part of the standard bridal costume for the rest of the century. It comes as no surprise that brides should have begun to appear in veils at the same time that women were being elevated to a pedestal by a culture that defined womanhood in terms of "purity, piety, submissiveness, and domesticity."[66] But the veil not only symbolized woman's distance, and protection, from the reality of life in the "world"; it also suggested the eclipse of a married woman by her husband. On her wedding day, a woman submerged her girlhood identity in the larger, more demanding, more invisible role of a wife.

The increase in the formality of middle-class weddings was part of a general trend in nineteenth-century America; life was becoming more highly structured on every front. Changes in politics, education, the banking system, domestic architecture, all attest to the pervasiveness of the organizational impulse.[67] But the development of wedding ritual also reflects the specific situation of young women and men on the threshold of marriage. The heightening of domestic expectations in the second quarter of the nineteenth century had made marriage the key to home and home the key to success in, and succor from, the world. Male providing was no longer a matter of seasoned wood for the bake oven and clean wool for the spinning wheel; house-wifely skills were no longer measured by the sweetness of butter or the quality of woven cloth. The extension of the husband's role into the increasingly complex outside world and the inten-sification of the wife's role in the home, and the separation of spheres that resulted, had the effect of making marriage appear to be an enormous step. All of the new rituals—the presents, the bridal veil, the white dress—first took hold in the 1830s and 1840s, at a time when the demands of domesticity, and the dis-junction caused by marriage, were at their greatest. The struc-tured behavior and patterned responses required by formal rit-ual offered support and direction for the participants—a predictable beginning for a life that appeared unknowable and risky. Furthermore, by establishing a connection between *all* brides and *all* grooms, the rituals helped to create a sense that a wedding, and the responsibilities that followed it, were shared experiences.

There were, of course, many couples who by choice or neces-sity still had small weddings, but they were an ever smaller mi-nority. In spirit if not in substance, the majority were like Ed Waring and Dora Hileman whose 1875 wedding Wilson Carpen-ter described in detail. It took place in a hotel in Altoona, Penn-sylvania, "where the bride's people were boarding. Over two hundred invitations were issued." There were four bridesmaids and as many groomsmen who were assigned to come and go in a particular way. The night before the wedding there was a re-hearsal—perhaps the surest sign of both formality and publici-ty. Wilson reported that he and his fellow attendants "made so many blunders that we all felt sure of repeating them at the wed-ding. I am sure we marched and countermarched . . . and then were worse prepared than when we had begun." When the time came—at seven in the evening—they performed "with beating hearts," but all went well; elaborate refreshments and dancing followed the ceremony.[68]

Wilson commented on the fact that the groom "seemed the coolest and most unconcerned one of all the party, he said he was unable to realize that he was being married."[69] It would be

172

interesting to know if Ed Waring's composure was the common state for a young man on his wedding day. Unfortunately, the evidence is limited since both correspondence and diaries were usually abandoned or at least interrupted at marriage. In some cases, a diary was resumed shortly after the wedding or at a later date, but only rarely did it record much of the subjective experience of the wedding day. Written reports from others who were present, however, offer some insight into the emotional tone of wedding celebrations.

It was a commonly held opinion that weddings were sad affairs. Champion Chase did not "see the least reason for unlimited mirth," but could not understand "why so much sadness need be present on the occasion as usually is." People expected to feel sad at weddings. Even when "all was mirth and enjoyment [and] not a tear was shed" at one New England wedding, it was not remarkable that "none were very gay." One bride told a friend, "I shall never forget your sorrowful countenance. One would have thought you were burying me." The report in a young New Yorker's diary that "most present at wedding cried" required no further explanation. It was the absence—or the concealment—of sadness that warranted comment, and sometimes commendation. At the wedding of a couple who were to move eight hundred miles away, Joseph Taylor noted approvingly, "Never have I heard distance once spoken of as a matter of sorrow, nor did I see a single tear at the wedding."[70]

A bride who managed to remain dry-eyed at her wedding might well give way once she had left the party behind. Persis Sibley revealed the effort required for her to maintain her composure: "I forced some of my cheerfulness, & thereby kept my spirits up & went through the whole with a bravery & fortitude that I could not have expected." Persis only broke down after she and her husband had made their departure: "As soon as our chaise had left the door I could no longer restrain my pent up feelings, but gave them vent in a passionate flood of tears. I could not help it." A Pennsylvania woman had a similar experience; she confessed to a friend that, on the ride to the railroad station, her "eyes were so filled with tears that [she] did not see much of the country." Not all women were so affected. The day after her wedding, Caroline Barrett White looked back and thought, "How like a dream it seems—a most pleasing dream." She had "felt sad" to leave her friends, but she realized that "those partings must come—they are part of our life." Caroline's acceptance was echoed by Mary Pierce, for whom "the parting . . . and bidding good-bye . . . was not accomplished without a struggle. Still," she added in her first letter home, *"some how or other I preferred going to staying."*[71]

Such conviction came more easily to women marrying after about 1840. They still suffered from "anxious thoughts of weakness and insufficiency," but they also experienced a "glad brightness" on the eve of their wedding. The night before her nuptials in 1851, Caroline Barrett expressed her mixed feelings: "This is the last night of my *girl life*. . . . A new life is to begin tomorrow—a life less free—more anxious—more responsible* it may be but nevertheless I trust it will not be less happy than the past has been." Caroline believed there was "something a little sad perhaps in all great changes in one's condition—whether that change be for *weal* or *woe*," but she felt "calmly happy" as well as "serious-sober in contemplating the step *we* are about to take." Although she knew that much of the "fancied happiness clustered about the consummation" of courtship "may or may not be fully realized," she reported, "My heart is firm." Caroline Barrett's equanimity was in part a reflection of the fact that her ties to home had already been broken by the deaths of her parents, but the mixture of positive and negative emotions she felt on the eve of marriage was shared by many middle-class women at midcentury. Now it was with "mingled feelings of hope & fear" that they approached the fateful day. Women still perceived the profound change marriage would bring about, but they accepted it more gracefully than their mothers and grandmothers had.[72]

This subtle difference in the way women handled the separation implicit in marriage affected the evolution of the

---

*In the original, Caroline first wrote, "less anxious, less responsible."

post-wedding tour. The trips to Niagara Falls, Cincinnati, New York, and other natural and man-made wonders that first gained popularity in the 1830s and 1840s had by midcentury become the standard sequel to a middle-class wedding. By the 1870s, "the conventional bridal tour to that delectable place [Niagara] was considered as much a part of the important event as a ring, orange blossoms, etc."[73] But while the destination of the journey did not change, there was an important shift in its function.

In the 1840s and 1850s, wedding trips were still an extension of the traditional visiting ritual. Many couples continued to be accompanied on their travels by friends or close relatives. One prospective groom suggested that he and his fiancée time their wedding to allow for a joint honeymoon with another couple: "We would all go to Cincinnati, or some place else, make our wedding trip together, and all return . . . together." Another pair of newlyweds met up with the groom's brother and his bride who were also making a wedding trip to Niagara. A couple who went to the Falls only at the last minute, when the groom "saw in the paper an advertisement of excursion tickets to Niagara," originally went to a hotel, but they had not been there long when an uncle's father-in-law "came with his carriage and insisted on [their] coming home with him."[74]

In the early 1850s, this would still have seemed more like an act of hospitality than an invasion of privacy; but over the next few decades, the wedding tour developed into an exclusive ritual in which bride and groom alone participated. The demands of exclusive romantic love superseded the need for affirming community ties. Friends and relatives now "went a piece" with the bridal couple or saw them off on the train, rather than joining them on the journey. It became less common for a friend or a relation to go along to Cincinnati or for a young couple to spend their wedding tour visiting friends and family. Beginning in the 1870s, etiquette books advocated that the couple leave the church—where middle-class weddings increasingly took place—together and alone, and that instead of the "harassing bridal tour," they enjoy "a honeymoon of repose, exempted from claims of society."[75]

There were still many couples who took traditional wedding tours, regardless of the fact that they were said to be "declining in fashion," and other couples who established themselves in their new home immediately after the wedding; but by 1880, honeymoon trips to "romantic" locations were expected to follow weddings. The bridal journey was no longer a ritual designed to integrate a new pair into the community, but, instead, it self-consciously isolated the couple. Although an ever-wider circle of friends and family participated in weddings as gift givers and as guests, bride and groom were expected to begin married life alone. The tour still delayed the assumption of married roles and responsibilities, but it no longer provided community support for the couple. Attendance at the wedding and the offering of gifts expressed the community's stake in the new marriage, while the solitary honeymoon demonstrated the couple's isolated position within that community. Young people could expect help in *getting* married—more help, in fact, than their grandparents had received, but once married, they were on their own.

PART III
1870–1920

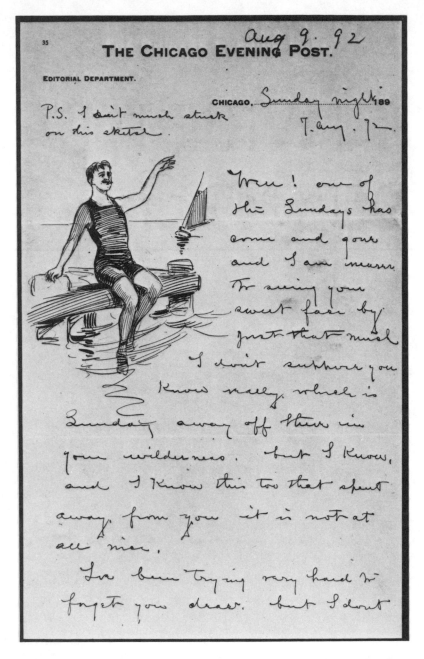

THE CHICAGO EVENING POST.

EDITORIAL DEPARTMENT.

Aug 9. 92

CHICAGO, *Sunday night* 189

P.S. I don't much struck on this sketch.

7. Aug. 92.

Well! one of the Sundays has come and gone and I am nearer To seeing your sweet face by just that much I don't suppose you know really which is Sunday away off there in your wilderness. but I know, and I know this too that spent away from you it is not at all nice.

I've been trying very hard to forget you dear. but I don't

While Raymond Brown was traveling in the West in 1892, he sent his fiancée a steady stream of letters and illustrated many of them with his own sketches. However, in the 1870 to 1920 period, even letters from home tended to read more like news reports than personal reflections. (Raymond Brown to Gertrude Foster, 7 August 1892, Gertrude Foster Brown Papers, SL.)

CHAPTER 6

"This Strong Fascination for Each Other"

W HEN John Franklin Jameson came down to dinner on September 18, 1891, the thirty-two-year-old Brown professor found a new face at the table. A decade of bachelorhood had hardened Franklin to boardinghouse life, to sharing meals with men who "would bore holes in solid rock," and with "maidens who [did] not speak until they were spoken to." But the newcomer to 55 Waterman Street was neither tiresome nor shy. Twenty-six-year-old Sara Elwell, called Sallie, had come to

179

Providence to teach music. Within a day or two, "the austere Jameson began to unbend sufficiently to 'take notice' of the frisky young thing." Before long she had become the "Universal Rejuvenator" of the household and "indispensable to the professor [who] began to think the world would whirl over if he couldn't have her."[1]

Through the winter and fall, it was "Miss Elwell" who "alleviated the miseries of morning beans, brown bread, and fish-balls" that were the all too familiar boardinghouse fare; she enlivened the table with her "cheerful impudence" and, when she was blue, aroused "masculine sympathy by the spectacle of her woes." Many an afternoon the young professor read to her, "pretending great interest in the poetry, but all the time watching the girl and feeling [his] way toward greater intimacy with her." By spring he knew he wanted her for his wife. Franklin was "slow to ignite," but when he was in love, he was "quite so." He set out to win Sallie's hand.[2]

There was one serious obstacle to his suit: Sara Elwell was engaged to another man, and Franklin was determined to do nothing dishonorable. When she gave signs of wanting to break her engagement, Franklin proposed. When she refused, Franklin assured her they would continue to be friends. He waited a few weeks and then asked again. Offering a detailed accounting of his income and expenses, he admitted, "On all pecuniary grounds a girl would be an utter fool to marry me." But his declaration of love carried more weight than his bank statement, and before the end of June, Sara Elwell had broken her first engagement and agreed to marry Franklin Jameson.[3]

Franklin had been in love once before, during his college days, and was thus "unable to give [Sallie] that first and freshest love which, though not at all necessarily the best, might yet seem to her the best." It was therefore "a sort of reassurance" to him that he was not the first man his fiancée had loved. "We shall give each other a fuller and happier love than we have known," he promised. For her part, Sara Elwell had already found a "completer happiness." Delighting in "the feeling of security [and] comfort" Franklin instilled in her, she was beginning, slowly, to let down "the mask of independence" which she had worn during her years as a self-supporting single woman. "I don't want to lean too heavily so that you will fall," she explained to her fiancé, adding, "Naturally I'm dependent."[4]

Sallie and Franklin both looked forward eagerly to the home they would have together. "I shan't 'marry for a home,' " as they say of old maids," Franklin wrote, "but it is an agreeable thing that having one is thrown in as part of the programme. Also that my young wife is so evidently capable in all housekeeping matters." Sallie wondered if his confidence might not be misplaced. "Do you know that when you mention my being a good housekeeper and getting up dinner and teas, my heart goes down in my boots. Why, man, where did you even get the idea that I knew anything about such matters?" she asked. Sallie suggested that to meet Franklin's expectations she would have "to spend the rest of the summer in the pastry kitchen and take a full course at Pratt Institute next winter."[5]

The next winter in fact found Sara Elwell recuperating from a serious illness at her sister's house in Brooklyn. In Providence, it was Franklin's turn to worry that his future mate's expectations were too high. It was not his culinary skill but his character that would prove a disappointment. "Ardently as I desire to make you happy," he wrote his fiancée in February, "there are kinks and twists and hardnesses and even meannesses in my character that you have yet to discover, and which will some time pain you." He urged her, "Look at me more critically, dear. It will be better for you in the long run if you do not expect too much."[6]

In the short run, Franklin and Sallie relied on correspondence and occasional visits to strengthen their relationship. The $1.75 it cost "to talk through the telephone to New York" helped Franklin resist the temptation "to get [Sallie] up to a long-distancer, just to hear that dear sweet voice." Instead, he wrote daily, using his "newfangled" typewriting machine; Sallie wrote less often, by hand.[7] Franklin kept his fiancée informed of his daily routine—the calls he paid, the classes he taught, the magazine articles he wrote and sold. He worried about the state of her health and pleaded with her not to exert herself, even if it meant going without regular letters from her.

In the winter of 1893, Sara Elwell received an inheritance which enabled them to purchase and begin building on a lot near the Brown campus. Franklin was delighted. He had long hoped they would be able to build a house to suit themselves. "Most men do their business out of the house; mine will be done inside," the young professor wrote, to explain why he needed "certain arrangements of a house which it will be difficult to secure in one that is bought." Franklin regretted that Sallie was too far away for daily consultation, but he was glad she would be "spared the worry of minor details." Although she was not "very fussy about those things," Franklin—as his builder would soon discover—had a passion for detail. In the winter and spring of 1893, with construction under way, Franklin's correspondence was filled with progress reports.[8]

They were to be married in Brooklyn on April 13, 1893, and as the date approached, wedding plans flew back and forth between Providence and New York. Franklin announced his opposition to a wedding cake—a "useless and nonsensical expenditure"—and his preference "to say simply 'to love and to cherish.' " He ordered "pins for the young gents" who would serve as his ushers and consulted with friends as to "who shall go in what carriages." Sallie was busy visiting dressmakers ("One for the [bridal] gown and the other for the make overs"), ordering the invitations from Tiffany, and keeping up with the steady stream of wedding presents. "I'm driving myself to drink with [thank you] notes," she wrote on a day that added a chocolate pitcher, a cut-glass berry dish, a pair of painted cologne bottles, silver sugar tongs, and a bonbon spoon to her accumulation of gifts.[9]

A few days before the wedding, Franklin left Providence for Brooklyn. He arrived in time to help with the final arrangements and to participate in the wedding rehearsal. On Thursday, April 13, his parents, sisters, and brother, who had traveled from Massachusetts, joined Sara's sisters for a "family breakfast." The wedding itself took place in Grace Church; over six hundred guests were invited, and police officers were hired to check tickets of admission at the door. Following the service and reception, the newlyweds departed for a honeymoon at the Shoreham Hotel in Washington, D.C.

Their house was still under construction when they returned to Rhode Island, so they spent the spring and summer in Wickford on Narragansett Bay, a long trolley ride from Providence. In September 1893, Mr. and Mrs. J. Franklin Jameson moved to their new home on College Hill, just a few blocks from the boardinghouse where they had met two years before.

"This vague hypnotism"

Soon after Sara Elwell had agreed to marry him, Franklin Jameson suggested they visit his family in Massachusetts. The prospect of meeting her future in-laws made Sallie uneasy. She felt sure that the Jameson men would welcome her. "I'm not very much afraid of that sex," she told Franklin, but she was "terribly afraid" of his mother and sisters. "It's only the women who are bright enough to see through my wiles and to judge me accordingly," she explained. When Sallie looked at her fiancé's family, she saw a line drawn down the middle. On one side were the men, who would be easy to win over; on the other, the women, who would "pull [her] to pieces."[10] Men might determine what went on in the world of business and politics, but the family was woman's domain.

Sallie Elwell did not, of course, invent the categories into which she placed her new in-laws. These categories were written into the catechism of middle-class life and had been for nearly a century. American children learned early that God had ordained a certain role for women and a certain role for men, and that they—the children—must prepare for the day they would play their parts with their own mates and offspring.

When boys and girls went off to school, they came under the guidance and control of female teachers who sought to shape them into manly men and womanly women. As children grew older and began reading novels and magazines, they found confirmation—and occasional criticism—of the gender arrangements and ideas that were in force at home and at school. By the time they were teenagers, young men and women had assimilated the basic principle that the sexes occupied unequal positions because they were endowed with different natures.

The association of women with domesticity, emotionalism, and purity, and of men with ambition, rationality, and sexual passion was almost as old as the century; but after the Civil War, there was an important, if subtle, shift in emphasis. The female sex retained its corner on moral purity, but male impurity assumed the proportions of a grave social problem. "The feminine mind is preoccupied with the original sinfulness of man," Kate Gannett Wells wrote in 1891 to explain "Why More Girls Do Not Marry."[11] While early nineteenth-century Americans had seen the disparity between male and female as a reflection of God-given differences, the late Victorians were more concerned with the external, circumstantial factors behind the double standard. The immoral behavior of men may have been natural, but it was also tolerated. The militance of the ante-bellum female moral reformers, who publicly confronted and exposed male patrons of brothels and saloons, re-emerged in the last quarter of the nineteenth century as a mainstream movement, involving thousands of women, and some men, in a national "purity crusade."[12]

At a time when the Women's Christian Temperance Union was clamoring for prohibition to save women and children from the scourge of drunken men, when campaigns were organized to eradicate the "Social Evil" of prostitution, young women looked at men through a dark glass indeed. "How can men bear to live double?" twenty-one-year-old Annie Winsor asked. "How can they be gentlemanly, of pure speech and right behavior at home and with ladies, and go to drink and swear and think foul thoughts, to see ugly sights . . . do ugly deeds and cover them over. And they know that there is a code of honour which will protect them from exposure." But Annie reminded herself "never to forget to what great temptations young men are open." When men succumbed to temptation, the outcome, according to Maud Rittenhouse, was children with "mothers but no fathers." It seemed to Maud, growing up in Cairo, Illinois, in the 1880s, that "vice of that sort is too generally ignored and condoned. . . . When boys are taught all their lives that purity is only for women (*some* women) and vice a necessity to them and 'natural' what better results could one expect." Maud was grateful she had "four brothers with no such notions."[13]

By excluding her brothers from her denunciation, Maud Rittenhouse resolved a problem that was implicit in the way her culture saw men. Women were taught that men were inclined, and allowed, to be impure and yet trusted, respected, and loved individual men. Kate Gannett Wells pointed out that, in "the great mass of literature," there were only two points of view:

One class of reformers has said that man is bestial, but capable of improvement; the other that the passions of manhood ally him to the forces of the universe and justify themselves. All have spoken so plainly or insinuatingly that the only refrain in which they agree, is, "Beware." . . . The girl starts with the notion . . . that all men are more or less explosive.[14]

Parents sounded the same admonitory note with their daughters. Eleanor Abbott remembered that she and her sister "were led to infer" that men were "turned into 'wild beasts' by the slightest departure on a woman's part" from modesty and decorum. But even as a child, Eleanor understood that this warning concerned the male genus rather than the men with whom she was personally acquainted. She and her sister were to guard themselves not against their "own father, of course, nor [their] brother, nor the bishop, nor the butcher, nor Mr. Lowell, nor Mr. Longfellow, but just men in general." Maud Rittenhouse had heard enough scandal to conclude, by the time she was seventeen, that "man, from the mightiest king to the humblest laborer is impure throughout—more animal than true man or honest love"; but she, too, realized that "*all* mankind is not depraved." Her father, his business associates, her brothers, and her current beau were all exceptions.[15]

Like most middle-class Americans of her generation, Maud believed that men were impelled by "animal instincts," but that they could overcome the impulse to act on those instincts if they developed their powers of self-control. Women could—indeed, *must*—help men in the struggle for self-control, but it was a struggle women themselves remained above. Their role was to restrain and, within marriage, to satisfy male passion. This, Helen Swett objected in 1899, was "the attitude of the world . . . woman capable of yielding man one pleasure . . . often not innocent—whole thing a nuisance—woman not much account anyway." The Stanford co-ed believed that ninety-nine out of a hundred men shared this "dwarfing androcentric view." (Ernest Schwartz, her fiancé, was "the hundredth man.") Helen realized that it was "a *man's* world" that created the double standard, but she acknowledged that "women, too, hold, or come to hold the same view." Even while attacking that view, she affirmed one of its basic premises. Condemning the "complaisance" of women because it meant "that their greater natural purity and sympathy and altruism avails the cause of moral progress but little," Helen Swett rejected the double standard of the "man's world" but accepted its central tenet: that women had "greater natural purity" than men.[16]

In the last quarter of the nineteenth century, some feminists and a minority of physicians suggested that women had the same sexual drives as men and were no purer by nature, but few young women adopted such an unconventional—and possibly self-incriminating—stance.* Most of those who attacked the status quo sought, like Helen Swett, to bring men "up" to the level of women, not vice versa. "The man I marry must *need* me . . . my influence must be *good* for him," a New Jersey woman wrote in 1892. To contribute to the elevation of male character was simply a duty women owed to themselves and to society.

---

*See chapter 8, pages 253–62, for a discussion of sexual attitudes in this period.

A woman's influence was by definition beneficial to a man; as a result, she had an obligation, Annie Winsor thought, to "bring [her] moral sense to bear upon" her relations with men. "God has put into us men and women this strong fascination for each other which most of us have. . . . We should try to find the way to use it." Although Annie believed that "women have a strong influence over men [and] men have a strong influence over women," she, like most of her contemporaries, clearly saw female influence as the more powerful and salutory force. If it were not for "the modesty of mien and deportment as exemplified particularly in the personality of all females, the world it seemed, was well-nigh lost," was what Eleanor Abbott learned growing up in the 1890s.[17]

The safety and security of the social order, then, depended on the modesty and virtue of the female sex. While this view fueled renewed crusades against vice (and *for* women's suffrage), most middle-class men had a more immediate and concrete way of understanding the effects of female influence. The women in their lives—especially their future mates—would keep them from the weaknesses, excesses, and errors that were their lot as males. "You are my ideal, my counselor, my confidante, the one who gives purpose and direction to every thought and effort," the Minnesota architect Cass Gilbert told his fiancée Julia Finch in 1887. "You are my *good influence* to keep me pure in heart. . . . Your influence makes me more manly." Frank Lillie, a young zoology professor, had similar feelings about Frances Crane. She would make him "more manly" by keeping him pure—not only in heart but in body. "You are the very incarnation of purity to me . . . and you shall help to cleanse me," he told her.[18]

For Frank Lillie and his generation, purity stood for sexual purity, and there was no form of female influence that was more important—and more full of conflict—for men. Young men, no less than their sisters, grew up in a world where the double standard prevailed. They were taught that the vigor of their "animal instincts" was what made them powerful, but that certain of those instincts were dangerous and had to be contained. A relationship with a "nice woman" was the best defense against a man's natural proclivities. Men could find an outlet for their sexual energies if they "raided the amusement parks or the evening streets in search of girls that could be frankly pursued for their physical charms," but these experiences only made a man more aware of his impurity in the eyes of the women of his own class. Henry Canby remembered that his generation, coming of age in the 1890s, "learned to associate amorous ardors with the vulgar, or worse, with the commonplace, and to disassociate them sharply from romance." Romance was for "nice girls," and nice girls who went too far were shunned. Canby recalled that "the men were more ruthless in characterizing them than were the girls." Men depended on women to uphold their half of the double standard.[19]*

Woman's most vital mission was to inspire and enforce sexual purity; she was also imbued with the power to make men "more manly" in other ways as well. Julia Finch moved Cass Gilbert to be more "gentle in life and generous in ambition." Franklin Jameson believed that "only a girl like [Sallie] can bring a man's life to its best performance." Ray Brown, a graphic artist in Chicago, loved Gertrude Foster for "making [him] work and stimulating [his] ambition." The effectiveness of his "darling taskmaster" lay not in any orders she issued, but in the inspiration she provided. "You don't *tell* me to be good, you go farther, you *compel* me," Ray explained to Gertrude. The Boston physician Richard Cabot attributed to his friend and later wife Ella Lyman a similar capacity to shape his future. "Seeing how utterly you hold my life in your hands you cannot let it go wrong," he told her.[21]

It was women who were imbued with this kind of power over men, yet it was men who in fact held the lives of women in their hands. A woman did not expect contact with men to have a transforming—and elevating—effect on her character; the

---

*This attitude was given empirical weight by two studies conducted among male high school and college students and college graduates in the early 1920s. Many of the subjects indicated that being with girls who were of a "better class" helped them restrain their sexual drive. "If with a decent girl I am o.k., but if she is indecent and tries to make me, I have to think of my ideals and use will to break and run," one young man reported. Christina Simmons discusses the fear among sex educationists that women "might decline this responsibility."[20]

change a man brought to her life was tangible, an alteration more in circumstances than in personality. If women made men more manly by helping them reconcile morality and instinct, men made women more womanly simply by choosing them to be their wives and the mothers of their children. No matter how much leverage a woman possessed by virtue of her sex—no matter how much men depended on women to preserve virtue—a woman's authority was exercised in and through her family.

This imbalance was nothing new. For a hundred years, the American woman had been conceded influence, even while she was denied the right to control her own property, study medicine, or earn equal pay. The doctrine of female influence had long served to justify the subordination of woman: she did not need the vote since her innate superiority gave her so much influence over her enfranchised husband and sons. A girl was "educated to believe," one social critic wrote, "that in place of an aggressive part in life, her power lay in her 'influence,' and with this vague hypnotism she expected to mold the life of her husband and to control her children."[22] In the late nineteenth and early twentieth centuries, female influence appeared increasingly as an argument in favor of, rather than against, a greater role for women outside the home. It was *because* woman was morally superior that she should be given the vote. Once it spread beyond the home, female influence would clean the streets, stamp out vice and crime, and restore order to the community. While this argument helped to enlarge the middle-class woman's sphere of action, it left in place—and reinforced—the assumption that women owed their stature to the differences, and not to the likenesses, between the sexes.[23]

"An honest friendship"

As their paths converged—on campuses and city streets, in trolley cars and dance halls—the belief persisted that women and men moved on different levels; however, shared activities might narrow, if not extinguish, the gap between manly men and true women. In 1912, Mary Roberts Coolidge observed, "Nowadays [boys and girls] grow up seeing each other every day, in school and college classrooms, in stores and offices, on boats and cars, as they travel to and fro about their work." This was precisely the situation that twenty years before had appeared to offer the best hope for genuine friendship between young men and women. "I think we ought to take the utmost pains to throw boys and girls together from childhood up—all the time. . . . We ought to be easier together. It is a great waste of opportunity," Annie Winsor wrote in 1884. A few years later, the editor of the *Ladies' Home Journal* made the same argument: "Let our girls have a chance to know our young men, and vice versa." Annie Winsor recognized that conventional sex roles made for long odds: "It is a pity for a boy to take up his time learning what drinking and gambling and betting, swearing, and flirting are like; just as it's a pity [for girls] to stay in a stuffy house and gossip when there's a fine sunset going on outside." Another midwestern college student, Madeleine Wallin, summed it up this way: "There is really little opportunity for an honest friendship . . . between a man and a woman."[24]

At twenty-two, Madeleine believed that "there is nothing so inspiring as a common work and common interest."[25] She saw some hope for friendship in the coming together of men and women to study, work, and play, but greater contact did not automatically produce easier relations between men and women. Compared with earlier generations, middle-class Americans of both sexes spent more time in school, had a wider range of occupational and mate choice, and moved in a more urban and more open society. Yet in spite of the fact that young men and women enjoyed greater proximity to one another, there seemed to be ever fewer points at which their lives intersected.

As the increasing specialization and bureaucratization of the economy demanded better-educated workers, more youths stayed in school through their teens. Home and school, rather than home and work, became the poles around which the lives of middle-class young people revolved. Early nineteenth century children had attended school when they could be spared from the farm or the house; they learned the basics of reading, writing, and ciphering, usually from a man or a woman not much older—or more learned—than themselves. The mid-century school-reform movement had succeeded in making teaching more professional and attendance more regular. The school year was lengthened, and absence was increasingly defined as deviant. After the Civil War, public high schools, most of them coeducational, opened in cities and towns around the country, and opportunities for higher education expanded as well.[26] The proliferation of normal schools and state universities meant that more and more men and women studied together throughout their school years. Sitting side by side in the classroom did not, however, necessarily increase informal contact between the sexes. Specialized curriculums (home economics for girls, woodworking for boys), organized sports, and after-school clubs made these high schools and colleges a great deal more sex-segregated than the ungraded, one-room schools of the early republic.

When Americans completed their schooling and entered the work world, they found a similarly mixed picture. Single women joined the paid labor force in unprecedented numbers, but they tended to concentrate in all-female occupations. Between 1840 and 1870, the teaching profession was feminized, and nursing and library work were clearly identified as female professions. Less well educated women followed more traditional routes, working as dressmakers, mill hands, or domestic servants. In 1880, four fifths of all women in non-farm occupations were teachers, servants, clerks, or dressmaker/seamstresses.[27] For a young woman employed in domestic service, the garment trades, or schoolteaching, the work world was no less (and perhaps even more) sex-segregated than the cooperative rural household in which her grandmother had labored without pay. In 1888, Annie Winsor, who had taught high school before she entered Radcliffe College, observed:

As women take work upon themselves more and more, the present social customs and arrangements will have to change. Women and men

191

must have each other's society, and as things stand now working women and working men cannot have more than an acquaintance with each other.[28]

Over the next three decades, "social customs and arrangements" did indeed change, but the obstacles to friendship between men and women did not disappear. Even with coeducational schools and offices full of working women, the late nineteenth century city brought men and women together in a context that demanded they keep their distance from one another. Between 1830 and 1870, the urban population increased by nearly 20 per cent a year; by 1880, one in four Americans lived in cities. One result of this rapid urbanization was to increase the range of potential marriage partners for city-dwelling youth; but because they were more likely than their country cousins to be choosing from among strangers, they were more likely to maintain a protective distance and reserve. The city was both a more open and a more hazardous place to find a mate than the small town from which it had grown; far more complex, heterogeneous, and dynamic, it was also more divided by class, geography, and gender.

The fact that the single most salient gender distinction derived from sexuality made friendship between men and women appear to be not only difficult but dangerous. Men's and women's separate spheres were contracting and overlapping, but the boundary lines were still highly charged and difficult to approach. Women were guarded; the sexual purity that was so important to their identity was at stake. "Young men soon lose their respect for a girl exactly in proportion as she allows them any familiarity," the *Ladies' Home Journal* declared in 1892. A New York man saw the same dynamic from a different angle: "Just in proportion to the real value . . . set on true friendship—there must be a certain so far-and-no-farther feeling which keeps locked up—on the girl's part at least—the deepest and the truest things, and the man has to get at them in a roundabout way."[29]

To protect her purity, a woman had to scrutinize not only her own behavior but that of the men she knew. When Maud Rittenhouse encountered a group of poor children whom she surmised were illegitimate, she was outraged. "It makes me want to *talk* to my men friends about such things. It seems to me almost sometimes that I *must.*" Annie Winsor felt that girls' responsibility toward young men went beyond talk: "We should be on the alert constantly that no word or deed of ours may encourage them in a poor standard." Young women who were "on the alert," like those who communicated a "so-far-and-no-farther feeling," would not find it easy to be friends with young men. No wonder Richard Cabot rejected the idea that "men can discuss the deepest realities of life with their girl contemporaries."[30]

Richard Cabot had "a craving for friendship" that he felt he could not satisfy with women. "The men friends which I am beginning to get now will give me something far deeper than I can get from women," he wrote while an undergraduate. Indeed, many middle-class men of his generation established close emotional ties with other men. Male friendship was highly valued for the companionship and closeness it offered. It afforded a transitional step between filial and romantic love, between childhood and adulthood. Men could give each other affection, without raising the expectations that inhibited openness with female peers. Even men who "always supposed [love] never existed between persons of the same sex unless they were brothers or some natural relation to one another," recognized the pleasures to be found in friendship with other men.[31]

Women, too, relied heavily on friendships with their own sex. Ties to other women were a primary source of love and intimacy for young women who turned, as their mothers and grandmothers had, to female friends for support, comfort, and strength before—and in some cases, after—marriage. Most women, however, expected that love for a man would eventually take the place of friendships in their lives. Frances Crane, who was part of a group of close female friends in Chicago in the 1890s, explained to her fiancé:

I feel such . . . sweet security that in you all my day dreams will be realized, of a true and tender husband, of children all *our* own, of a home in which both of us can work out our lives, with the other's help and sympathy. Just *think* that is what a man's and woman's love means! It is so different from loving a girl isn't it? I mean for *me* loving a girl.[32]

As one midwestern man put it, "Persons of the same sex form great loves," but "it accords with all nature that man and woman should love each other with a greater love than does woman and woman or man and man."[33] Ever since this "greater love" had been enthroned as the exclusive agent for individual (and familial) fulfillment, friendship between men and women had been difficult to sustain. Even if women and men managed to bridge the distance between their separate spheres, and to overcome the obstacles created by the definition of woman as "pure" and man as "animal," they had to contend with the ever-present possibility that "more than friendship" might be expected.

The editor of the *Ladies' Home Journal* decried the fact that "there is absolutely no halfway station between being a stranger and a lover. Friendship is never thought of." On the contrary, friendship was thought of and longed for, especially by young women who wanted to enjoy male companionship and attention without the demands of romantic love. They sought to reclaim "common friendship" from the lowly place to which their parents had relegated it. "What can a girl do with young men?" Annie Winsor wondered. "If she treats them merely as other friends . . . she is more than likely to make unhappiness." On the other hand, the twenty-one-year-old reasoned that "if she guards constantly against this evil, her free action and speech are gone, she cannot be even half a friend." Madeleine Wallin phrased the problem more simply: what made friendship awkward was that "it either develops into something stronger on one side or both, or it is hampered by conventionality and insincerity."[34]

If it did "develop into something stronger" on the woman's side, she was unlikely to declare herself; but if it was the man who wanted more, he might be bold enough to say so. When he did, it often left the friendship strained and the woman with a sense of loss. Eighteen-year-old Maud Rittenhouse was distressed when two of the young men in her social circle fell in love with her. "Oh, dear. I like boy friends, not boy lovers," she complained to her diary. A more mature woman described her feelings when "an old friend . . . disappointed [her] by turning into a lover. . . . All the spirit of freedom seemed to leave the relationship between us," twenty-seven-year-old Caroline Drayton wrote: "He was desiring something from me, which I could not give, and the feeling was suffocating and terrible to me—and made me want to fight like some wild creature."[35]

Some young men sensed that a confession of love to a woman friend might cause her pain. A classmate at the University of Wisconsin asked Edna Rankin, "Forgive me if . . . I have or am trespassing on grounds which I have no right to enter. . . . I need to be able to tell you I love you so forgive me if I hurt you in any way." Edna had once told this young man that "the love of a friend for a friend is the most wonderful feeling a man can have for a girl," but what he felt was "far more . . . than the love of a friend": he loved Edna "as a man can only love a girl."[36]

"Ideals are of some moment"

Men had been offering women "more than the love of a friend" for a century; this generation considered it "a generally accepted fact . . . [that] it is the addition of passion . . . which constitutes the difference between Friendship and Love." Women found it much harder than men to come by that all-important element; they were more eager for friendship because they were more wary of love. Theirs was not the caution of the early republic, on guard against the dangers of unchecked passion. These turn-of-the century women worried more about an insufficiency than about an excess of feeling. A woman expected to be drawn to a prospective mate with all the force of a powerful magnet; if she was not, she was likely to judge herself a failure. Even women who thought that "love should be *founded on respect* instead of *passion,*" believed that lovers "should have a magnetic attraction for each other." "If real true love should come there won't be any doubts about it," wrote Caroline Drayton in 1908; but she and many other women found that outside of novels, "real true love" was not so easy to detect.[37]

In the 1880s, Maud Rittenhouse filled her diary with questions about her feelings for each of the men who courted her. "I look into the very depths of my nature, I analyze every thought and feeling, and still I *cannot* find whether I truly love him or not. I wish I did," she wrote in the midst of one relationship. On another occasion, when a suitor asked if she loved him, she responded, "I *do* love you. I always shall. But all the time I feel within me that I do *not* love you with that intensity of love of which I am capable." (Maud claimed not to know if that was "how a wife *should* love her husband," but she agreed to marry only after she had decided that she was "in love.") Concern about what they were *supposed* to feel nagged at many women. A New Yorker questioned whether she felt "the love [she] ought to have" for the man who wanted to marry her; her wish, she told him, was to "just wake up some morning and find I love you with all my heart & all the horrid old worry is gone." Until that happened, she was left suspended in a state of indecision and self-denigration. She belonged to a generation that "could not imagine ever being able to marry anyone without" first falling in love. A young Washington lawyer wondered if in some cases that might not be "the way to happiness," but he could see that "it's not one's ideal and ideals are of some moment."[38]

Ideals were a powerful force indeed; they acted on both women and men but in different ways. For women, ideals of love were an abstraction, often an obstacle to the thing itself; while men tended to personalize and internalize their ideals. Evangeline Walker, a student at Bryn Mawr College in the 1890s, described how her ideals had preserved her from a loveless marriage:

I had given up finding any one whom I would really love. . . . At times I almost came to the conclusion that it would be better for me to marry someone who loved me and whom I did not love, than never to marry at all. But my respect for my ideals, for my self and feelings of justice towards the poor man who might fall victim, saved me.

If Evangeline was "saved" by her ideals, other women found themselves misled or paralyzed by theirs. "If I didn't do quite so much idealizing I shouldn't meet with quite so many disappointments," Maud Rittenhouse observed in 1889. Idealizing led Eugenie Homer to disappointment, too—in herself. She explained to her suitor why she had not accepted his proposal: "My ideal of love comes to me and tells me that I am not living up to it, that the love I have for you is not worthy of it— and that seems terrible to me. There should be no doubt," she concluded.[39]

But, of course, there often was doubt. The voice that told women what they "ought" to feel was difficult to silence; a great deal was at stake. Caroline Drayton wished desperately that she "could fall in love & marry," but the risks of making a mistake held her back. "I know I could be so blissfully happy with the right man, and so frightfully miserable with the wrong one & have so little confidence in my own judgment of men, that I don't know what to do. If only I could make myself love ———— enough to marry him," she wrote when one man was attentive to her. Women tried hard to "make" themselves love the men who loved them and to keep themselves from loving men who did not. "Oh, why can't I feel as I want to, as I *ought* to?" nineteen-year-old Nella Hubbard asked.[40]

In 1786, Elizabeth Sherman was perfectly comfortable with the idea that "the sensations of the heart in these respects are not Controulable." Young women coming of age a hundred years later felt they should be able to direct their emotions into the proper channels, but they were not sure how to chart a course that would bring them into the safe harbor of a happy marriage. They knew that they could not rely on rational thought to guide them, although they often wanted to. Nella

Hubbard's strategy was to "try to stop thinking and just work." Several decades later, Dorothy Kirchwey came to a similar, if more sophisticated, resolution. Worried that she did not love LaRue Brown "quite the way" he loved her, she promised to accept things as they were. "The measure & kind don't matter as a subject for analysis & the less self-analysis that goes on the better," she declared. When the Philadelphian Margaret Lesley had similar doubts after her engagement to Henry Bush-Brown, it seemed that her problem would "be solved only by anxious thought," but she admitted that "the intellect had little to do with love."[41]

In fact, it could inhibit love. Caroline Drayton understood that her detached perspective on love and marriage kept her from falling in love with the men who admired her. "The trouble is I can see too clearly and critically the pros and cons of the question, so that I do not seem to be able to arouse in myself any more romantic feelings on the subject." One could simply not *think* one's way into love. Barriers that were open to the heart proved impermeable to the mind. If one *tried* to love, one was destined to fail. "Real love is to me intensely active and without effort . . . if worthy of the name," Eugenie Homer declared.[42] "Real love" and "ideal love" were defined as one and the same thing; no compromise was possible.

Imbedded in women's images of ideal love was the figure of the ideal lover. In an age when men were both condemned and celebrated for the power of their "animal instincts," young women cast their ideals in the anachronistic tradition of medieval chivalry. Mary Bulkley remembered that, growing up in St. Louis in the 1870s, she had "a romantic notion, as to the only sort of man who would be good enough" for her: "He was a beautiful combination of Sir Lancelot, Sir Galahad, and Robert Elsmere." In New York, Emily Smith thought she had found just such a man in Henry DuBois, whom she addressed—much to his embarrassment—as "My Knight" and "Vigilans." Thirty years later, Caroline Drayton inscribed her diary "Dedicated to my Knight," the nameless man who appeared in her "vision of what true love must be." She imagined that their love would

"This Strong Fascination for Each Other"

"be Kingly and Queenly when it comes, full of courtesie, nobility and gentleness."[43]

But the man must be forceful as well as gentle, assertive as well as courteous; the man who succeeded "in meeting the world and whipping it into line" was the one who would win a woman's love. Women who were unsure of the strength of their own feelings looked for self-assuredness in a lover. Caroline Drayton believed that "God had kept [her] for [her] knight," but admitted, "If some strong minded, determined man came along & made up his mind to marry me, & told me in a perfectly convinced way, that it was going to happen, I would probably do as I was told . . . I really believe," she continued, "what I need & what most women need, is a master, a kind but firm one, & one who loves her with all his heart." Another woman who "never intended to marry until [she] found a real hero" knew she "had met [her] fate" when she was courted by a man who "at once assumed a very commanding manner." It was not just old-fashioned women who expected domination from a man. A midwestern co-ed admitted to her fiancée, "Modern ideas to the contrary, . . . much of the same old dependent spirit still remains in most women, out of sight perhaps but still there." Indeed, even Lucy Sprague (the first dean of women at Berkeley), who was looking neither for a "knight" nor a "real hero" and who certainly did not agree with Caroline Drayton that "what most women need is a master," doubted that Wesley Clair Mitchell would make a good husband because he was so unaggressive in his pursuit of her.[44]

A man who was less than ardent in his wooing of a woman risked appearing weak and unmanly, but one who was too passionate might seem to lack control over his baser instincts. A man's headlong rush into love could carry along a woman whose own feelings were uncertain, or it could make her feel as though she, with her slower pace, would never catch up. The sheer intensity with which they loved made men suspect. Men were possessed of a conviction and self-confidence that eluded the women who were the objects of their pursuit. "If you only care as much for me after we are married," one woman worried out loud to her impassioned fiancé, "I think I shall be satisfied." But she had grave doubts: "It is a man's nature not to value what he has as much as what he wants and has not. And a woman is so much at a man's mercy."[45]

The ideal man, then, was a contradiction in terms: he must be aggressive, masterful, and sure of himself; yet he must be deferential, gentle, and pure. The same tensions that characterized men's own ideals of manhood appear in the way women conceived of the ideal lover and mate. Finding a man who was both a "Christian Gentleman" and a "Masculine Primitive" was a difficult task; a man who possessed one set of strengths might seem to lack the other.[46] Thus, one can see why many women were guarded, even fainthearted, in their feelings for men. Dorothy Kirchwey's fear that she did not love LaRue Brown "with quite the absorbing love" he had for her was such a common concern that a University of Michigan co-ed was led to wonder "if a woman *ever* loves as a man does."[47]*

The late nineteenth century view was that women, although more emotional and sensitive than men, loved less intensely. Where women in earlier generations lacked confidence in their worthiness to *be* loved, these women were more likely to question their ability *to* love. The self-doubts that plagued many women—the uncertainty about whether the man and what she felt for him were worthy of her ideals—served as a powerful constraint on a woman's feelings. When Alice Stockham observed, in the 1887 edition of *Tokology*, "We teach the girl *repression,* the boy *expression,* not simply by word and book, but the lessons are graven into their very being by all the traditions, prejudices, and customs of society," she was referring to sexual feelings; but her analysis applies equally well to other emotions.[49] Young women were expected to be at once the patrons and the regulators of emotional life. Many found it difficult to exercise the great power men granted to their sex: the power of love.

*This co-ed wished she "hadn't read so many crazy novels. Perhaps," she speculated, "I shouldn't be so unreasonable and uncertain about myself if I hadn't imbibed such a quantity of fin de siecle notions." Mary Bulkley blamed novel reading for the "preposterous idealization" of her youth.[48]

"This Strong Fascination for Each Other"

Perhaps because they saw themselves as having greater control over their future than women did, middle-class men were better able to trust their feelings. They put far less faith in the power of reason than had their midcentury forebears. Man was now a "Civilized Primitive" who relied on instinct and physical strength as much as on rationality and honor to survive in the "jungle" of the modern world. There were "seasons in human affairs," the minister Sydney Smith observed, when "men must trust to emotion for that safety which reason [cannot always] give." Courtship was such a season, and men did indeed "trust to emotion." They disdained reason as a weapon in the fight for a woman's affections, and they encouraged women to use their hearts, and not their minds, to measure love. Men did not want women to make an *effort* to love them. "I don't want to force love—or try it—but Oh let it come if it will," the young physician Howard Taylor Ricketts told Myra Tubbs.[50] It was women who were expected to be comfortable with and motivated by emotion, but in courtship it was men who placed greater trust in their feelings.

A man responded emotionally to a fit between a long-cherished image of the woman he would love and a real woman who appeared in his life. The Cleveland lithographer William Zorach met Californian Marguerite Thompson when both were studying art in Paris. "I wish I could . . . tell you what I felt when I first saw you. How you fulfilled all that I have thought of and dreamt of in my boyhood dreams," Bill wrote when Margeurite had left Paris. The Harvard-educated lawyer LaRue Brown explained to Dorothy Kirchwey how the process worked for him: "Since first I came to think as a man thinks there has been ever with me in my heart a picture of a kind of girl. I could love that kind of girl and be to her what I wished to be to the woman whose life was linked to mine." LaRue concluded "that when one does come to know *the* girl one knows that he has really cared for her a very long time indeed." For Bill Zorach and LaRue Brown and many of their male contemporaries, love was the "shock of recognition" they felt when they encountered the woman familiar from "boyhood dreams" or from the "picture of a kind of girl" one wanted for a wife.

This did not mean finding someone else's idea of the "perfect woman." Bill remembered that his family and friends never understood "the kind of a girl [that] appealed to" him, and LaRue announced that he "greatly preferred to marry a human woman and not an abstraction from the Ladies Home Journal."[51]

Men coming of age between 1870 and 1920 still idealized women, of course, but they were looking for a woman who had the qualities of a *personal* ideal rather than for one who seemed to be the ideal representative of her sex. They dreamed not of a mate with the virtue, purity, and domestic accomplishments extolled in the Cult of True Womanhood, but of "the kind of a girl" pictured in their own fantasies—"a charming woman to whom one can *talk*, upon whose experienced judgment one can place confidence and with whom one could share problems," in LaRue Brown's case.[52] The designs were never entirely original: they reflected popular notions of female beneficence, sympathy, and purity and the psychological needs of men raised in mother-dominant families. Nevertheless, the ideal woman whom a man of this time hoped to marry was less a stock character of midcentury reveries—ideal for all men—and more an individual creation—ideal for the man in whose dreams she appeared. When a man recognized this image, he did not need to think: he had, as LaRue Brown said, "cared for her a very long time indeed." She was familiar; she was known; she was loved. He could "trust to emotion."

The search for the ideal in love was not an academic exercise. Gender ideals could be adjusted; indeed, they had to be, for ideals of manhood and womanhood were often self-contradictory. But ideals of love could not be compromised, no matter how difficult of achievement they seemed to be. They were the only foundation—the only chance—for a happy marriage.

CHAPTER 7

"Going Somewhere"

I N *The American Husband and Other Alternatives,* a 1925 collection of magazine pieces, Alexander Black recounted this story: A young man asked a young woman if he could pay a call on her. As he traveled to her flat, his mind was full of images of a "homelier era" when girls made fudge or played the piano for their suitors. But when he arrived, he realized at once that he had been mistaken: "*She had her hat on.*" Black offered only the merest sketch of these two figures: The young man, nostalgic for the time when a woman entertained her beau at home, was regretfully making quick calculations of what it would cost him to "meet the presumptions arising from the fact that she had her hat on." The young woman who came to the door dressed for the street was a "city girl"; she spent her days at a typewriter, blackboard, or file cabinet and was eager to get out and enjoy the pleasures of life in the metropolis.[1]

By 1920, "going somewhere" had become the favorite pasttime

of middle-class young Americans. "Home and its arts went out of date," Alexander Black believed, as a result of the automobile. "Doing anything without a car became equivalent to doing nothing at all."[2] The car did indeed transform American life. It affected where people lived and worked, what they did for fun, how they defined success, and, not incidentally, the way they conducted their courtships; but the "homelier era" was already waning when the first Model T rolled off the assembly line. Even before the automobile provided unprecedented—and to some observers, alarming—mobility and privacy, young people had discovered the joys of "going somewhere." In the last quarter of the nineteenth century, social life was moving into new channels; the old ones were not abandoned overnight, but they gradually carried less of the flow.

"A warning of the new age"

Ina Smith and John Marean lived with their families on adjoining farms near Glen Aubrey, in the Nanticoke Valley in Broome County, New York. Ina was eighteen and John twenty-four when they began keeping company in 1899. Their usual pattern was to see each other three times a week: going out on Friday or Saturday evening, John calling on Ina at home on Sunday, and visiting together on one other occasion during the week. Although they spent much of their time at the Smiths' house—playing cards or tiddlywinks, reading aloud, making fudge—they also attended parties and dances, church socials, and musical events. In this, they were not very different from couples who courted in the 1830s or the 1860s.

But John and Ina were not limited to these traditional activities; they had access to new forms of entertainment which had recently spread from the city to rural areas like the Nanticoke Valley. On July 4, for example, they went with four of their friends "to the Casino in the evening [and] played croquet." The Casino was in Union, seven miles from home; less than two weeks later, the same group went to the Buffalo Bill Wild West Show in Binghamton, fifteen miles away.[3] What distinguished these excursions from band concerts, church fairs, and taffy pulls was that they were commercial—"going somewhere" cost money—and that they took place outside the confines of the local community. Taking a train or streetcar to a nearby town to see a show, ride a carousel, or dance in a cabaret was both a more expensive and a less communal form of leisure than strolling down to hear the band play.[4]

For Ina Smith and John Marean, visits to the Casino meant mounting major expeditions and returning home late at night (after the July 4 trip to the Casino, Ina wrote, "Got home at half-past three. . . . I have been awful sleepy today"[5]). In the city, a variety of amusements was only a trolley ride away. By 1910, the girl who met her caller at the door with her hat on could have been looking forward to an evening at the movies, in a dance hall, or at the vaudeville.* Young people who lived at home still had their friends in for cards, dancing, refreshments, but these evening socials now had to compete with an increasing array of leisure-time activities that took place outside the home. Men had always had the run of the city's saloons, theaters, and red-light districts; but after 1900, a woman could frequent cabarets, restaurants, and movie houses without jeopardizing her reputation.[7]

Henry Canby thought he detected the first seeds of this change when he was growing up in Wilmington, Delaware, in the 1890s. Two decades before the sound of the car horn filled the evening air, the sight of bicycles signaled the sharp turn that lay just ahead. "When bicycles came in and flocks of young people wheeled through twilight streets past and past again the porches where the elders were sitting, it was the first breakaway from home, a warning of the new age." The bicycle, as Canby

*Or, as Linda Gordon has suggested, the girl could have been looking forward to a free meal: "Many independent women workers had to count on being taken out to dinner several nights a week in order to make ends meet."[6]

observed, was an instrument of independence and, like the automobile, could create new opportunities for intimacy. In 1895, the
Chicagoan Otto Follin explained that his friendship with Laura
Grant was "not an ordinary affair . . . it cannot be considered
as such because we are nearly always on our wheels and people
aren't what Laura would call foolish on wheels." But Otto and
Laura were not pedaling around the familiar streets of Wilmington, where parents sat watchfully on their porch swings; this
twosome was living in Chicago, where it was easy to be alone.
Otto described an evening they spent together:

We rode till half past nine and then we sat down to rest by the lake
and were all alone and I knew that I could touch her if I wanted to
and I did, just a little, and then I couldn't help saying something to
show her what I was thinking about and she understood it and then
we talked about it a little while and then we got up and rode away
and kept talking for about an hour and then we stored away the wheels
and the little girl walked the streets with me until about twelve
o'clock.[8]*

In Chicago, as in the Nanticoke Valley, one could observe the
"free association of boys and girls in their teens and early twenties" that Henry Canby remembered from his youth in Wilmington. Looking back from the 1930s, Canby thought that the
members of his generation owed their freedom to the fact that
"one met one's girl not in the transitoriness of a week-end, or
at the end of three hundred miles of auto road, but for long acquaintance. . . . She was one of a family and that family part
of a community which was yours." In Canby's account, young
people fell "in and out of love with never a crude pang of sex,"

*Otto Follin's reference to Laura Grant as his "little girl" was not unusual. Begin-
ning around 1880, couples began to use "little girl" and "little boy" as terms of endear-
ment. It seems logical that men and women raised in the increasingly child-centered,
emotionally dependent families characteristic of the late Victorian middle classes would
associate intimacy with the parent-child relationship and feel comfortable addressing
each other by a term that evoked the closeness and dependency of childhood. As courtship developed in a direction that inhibited the equality born of openness and candor,
couples may have turned to the more passive intimacy little girls and boys experienced
with their parents.

but other images of the 1890s suggest that the "free association of boys and girls" was not so sexless. After all, Otto Follin took advantage of his moment beside the lake to caress Laura Grant. In the small Indiana town of Warsaw, where Theodore Dreiser grew up in the 1880s, boys and girls were constantly seen "walking under the trees or rowing on the lakes, holding hands or kissing or whispering sweet nothings." Dreiser recalled that the town was "rife, in boyland at least, with stories of who was in love with whom, of who was going with whom, and those darker, more fiery tales of sweet trysts and doings in unlighted parlors and groves."[9] Still, whether out on the lake or in "unlighted parlors and groves," the young lovers of Warsaw were far more visible to each other, and to their elders, than the couples who a few years later could go for a drive in the country or to a movie, restaurant, or dance hall.

In the last quarter of the nineteenth century, some middle-class people sought to counter the forces that were pulling children out of the home. Young Americans had traditionally enjoyed a great deal of privacy and autonomy; they had been free to sit up late at night, to go on picnics, sleigh rides, to dances—all without adult supervision. But as they pursued these pleasures, they had rarely gone beyond the reach of the informal oversight of family and community. When this situation began to change—when young people spent their time in darkened nickelodeons, smoke-filled dance halls, and public tea rooms rather than at church socials or neighborhood parties—parents responded by increasing their attentiveness to behavior that still fell within their purview. The new forms of leisure presented both a stimulus to and an escape from heightened parental control. Autonomy was too firmly established for middle-class parents to feel comfortable monitoring their children's every move, but the world of the 1880s and 1890s seemed to require tighter controls.

The increase in adult supervision was evident first among the well-to-do, especially in the eastern cities. Even in the fashionable boroughs of New York, young people had moved freely, without chaperonage, in the first half of the century. About 1850, however, the arbiters of "Society" began warning young people to avoid "newly forbidden things" and to accustom themselves to the presence of a chaperon. By the 1880s, the chaperon had become an "unbudgable fixture" of the social scene in genteel circles. One authority explained in 1884: "She must accompany her young lady everywhere; she must sit in the parlor when she receives gentlemen; she must go with her to the skating rink, the ball, the party, the races, the dinner, and especially to theater parties."[10]

The "primitive custom," which had permitted unmarried men and women to go about together unescorted, still prevailed outside of big-city "Society"; but even there, young people were more closely watched than earlier generations had been. John Marean and Ina Smith kept company for a full year before her parents allowed them to "set up" alone; while in Muncie, Indiana, the 1890s were remembered as a time when "a well-brought-up boy and girl were commonly forbidden to sit together in the dark."[11]

Young people living on their own in the city had greater opportunity for privacy and mobility than their cousins in Glen Aubrey or Muncie or their neighbors who still lived at home, but their freedom had a price. Unconstrained by parental or campus discipline, independent city youths could, with an occasional nod to convention, go wherever and in whatever company they liked (and could afford). However, when they sought privacy, not in the din of a nightclub or the darkness of a nickelodeon but "at home," they often faced more obstacles to intimacy than they would have under their parents' roof. Even Mrs. Burton Harrison's *The Well-Bred Girl in Society*, which decreed that a girl have a chaperon whenever she was in a public place, recognized that at home a girl enjoyed certain long-standing privileges:

To lay down any law of restriction or limitation for the American girl with regard to receiving calls without the presence of a chaperon in her own home, from a young man with whom she associated by her parents' sanction, would be to revolutionize a state of things firmly established long before the political liberties of our republic had been secured.[12]*

When a young woman was not in her own home but in a rented apartment, boardinghouse, or dormitory, more stringent laws were in effect. In Chicago in 1892, Raymond Brown complained of the "ague-eyed landlady important with proprieties" who "separated" him from his fiancée (he would have preferred "a flinty old father or some Robber Baron of a brother"). And in New York, when Hutchins Hapgood wanted a woman friend to come to tea at his flat, "she could not do so without a chaperon."[14]

It was, however, not an easy matter to curtail the autonomy that young adults had enjoyed for well over a century, especially when the telephone, automobile, coeducational campus, and commercial leisure were all creating new settings in which people could socialize. Few middle-class parents attempted to monitor their children as closely as "Society" considered necessary. When a young woman traveled, especially in male company, she was expected to be accompanied by a chaperon (although one mother felt compelled to explain that, in insisting on a chaperon for her daughter, she was "not more careful than every Mother *ought* to be" [emphasis added]). But other than in fashionable circles, young people were rarely supervised on local, routine excursions. Ina Smith and John Marean were on their own when they attended parties, dances, concerts, shows, or ventured into Union or Binghamton. More than half of a group of Ohio women who courted around 1900 reported that they were *never* chaperoned.[15]

Even when chaperons were present, their role was often more decorative than protective. One midwestern college professor remembered a time in the early 1900s when he and his wife "averaged about two social gatherings a week during the season."

*Some parents heeded the letter more than the spirit of this unspoken law. Until the week before Frances Wheeler's wedding to Harry Keyes in 1906, "when the house became so full of guests that . . . there was safety in numbers," Mrs. Wheeler "always sat in the dining room . . . while [Frances] received [her] fiancé in the connecting library."[13]

But their duties were minimal—to greet the company and man the "chaperons' booth"; they thought of themselves as "guests." "It was a pleasant state of affairs, which brought us a good many friends and a good deal of pleasure. The young people seemed to like it," he added.[16] Indeed, the men and women who paid their respects to the chaperons in the receiving line may have welcomed their presence as providing a middle ground between the watchfulness of their parents at home and the complete freedom of the world beyond.

The college campus was itself such a middle ground, and between 1890 and 1920, its population grew enormously. In 1890, 174,000 students were enrolled in colleges and universities; by 1920, the number had tripled. Many of these students were women. A declining proportion of them attended women's colleges; the majority studied alongside men at land-grant universities, private colleges, and normal schools, although most co-eds were segregated into teacher-training and home economics programs.[17]

Outside of the classroom, men and women mixed more freely and with minimal adult supervision. Women who lived in dormitories were subject to greater discipline than those who did not, and women were in general more restricted than men. But there were limits on the ability (and the inclination) of college authorities to regulate student conduct. Especially at urban universities, where many students lived off campus, and where the city made it difficult to keep careful track even of those who did occupy college housing, collegians could lead a life largely free of adult control. A survey in 1900 of how women students were governed at six women's colleges and four coeducational universities (Chicago, Cornell, Michigan, Wisconsin) found that "very little social control [was] exercised over" those who lived at home or in boardinghouses. The report concluded that, in general, women who attended coeducational schools enjoyed greater freedom in every aspect of social life: "They are trained to depend for guidance upon their own judgment and good sense, and are expected to themselves control the details of their lives."[18] A dean might require women students to live only "in houses or flats where a reception room is provided," and reprove them "for spooning in the dormitory," but there was little she could do to keep them out of the dance halls and movie theaters.[19]

Even students who preferred mission work to dancing the one-step subverted college discipline. Many couples who met as fellow students would have recognized themselves in Madeleine Wallin's playful description of the beginnings of her relationship with her Northwestern classmate George Sykes. She asked him:

You remember . . . when you began coming to see me on Sunday nights when there were special meetings of the Students Christian Association or was it the Y.M.C.A? Anyway you ought to have been there, and instead you were up in my room, and sometimes you found it necessary to take off your glasses—the better to see the truth.

When George Sykes was courting Madeleine Wallin, he "ought to have been" at a meeting of the Northwestern Y.M.C.A. or of one of the other reform groups in which he was active. While Madeleine could tease George that he had "strayed from the path of righteousness," most of their classmates never took it in the first place.[20] During the height of Progressivism, when spiritual and social movements commanded a large following on college campuses, fraternities were already emerging as the dominant organizations—and organizers—of the "extracurriculum." The fraternity house was always more of a draw than the settlement house. The great expansion of fraternities (and the establishment of sororities) occurred after 1900, especially in the 1920s; but as early as the 1880s and 1890s, fraternities were shaping college life.

It was a life of teas and dances, rites and rivalries, sports and secrets. In 1904, the visiting board of the University of Wisconsin deplored the "seasons when the social life of the university amounts to an undesirable dissipation for all students." Since each of the twenty-five "secret societies" on the campus sponsored at least two formal dances, parties had become "too prevalent in the middle of the week." Not only were there too many dances, but the dances themselves could no longer be regarded as decorous events. Men and women had begun to forsake the "look but do not touch" of the waltz for the one-step, bunny hug, and other new dances that "allowed a lingering close contact." After 1912, a "mania" for social dancing took hold.[21]

By 1920, collegians were less interested in debating the causes of—and working to alleviate—urban poverty, municipal corruption, or the concentration of capital than they were in pledge parties, athletic contests, and the latest dance step. Rather than meeting at a lecture on public health or at a Bible class, men and women structured their social lives around teas, smokers, dances, and football games. One man who attended the University of Chicago in the late teens described the "social system of the undergraduate world" as "a couple of thousand young nincompoops, whose ambition in life was to get into the right fraternity or club, go to the right parties, and get elected to something or other."[22]

Parents watched—and worried—from a distance. Everett Baker attended Dartmouth College, in Hanover, New Hampshire; his family lived in Cleveland, seven hundred miles away. In 1923, Mrs. Baker was dismayed by a report of improprieties at a Dartmouth ball, but all she could do was send off a concerned letter to her son. In his reply, he insisted that only a handful of guests had behaved badly. "There will always be those boys who will invite immodest girls to house parties and who drink," he admitted, but he assured his mother that he had shunned their kind in high school and "didn't play with the immoral crowd" at college either. Finally, he declared that "a Dartmouth Prom is no worse than any other & the life here the rest of the time is a great deal more wholesome than any other college I know of."[23] Whether or not Mrs. Baker was convinced by Everett's arguments, there was little she could do about it; she might wish to control her son's behavior, but there were few opportunities for her to do so.

In spite of the rise in college enrollments, children who lived at home remained the majority of young adults, and sometimes their desire for autonomy produced serious conflict with parents. This was the case for Marian Curtis, who lived with her family in suburban Boston. After graduating from high school in 1916, she went to work as a card puncher at the John Hancock Insurance Company. In June of that year, she became engaged to Lawrence Gerritson, who also worked in a downtown office. Through their stormy six-month courtship, Marian struggled to assert her independence while still under her parents' roof.[24]

Sometimes the couple rode the streetcar together in the mornings; often Marian stopped by Lawrence's office, or vice versa, so they could have lunch or dinner together. They spent occasional evenings at the Curtis's, playing records on the gramophone or duets on the piano. More often, they went out—to the Modern Movie Theater, to the beach at Nantasket, for walks on the Common or along the Esplanade; and many of these outings ended late enough to arouse the ire of Marian's parents. One day Marian took a vocal lesson after work and did not get home until seven o'clock; the result was an "awful scolding." Later that evening, she and Lawrence went for a walk and "had a good talk. Another scolding," she reported, with the comment: "Am going to leave home." A few days later, Marian told her father she was going to leave home; but after he and Lawrence "had a talk in the office," the situation improved. Even so, when she and Lawrence broke off their engagement in November, she wrote "I guess I will live by myself now."[25] At eighteen, Marian was clearly ready to leave home. For a young woman like Marian Curtis, the city offered new opportunities for employment and entertainment; to her parents, it might seem a dangerous place, where their daughter was constantly at risk and in need of protection. The conflict was resolved when, in December, Marian and Lawrence reconciled. On New Year's Eve 1916, they eloped.

"The Folks are awfully nice"

When Marian Curtis clashed with her parents, it was because she wanted, and showed, greater independence than they thought appropriate. If they objected to Lawrence Gerritson, they never said so. While Marian may not have been old enough to be spared an "awful scolding" when she stayed out late, at eighteen she was old enough to chose a husband. And it was her choice to make. In 1901, the author of *The Spinster's Book* observed, "It is only in the comic papers that a stern parent waits upon the continuous caller and demands to know his 'intentions,' so a girl must, perforce, be her own guide." Even as parents sought to regulate the behavior of their young-adult children, they did not encroach on the process of mate selection. Thus, middle-class Americans continued to exercise the freedom they had enjoyed for more than a century. The woman who told her children in the 1870s, "When you want to marry you are to make your own choice and not come back home afterwards with any complaints" might well have been repeating the message she heard from her parents in the 1840s.[26]

But as young people spent their late teens and early twenties outside the home circle—in schools and colleges, in offices and settlement houses—they increasingly made their choices from among strangers; and parents might feel concern about the outcome. "How much anxiety parents suffer for their children," nineteen-year-old Annie Winsor reflected in 1884. She assumed that, even as parents experienced "constant anxiety," they would not interfere; they were "helpless . . . when they must let the child—now grown—act mostly for itself." She sensed that it was painful but inevitable for parents to see "all their advice and long experience scorned by the rash youth." But once the choice was made, the anxiety was at an end and parents could tell themselves that their children were "on the right road."[27]

While there were those who disapproved of (and doubtless some who sought to disrupt or delay) their children's engagements, most middle-class parents expressed confidence in the rightness of their children's choices. Marion Watrous formed an engagement with James Angell while they were students at Ann Arbor in the 1890s. Although her father had never met her intended, he was "quite satisfied that [she was] satisfied." Twenty years later, when Marguerite Thompson agreed to marry a fellow art student in Paris, it came as a shock to her parents, but they did not question her judgment.* She reported, "The Folks are awfully nice and want me to do just what I want to in such things—they say that they guess after all anyone I like must be all right (me being the precious & wonderful daughter of fond parents)." In September, with her marriage and departure approaching, her father was visibly saddened, but he assured Marguerite, as she told her fiancé, "If I care for you and want to marry you, he knows you're alright because he has so much confidence in me."[28] Occasionally, family members made inquiries about the character of a prospective relation, but even such minor intervention was rare in middle-class circles.[29] In spite of the wider world in which their children were seeking mates, parents did not restrict the freedom of choice which they—and their own parents—had enjoyed.

When Leander McCormick proposed to an Englishwoman in 1886, he explained that it was the American custom for a man "to seek the consent of the young lady first," then to consult her parents.[30] Although requesting parental approval had long since become a formality, it was one that most couples continued to observe. The usual practice was for the young man to call on or write to his prospective father-in-law. Many men agreed with the journalist George Sykes that "asking a man for his daughter is one of the unique and trying experiences of a man's life."[31] The discomfort many men felt reflected two contradictory feelings. As he approached his prospective in-laws, a young man must have dreaded the possibility that they might disapprove of their daughter's choice. But there was another dimension to the awkwardness a man felt as supplicant for a young woman's hand: he already possessed what by long tradition he was asking to be given. When Daisy Chamberlain explained to Horace Allen why her father did not wish the young lawyer to write to him, she observed, "He looks upon it as asking for something you already have—he thinks you have a certain advantage over

*Marguerite's parents did not appear to be disturbed by the fact that William Zorach was the son of Jewish immigrants.

him, I imagine." Having one's future father-in-law at a disadvantage could not have been a comfortable position for a young man.[32]*

Fathers found it difficult, too. After an interview with his daughter Maud's suitor, Wood Rittenhouse, a commission merchant in Cairo, Illinois, remarked on "how strange it had seemed to think of [her] as a *wife* for anyone—his little daughter." Mr. Rittenhouse may have concealed his feelings from the young man, but other fathers made their discomfort plain. When William Allen White and Sallie Lindsey reached the point of house hunting and setting a wedding date, Sallie insisted that Will have a talk with her father. The young newspaperman remembered the day he went to the stockyard where Mr. Lindsey was superintendent as "probably the most embarrassed moment of our lives." After listening to Will's carefully rehearsed request, the older man

spat desperately into the pen, turned his wide, sweet blue eyes on [him] that were watering, and cried: "God 'lmighty, man, God 'lmighty!" That was as far as he could get for a moment. Then he added desperately: "I don't know about these things. Why don't you go and talk to her ma!"[34]†

Although a mother was the person most affected when a daughter married, she was rarely the object of a prospective son-in-law's supplications. The ritual required a man to receive his bride's hand from another man. When he could not do so directly, for reasons of logistics or strategy, the young

*One young man reported a fantasy in which he took advantage of his future father-in-law in a dramatic and humorous way. When Gertrude Foster's father was in Chicago on business, Raymond Brown "went hunting him . . . with great elation. . . . My plan was to use my influence as a newspaper man to get my future F. in L. arrested and then go round to the Central Station and talk to him through the bars, as I had been horseback riding and was not in condition to meet him in open field. When he proved amenable to reason (my reasons) I would get him out again."[33]

†When Will White did as he was told and approached Sallie Lindsey's mother, she "took a practical view" of the matter and concluded, "Well, if you must, you must. Sallie generally has her way." Mrs. Lindsey had hoped for a better match for her beautiful daughter, but she laughed and said, "Well, Mr. White, I always told Sallie she would go through the woods and pick up a crooked stick."[35]

woman might approach her father on her suitor's behalf. In 1886, Ruth Huntington sought her father's consent to marry her cousin Archie Sessions. Mr. Huntington did not object to Ruth's choice (although he was surprised that she had not gone "farther afield for [her] love-affairs"), but he thought the couple should not become engaged until their prospects in the world were more settled.[36]

Fathers who withheld their consent or gave it conditionally generally cited financial or other external factors; like Mr. Huntington, they were concerned with a young man's business or professional situation. It was a mother who was more likely to perceive—and, in some cases, to create—emotional obstacles; and her role in the decision to marry was both less formal and less circumscribed than her husband's. One woman who was in the unusual position of being asked for her consent refused it on the grounds that her daughter did not love the man enough. It is not hard to imagine that had other women been formally asked to give their permission for a child's match, they might have raised similar objections, for many mothers were emotionally involved in the progress of their children toward marriage. A woman played a different part in the courtship of her male and female children, but in both cases, she was likely to be a more active participant than her own mother had been. In the last quarter of the nineteenth century, mothers, who had remained largely offstage in earlier generations, took supporting, sometimes even leading, roles in the drama of courtship. Although this quirk of casting was short-lived, it was, for a few decades, the norm.

Middle-class girls coming of age after the Civil War were accustomed to seek advice and direction from their mothers. Maud Rittenhouse, for example, turned to her mother often during her two-year courtship with Elmer Comings. When Elmer proposed, Maud, "laughed and cried a while, and then sent the whole letter post-haste to Mama telling her all about it and asking her advice." Two days later, Maud wrote to Elmer telling him that they were "too young to take any decided step"; she explained that she was acting "upon her [mother's] advice." A year later, with Elmer still in pursuit, Mrs. Rittenhouse continued to urge caution. Maud reported in her diary:

Yesterday while Mama and I were sewing together I told her all about it. She seems to doubt my love for Elmer and persists in asking me if I love him as well as I did Robert [her high school beau who jilted her], . . . and such questions as that.[37]

By the end of the nineteenth century, Laura Rittenhouse's involvement in her daughter's courtship was not unusual. As family size decreased, middle-class women were in a position to develop confidential relationships with their daughters. A woman with seven or eight children was unlikely to have time to involve herself in their adult lives to the extent that became common in the last quarter of the century. Now more and more young women looked to their mothers to help resolve the questions a courtship could raise. When Richard Cabot, a young Boston physician, declared his love for his close friend Ella Lyman, she wrote to her ailing mother:

I wanted to tell you that Richard loves me—perhaps you knew it before & it was easier for you to see than for me who was too close. . . . Dearest Mamma, I felt as if I owed it to you to tell you all and if you are willing I would rather no one else knew it. . . . You told me to tell you everything & now that I have you must not let it make you worried or I shall regret it.

Two years later, when Richard proposed once again, Ella asked her mother, "Do you think now dearest that I ought to wait or not? I feel first one way then the other & I want your help."[38]

If Ella had been a boy contemplating marriage, Mrs. Lyman would probably not have received such heartfelt pleas for advice, but neither would she have kept her distance. The last decades of the nineteenth century were a time when middle-class women involved themselves in the courtships of their male *and* female children. Positioning themselves at or near the center of their sons' emotional lives, mothers were at risk when love and marriage entered the picture. A son's decision to marry meant that his mother would be displaced from her "position as the chief object of his affection." William Allen White understood his mother's "inner fear . . . at losing the apple of her eye." Young men rushed to reassure their mothers, as Waldo Leland did, that the loss would be assuaged: "You shall not lose one single bit of me—but rather gain from my increased power of loving. I shall always belong to you . . . and never more than when I am promising to love honor and cherish the newest addition to the family."[39]

Waldo was, by his own admission, a "Mother's boy," but his mother welcomed his marriage to his long-time sweetheart Gertrude Dennis. "I'm ready for it any day," she declared in 1903. Other women had a harder time accepting a son's new commitment, especially if his future wife was a stranger. The young historian Charles Andrews, for example, was still writing weekly letters to his mother after he joined the faculty at Bryn Mawr. In November 1893, he became engaged to Evangeline Walker, a student at the college. Like most young men, he informed the female members of his family first. In conveying the news to his mother, he admonished her: "This is for you and Bessie [his sister] alone to know." Before their engagement, Charles had scarcely mentioned Evangeline in his letters, but now he was singing her praises. "I am more than ever certain not only that I love her for life and eternity but that she is more than worthy of that love," he told his mother and promised her, "You will know all this some day, for she will come into my life and not I into hers." Mrs. Andrews was not reassured, however, in spite of the fact that Charles's fiancée was an orphan whose only family tie was to a sister. It was not another *family* she feared would deprive her of her son.[40]

At first, she responded only indirectly to Charles's momentous news. When the Christmas holidays approached, she wrote her son, "It has occurred to us whether it would not be better for me to write to Evangeline and invite her here for a certain time . . . than for you to talk to her about it." Although Charles reported, "Evangeline agrees heartily with the plan as you wish it," he asserted his independence and informed his mother that he would stay in Bryn Mawr over Christmas and then come to Connecticut with his fiancée. This decision prompted the first direct statement of his mother's feelings:

I hope you will be persuaded to change your mind [about Christmas]. Little Charlie dear—you must let me down gradually—I shall get used after a while to feeling that your interests are elsewhere more certainly—as certainly as they ought to be—but just at the beginning I want you to myself for a little bit of time.

Charles, interestingly enough, felt "cheered" by this letter and agreed to "let some of the work go and go home on Saturday." He accompanied his concession with a statement of devotion to his mother:

I will never be the less to you now than before. . . . It is true that I can no longer come to you quite alone, another will now come with me, but I know your heart is large enough and your love wide enough to take us both in. Love for a mother is in no way curtailed in love for a wife and you must never feel even in the least that you have lost a son or that someone else has taken away anything from you.

He concluded, "Dearly as I love my sweetheart I cannot love my mother any the less for it."[41]

Another man whose mother felt threatened by his approaching marriage took a slightly different tack: Cass Gilbert told his fiancée, "My love for my wife can not be less strong or pure, because of the love I shall always have for my mother." Cass had gotten a painful glimpse of his mother's grief. Returning from a visit to Julia Finch full of wedding plans, Cass found his mother in tears. He described the scene to his fiancée:

She broke down entirely [and] wept as though her heart was broken and for the only time in her life she told me I was excluding her from my plans and withdrawing my love from her. Once having spoken, I insisted that she should keep nothing back from me and I learned what I had not suspected before, that she felt as though we had coldly passed her by in all our calculations and that she was left out in the cold. . . . Mother has carried this in her heart for months until she could bear it no longer.

Cass believed that he had not in fact excluded his mother, but he understood immediately what lay behind her tears. He explained to Julia that he and his widowed mother had been extraordinarily close: "More to one another than Mother and son ever were before. . . . I have been her favorite son . . . and now she feels that I am leaving her." Cass realized that his mother felt dispossessed; he told Julia, "she seemed to think you were taking me from her." Where Charles Andrews had asked his mother to love his bride as she loved him, Cass Gilbert put the responsibility on his fiancée: "Write to her and assure her of your love and win her for yourself . . . open your heart to her."[42]

After 1900, such close ties between middle-class mothers and sons would become less common, and such painful scenes would be more easily avoided. The intensity of women's emotional involvement in their children's courtships was not sustained. The twentieth-century mother was not such a dominant presence in the lives of her children as they reached adulthood (although, as we shall see, she increased her control over the rituals surrounding marriage). Sons might seek, and mothers might give, advice without arousing the deep feelings with which Charles Andrews and Cass Gilbert had to contend. In the summer of 1905, for example, James Laidlaw was trying to persuade the New York schoolteacher Harriet Burton to marry him. One evening when all of the family except his mother had gone to bed, he decided to confide in her. He later relayed the conversation to Harriet: "I told her I love you & had asked you to marry me & that you refused me many times & still kept on doing so." His mother urged him not to give up. "Well, she was lovely & we had quite a long talk. . . . She is fine, Harriet, she is *fine!*" Jim concluded.[43] He felt independent enough of his mother to use her as an ally in his campaign to win the woman he loved; he was not afraid that his mother would feel betrayed.

Women who came of age after 1900 were also more independent of their mothers. In 1913, the popular columnist Dorothy

Dix saw the situation as one of "estrangement between mothers and daughters" and judged it "a grave problem." She chastised mothers for failing to earn their daughters' love and confidence and for being overly critical. The result was that a girl was "miserably conscious that she and her friends fall far below [her mother's] exalted standard . . . and she protects herself as best she can by silence and by keeping her chums, male and female, out of her mother's sight." Not all girls adopted this policy of silence by any means. One college sophomore assured her mother, "If there is anything you want to know just ask because there is nothing I wouldn't tell you, you know"; but the distance between mothers and their young-adult daughters was indeed widening. Mary Elliott described the afternoon in 1914 when she told her mother about her intention to marry Harold Foster:

Mother and I had a talk yesterday it came about by our talking of some sheets I was embroidering for her. She said I had better keep them for myself I might need them some day. I said "think so." Mother said Nora [their hired girl] would say it looked like it. So forth and so on. She asked if anything had been said about it and I said yes.[44]

Why was the active involvement of women in their children's courtships so short-lived? Why did the pattern begin to disappear almost as soon as it took shape? Surely the women whose children married in the last quarter of the nineteenth century were not unique in feeling a desire to be involved in, even maintain some control over, their children's courtship experience. We can only speculate that the emotional climate of middle-class life in those years was particularly conducive to close, in some cases intrusive, mother-child relationships. Fathers worked long hours away from home; family size was shrinking; children remained in school, and therefore dependent on their parents, to a later age than ever before. Yet new forces were beginning to draw children out of these close-knit, mother-dominant families. Commercial leisure, extracurricular activities, competitive sports, and the open spaces of the city all threatened to erode the ties binding the home circle.

"Going Somewhere"

In this world of new possibilities and new dangers, a mother's involvement was an expression of a deep, perhaps universal, wish to keep her children safe by keeping them close. But the new world was soon disarmed by familiarity. If mothers had increased their involvement in their children's lives to counter the centrifugal forces of the time, it soon became clear that these forces could not be stopped. Children were going to go for automobile rides, frequent dance halls and movie theaters, join fraternities and sororities, no matter how close they were to their mothers. Young people belonged ever more to a peer society where parents had less opportunity, and less authority, to take an active part in the lives of their young-adult offspring. This was the context not only for changing relationships between parents and children but between men and women as they moved toward marriage.

"You will be water proof"

Whether young men and women spent their time together at fraternity dances or settlement houses, listening to the gramophone or watching a movie, their courtships differed from their parents' and grandparents' in ways both immediately recognizable and almost imperceptible. One concrete change was the telephone. Marian Curtis and Lawrence Gerritson saw each other several times a week (except when they were at odds) and talked regularly on the phone. Some days they wrote, spoke on the phone, *and* spent the evening together. The telephone was an important ingredient in their relationship. They used it to make plans—"Called up Lawrence and he met me and we walked in the Common"—or to make peace after their frequent squabbles—"Lawrence called me up tonight and I feel a lot better." (On one occasion, the telephone was itself the cause of strife: "I called Lawrence up and asked him to go to [Billy] Sun-

223

days with me. He didn't want to go and shut the telephone off which made me sore," Marian wrote in November 1916.)[45]

The telephone was more than a convenience: it allowed a couple to create a common life, even while they were living apart. In 1898, John Lewis told his vacationing fiancée Sophie Borel, "When you were here I could connect myself with your telephone and talk with you at any time. . . . The medium of the mail," he complained, "is not half so satisfactory as the actual presence and the medium of the telephone."[46]* A Chicago couple, Katharine Dummer and Walter Fisher, were not sure they preferred the telephone. Katharine once remarked that she felt "like Dr. Jekell & Mr. Hyde, one side living by telephone & one by letter"; and Walter agreed that "there are lots of things we don't tell over the telephone." Katharine realized it might seem odd for her to sit down and write a letter just after she and Walter had talked on the phone; she tried to understand why "the telephone which seems more intimate [is] in reality more formal? We say something just to say something & yet underneath are striving to make our voices bridge even with our eyes." Katharine and Walter gave each other mutual assurances that they "wanted to know everything" that went on inside the other's head, and they felt that some of those things were simply not suitable for talking about over the telephone.[48]

How many couples demanded and encouraged such complete openness? For most of the nineteenth century, the sharing of confidences had been important both as a guarantee and a measure of intimacy between engaged men and women. Now, in the early twentieth century, a style of courtship was emerging that inhibited candor and frankness. Increasing contact between the sexes did not necessarily mean greater openness. Cabarets,

---

*One reason John Lewis may have found the mail unsatisfactory is that Sophie's letters were unrevealing; he told her he wished they "might contain some of [her] inner thoughts & feelings as well as [her] outward existence in the world."[47]

Much of the correspondence of this period has the perfunctory, formal, superficial quality of Sophie Borel's letters to her fiancé. Even the paper on which letters were written changed: the large sheets of which earlier correspondents used every square inch were replaced by paper half as large, and these smaller sheets usually showed a large, bold hand, further reducing a letter's length.

dance halls, movie theaters were settings that lent themselves to sexual experimentation but not to emotional openness. Dancing cheek to cheek or sitting side by side in a darkened nickelodeon may have invited new physical freedom, but neither encouraged the heart-to-heart talking that had occupied couples in earlier generations. In the mid-1920s, Duncan Aikman reminded the readers of *Harper's* that "until about 1913, the rule for young couples was conversation in pairs about serious things. There weren't many cars, most movies were not approved of, church socials had lost their appeal. Couples would spend hours discussing each other."[49]

It was not only how and where young people spent their time that discouraged the mutual explorations of an earlier day. A growing emphasis on personality and physical attractiveness made self-exposure a risky proposition. "Catching" a mate had become a matter of wearing stylish clothes and knowing the latest dance step, rather than of demonstrating certain attributes of character. In 1920, Everett Baker reported to his mother that he "wasn't very favorably impressed" with a girl he met at a dance. She was "not especially pretty and didn't have much to say—that is, her 'line' was weak," he explained. At a time when young people were expected to woo each other with the right look and the right "line," candor and openness were outmoded virtues. This was the message of popular fiction, movie romances, advertisements. Even the marriage counselors of the period advised young lovers to "get over any habit of thinking that they must be frank and tell everything they know."[50]

Of course, many couples declined to break what had indeed become a habit of candor. Lucy Sprague and Wesley Clair Mitchell, who met at Berkeley where he taught economics and she was dean of women, were one such pair. Like many nineteenth-century couples, they "spent long days together [and] talked of many things." In the fall of 1911, Wesley reminded Lucy, "You have told me and I have told you of experiences and feelings of which we do not tell others." Lucy assured him, "I am not afraid of your discovering new and unlovely 'me's.'"

Quite the contrary. She explained, "I have rather ruthlessly shown you my worst traits in a sort of passionate desire to have your love founded on realities and not on dreams." The young attorney LaRue Brown was of a similar mind. After a motor tour with Dorothy Kirchwey, he looked back on all the mishaps and short tempers and declared, "I am not sorry . . . to have let you see whatever you have seen. I want you to marry me and I am unwilling to win you under false pretenses." But in the second decade of the twentieth century, Lucy Sprague and LaRue Brown were going against the tide. The desire to avoid illusions was increasingly submerged in the need to create and preserve them. Dorothy Dix told her readers: "What we don't know doesn't hurt us in domestic life, and the wise do not try to find out too much. . . . Nothing does more to preserve the illusions that a man and woman have about each other than the things they don't know."[51]

This advice stood on its head the ideal of openness that had guided middle-class couples in the transition to marriage throughout the nineteenth century. In the 1880s and 1890s, the necessity for frankness—and the danger of illusions—were still major concerns during courtship. The woman who in 1880 expressed her belief "in as perfect an understanding as is possible between engaged people" was typical; her generation thought it "a right & duty to know the exact nature of the future partner." Or, as one couple put it in 1894, "it is our duty to each other and to ourselves to be true and frank." Lovers not only had a duty to tell but a right to be told. When the artist Henry Bush-Brown sensed that his fiancée Margaret Lesley wished to hide "some of [her] passing feelings" from him, he urged her not to: "If you ever do . . . I shall be obliged to tell you I have a right to know them."[52]

The requirement to share "passing feelings" applied to fears and failures as well as to joys and successes. Henry had unburdened himself to Margaret already, and he wanted to continue doing so. He suggested that she become "a little duck and oil [her]self all over with faith and hope. Then," he concluded, "you will be water proof and I can pour my cares and anxieties all over you." Gertrude Foster made herself into just such an all-weather support for Raymond Brown. "Don't be afraid to tell me of any failures dear," she wrote in 1892, when his career was foundering. Sometimes there was no particular trouble to be shared but just a general letting down of reserve. "How lovely it is," one woman told her fiancé, "to write to you *just* as I think and feel, knowing you will understand and not laugh at me thinking I am weak and silly."[53]

But even while they believed candor was the best guarantee of happiness in marriage, many late nineteenth-century men and women found it difficult to meet their own standards for openness. The difficulty with which people had expressed their feelings in earlier generations had not diminished. The stability of middle-class society depended on the self-control of its members. Immigrants, industrial workers, manual laborers might require external direction and oversight, but middle-class children were raised to obey internalized standards. As they matured, expectations of openness and frankness had to compete with expectations of self-control. A young architect's letter to his Boston fiancée made the tension explicit:

I am very glad you did send me your downhearted letter instead of destroying it as you thought you ought to have done when you wrote the next morning. Doubtless a certain amount of self-control is desirable, even sometimes when it becomes self-repression, but it is good to know and share our innermost consciousness and we need more than anything else to get acquainted—to really know our own and each other's true selves.

Men and women alike suffered for their inability to express feelings and to control them.[54]

The experience of Howard Taylor Ricketts and Myra Tubbs, who met when both were students at Northwestern in the early 1890s, vividly illustrates this dilemma. In 1894, Howard wished he had "that constant self-control which can consider, appreciate and put in its proper place, every feeling and idea, and yet not be visibly affected itself, i.e., in an emotional way." But he also censured himself for not being more open with his feelings.

"Don't be as I am, a clam," he told Myra; "two clams would be a miserable combination." The feelings Howard found it most difficult to express were those he had for Myra. "When I tried to tell you how I love you," he once admitted, "I thought I was a kind of criminal and felt just a little as though I were confessing some wrong I had done you."[55]

The constraint was not all on Howard's side. Myra confided to him that "telling a real live man that [she] loved him made [her] feel guilty." She felt his maleness to be an obstacle to her openness. "When you can't say things to me because I am a boy just imagine I am not," he suggested. In a more serious vein, he told her, "You have a right to say anything to me that you wish—even if I am a man. I am more than that to you." Clearly, the boundaries between men and women account, at least in part, for Myra Tubbs's "vow not to express [her] thoughts and feelings" to her fiancé. She was honest enough to admit her vow and—with an apology for her "boldness"—to break it, but she had difficulty meeting both the standards for candor and those for emotional self-control.[56]

Howard and Myra's ambivalence may have been an extreme case, but the issues that troubled them are those that defined the experience of intimacy in the last quarter of the nineteenth century. Like Howard Ricketts, many middle-class young men struggled with the often conflicting demands for self-expression and self-control. Their struggle was not unlike the one waged by their fathers and grandfathers; it was simply more intense. Men continued to be torn between the need for candor in their personal lives and careful self-regulation in the world outside the home. Charles VanHise expressed his dissatisfaction with the results: "I have always so lived within myself, never having confidants that it [is] almost impossible for me to speak of my personal affairs to anyone." He added, "My reticence I know has often pained my mother, but I don't know how to regenerate myself." Another man reflected that "years of having no confidants" had made him "a pretty secretive person."[57] Male reticence was hardly new, but it was more deeply ingrained and more conflict producing than ever before.

"Going Somewhere"

For Myra Tubbs and other women of her generation, openness with men represented both a responsibility and a risk. Apologies for "boldness" or "unmaidenly confidences" expressed women's feeling that candor could be a liability for them. Although it seemed to Marguerite Thompson "as if one ought to be able to talk things over no matter what they are," it was difficult for her because she had "inherited a kind of frightful reserve that hems one around and which one seldom gets beyond." She finally overcame her hesitation and told her fiancé about her family and financial problems, but she worried that she would regret it. She had "never told a word of this to anyone before"; it was her nature "never [to] tell anyone anything," she explained. "Sometimes I feel I would like to but I never acted before on the impulse." It was only in a premarital relationship that many women felt safe enough to test the limits, and strongly enough to see the dangers, of womanly reserve. When Katharine Dummer acted on her impulse to tell Walter Fisher how upset she was when his parents objected to their spending the summer together, she explained, "If I kept . . . sitting on the safety valve all the time I'm afraid there might be an explosion some time and maybe that would be worse." Katharine revealed that she had once been "rather proud of the fact that [her] feelings never got the better of [her] physical self," but confessed that such self-mastery was a thing of the past. She allowed herself to feel the "hunger" that came from missing her fiancé.[58]

Although Katharine Dummer believed it was dangerous to keep her emotional "safety valve" closed, and Walter Fisher was of the opinion that "Life's best slogan" was to obey one's impulses, neither doubted that sexuality demanded considerable self-control. Walter wondered if what he felt when he wanted to kiss Katharine was "an insane desire." "If it's true then I've been out of my head several times," Katharine replied. But while she might declare it "the sanest because the most natural thing in the world," Katharine recognized that their sexual feelings—unlike their loneliness or disappointment—could not be freely expressed.[59] The sexual potential of casual relationships may have been easily denied or contained, but in serious court-ships, sex often proved to be an explosive issue.

"To spoon or not to spoon"

In June 1915, the year after Katharine's graduation from Rad-cliffe, the Dummer family set off on a long camping trip in the West. Walter was midway through law school, and his parents were opposed to an early marriage, so the Dummers decided that it would be better if the young couple spent the summer apart. Katharine described the result as "starvation," and both she and Walter doubted that they had been right to accept it "without revolt." "I'll be patient, dear, but I'm awfully hun-gry," Katharine wrote at the start of their separation. "If this hideous restless feeling keeps up I don't know what I'll do." A few weeks later, she warned, "If I get much hungrier I'm aw-fully afraid I'll start something." It is not clear exactly what Katharine had in mind, but in mid-July her parents relented and invited Walter to join them in California. Katharine explained, "If we have this . . . seeing & doing things together this summer with my family then we can have a natural good time. Things will be as normal as possible." If they remained apart, the sys-tem of sexual safety valves they had constructed might not hold. "If I only see you for two weeks in September with nothing par-ticular to do & the thought of separation again the uppermost thing," Katharine conjectured, "we may have more or less of a debauch, we'll be a lot more likely to do crazy things."[60] Katha-rine was not specific about the "crazy things" they might do, but she sensed that their circumstances made them vulnerable to a dangerous failure of self-control.

The conflict between self-expression and self-control was not limited to the sexual arena, but the stakes were greatest there. Men and women both experienced the struggle, but the strate-gies and the costs were different for each sex. A man knew that one of the tests of his manliness was the strength of his instincts. Late nineteenth century men were "to be counted . . . by the fire and vigor of the passions," and yet it was a man's sexual instincts that made him dangerous to women.[61] Even in an era of purity crusades and temperance marches, young men had easy access to red-light districts, to the excitement of the dance hall, the darkness of the movie theater, and, soon, the privacy of the automobile. Temptation was everywhere; self-control was everything.

If in reality he must be more restrained, in fantasy a man might allow himself unchecked embraces of the woman he loved. Manus McCloskey was a young army officer stationed overseas. His letters to his fiancée Sara Munro, at home in Pittsburgh, were full of expressions of physical desire for her. He remembered "the sand dune at old E.H. [East Hampton, N.Y.] where I could kiss your lips, fondle your soft cheeks and clasp you to my poor hungry heart," and thought about what it would be like if they were back there again: "I would kiss you and fondle you and hug you and pet you till you would be like a spoiled child and cry when I stopped." Manus realized that this picture might have less appeal for Sara than it did for him. "What if you should not like to be kissed so much?" he asked in another letter. His response would be to hold Sara on his lap and confess his love. "My eyes will plead so humbly and my lips speak so plaintively that of your own accord you will clasp your dear arms about me and cover me with kisses, calling me all dear names."[62] Manus McCloskey was unusually open about how much he wanted Sara; with thousands of miles of ocean between them, there could be no immediate threat to her womanly virtue or to his manly self-control.

When a man met his love not in imagination but in the real world of train stations and sitting rooms, he could not express his passion so unreservedly. Even when social sanctions were missing—when no onlookers stood on the next platform—a harsh inner voice told him that he must control himself. A young woman who pressed Theodore Dreiser to consummate their relationship found him unwilling. "I had not the wish. I did not think that I ought to do that thing then," he remembered. The radical writer Max Eastman recalled a similar reluctance in himself. In his dreams, he would "undress and ravish" one of the "free-hearted girls" he knew in New York, but in reality he "could not bring this to pass. It was not they who stopped me, for although captive to virginity they were not unwilling to be set free. The trouble was in the interplay of my own instincts."[63] As Dreiser and Eastman told it, the impediment to their first sexual conquests came not from the objects of their desire but from within themselves.

Because men could not always be expected to heed these inner calls for restraint, women were well advised to impose their own sanctions. In 1882, a midwestern girl reported a typical conversation with an ardent suitor:

I told him he might call another night soon if he'd leave *very* early and not expect me to stay on the porch alone with him when he leaves. He says, if I loved him as he loved me I wouldn't care for the whole world to know that he held me in his arms and kissed me good-night. But I told him it was highly improper.

If some girls appeared eager "to be set free," most women of this generation maintained a strict guard against the dangers of impropriety. A New Yorker advised her fiancé before a visit, "When you come up again, we had better sit on the piazza and be dignified. . . . there will be lots of things I will tell you 'you mustn't do.' "[64]

While the years from 1870 to 1920 saw a liberalization of the middle-class code of sexual conduct, it remained the woman's role to post the "do's" and "don'ts." In the 1870s and 1880s, the presumption existed that "nice girls" desired, and permitted, only the most decorous demonstrations of affection. Growing up in the 1870s, Mary Bulkley learned that "no nice girl was ever supposed to have her senses stirred. If she did, she was perilously near being not so nice." After the turn of the century, a nice girl might have "her senses stirred," but she still must keep herself in check. In the summer of 1906, Emma Lou Story was angry when a suitor violated her standards of decency. "I didn't think that you thought me that sort but now you know that I'm not," she explained. She could not approve of his behavior, but she viewed it philosophically: "Everyone has impulses now and then and I think . . . you probably had one and gave way to it without thinking. I haven't any doubt that girls have the same feelings at times but being girls can't give way to it the way a fellow can."[65]

What happened if they did? They sacrificed not only their chastity but their authority as well. When George Child went "too far," his schoolteacher fiancée was surprised and disturbed; but Sadie Treat conceded that her own actions—the "favors" and "privileges" she had allowed him on other occasions—had weakened her position. "I cannot say anything to you when I feel that I at this late date should think I ought to draw some indefinite [sic] line. I should have insisted on my own ideas long long ago," she wrote in 1890. In Wilmington, at this time, girls like Sadie who "yielded just enough for too tight embraces in the dance or permitted fondlings . . . lost caste."[66] Twenty-five years later, when, in the words of the columnist Beatrice Fairfax, "making love lightly, boldly and promiscuously" had become "part of our social structure," this equation still held. Fairfax reminded the readers of the *Boston American* that "the girl who lets every man she likes make light and facile love to her loses her power to kindle high and lofty feelings. . . . The path [to marriage and motherhood] should not be strewn with cheap emotions, light flirtations, and meaningless caresses which express casual desires of a fleeting moment." But even as she advised young women to maintain high standards "of dignity," Beatrice Fairfax acknowledged that they *had* desires. It seemed to her in 1917 that there was "no question with which young America is more concerned just now than 'to spoon' or not 'to spoon' "; and she recognized that, for women as well as men, the answer involved a conflict between inclination and training.[67]*

Although female sexuality was only beginning to win wide-

---

*Frances Dummer was one young woman who struggled with this question. "Is it wrong for a girl who has not been given all kinds of intellectual and other interests to spoon, if she herself does not think it wrong?" she asked her mother during her sophomore year at the University of Wisconsin.[68]

spread "official" recognition, women had been struggling to control their sexual feelings long before these feelings were legitimated in medical and popular literature. Mira Bigelow, Mary Butterfield, Annie Cox, and Lu Burlingame had all dealt with the consequences of their sexuality in the mid-nineteenth century when female passionlessness was the prevailing ideology. Although a more positive view of female sexuality was gaining acceptance, girls who came of age after 1900 were not spared the struggle against their own desires. Some women held themselves in check, presenting their suitors with an image of a woman devoid of sexual feelings; but as a courtship progressed, they often found it hard to stay within the narrow bounds of passionlessness. During the early stages of her relationship with Howard Taylor Ricketts, Myra Tubbs was so sexually restrained that she wondered if Howard thought of her as an "iceberg." He assured her, "You are a warmth I have never felt before," but realized that he was "demonstrative about some things more . . . than [she] really liked." Their relationship managed to accommodate the differences. Two years into their lengthy engagement, Howard wrote, "Sunday evening you'll give all the 'my kind' [of] kisses I want. Of course I'll not be selfish and shall give you some of your kind too." It took another two years before Myra kissed as passionately as Howard, who could then refer approvingly to "those good soul-thrilling kisses which we both like *now*."[69]

As far as we can tell, Myra and Howard's sexual relationship developed slowly and without much open conflict. For many other couples, the journey to sexual intimacy was marked by a series of steps taken and regretted, of leaps forward and sudden scurrying for cover, of resolutions made and broken. This path wound through the interior of the relationship, a landscape that offers little access to a contemporary observer, even less to the historian. In some cases, there are merely the hints that appear in cryptic diary entries; in others, events are rehashed, promises are given, confessions made. From the evidence that exists, it appears that the pattern of advance and retreat was widespread. In his autobiography, Max Eastman provides a capsule description. While he was in college, he courted a young woman who lived nearby. They "kept making high resolves against embraces and patching these when broken with still higher resolves."[70] The scene that was enacted and re-enacted over and over again between Max and his girl was the signature of most late nineteenth and early twentieth century courtships.

In the summer of 1885, John Ripley Freeman met Bessie Clark when both were vacationing in New Hampshire. The following summer and again in the spring of 1887, the young engineer traveled from Boston to visit Bessie at her home in Muskegon, Michigan. On March 9, John entered in his line-a-day diary: "Talks on relations" followed by a small drawing of two spoons crossed. Two days later, on March 11, he noted, "Swore off—confessions—solemn lectures." At the end of his March visit, John and Bessie became engaged; when he returned to Michigan at the end of May, his diary indicates that the couple's new status had not affected their behavior. On the twenty-ninth, they went riding and John reported "Behavior Good!" but the next day, he noted simply "Repetition of March 11."[71]

Bessie Clark's part in these episodes is unclear. It seems likely that it was she who delivered the solemn lectures on March 11 and May 30, but was she a willing participant in the spooning that went before? John Ripley Freeman's diary tells us nothing more of Bessie (until she appears in the next volume as "wife"), but other evidence suggests that many middle-class young women played a double role in the sexual dramas of courtship: they went along for the ride, although they rarely took the wheel, and acted as traffic cops; they both broke the rules and imposed the penalties. Take, for example, Gertrude Foster, a music teacher in Chicago, and Raymond Brown, the Connecticut-born graphic artist whom she married in 1893. Ray loved Gertrude "madly, wildly, even improbably for this day and age"; and when they were together, he had a hard time suppressing his physical impulses. He regularly promised to do better. "I am very glad that you do love me enough to forgive and forget," he wrote her in the summer of 1892. "I am very sincerely penitent dear and between us both I think any future bother can be avoided, don't you?" A few weeks later, he was feeling less sanguine. He wanted to see Gertrude, but he feared that if he came it would be "the same story—paradise for an hour or two that go like moments and then—a purgatory of unavailing regret." But Ray realized that distance from Gertrude, who made him "dizzy with feeling," was not the answer. "The only way to become an Athlete is by continued exercise, one never did it yet by staying away from the Gym because one couldn't do the Giant swing, and I suppose moral strength grows in much the same way."[72]

Ray counted on Gertrude to help him develop his moral strength. "Help me fight myself—my worse [sic] self that has so long had the mastery," he pleaded. Apparently, Gertrude could not always be relied on. In a letter addressed "My capricious Sweetheart," Ray teased her: "The girl I parted with [last night] . . . undermined all efforts to be proper, . . . alternatively scoffed at me and entreated me, . . . laughed and loved and disdained all in a moment." Another night, when Gertrude "hung over [him] kissing [him] with little tender touches," he could not resist the urge to "jest about [her] conscience." Whatever her actions, in her words Gertrude urged her fiancé to "be strong, patient, self-denying." Although she told him, "I want to feel absolutely certain that when you promise me anything, I can rest since it is kept," she claimed not to find his behavior worrisome; she did not think he should be "blue, 'on the brink of despair' about these things." Some of the problems would disappear once they were married, she suggested, and others would "be very much better." In the meantime, he should "work hard . . . it is the best cure for *everything*."[73] In most of their correspondence, Gertrude and Ray ascribed their lapses to Ray's weakness or to the intensity of his feelings for her; but on at least one occasion, she admitted that she bore some of the responsibility for their behavior. Before one of Ray's visits, she wrote, "I made up my mind that if I allowed things I knew I should regret that I should not allow you to come out for two weeks as punishment for myself. . . . The only thing we can do," she concluded, "is to practice and learn self control & self denial." (She added, cryptically, "We are not too old for that yet.")[74]

Gertrude Foster saw self-control as a skill to be mastered by women as well as men, but a woman was under an additional obligation—to help a man control himself. A man, who, like Ray Brown, could not restrain his feelings might suffer a "purgatory of unavailing regret" or label himself a "brute," but his manhood was not in question. It was, if anything, only confirmed by the power of his "animal instincts."[75] For a woman, however, the situation was more dangerous. If she failed to exercise her own, and to enforce her man's, self-control, she put herself—and her womanhood—at risk. The crisis that shook the relationship between Frank Lillie and Frances Crane provides a stage on which to observe a woman taking and then retreating from this risk. Frank Lillie, a zoology instructor at the University of Michigan, was teaching at the Woods Hole summer institute on Cape Cod in the summer of 1894, when he fell in love with one of his students, Frances Crane, the daughter of a midwestern manufacturer. In the fall, Frances returned to her studies at the University of Chicago and Frank to his duties at Ann Arbor.

Frances's correspondence while they were apart is full of sexual fantasies. Two weeks before Thanksgiving, she wrote, "My mouth wants to be kissed so much that I cannot make it behave and it's always tipping up just as though your hand were under my chin." While Frank was at the Cranes' for the holiday, Frances's fantasies were realized. Once again we cannot know the precise nature of their sexual interaction. Frances referred to "our big secret" which she had "buried . . . deep down in [her] heart to go to sleep" until they were married, while Frank viewed their visit as "a new bethrothal . . . a new bond of union, a new pledge of faithfulness." At the end of the visit, Frank told Frances, "My love for you was never so strong as now, and I never was so little ashamed at any aspect of it; for I have now shown it to you in every light and you not only pardon my passion but love me the better for it."[76]

Frances's acceptance of her fiancé's passion—and her own—was short-lived. Although Frank left her "quiet and peaceful . . . and more loving than ever before," a conversation with her foster mother Ellen Halstead "awoke all [her] fears and left [her] in such a state of uncertainty." Frances reported the scene to Frank:

As I was undressing my little mother said I'm so glad you are safe my precious child. I had never feared for you somehow, with Frank until Saturday night when I awoke suddenly at three o'clock and felt that you were in danger. . . . Even honourable men have been known to forget themselves and harm the girl they love truly even if they hated themselves afterwards. . . . You do not know how a man loves, and you must be very careful how you let Frank love you. You must help him too.[77]

Frances felt as though Ellen Halstead was her only "protection in the whole world" against Frank and, perhaps, against herself. She made him promise to control himself—"keep your hands just to hold me to you *nothing else*"—but one suspects that it was her own behavior, as much as Frank's, that frightened her. "I cannot resist your love," she told him, "but if you take it away, the strong kind that for the last week has frightened me, and made me so weak, and replace it by the protecting love then I shall be able to work and wait for you." She closed her letter by asking him, "Please don't write me any more love letters only the kind you write Millie [his sister]." This only a few days after she had pleaded with him to give her "not the kisses you give Millie nor anyone else just your kisses for your betrothed."[78]

In the face of Frances's ambivalence, Frank Lillie retreated. He conceded that Ellen Halstead had "said much that was true," but he believed Frances was "wrong in feeling frightened." She was safe with him. He assured her, "You have only to ask me (what you have never done) that I recede from any given position or privilege and I shall do so." Declaring that he would willingly return to the way things were before they had exchanged their first kiss, Frank calmed his fiancée. "I feel my trust coming back," she wrote a week later. "Even your unmanageable hands seem so dear. . . . I'm glad they're way off though. They're going to be very good and mind me after this, aren't they?" she asked.[79] When Frances Crane reasserted her right as a woman to control the sexual relationship, Frank Lillie respected it. He readily withdrew to a position of self-righteous restraint.

Not all men were so ready to retreat to continence. Delbert Boston, for example, was an Indiana barber who refused to observe his fiancée's limits. He told Ella Furley, "I wish I could see you. I do believe I would kiss you—that is if you didn't object too strongly." Ella was hardly an asexual woman. When she found herself gaining weight (during what appears to have been a pregnancy scare), she fretted to Del, "I'm afraid you can't hardly hold me. If you can't I'll take something to reduce flesh, for I couldn't live happily, if you wouldn't let me sit on your lap." Still, she obviously drew limits Delbert found too confining. He once told her that the date of his next visit would have to depend on her:

To suffer what I did the last time . . . is rather hard but Ella dear I cannot help it, perhaps you get mad and offended and feel hard towards me and think I have no respect for you—but such is not the case . . . but I have one little weakness which it is impossible to overcome.[80]

Delbert Boston made no effort to cure or analyze his "one little weakness," but Oakes Ames, an earnest young botanist with a similar problem, did try to. Like Delbert and Ella, Oakes and his fiancée, an 1899 Smith College graduate named Blanche Ames (no relation), continually pressed against the bounds of propriety. After one of what Blanche referred to as their "oh Naughty episodes"—this one on the windowseat in Oakes's family's house in Boston—Blanche "assumed a forced gaity for a time then bade Oakes a formal good-night and retired . . . to do penance for two hours." The remorse she felt was "entirely her fault." The next morning, the couple "talked of certain resolve": the "condition of old friendship" was their goal, but it was abandoned soon after lunch.[81]

Oakes was ashamed that he had allowed himself "to cry in [Blanche's] ear the dreadful dictates of a vulgar tendency," but he went beyond this conventional admission of male guilt. He devised a "strange and wonderful plan in his head, in regard to our relation," Blanche reported in her diary, noting that at first it made "little difference." She resolved to mark "every day that it continues . . . with a circle." (Unfortunately, if she kept a diary over the next few weeks, it does not survive.) Two months later, Oakes at least seemed satisfied that their "strange agreement" (which is never described) was working. He resisted the temptation to make Blanche "do something to prove that [the] arrangement really exists . . . I dare not, for the simple reason that there are animal passions which might rise and cause me too much anxiety." Oakes had succeeded in suppressing these passions, but only with great difficulty; and the result was a "strained condition of mind and body . . . a certain unrest which is extraordinarily peculiar." Like Gertrude Foster, he thought there must be something "in the intercourse of married life that brings balance of feeling." He suspected that it was a "physical phenomenon" and wondered if the "unrest" was not "due entirely to a resistance to the laws of sexual affinity."[82]

In his roundabout way, Oakes Ames was raising questions that would preoccupy the century just beginning. How did the "laws of sexual affinity" work? Did they apply equally to men and women? What were the consequences of breaking them? In 1900, Oakes's search for "answers that withstand the scrutiny of scientific investigation" would yield little, but such investigations were already under way in Europe and in a few corners of American psychology and medicine.[83] In the next decades, the work of sex researchers would have a profound effect on the attitudes and behavior of a wide spectrum of the American population. Havelock Ellis's first *Studies in the Psychology of Sex* would be published in 1901. When Madeline Doty, a young New York lawyer, sought to resolve her own sexual confusion in 1908, she could turn to Ellis's volumes on sex and to August Forel's *The Sexual Question*, published that year. Unfortunately, "the knowledge didn't help" her much. She was still torn by "an intense conflict between body and spirit." Madeline had fallen in love with the novelist David Graham Phillips, a man who "didn't believe in marriage for himself." Although she loved him "so much that nothing else mattered," Madeline found that she was unable to accept the relationship on his terms. She remembered one night at her apartment: "He remained until 3 AM without the ultimate union. Such a state of affairs could not go on. We agreed not to see each other."[84]

Oakes Ames's struggle to stay within the bounds of sexual propriety left him with "a certain unrest." It was only eight years later that Madeline Doty suffered "gastric attacks," for similar reasons, but the difference between the "oh Naughty episode" on the windowseat in Boston and the crisis at 3:00 A.M. in Greenwich Village was the difference between the nineteenth and twentieth centuries, between what had been in the past and what would be in the future. Oakes Ames saw his sexual desires as "the dreadful dictates of a vulgar tendency" which must be ignored before marriage and heeded only in moderation after. For Madeline Doty and her compatriots in New York's bohemian subculture, sexual impulses were repressed only at the expense of mental and physical health. The freedom of sexual expression and action which free love reformers and utopians had advocated in the nineteenth century was a way of life for the well-educated, iconoclastic young women and men who gathered in Greenwich Village before the First World War. They had "stepped out of the circumspect life of small-minded, mild-mannered communities" and into a world that scorned the conventions of bourgeois domesticity. Here, women could be breadwinners and men could be artists, unmarried couples could sleep and live together openly, love could be sexual, and sex could be playful.[85]

But even in Greenwich Village, where there was "none of the college-dormitory talk about the ideal husband," and where marriage seemed an "intrusion on the part of the state and society into the intimacies of a private romance," marriage exerted a powerful pull.[86] It was David Graham Phillips's unwillingness to marry her if she became pregnant that kept Madeline Doty from experiencing "the ultimate union": she could not bring herself to break the link between intercourse and marriage.

When the new sexual norms spread from bohemian circles to the rest of America in the late teens and twenties, the connection between "the ultimate union" and legal union remained strong. What had been reserved for those who were married became acceptable for those who were engaged to be married; engagement functioned like the safety net under the trapeze artist: it did not eliminate missteps and falls, but it minimized the cost of mistakes.

As sexual fulfillment became important to marriage, it became important to the transition to marriage as well. If marital happiness rested on sexual compatibility, a couple would benefit from sexual experimentation and exploration *before* marriage: thus, the increase in sexual expressiveness among the young in general and of coitus among couples who were engaged.[87] Opportunities were plentiful: the automobile, the movie theater, the cabaret, the coeducational campus had all become fixtures of middle-class life. The intellectual justification was available: the popularization (and misinterpretation) of Freudian psychology transformed sexual repression from a necessity into a danger. And the risks of pregnancy were greatly reduced: contraception was accepted by middle-class doctors and widely practiced by their patients, in spite of legal restrictions.

In 1915, Dorothy Kirchwey resisted the "combination of moonlight and physical attraction" so that she could come to LaRue Brown "satisfied in mind." Intercourse would be sweet, but it would be "all the sweeter for having been waited for."[88] Dorothy, born in 1888, belonged to a transitional generation. The first surveys of sexual behavior found that women born after 1900 were almost twice as likely as those born before 1900 to forego the sweetness of waiting. Dorothy's insistence on preserving her virginity made her appear "mid-Victorian" to her younger sister Freda; but to her fiancé, their discussions about menstruation, contraception, and sexual pleasure were "distinctly radical."* Both were right. By 1915, when this exchange

*Dorothy (b. 1888) and Freda (b. 1893) Kirchwey illustrate a phenomenon which appeared in the data collected by G. V. Hamilton in the early 1920s. Hamilton found that

took place, there were already many women and men—in and outside of Greenwich Village—who saw engagement, not marriage, as the green light for sexual intercourse, but they were still greatly outnumbered by those who shared Dorothy's "mid-Victorian" standards. On the other hand, in 1915, Dorothy and LaRue's approach to sexuality would have appeared "distinctly radical" to most Americans, especially to their elders; but within a decade, it would be widely practiced—if not accepted. Seeds were sprouting in the teens which would, when they flowered, give the 1920s the appearance of a sexual revolution.[90]

The First World War provided ideal growing conditions for this unruly crop. In the army, young men's knowledge and experience of the world in general, and of sex and contraception in particular, would transcend the boundaries of civilian life. One and a half million women joined the wartime work force, many of them stepping into jobs that were "men's work" in peacetime. Many others made more traditional contributions to the war effort—rolling bandages, nursing the sick, running canteens and bond drives, and entertaining the men in uniform. Under the "lure of the uniform," girls were "picking up soldiers on the street, going to shows and ice cream parlors with them, and gradually becoming demoralized," one reform group reported in 1917. At the end of the war, a study of the adolescent girl concluded that the war "wrought its greatest influence . . . in the field of sexual relationships." It produced "a vast emotional tension which tends to break the conventionalities and outer restraints."[91]

Indeed, the excitement, the dislocation, and the eventual disillusionment of fighting "the war to end all wars" did cause young men and women to abandon old standards of conduct, but for

---

couples born in the 1880s had a higher rate of virginity at marriage than those born before 1881 or after 1891. In 50 percent of the couples born before 1881, the women were virgins at marriage; the percentage rose to 62 for those born between 1881 and 1885 and then to 67 for those born between 1886 and 1890. However, a sharp drop occurred for women born after 1891, with only 30 percent virgins at marriage. Hamilton's sample was tiny—one hundred married men and one hundred married women—but the pattern it suggests is interesting, especially in light of the Kirchwey sisters' attitudes. Rosalind Rosenberg speculates that "greater sexual freedom meant, at least initially, greater sexual experimentation short of intercourse."[89]

many this was like discarding a pair of shoes they had long ago stopped wearing. Even in the tumult of wartime and in the "roaring" decade that followed, however, they did not reject the old rules entirely. A middle-class young woman might smoke in public, dance the latest jazz step, and spoon with the boy who drove her home, but she would sleep only with the man who promised to marry her.

CHAPTER 8

"A Season for Show"

Sᴇx in the early twentieth century remained the prerogative of married couples or, among the more adventuresome, of those who were engaged to be married. In spite of all the territory that had been added to the domain of middle-class youth, marriage retained its place in the social geography as the one setting in which sex was safe. No banners of sexual liberation were unfurled over the heads of the newly wedded; this was largely a tacit safety, recognized both in Greenwich Village, where it was scorned, and in Gopher Prairie, where it was sanctified.

There were other constants, too, in the late-Victorian picture of marriage. Although middle-class marriage was, by design and necessity, a partnership, there was general agreement that the partnership was rarely equal and all-too-often bankrupt. Women were still required to make the greater investment; and while a minority declined to do so, most accepted marriage as the natural, if no longer quite so inevitable, path to the rewarding role of wife and mother.

But the shifts in the contours of courtship could not help but affect the way marriage appeared to young men and women as they approached it. Marriage still dominated the landscape, but it was less heavily shrouded with sentimentality and cast a less ominous shadow than at midcentury. Between 1870 and 1920, changing attitudes toward sexuality and domesticity reshaped the experiences and the rituals surrounding the transition to marriage into a reflection of modern America.

"Concessions on both sides"

Even before they began the new century, Americans seemed to be leaving behind the ways of the old. Women attended medical school, lived among the immigrant poor, and took to the road on bicycles. Men learned to drive cars, built skyscrapers and steel bridges, and played football. But not everything was new. This generation saw no reason to alter certain tenets of faith: Marriage was the key to virtue and to pleasure, but it was a rare marriage that bore any resemblance to the ideal, an ideal that had changed only slightly in fifty years. Madeleine Wallin believed that "complete satisfaction was . . . the ideal and the dream when people are thinking of the infinitely solemn relation of married life," but at twenty-four she wondered if it was not "vain to expect that." She had observed many married couples and concluded simply that "part of the time it is nice, and part of the time it isn't, and you never can tell which way it is going to be." Madeleine reflected that "no one ever learns by the experience of anyone else . . . that marriage brings a thousand complications and trials." The century-old lament was familiar: Americans bemoaned "the great number of unhappy marriages we see on every side."[1]

To the informal assessments of marital unhappiness was added a new public preoccupation with the issue. Every time men and women picked up a newspaper or magazine, they read about marriage—articles on the "growing frequency of unhappy marriages," editorials on "the marriage problem," catalogues of the "disagreeable surprises which succeed the wedding day," and stories in which newly wedded couples had their ideals dashed by the day-to-day realities of married life.[2] In 1895, the editor of the *Ladies' Home Journal* decried the fact that "marriage has been made too much of a problem," and he proposed:

Let us keep complex questions out of it. Let us get it back to the simplicity of the days of our forefathers. Our conditions of life have changed, it is true, but the basics of true marriage cannot. Let it be what God intended it should be: the union of two confiding, loving hearts. . . . That does not make a problem of marriage. And if it has the purple light, as well as the pink hue, let us still leave to the young their ideals.[3]

Indeed, even as the polemical storm swirled about the subject, young people hung on to their ideals.

Like the couples who courted at midcentury, this generation subscribed to sympathy and mutuality as the basis of an ideal marriage. They agreed with Bostonian Eugenie Homer, who believed in the importance of "tolerance and large-mindedness" but cherished "far more the ideal of unity of thought and purpose." For Eugenie, "the thought of loneliness and solitude deep down in this relation [was] crushing." Along with many other Americans, she shared the vision expressed by a young college professor to his fiancée: "We'll think the same thoughts, have the same emotions and together work out our little tasks." Another couple agreed that "the ideal way would be to have all cares mutual." Madeleine Wallin observed, "It is the togetherness of the marriage relation that makes it blessed." She looked forward to "mutual joy . . . mutual forbearance, confidence, enjoyment and the mutual burden and sorrow" in her life with George Sykes.[4]

Madeleine was well aware that there were practical obstacles to this lofty ideal, but she believed they could be overcome by mutual effort. Twenty-five years after Mary Ann Smith had suggested "Bear and Forbear [as] the motto for all husbands and wives," Madeleine Wallin proposed a more active model. "Concessions on both sides are needed," she declared.

The woman should identify herself with her husband's interests, should be in every sense a help-meet and in no sense a deadweight, should renounce her pleasure when it is for the common interest; should accept her share of the burden. . . . And the man should see to it that in her zeal for his interests she is not wearing out her life; that she has some time and some money that she can call her own; should regard her as an individual with tastes, convictions, and desires as strong . . . as his own. He should accept the sacrifices and the efforts she is called upon to make in a large and noble spirit, . . . never treating her endeavors as a matter of course, but allowing her always to feel that she fills a large and recognized place in his life, giving her strength and courage she could not otherwise have.[5]

Concessions might be mutual, but it was as obvious to this generation as it had been to the generations that came before that "the sacrifices and the efforts" were greater on the woman's side. Social critics analyzed and attacked what women had long recognized as the truth about marriage: that it was perfect in the ideal but flawed in reality, and that it was women for whom the reality was most burdensome. Few men questioned this view. "A great trust is committed to a man when he accepts the all a good woman gives him," a New York man wrote to a friend. "The man's feeling is one of triumph, hers is one of self-surrender and abnegation. Hers is the nobler part," he concluded.[6]

The nobler and, he might have said, the more difficult part. Men and women alike recognized that women paid a higher price for the satisfactions of wedded life. "Marriage makes such a difference to me—while with you it's all gain," twenty-six-year-old Sadie Treat explained to George Child in 1890; "I must give up more than you." Saide did not "want to go into it as a sacrifice. . . . I want to be just as willing as you are," she told George, adding, "But all the same yours is easier." George Child understood "what an awful awful thing it will be for my dear girl to really have to surrender." He had heard Sadie's "old motto" often enough: "I don't want to be married. I can take care of myself."[7]

Women like Sadie Treat, who was a college graduate and a high school teacher, were better able to take care of themselves than their mothers and grandmothers had been. The numbers of women attending high schools and colleges was rising steadily in the last quarter of the nineteenth century; many educated women joined the almost thoroughly feminized teaching profession. Although less remunerative and prestigious than law and medicine (from which women were still largely excluded), teaching had become a satisfying—if short-lived—career for many middle-class women. Where their ante-bellum counterparts had looked to marriage as a release from the isolation and insecurity of school keeping, these women were more likely to see marriage as bringing an end to something they enjoyed. Many of them chose to delay marriage or to remain single. Of women born between 1860 and 1880—in other words, those courting between the late 1870s and about 1910—11 percent never married, the highest proportion in American history. And among the first generation of college women, the age at marriage and the proportion of women never marrying were even higher than in the general population.[8] Some well-educated women regretted the fact that, in the eyes of many men, college training made them unattractive candidates for marriage and motherhood, but others viewed marriage as a threat to the independence and self-esteem derived from a professional career.

This was the case for Harriet Burton, who taught school before and after her graduation from Barnard College in 1902, when she was twenty-nine. In 1904, she met James Laidlaw at a New York charity ball. A year later, he proposed and after refusing him several times, Harriet finally agreed to marry him. Harriet Burton "really cared about her work," but her wedding—"the fatal event"—would mean the end of her career. Only a small minority of women continued to teach after marriage; public policy (and prejudice) and personal preference acted to keep most married women out of the work place. The

Illinois woman who urged a young male acquaintance not to "entertain any idea of stopping" his fiancée's work after they were married was ahead of her time. Her declaration that "the old feudal time when a girl was a mere dependent of a man are gone. A girl doesn't belong to a man any more," was premature in 1892.[9] A girl might not belong to a man, but a wife still belonged at home.

A woman's experiences and achievements in the world could not be allowed to interfere with her devotion to her home. Typical was the woman who possessed "an unreasonable thirst for knowledge" but was "content to have [it] by proxy" once she married. "Do not worry over my defunct ambitions," a University of Michigan co-ed assured her fiancé in 1892. In a striking metaphor which suggests the destructive power of her ambitions, she reported their demise: "Of course, I've had quantities of them, but they are all deader than extinct volcanoes and show no signs of re-erupting." All women were not so confident. When Florence Finch agreed to marry her fellow journalist Allen Kelly "some day," she thought she "had fought and finished" what she called "the battle between love and ambition." Florence had "never envisaged [her] future without the accompaniment of marriage and motherhood," but when the time came to fulfill her promise, her "innermost heart" was once again the scene of an intense conflict.[10]

The battle Florence Finch described usually took place in the depths of a woman's consciousness, and the loser was quickly and quietly interred there. A more visible struggle was waged over another loss associated with marriage. Just as a woman extinguished her ambition (if she had acknowledged it to begin with), so did she surrender her independence. The emotional confinement of marriage made one Massachusetts woman exclaim: "Even if you loved any one enough, it would be imprisonment in a garden! How can you *belong* to anybody, *anybody!*" she asked herself. Margaret Lesley did love Henry Bush-Brown; but when she found her "freedom gone, [her]self belonging to another," she wondered if she had made a mistake in accepting his proposal of marriage. "Sometimes it makes my heart beat

with fear," she told her fiancé, who promised her, "In after years
you will find that your freedom has returned to you, not the
same sort of freedom of course, but none the less free." A similar
exchange took place between Frank Lillie and Frances Crane.
In response to Frank's query, "Would you rather be free?" Frances posed some equally rhetorical questions of her own: "You
wouldn't take my freedom from me would you? You don't want
to do anything else do you dear? You frighten me," she added.
Frank hastened to assure her that "marriage should not mean
less but in many ways more freedom."[11]

Frank Lillie was not specific, and Frances might well have
wondered what he meant. Perhaps he was thinking of the social
acceptance a married woman enjoyed. That seems to be what
Annie Winsor had in mind when she remarked, "One of the
main advantages of marriage is the right it gives you to live exactly as you please." The advantage, however, was available only
when husband and wife were "one in belief. . . . I will be in exact
accord with my husband or I had much better have no husband," she resolved. This idea was not a new one for Annie. A
few years before, when she was eighteen and teaching school,
she had written, "How infinitely better a loving helpful life
without a mate—free to think and feel and do—not cramped
. . . by a necessary unsuitable companion."[12]

There had long been agreement that a woman was better off
single than unhappily married; now there were women who regarded marriage, by definition, as unsatisfying for an independent woman. Ruth Huntington chose (temporarily as it turned
out) "a life of single blessedness. . . . It seemed to me," she later
recalled, "that the prospect for usefulness in the community was
broader on that basis than to devote my strength to the management of a house, not to say a husband and children." She would
have been sympathetic to the Indiana woman who planned "to
accomplish so much alone and single" and set out "to be a model
old maid." Newspapers and magazines were full of paeans to
the single woman. (Indeed, she was more praiseworthy, because
more useful, than the woman who married but contrived to have
no children). A typical one, written by Louisa May Alcott, ap-

peared in the September 1887 issue of the *Ladies' Home Journal:* "Spinsters are a very useful, happy, independent race, never more so than now when all professions are open to them, and honor, fame and fortune are bravely won by many gifted members of the sisterhood," wrote the unmarried author of *Little Women,* a year before her death.[13]

In spite of the recognition that all spinsters were not destined to lead lives of dependence and loneliness, and that marriage, even when it was based on love, demanded enormous—and unequal—sacrifices from women, most middle-class Americans continued to see marriage as the only natural and desirable state for an adult woman. A magazine writer complained in 1889 that "women are trained into the idea that their lives would be awry and unfinished without marriage." Indeed, few would have quarreled with the woman who wrote "that life, alone & especially for a woman, is not a complete existence, no matter how full of other interests and work it may be." But it was not just a matter of completeness; marriage also signified normalcy and health. Even people who advocated the higher education and advancement of women shared this perspective. Professor Harry Judson at the University of Wisconsin assured a recently engaged female student: "No avocation for a good woman is higher than being a good wife for a good man. . . . It is my notion that only abnormal women think otherwise. . . . In her heart of hearts no woman thinks otherwise," he concluded. The radical feminist Charlotte Perkins Gilman agreed that "all girls ought to [marry] unless there is something wrong with them." Often this was only an implicit assumption, as it was, for example, in the young physician Richard Cabot's observation that "a lot of nervous diseases and psychosis, and morbid ideas of all kinds, are peculiar to unmarried women and widows. . . . How often they all disappear like a shot at marriage."[14]

It was marriage, and only marriage, that completed and fulfilled a woman—a notion recognized even by women who defended and enjoyed the benefits of singleness. When Harriet Burton decided to forsake her "antimatrimonial principles" to marry James Laidlaw, she received many letters of congratula-

tion from former schoolmates and colleagues. "Let your unmarried friends jeer—it is their only consolation in their miserable state, and they are actuated by envy," wrote a married
friend from Buffalo. In fact, Harriet's single friends did not
jeer; they greeted her news more as a victory than a defection.
"I hope you will both be very happy and that you will prove
to any 'doubting public' that the best thing in life is your other
half—after all the scoffing at married life that we bachelor
maids indulge in generally," one unmarried friend wrote. Another asked, "How could [you] desert the ranks of Bachelor
women . . . when you have sworn that no man under the sun
would ever get you to pay allegiance to him," but she pronounced Harriet "a sensible, lucky girl to make up [her] mind
to lead a domestic life."[15]

"Our very consciousness in the matter"

A domestic life meant not only a home and a mate—which
some women found with each other outside of marriage—but
children as well. Women who remained unmarried, whether
from choice or circumstance, also remained childless; and if, on
one level, children represented the risks of marriage, on another, they were its greatest reward. In 1895, a young Connecticut
woman composed a poem of welcome to "the band of spinster-
hood":

> I am sure you don't miss anything
> Most women are fettered & chained,
> Just because of their fine wedding ring.
> But one thing does seem a mistake,
> The babies don't fall to our share,
> 'Tis sad to be always alone,
> They too would have much better care.

The next verse sings the praises of the new woman: "The college is open to us./ We're lawyers and doctors and deans" and

closes with the question "To join us why are you afraid." Two decades later, a woman who was in fact a university dean offered her answer. "The fear of being *only* a professional woman had clutched" at Lucy Sprague all through the years when she was studying and working at Berkeley. She, too, expressed her feelings in verse:

> Free! I'm neither daughter, mother wife—
> (But oh, this treasured freedom costs me dear!)
> And I who've welcomed other burdens, fear
> To bear the burden of this unbound life.[16]

Lucy Sprague wondered if being only a professional woman would be enough for her. Caroline Drayton was more typical; like the majority of middle-class women, she had no profession. She had her "causes" but felt "no interest in any one." She admitted, "I have *made* myself pretend interest . . . for all these charitable institutions." What she really wanted were a "husband and children which is the only true form of happiness & usefulness I (for one woman at any rate) am capable of." At the beginning of 1908, the year she turned twenty-seven, Caroline Drayton resolved not to worry about her situation: "It makes very little difference whether I marry or not & I must try to put it all out of my mind as much as possible." But her efforts were futile; hardly an entry in her diary does not contain some reference to her desire for marriage and children, especially the latter. In March, she exclaimed, "I do *so* much want to have babies of my own, and I do not see how I am ever going to be able to get any without having a husband first." "Oh babies, babies, babies. I just die of heart-hunger for one," she exclaimed a day later.[17]

As much as Caroline Drayton longed for a child, the prospect frightened her. "I would be broken-hearted if I thought I was never going to have a baby of my own, & yet when I am brought face to face with the realities I feel as though they were too strange and terrifying to undertake." Caroline Drayton named her fear but not its cause. What was it that made having children seem at once natural and strange, something to be longed for and dreaded? If it was childbirth that held the terror for women, few betrayed their feelings. As Mary Bulkley learned, growing up in St. Louis in the 1870s, "the risk was quite apart from the travail of childbirth, which all the young mothers took in their stride . . . and made no fuss about." The danger lay instead in the "indignities" to which a wife submitted. Sexual relations, Mary was taught, were "necessary for continuance of the race," but they put " 'nice women' . . . in jeopardy."[18]

Not everyone shared this negative view of sexuality. An alternative interpretation, which recognized that women needed—and enjoyed—sexual intercourse was available in the last quarter of the nineteenth century, and we know that at least some women adopted it. Dr. William Acton's oft-quoted assertion that "the majority of women (happily for them) are not very much troubled with sexual feelings of any kind" was implicitly and explicitly contradicted by medical experts, reformers, and women themselves.[19] Even those authorities who affirmed female sexuality, however, agreed that women's sexual needs and desires were different from—and in most cases less intense than—men's. When Dr. Alice Stockham published *Tokology: A Book for Every Woman* in 1883, she summed up the different views then prevalent: First, there were "those who hold that sexual intercourse is a 'Physical necessity' to man but not to woman." Second were "those who believe the act is a *love* relation, mutually demanded and enjoyed by both sexes and serving other purposes besides that of procreation." And third were "those who claim the relation should never be entered into save for procreation." Stockham concluded that the first view was the most widely held: "Physicians and physiologists teach, and most men and women believe: That sexual union is a *necessity* to man, while it is not to women."[20]

It is impossible to judge the accuracy of Stockham's assessment. Only the most fragmentary evidence exists on the sexual attitudes of late nineteenth century Americans; most of what we know is drawn from prescriptive rather than descriptive writings. One exception is the survey of married women conducted by Dr. Clelia Mosher between 1892 and 1920. Of Mosher's forty-five respondents, forty-three were born before 1890, thirty-three before 1870.[21]* For 20 percent of these women, "the true purpose of intercourse" was reproduction; most of the others indicated that coitus could serve for pleasure as well as reproduction. Only two women believed that intercourse was necessary just to men, while eighteen considered it necessary to both men and women, and twenty to neither sex.[22]

Mosher's respondents were all married when they completed the questionnaire. We can only speculate about how experience may have affected the ideas with which they had approached marriage. One woman in the Mosher Survey "thought reproduction was the only object" of sex before her marriage; but at the time of the survey, a year later, she believed that "mutual bodily expression of love has deep psychological effect." The novelist Frances Parkinson Keyes described what happened after her 1904 wedding: "Soon I was gladly conscious that I myself had desires and needs, of which I had not known before. Marriage was no longer a mystery but a revelation."[23] Frances recalled the "puzzlement and dread," the "dismay and doubts," which she had felt as a nineteen-year-old bride. She came to marriage with little knowledge of its sexual dimension. Her mother had not helped to enlighten her. Although a woman was expected to have "a little talk" with her daughter before she married, most women were like Frances's mother and too embarrassed to offer much information, and many "felt strongly that prenuptial revelations about the marriage relationship would sully a young girl's innocence and make her less desirable to 'the right man.' "[24]

The woman in the Mosher survey who "never *talked* with anybody on the subject" before her marriage in 1896 was typical. Only fourteen of the respondents indicated that they had discussed sexual physiology before marriage; of these, six had broached the subject with their mothers. One woman, married in 1882, remembered that her mother, who was herself a physician, "refused to instruct" her; another's mother "taught her

*Unfortunately, no comparative data exists for men in these early cohorts. The youngest men studied by Alfred Kinsey and his associates were born between 1890 and 1900.

that such things were not only not talked about but also not thought of." There were exceptions: one woman reported having a "very frank talk" with her mother; another had acquired "some knowledge from her mother and other friends"; but it seems clear that most mothers were like Mary Bulkley's whose "tabus prevented her from teaching her daughter about sex."[25]

As a result, many women approached marriage with little or no knowledge of its sexual side. The minister who advised young men that "many women, even at the time of their marriage, are totally ignorant of all questions relating to sex," may not have overstated the case; it was clearly not unusual for a woman to receive her first real "sex education" from her husband. Fully half of the women in the Mosher survey reported that they knew little or nothing about sex before marriage. One was "so innocent of the matter that until [she] was eighteen, [she] did not know the origin of babies."[26] Her only source of knowledge was books. She was one of nine respondents whose knowledge came solely from books; ten others relied on books as a primary, if not exclusive, source of information.

Those who consulted books might still come to marriage in a state of ignorance. Several who depended on books for their understanding of sexual physiology reported that nevertheless they had "very little" knowledge.[27] This predicament is not difficult to understand. While many of the marriage manuals available in the early nineteenth century had contained explicit descriptions of human sexual anatomy and even of intercourse, most of the works published after the Civil War were vague and incomplete. Even those that discussed menstruation, conception, and human anatomy rarely offered the reader much insight into the sexual act itself. Most cast their explanations in terms of plant or, at best, animal biology and presented a moral, rather than a practical, message.[28]

Women who received so little information from published authorities and from their own mothers had one other alternative to ignorance: they might turn to their fiancés for guidance. Although young men were urged from every quarter to maintain their chastity and come to the marriage bed unsullied by experience, it was assumed that even the most upstanding groom would be more knowledgeable abut sex than his bride was. However, few men felt comfortable enough to share what they knew with their sweethearts. Only two of the women in the Mosher survey reported that they had talked about sex with their future husbands; and while discussions of both menstruation and contraception do appear in courtship correspondence (especially after 1900), they were never common.[29] In *Ideal Married Life*, one of the few advice books directed to both men and women, Dr. Mary Wood-Allen insisted that it was not "indelicate" but essential that a couple discuss before marriage the sexual relations that would follow it: "The prospective husband and wife should study this matter with open minds and should know each other's opinions." Helen Swett and Ernest Schwartz, two Stanford students who became engaged in 1899, agreed. After a lengthy exchange on the subject of birth control, Helen wrote, "Unless the views of one of us change we need not discuss this matter further unless we both care to. For myself, I think it a very hopeful symptom that we can, . . . but we do not want to overdo this."[30]

Helen Swett had also raised the issue indirectly with her mother, and reported to Ernest, "Mother told me she hoped I would not place myself in a position where I would have to work when I was 'not in a condition to do so.' " In response to Helen's claim "that there was no need to begin raising a family until one was ready," her mother informed her "quite gravely that 'that was a matter some people could regulate and others could not . . . .' She herself never could."* Helen assured Ernest, "We will be able to keep our domestic relations well under our control, doubters to the contrary notwithstanding."† Helen Swett and Ernest Schwartz saw themselves as trailblazers. "There will be more cases to parallel ours in the future . . . than there have been in the past," Helen predicted in 1899. "Our very

*Another mother-daughter difference on this issue appears in Maud Rittenhouse's journal. "I have extreme notions about purity in the marriage-relation. Even Mama thinks them extreme," Maud wrote shortly before her marriage in 1894. Apparently, Mrs. Rittenhouse did not share Maud's "ideal of happiness . . . a white life for two."[31]

†Helen provided a hint about the source of her confidence when, after this conversation with her mother, she wrote Ernest, "I thought it better not to rouse her curiosity by making any boasts."[32]

consciousness in the matter is, I fancy, a modern phenomenon," she concluded.[33]

Helen and Ernest's attitude was indeed a modern—if not completely unprecedented—phenomenon, but it was based on a nineteenth-century assumption. Helen believed her immunity to "sex problems" was due to Ernest's unusually strong self-control: "It is because 'my man' is a man in whose stern self command I can rely at all times," she explained. What made sex appear safe to Helen Swett was the conviction that she and Ernest could set their own course and pace. "Where other people *drift*, we shall *steer*, and know whither we go," she declared.[34] Self-control had long served to keep couples out of the dangerous waters of sexual intimacy. Increasingly after 1900, pleasure would replace self-control as the guiding principle first of marital and then of premarital sexual relations.

In spite of the 1873 Comstock Law, which defined birth control as obscene and then prohibited the interstate mailing of obscene material, more and more Americans were using contraception to limit fertility. Participants in the race-suicide controversy, physicians, and the census takers all agreed that birth control was widespread.[35] The spread of contraceptive practices—the rhythm method, condoms, douches, pessaries—meant that couples could limit family size without relying on abstinence and *coitus interruptus*. The nineteenth-century middle class had valued continence as both a means—to smaller families—and an end—a virtue in itself; but as the century waned, the medical and moral benefits of continence were at first disputed and, within a few years, rejected altogether.* "The ability to enjoy sensuous things was tolerated, encouraged, even romanticized."

*A rare insight into the way physicians promoted their view of sexuality is furnished by the Philadelphian Mary Smith, in a letter to her mother. When Mary told her doctor, Elizabeth Garrett Anderson, that she and her husband of three years, the London barrister Frank Costelloe, were using abstinence as a means of birth control, Dr. Anderson lectured her harshly. "She said if I was *her* daughter she would warn me most seriously that such a way of life was wrong and wicked and all sorts of terrible things," Mary wrote home. In time, Mary Smith Costelloe, later the wife of Bernard Berenson, would change her mind; but in 1888, at the age of twenty-four, her response to being told that "there are plenty of other ways besides abstinence" was to declare, "It is *wicked* in physicians to give such advice to their patients. It is a fortunate thing I married a man who agreed with my principles—I think it would almost have turned me to *hating* my husband if he had wanted me to use any of Dr. Garrett Anderson's 'other ways.'"[36]

Marriage manuals published after 1900 took a more positive stance toward sex. By 1920, "more expressive, emotional, recreative sex inside marriage was almost universally called for."[37]

When Walter Fisher's parents insisted he delay his marriage to Katharine Dummer, the decision seemed to Katharine's mother Ethel "a risk of both health and happiness." A free thinker, Mrs. Dummer believed that "the contentment brought by the consummation of love is the right of these young people. In the sex relations great creative power is developed for art and literature." Ethel Dummer recognized that "the world would stand for conservative opinion rather than for [her] belief in Nature." "The time is not ripe for preaching these things yet," she admitted in 1915; but even as she wrote, sex was being portrayed as a "source of individuality, creativity, fulfillment." A 1912 volume of *Facts for the Married* declared, "No other state but that of happy and joyous sex relations can keep the world moving and progressing." Another adviser asserted that "the sex instinct has other high purposes besides that of perpetuating the race, and sex relations may and should be indulged in as often as they are conducive to man's and woman's physical, mental and spiritual health."[38]

It was not just in marriage manuals that young people found this new view of sex set forth. The explosion of popular writing about sex, especially after Sigmund Freud's visit to the United States in 1909, was impossible to ignore. In the years between 1905 and 1915, sexual hygiene reformers had, in the words of one historian, opened a "Pandora's box of sexual discussion." From to 1910 to 1914, magazines carried twice as many articles on prostitution, divorce, birth control and sexual mores than they had from 1905 to 1909—a level that would not be exceeded even in the "Jazz Age" years of 1915 to 1924 or 1925 to 1929. While almost 90 percent of these articles were hostile to the liberal trend, they nevertheless had the effect of opening doors long guarded by propriety.[39] "Sex o'clock" had struck in America, as a clever editor noted in 1913. Another writer hailed the "repeal of reticence": "Knowledge is the cry," Agnes Repplier wrote in the *Atlantic* in March of 1914; the sources of sexual knowledge for "the rising generation" were abundant and "astoundingly explicit." But while Repplier was glad to see "the conspiracy of silence" broken, she complained that "it was never meant by those who first cautiously advised a clearer understanding of sexual relations and hygienic rules that everybody should chatter freely respecting these grave issues."[40]

This increase in public discourse carried over to personal communication.* "A kind of healthy new frankness was in the talk between men and women, at least an admission that we were all at times torn and harried by the same lusts," remembered Sherwood Anderson.[42] Engaged couples discussed sex more comfortably. Instead of the oblique dialogues on "domestic relations" in which Helen Swett and Ernest Schwartz had taken pride, one begins to find direct and open discussion of sexual actions and choices. A particularly revealing exchange between LaRue Brown, a thirty-two-year-old lawyer, and Dorothy Kirchwey, his Barnard-educated fiancée, suggests that the new attitude toward marital sexuality was resisted by some people and welcomed by others.

When a "serious-minded young matron" presented "an extended homily on matrimonial matters" to LaRue, he gave Dorothy this synopsis: "Wives hate their husbands for months. Men are brutes. Women wholly unused to what happens. Men consider only their desires. Women find the whole thing unspeakably horrid because no knowledge or preparation for complete overturning of all existing canons of modesty and behavior, etc." LaRue doubted "how many wives hate their husbands," but he admitted that the woman was "fundamentally right" about "the conditions she described." Although he was sure that he and Dorothy were better prepared than many couples "to undertake the great hazard," he felt moved to promise his future bride: "I'll be just as considerate as my nature will let me." [43]

---

*At least one physician noted a marked increase in the frankness of his women patients in their conferences with him. "In the early years of the century," Robert Latou Dickinson wrote, "the patient was denying sexual experience." After the First World War, there was a "perceptible difference in sexual frankness."[41]

Her reply makes it clear that a more positive view of sexuality was taking hold. Reflecting on how well suited she and LaRue were to each other, she included physical attraction among "the essential ways." "I like you & I admire you & I respect you very very much; and my body wants to be the mate of yours, more & more," she told LaRue soon after they became engaged. In response to "the jealous and kindly young matron" who had lectured her fiancé, she conceded that "there is some truth, probably a great deal in all that. But it is not a thing to generalize about." In her own case, Dorothy expected—and hoped—that there would be no "inequality of desire or of joy in its gratification." She believed that it was "a little harder for a woman to know beforehand just how much that side is going to mean to her than it is for a man," but she declared, "I have absolutely no dread of that phase of our married life, except possibly a little inevitable hesitation on the threshold of any new experience, and aside from that I welcome it as you do, & look forward to it as to all the other sides of our life together serenely and gladly." But Dorothy Kirchwey went still farther. She took for granted that LaRue would be considerate of her, but she wondered why she needed such careful treatment. "Somehow I resent the idea that it is a thing that will be easy for you & hard for me . . . as if somehow it were a thing I had to endure—the eternal sacrifice & all that—which is wrong and absurd. I want it just as much as you do," she concluded.[44] We have no way of knowing how many women found "the whole thing unspeakably horrid" and how many looked "to it . . . serenely and gladly"; but as the first quarter of the twentieth century drew to a close, ever more women regarded marriage as offering them as well as their mates an opportunity for sexual fulfillment.

"The final end and aim"

In addition to these new forms of self-expression and intimacy, the traditional source of fulfillment—the home—remained central to the middle-class ideal of marriage. In 1905, the *Ladies' Home Journal* sounded the familiar refrain: "One of the dearest ideals [of a bride] is a home of her own, for home is her true sphere." There had always been women who had departed, out of conviction or necessity, from their "true sphere," and there would soon be many more, but most middle-class Americans growing up around the turn of the century accepted the traditional premise on which married life was based: home provided a man a retreat from and a reason for his work; home *was* a woman's work. A man made a living so a woman could make a home. "Our home will be our alter [*sic*]," Howard Taylor Ricketts announced to his fiancée in 1897.[45] The altar would be destroyed if men were too engrossed with worldly affairs to worship there. A man must not only provide for his home, he must *come home.* The image of a man returning home from his labors in the world had long been part of the middle-class picture of marriage, but in the last years of the nineteenth century, it took on new poignancy. The figure remained in focus, while everything else about the composition changed.

In Frances Crane's 1894 fantasy of how life would be after marriage, the climax of the scene comes when the husband returns to his wife at the end of the day: "He will put his arms around her, and hold her close to him, and say 'This is my very own little girl and oh! I'm so glad to get home to her.' " Twenty years later, when another young Chicagoan imagined herself married, her husband's homecoming was what gave meaning to her daily tasks. In 1915, Katharine Dummer was in Madison, Wisconsin, filling in for her sister's ailing housekeeper. As she was washing dishes, scrubbing floors, "wringing out greasy dish rags," she reported to Walter Fisher, "What I'm really thinking about is you coming home every night—forever!"[46] Frances Crane's reverie, set in "a little library with a fire on the hearth and a lamp on the table," was a highly artificial vision of married life. For Katharine Dummer, her husband's return home every day still represented the quintessence of being married, but her imagery was more down to earth: home was located in the everyday world of dirty floors and greasy dishrags.

Richard Cabot would have been pleased. In 1886, while still

a college student, he complained that "there is a great deal of talk about the necessity and desirability of 'home life' that is largely tainted with guff and sentimentalism." What the young Bostonian found even more deplorable than sentimentalism was the distorting effect of domesticity. "People . . . sometimes seem to twist the world around," he complained, "until the home, the place to which we . . . return . . . *after* and *from* our work . . . [becomes] the final *end* and *aim* of the whole process, the whole and not one element, that for the sake of which we do or ought to do all the rest." Richard Cabot realized that, as long as women were defined by and confined to the home, they would insist on its pre-eminence, and that it would dominate and, he thought, constrict married life. His solution: "Women have got to make themselves able to be real equals and companions . . . in the breath and depth of their *hold on the world* . . . which is what men have too much and women too little of," he declared in 1886.[47]

After about 1900, this imbalance, which had been growing steadily more pronounced throughout the nineteenth century, began slowly to diminish. As middle-class men found that their jobs were demanding less of their time and offering less gratification, they looked for other sources of self-worth and satisfaction. A rising standard of living and a shorter work week combined with the anonymity of the corporation to loosen, if only slightly at first, men's tenacious "hold on the world." While their fathers and grandfathers had come home seeking repose, these men sought interaction and stimulation. The mother remained the primary, even dominant, parent, but fathers claimed a greater role in the raising of their children. Although there was concern in the popular press about the effect absent fathers had on the manliness of their sons, many middle-class fathers were in fact moving back into the mainstream of the family's emotional life. The father maintained his traditional role as economic provider, which required him to spend long hours away from home, but there was less emotional distance between him and his wife and children. Women, of course, retained the day-to-day responsibility for child rearing—just as men continued to be the breadwinners—but the roles were less rigidly defined than they had been at midcentury.[48]

There was, however, a painful irony here: just as middle-class men turned toward home for the satisfactions missing in the modern work world, their wives—and children—were becoming less and less home-centered. A man's homecoming might serve as a symbol and validation for married life, but more men were returning to homes that had been empty for much of the day. Rather than spending her days sewing, the middle-class woman shopped for her family's clothes in department stores; rather than supervising the weekly laundry ritual, she patronized a commercial laundry; and rather than harvesting and canning vegetables from her own garden, she made daily trips to the neighborhood grocer.[49]

The smaller size of middle-class families also had the effect of loosening a woman's ties to home. The average number of children born to a white woman surviving to menopause continued its steady decline, falling from 4.24 in 1880 to 3.56 in 1900, and then to 3.17 in 1920. While every segment of the population registered a drop in fertility and household size, the change was most dramatic among the urban middle classes. The size of business and professional men's families contracted more rapidly than did other occupational groups. In 1890, business and professional men already had significantly fewer children than skilled or unskilled workers or farm owners: almost half had no more than two children; 60 percent had no more than three; and less than a quarter had five or more offspring.[50]

The increase in women's mobility beyond the home was not just a function of new goods and services or of falling fertility. A subtle change had taken place in the relationship between a man's work in the world and his wife's life at home, and the effect was to transform the nature of middle-class domesticity. In 1850, the more successful a man was, the more elaborate his household and the greater the demands on his wife. The fruits of a Victorian man's labors in the world did little to ease—and in fact may have added to—the burdens of his wife in the home.

If her husband prospered, a woman could afford carpets (which had to be cleaned), bric-à-brac (which had to be dusted), silver and silver plate (which had to be polished), an extensive wardrobe (which had to be kept up-to-date and clean). Even if the household included one or more servants, the result was to increase the managerial burdens on a woman. By 1910, the situation was very different: the more success a man had in the world, the more labor-saving devices and store-bought goods his wife could afford. Now her husband's earnings bought linoleum for the floor, indoor plumbing, a telephone, a vacuum cleaner. Although the impact of these changes was mixed—many "labor-saving" devices only raised housekeeping standards and shopping was a time-consuming task—the overall effect was to lighten the burdens a successful man's wife carried at home and to reduce the time she had to spend there.

Innovations in domestic technology and marketing were not the only solvents acting on women's ties to home. As the sphere of female benevolence expanded, middle-class women ventured abroad not only to meet household needs but to promote the public good. The transformation of women's clubs from forums for intellectual self-improvement to instruments of social reform enlisted thousands of women in organized campaigns against liquor, prostitution, child labor, and unsanitary conditions and for suffrage. Children, too, were less home-centered. Not only did they devote more years to school, they spent longer hours there as well. After-school activities occupied more and more of young people's time; and as they got older, cabarets, movies, athletic contests, amusement parks all offered stiff competition for an evening at home. In the 1890s, the middle-class home was still relatively isolated. "Neither radio nor phonograph brought the outer world into its precincts," Henry Canby recalled; but the new attractions of the "outer world"—commercial entertainment, political meetings, museums, department stores—created powerful centrifugal forces.[51]

When the world was seen in terms of the sacrifices it demanded of and the rewards it offered to men, home was venerated as a retreat and refuge. When the world became a place where men *and* women worked for wages, and where they played—often together—when work was done, the definition of home had to change. Couples courting after about 1900 no longer identified home with the transcendent power of marriage. Now it was sexuality, rather than domesticity, that united and up-lifted a couple. Discussions of home emphasized its concrete and tangible elements. It was the mundane details—an electric range that would mean "no smut on the dishes . . . no coal to carry"—rather than the mystical qualities of home that couples cared about; and even these aspects of domesticity seemed less important than they once had. " 'Cooking & keeping house' etc. are things we have to think about but they are things to not bother about & to not regard as the whole thing in life," Marguerite Thompson wrote in 1912.[52]

Marguerite's statement that she was not "one of those good housekeeping kind who make out the menus for the week on Sunday" was not an admission of failure. By the second decade of the twentieth century, there was more leeway and less invest-ment in the "how to" of homemaking. Engaged women might, like Mary Elliott, resolve "to work hard now on [their] cook-ing," but they would not hesitate to send their fiancés playful reports of "maple biscuits [which] tasted good but looked kind of funny," or—like Katharine Dummer—to sum up their cook-ing experiments: "None of us have starved yet."[53]

Shrinking family size, the presence of hired help, and the ex-tension of formal schooling all had the effect of reducing the amount of domestic training middle-class girls received at home. Frances Parkinson Keyes recalled that, in a family of "comfort-able circumstances," a girl might "make her own bed, do a little light dusting, arrange the flowers and sew a fine seam, [but] she rarely strayed into the kitchen, except to make fudge on the maid's afternoon off."[54] Such a girl might, like Frances, be "in-adequately prepared for marriage," but the result was hardly disastrous. It was no longer necessary for a bride to master the complexities of kitchen and dairy, parlor and pantry. It was more important that a man think his mate was good compa-ny—and a good lover—than a good cook. Domesticity no longer defined the essence of marriage. Companionate marriage was more highly valued than ever, but this companionship counted for more in the bedroom than in the parlor.[55]

The generation courting in the early twentieth century envisioned marriages that were more open to the world beyond the home than the ones of their parents' and grandparents' day. Where the nineteenth century prized marriage for the refuge it offered from the world, the young men and women of the 1910s and 1920s assured each other that marriage would not isolate them at home. As early as 1893, Franklin Jameson thought he and his bride would "have such happiness and delight, and amusement too, inside the house" that they would not "care much about . . . good times outside," but Sallie Elwell worried that she and Franklin would " 'settle down' into stupid old people at once" after their marriage. Three decades later, when a young businessman told his fiancée how much he liked the idea of "just being at home evenings with you," he was quick to add, "Of course, we'll have to step out now and then . . . just to keep us youthful."[56] "Stepping out" together was a new form of leisure. Married people need not entirely forsake their youthful pleasures for domestic confinement; the home was important to them, but it was not their "all." The realignment of home and world did not happen all at once. It took place gradually in the decades after the Civil War; by 1920, the middle-class home had become more a "base of operations" for the family than an altar at which they worshiped.

"Pulled in two ways at once"

For couples in the late stages of courtship, home was both their destination and the place they were leaving behind. The expectations of their families created powerful constraints on their behavior and prescribed a route to be taken from the announcement of the engagement all the way to the honeymoon suite.

On the day a couple revealed their intention to marry, they

acquired the privileges, and were bound by the conventions, of engagement. By 1890, engagement had become a distinctive stage in the transition to marriage—a stage with its own rites of initiation (the announcement), its own ceremonial object (the ring), and its own rules of conduct. Intimacy was allowed but, like everything else about engagement, was kept within lines demanded by propriety. Helen Swett wondered if it would not be better for her and Ernest Schwartz to spend a year "working tooth and nail apart to bring about an early marriage" than to live engaged in the same city. "How tiresome and exasperating . . . to have to preserve the outward appearance of a reserve we do not feel," she complained in 1899. As she saw it, they could either "conform or suffer a withdrawal of social approval and social 'backing.' " She explained to Ernest, "As a married couple we would be 'good' beyond any recognized social necessity, as an engaged couple we would be constantly overstepping the simplest social requirements."[57]

Helen Swett thought of her home as one place where she and Ernest "could disregard the conventions," but for many couples, the family was the chief arbiter of convention—and the source of conflict. Walter Fisher found himself constantly "scraping" with his parents; he admitted, "We all three make mean remarks in reference to the conduct of dependent persons engaged to be married. . . . When I am guilty, I excuse myself by saying that this isn't any of my infernal system." Oakes Ames railed against the "system," too, and resented the fact that he was forced to "suffer for the sake of appearances." When he returned from a trip to Cuba in January 1900, his fiancée, Blanche Ames, wanted to come down from Lowell to meet him in Boston. Her parents opposed the plan. "I entered one of the hottest discussions of my life," Blanche reported in her diary. Her parents prevailed, and she concluded in disgust that "being engaged is useless as far as privileges are concerned." Two weeks later, when Blanche's parents refused to allow her to stay overnight at the Ameses in Boston, Oakes was outraged. "It may be . . . the violation of all that is good in the eyes of Propriety or common sense, yet I fail to find out why," he wrote angrily. He insisted that he had "tried hard to learn to conform to the apparent laws of [Blanche's] house, but . . . cannot account for their existence."[58]

Oakes Ames could appreciate that his "being a man and all that makes a deal of difference," but he still could not understand, he told his fiancée, "why our little outings should give rise to such strong objections in your mother's estimation." His own mother had counseled patience; she had explained "that people differ radically in their views regarding engagements." Hers was that it was not proper for him to spend so much time in Lowell, although in deference to yet another convention, she allowed that, if Blanche's family had "no objection she of course can not have any." Oakes's sister added her opinion, too, announcing that Oakes "ought to go to Lowell just twice during each week." No wonder he longed for the time when he and Blanche could enjoy their "love and companionship without the dread of intervention."[59]

In families with less wealth and social status than the Ameses of Boston and Lowell—Oakes's father had been governor of Massachusetts, Blanche's a U.S. Senator—the comings and goings of engaged couples were not subject to quite such careful scrutiny. Nevertheless, engagement was generally a stressful time. "This way of loving under a constant if unconscious strain is not a good way for either of us," Helen Noyes told her fiancé in 1891. Oakes Ames suggested to Blanche that the strain came from "living as much in each other as in ourselves and our thoughts can not for any length of time be free from a certain unrest." While Oakes may have experienced that unrest more keenly (and certainly probed its causes more deeply) than most young men, the feelings he described afflicted many couples. An Indianapolis lawyer marveled to his fiancée, "Ours could not be the usual life of engaged people just antecedent to marriage . . . we seem so happy with each other."[60]

While men chafed under the restrictions of engagement and felt the strain of keeping their balance on the sexual tightrope, it was women for whom engagement was most stressful. A girl had to consider herself "quite unorthodox" if she did not have "some tremors and fears as most engaged girls have." Engagement fulfilled girlhood fantasies and promised the still greater felicity and security of marriage, but for many women, it was also a time of public exposure and personal doubt. "Such a public announcement . . . is almost as irrevocable as marriage," Marion Watrous told her fiancé to explain her uneasiness. In fact, what seemed to trouble Marion more than anything else about the announcement of her betrothal to James Angell was that it might *not* be "irrevocable as marriage." Once her engagement was public knowledge, the potential existed for public humiliation. "I haven't the faintest intention of going to Ann Arbor in state and then having you turn around and break the engagement," she told him in one of many only half-teasing comments on what she referred to simply as "the announcement."[61]

When a woman appeared with a man's ring on her finger, she declared her commitment—and her desire—to become his wife. Inwardly, however, her struggles might be just beginning. Only after her engagement, did Blanche Ames experience "a disagreeable realization of [the] responsibilities before me." Similarly, Dorothy Kirchwey's doubts came to a head when marriage approached. "I thought how ghastly it would be if I should find out I had made a mistake . . . and suddenly getting married stopped looking simple & easy & began to seem like a big & puzzling sort of undertaking with big & unforeseeable responsibilities attached to it & that frightened me." In their anxiety about what lay ahead, Blanche and Dorothy echoed the women of an earlier time; but there was a difference: Perhaps because they tended to worry less about their own fitness for marriage and more about the worth of the men they had chosen, these women found their doubts dispelled by the presence of their future mates. Blanche was reassured and comforted by her fiancé—"when Oakes is with me such thoughts do not exist"—and Dorothy observed that when she was with LaRue, "the trouble is pretty nearly all in retrospect.[62]

Although engaged couples were still tied to their families and subject to a measure of parental control, they were already intimately connected to and dependent on each other. "I am pulled in two ways at once and I do not quite know whose I am," Helen

Noyes complained in 1891. She belonged both to her family and to the man she was pledged to marry. By becoming engaged, she had taken a step toward him—in her own eyes and in the eyes of the world—and a step away from the bosom of her family. When Blanche Ames was separated from Oakes, she felt alone: "Now that I have known his sympathy, the family, though very dear of course, does not suffice."[63]

Not only were an engaged man and woman closer to each other than to their families; they also occupied a special status which isolated them from their peers. When Maud Rittenhouse became betrothed in 1885, she "wanted to be not like all engaged girls, but to have friends like ordinary girls, to be sociable and see that Elmer [her fiancé] was too."[64] For a middle-class woman of Maud's generation, engagement brought a sense of social isolation but also, perhaps as a result, greater intimacy with her future mate. The conventions of formal engagement united a couple, even as they hemmed them in with restrictions and set them apart from their peers. So united, most couples passed easily through the final stage in the transition to marriage. There were rough spots, especially when convention and inclination conflicted; but the structure of engagement provided support and stability. Some women still found the ride a rough one, but these tended to be older women who had delayed or had difficulty making the decision to marry.[65] Most women coming of age in this period had already lived or worked outside the home; they had traveled at least a short distance under their own steam, and during engagement, they had tied up alongside their future mates in the channel marked out for the passage to marriage.

"The last gun"

Although the close of courtship involved less emotional conflict than it had in ante-bellum America, there remained in place rituals and conventions that had developed to smooth the transition. They were thoroughly integrated into expectations of wedding etiquette; to abandon them would have meant going against the stream of late-Victorian society that flowed steadily in the direction of increasing formality, regularity, and structure. Furthermore, it would have created an impression that one's means were insufficient to provide what had come to be expected of a middle-class wedding. So couples who married around 1900 continued to follow the rituals that had emerged out of the social changes of the midcentury.

Engraved invitations were sent to guests who, upon their arrival at the church, would be escorted by formally dressed ushers to pews draped with satin ribbons. The bride, dressed now almost invariably in white, was attended by numerous bridesmaids as she proceeded to the altar.* Some couples, of course, were married more simply, at home, in the presence of a few friends and relations; but they were conscious that they were either too rebellious or too poor to observe the conventions. The latter was the case when William Allen White married Sallie Lindsey in 1893. It was, he remembered, "not a formal wedding." With a small group of their friends in attendance, they were married in the Lindseys' parlor and then "all sat down to a lap breakfast," which was all that the bride's family could afford. In families with more ample means or greater pretentions, weddings were rarely such modest affairs. The woman who referred to her approaching wedding as a "dreadful botheration" expressed the sentiments of many young people who saw themselves about to be submerged by the tide that would carry them to the altar.[67]

As the layers of ritual increased, so did the demands on the couple and their families. Guest lists had to be compiled—slights avoided, debts repaid; invitations had to be printed and sent; the church, the minister, the organist had to be booked, and cutaways fitted for the men, gowns for the women; the reception had to be planned—and all of these tasks

---

*In 1892, a young Chicago woman reported to her sister: "The bride was dressed in yellow . . . must have looked queer."[66]

presented opportunities for conflict. Tension between the prospective bride and groom, between children and parents, even between parents and parents multiplied along with the decisions to be made, the conventions to be observed. If parents lacked authority over their children's mate selection, they asserted it very effectively over the events that celebrated and legalized the match.

The autonomy children enjoyed in courtship seemed to disappear when wedding plans were being made. Julia Finch explained to Cass Gilbert, "I doubt if we shall have anything to do with the managing of our wedding, there are so many others to do it for us. If we are on hand to say 'I will' at the right time, that will be all that will be necessary." Julia seemed to accept this state of affairs; Oakes Ames found it infuriating. Realizing that "weddings are but the last gun that a family can fire off over the heads of children," he saw "clearly that all opposition is out of order and apt to create ill feelings if indulged in." Yet in spite of his promise to his fiancée not "to give advice nor . . . object to the arrangements you may see fit to adopt," he could not control his anger. He understood exactly what his responsibilities were, and he fulfilled them: he made up his list of people to be invited to the wedding, wrote to the men he wanted for his ushers, and set about looking for the gifts he was expected to give them. "When I have done these things and made arrangements for the music, I shall feel that I have done all you could expect," he told Blanche.[68]

While she was satisfied, Oakes clearly was not. He resented the fact that "all the older people are so set on making a wedding a season for show and noise," and was outraged that he and Blanche had to observe "one of the most ridiculous customs of crystallized society." Why, he wondered, could they not just "run off together and get married?" Although he bristled at his own mother's interference, Oakes reserved his greatest wrath for Blanche's family. They had been "considered in everything," he thought, and was disappointed in Blanche for having "conformed with all [their] ideas." Blanche was opposed to "the silliness of rice and old shoes and the assenine temprement [sic]

of people who indulge in such things at weddings," but she did
not take issue with her parents and their views of the wedding
service. While Oakes wished his fiancée would "brace up and
do some real kicking," what really irked him was his own pe-
ripheral role in the whole business. He rejected "the prevalent
idea that in arranging a marriage, the man is of no account and
that the woman is the only person to be considered." He found
it galling that "crystallized society" gave the woman "the set-
tling of such matters" and required the man "to yield gracefully
and without objection."[69]

This basic rule remained in effect through the first quarter
of the twentieth century. The bride was the center of the show,
and she and her family were in control. But among couples who
adopted a more companionate, less formal approach to engagement, the man was allowed a wider role than the one Oakes
Ames was playing when he checked items off his all-too-short
list in 1900. As she neared the end of the mountain of unhemmed
sheets that lay between her and her wedding to Harold Foster,
Mary Elliott exclaimed, "Its lots of fun getting things done. I
wouldn't be the man for anything. You miss so much." But
when faced with decisions about their wedding, Mary wanted
to include her fiancé. "There is so much to say and plan. Mother
keeps asking me about things I can't decide alone. The time of
the wedding and all," she wrote Harold from her home in the
Green Mountains. "I know you will say that its up to you but
it isn't entirely dear for you have some choice in the matter and
there are lots and lots of other things."[70]

But even men who were given an active role in the wedding
preparations found that there were limits to their
self-determination. Many men asserted themselves on the issue
of what they would wear, but few prevailed. They were out-
voted by the bride and her mother, who often seemed to have
all the power of an absolute monarch. When Harold Foster
balked at wearing a Prince Albert, Mary explained that her
mother did not "think anything else would do at all." She was
sorry that she could not take his side, and consoled him with
the promise that he would "only have to wear it a few minutes."

275

As far as LaRue Brown was concerned, even a few minutes was too long. "I do revolt at the cut-a-way for I don't want to be conscious of my clothes and I *hate* . . . the idea of being married in that scare-crowy garment." LaRue realized that his fiancée's mother might not understand: "I want to please [her] and I think we've gone quite a way in that direction but I certainly do want to duck that cutaway coat."[71]

Whether in the New Hampshire hills or the west side of Manhattan, the mother of the bride viewed herself as the final arbiter of wedding convention. This was the last scene in her daughter's life a woman would direct. She might have remained slightly offstage for most of the courtship; but it was her right and her responsibility to stage, costume, and choreograph the finale and to be sure it followed the script. Even couples who had been left free to find their own way to the altar were not allowed to improvise the final steps. They must observe the rules; and the more rules there were, the greater a mother's power of enforcement. Few young people chose to fight this alliance between social custom and maternal authority. Men might protest cutaways, and women might hope to avoid the shower of rice and old shoes, but most middle-class children accepted the inevitable.

The approach to marriage, then, involved a certain surrender of autonomy. There were things to be done, and they had to be done in a certain way. Presents, which were universal by 1900, could not simply be given and received. They had to be carefully chosen and just as carefully catalogued and displayed. Mary Elliott and Harold Foster were enthusiastic about a book "all numbered with a place for description, giver, where bought, etc.—and pages of corresponding numbers to tear off and stick on the present so there can be no mistake." This was the logical extension of the custom by which Florence Hemsley received presents in 1889 from school friends, old family friends, and "so many people from whom [she] did not expect any." Florence was the daughter of a prosperous Philadelphia family; but, by the 1890s, in country towns and small cities too, bridal gift giving had reached epidemic proportions. One woman reported on a bride's bounty in Corydon, Indiana:

The men in the store where [the groom] works sent them a set of dishes
. . . then others gave her dishes, water bottles, cracker bowls, vases,
she got three or four fine pictures, three or four rocking chairs, opera
glasses, table clothes and napkins, doilies, a fascinating carving knife
and fork, a lot of books and I don't know how many silver spoons,
. . . silver toothpick holder . . . and a whole lot of other things.

Even among the iconoclastic denizens of Greenwich Village,
the virtues of a traditional wedding were acknowledged: "That
way you get more presents," Neith Boyce was told when she
married Hutchins Hapgood.[72]

But silver spoons and opera glasses, cut-glass bowls and toothpick holders did not furnish a household. In fact, it was because
they were unessential items that they were considered suitable
wedding presents. Parents and other relatives who could afford
to gave their children money, but otherwise most gifts were of
little use to a couple just setting up house. They would have to
supply the necessities themselves, but first they had to arrive at
some understanding of what these might be. Like the young
physician who made "the round of all [his] newly married acquaintances," engaged couples interrogated their friends, studied their parents' households, and consulted the popular press.
In July 1899, Helen Swett urged her fiancé to read an article in
Cosmopolitan on "the Ideal and Practical Organization of a
Home." She suggested that the estimates the author offered
might be a "convenient basis . . . to reckon up our probable
expenses upon."[73]

In the process of "reckoning" their expenses, people revealed
the approach to domestic decisions that would characterize at
least the beginning of their married life. Many couples found
that they could collaborate on their household in a way that they
could not on their wedding.[74] There were interfering parents,
of course, but generally an engaged man and woman negotiated
the details of their living arrangements between themselves.
This involved a complex calculus of expense, taste, and convenience, which varied according to a couple's circumstances.

When Harold Foster and Mary Elliott were deciding where
to live after their marriage, Harold sent Mary regular reports

on the various possibilities. "It is nice to hear all about them and also nice to leave all the deciding to you," Mary wrote in May 1915. But she was hardly leaving it all to him. She was quick to tell Harold when a house sounded too small, or too hard to heat, or to reject the idea of a furnished apartment. It was his job to find them a house they could afford, but he would have plenty of help from her. Likewise, it was her role to select the furnishings, but because she wanted Harold to have a say, they both went to inspect the furnished rooms at Jordan's department store in Boston. On the question of kitchen appliances, Mary made sure Harold knew the virtues of electric ranges—"they are not much more expensive than coal stoves . . . and it would be wonderful if it was practical"; but she agreed with him that the cost of electricity exceeded their budget. Mary left the final decision about *where* they would live to Harold, since it was largly a question of what they could afford on his salary; she expected him to let her control *how* they would live, since that was a matter of household management. "As to finances . . . don't you worry dear man about this side of it. . . . I am going to be a wonder."[75]

Even for a woman who could have anything she wanted, "without thinking for a moment whether she can afford it or not," there were still countless choices to be made.* When Helen James and Harry Sommers, the son of a wealthy St. Paul

*One item of furniture required by every married couple was a bed, and beginning in the 1910s, some newlyweds chose twin beds rather than the traditional double bed. Because twin beds represented a break both with long-standing custom and with the movement toward acceptance and affirmation of marital sexuality, they present something of a paradox. The explanation for their popularity may lie in several directions: First, by allowing a husband and wife greater personal space than a double bed, twin beds satisfied the growing desire for personal space. Second, twin beds may have been an expression of "domestic feminism." Sleeping in her own bed may have contributed to a woman's sense that she was in control of the sexual dimension of her marriage. Third, it may be that twin beds appealed to some couples who wished to demonstrate that, although they may have enjoyed sex and considered it important, they were not in any danger of being carried away by it. Finally, twin beds may have been a form of conspicuous consumption. Two beds cost more and required more floor space than a double bed. Furthermore, as objects that would have been alien in an immigrant household, twin beds were testimony to a couple's membership in the all-American middle class. Further research to establish the extent and nature of the market for twin beds is needed before these hypotheses or others can be confirmed.

merchant, were married in 1909, both participated in finding and furnishing their first house. But the collaboration was on Helen's terms: "Harry and I are working everything out together," the bride reported to her sister a month after the wedding; "he is lovely about everything and adopts my ways without protest." Helen had only recently discovered that she *had* ways of doing things: "I am amazed at how absorbed I am in the decorating, because I never cared about a house and its details at all before I was married."[76]

Women were not, however, the only ones who cared about "a house and its details." While all men were expected to be concerned about how much things cost, some also attended to how things looked. Walter Teller Post, for example, was a poorly paid clerk for the Northern Pacific Railroad in St. Paul when he married Lillie Carl in 1894. They began their married life at Walter's old boarding place, but within a few weeks, they had rented a house and were shopping at the downtown department stores for furniture. Walter was more attentive than Lillie to the advantages of ingrained carpeting and to the rage for all things oak; he took equal pride in the appearance of his "real cozy and pretty house" and in the financial arrangements that lay behind it. Walter was the more status-conscious and extravagant of the pair; here was a wife who restrained a husband from purchases that were beyond their means. On Lillie's insistence, they furnished their parlor only with rocking chairs: "a handsome polished and carved oak $7.25, a rattan $4.95, 1 upholstered $3.95." Walter was disappointed but, on this occasion, he deferred to Lillie's judgment. "That is all we will have in the parlor, until we get rich enough to have more," he concluded. Walter's father responded by suggesting that his son turn his pay packet over to Lillie, who he felt sure would spend it more sensibly. Walter rejected the idea out of hand: "Lillie knew before I married her what I thought about all that. She does not believe it either. I buy all the groceries, etc," he replied indignantly.[77] While it was clear that husbands earned the money and that wives maintained the household, there was, within those well-defined boundaries, great variety in the way middle-class couples made and implemented domestic decisions; and this variety was in evidence at the very outset of a marriage.

Another decision that a couple had to make in the last weeks before the wedding concerned the bridal trip, or honeymoon as it was now called. The route was no longer determined by visits to family and friends; the bridal tour had lost its communal basis. Rather than an affirmation of family and community ties, it had become a rite of initiation for the couple as a self-contained, sexually complete unit. By the close of the nineteenth century, the common practice was for newly wedded couples to disappear to some romantic—and secret—destination. It was not good taste to ask where the honeymooners would be, according to one 1886 adviser. Indeed, when Charles Andrews revealed the itinerary for his bridal trip to Lake Champlain in 1895, he instructed his mother, "You must not give it away."[78] The secrecy surrounding post-wedding plans ensured privacy for what had once been a highly public ritual.

If the bridal tour had been a time for newlyweds to affirm their ties to others, the honeymoon was a time for consummating—literally—their tie to each other.* At least one writer detected a "great and generally unrecognized source of danger to wedded happiness" in the isolation and sexual indulgence of the honeymoon. The problem, Dr. Mary Wood-Allen suggested in *Ideal Married Life*, was the same one faced by the new clerk in the candy store:

---

*Most advisers suggested that wedding dates be chosen to coincide with the least fertile part of a woman's menstrual cycle. However, as late as the end of the nineteenth century, most lay and medical writers misunderstood the timing of ovulation and considered the safe period as falling in the middle—and, in fact, most fertile—part of the cycle. One physician who did not share in the common misconception was George Napheys, who advised newlyweds to arrange things so that "one profound change should not too quickly succeed the other."[79] By the 1910s and 1920s, some couples began to discuss the woman's menstrual cycle as a factor in the scheduling of the wedding, although it is not entirely clear whether they were seeking to avoid the embarrassment or the inconvenience a woman may have felt at having her period during her honeymoon, or to ensure that the honeymoon would fall during what they believed was the time of natural infertility.[80]

"A Season for Show"

Young married people, during the honeymoon, away from friendly association, with no occupation, wholly dependent on each other for society, cloy themselves with sweetness; they are satiated with caresses; they have exhausted their mental resources; they have possibly worn themselves out with sexual excess, and imagine they have made a mistake and do not love each other.[81]

The sexual agenda of the honeymoon was an explicit concern of advice books beginning in the 1870s. Even those writers who treated the matter in the abstract, often imponderable, terms favored by marriage manuals stressed the importance of the wedding night for the success of the marriage. They sketched a uniformly alarming scene. In the popular *The Physical Life of Woman*, George Napheys advised his readers that "more or less suffering" accompanied "the initiation into marriage." Eliza Duffey's *What Women Should Know* explained that "the consummation of marriage is frequently attended with inconvenience, and even physical prostration." It was not just women who received such uninviting glimpses of the sexual transition to marriage. Sylvanus Stall warned young men that "scores of wives . . . annually confess to their physicians that the only rape that was ever committed upon them was by their own husband the first day of married life." Husbands were widely denounced for their "brutal and impulsive behavior . . . on honeymoons."[82]

No wonder Waldo Leland worked himself into such a state about when and where he and Gertrude Dennis would spend their first night together. "Confound it all. I get so mad when I try to think out the best way of doing it," the young teacher exclaimed in March 1902. If they went to a hotel after the reception, they would "look foolish and . . . feel sort of queer" when they came back to the house the next day to finish packing and say good-bye. On the other hand, he felt sure that Gertrude would not want to spend the night with him at her home or his, so he proposed that each of them sleep in their own beds that night. That way they "would have plenty of time to get a little rested and . . . needn't feel at all embarrassed the next morning." For Waldo, the problem was how to avoid the embarrassment of facing family and friends after the first night together. Dr. Mary Wood-Allen questioned why a couple should "at the very outset of their new and untried life together . . . be sent out into the world among the prying eyes of strangers," but Waldo preferred the anonymity of the journey to the scrutiny of his family.[83]

Men and women understood that they were *supposed* to be scared; it was as much a part of the wedding ritual as rice and cake. When Gertrude Foster imagined herself and new husband driving away from their wedding, "holding each other's hands and feeling very happy," she corrected herself. "No, I forgot, you will be scared—I alone will be happy. I wonder if I will try to make you less frightened," she wrote to Ray Brown. Ray was amused by "the idea of a mans getting scared, and the girls comforting him at such a time." He admitted that he might "be a bit nervous," but he doubted that Gertrude would be much calmer when the day arrived. Two weeks before his wedding, Waldo Leland admitted, thinking perhaps of the wedding night, "I pretend to feel sort of scared and nervous, but I truly don't—only glad and impatient." He and his bride had known each other since high school, and for Waldo, their marriage was "just a step further in the direction we have long been traveling together. There are no doubts, no fears, no hesitancy, as I look ahead."[84]

Whether or not Waldo Leland was unusually confident on the eve of his wedding, young people who married around the turn of the century do seem to have approached their wedding day more with nervousness than real fearfulness. After 1890, marriage appeared a less fearsome prospect than it had for most of the past hundred years. Why? What accounts for the greater sureness and self-confidence with which women especially reached the close of courtship? Several different threads came together to give the fabric of courtship a softer texture and make, once again, a smoother seam between single and married life.

First, there was the growing acceptance of contraception. The practice of birth control had increased steadily throughout the nineteenth century; and by the early 1900s, historian Linda Gordon has concluded, small families and birth control were "not a temporary aberration but a secular trend, and possibly even a new norm." Marriage no longer required repression and risk as the price for sexual intimacy. Although both partners stood to gain, women had faced the greater risks and experienced the greater gains. Contraceptives could give a woman control not only over the size of her family but over the quality of her life.[85]

While birth control is a significant factor, it should not be overestimated. There were, after all, "no significant technological improvements of importance in this period."[86] Increasing use of contraception was as much a result as it was a cause of woman's improved position in and perception of marriage. The diminution, if not disappearance, of women's fearfulness about marriage reflected other less easily measured changes.

Women who came of age around the turn of the century were less likely than those in earlier generations to associate marriage with separation from one home and isolation in another. As the opportunities for higher education and paid employment for women expanded, the daughters of the middle class moved beyond the family circle more freely and left home more gradually. While the fact that a record percentage of those born between 1870 and 1890 waited to marry or never married at all may seem to indicate a negative attitude toward marriage, it may on the contrary be a sign that marriage represented a woman's choice rather than her destiny—one, rather than the only, option available. The decline in the marriage age and the increase in the marriage rate after 1890, even among college and professional women, suggests that the "new woman" believed she could enter into marriage on new, and better, terms. She would not be nearly so defined by and confined to the home as her mother and grandmother had been. The world of mass entertainment and commercial leisure, of department stores and steam laundries, of women's clubs and movie matinees not only loosened the ties of children to the home but of their mothers as well. These new conditions may have inhibited openness and emotional intimacy during courtship, but they could have the opposite effect on marriage.[87]

If young women looked around and saw that marriage did not preclude the mutuality and companionship that middle-class Americans had long idealized, they may well have approached it with a quicker step and a lighter heart. An 1876 bride used this analogy for "the trembling feeling inside" just before her marriage: It was "as if I were going to jump in the river trusting to the chance of my knowing how to swim."[88] Many of the women who wed in the century after Independence hesitated before they jumped; the river would carry them away from what was familiar and safe and take them to a new life that promised happiness but might bring bitter disappointment. Women who made the transition to marriage after about 1890 might fret when the day came, but the "trembling feeling" was an expression of excitement more than of anxiety. They were confident of their ability to stay afloat and to enjoy the journey.

EPILOGUE

In Our Own Time, 1920–1980

IN RECONSTRUCTING the history of courtship from 1770 to 1920, I have relied on personal records left by individual men and women and have ventured into the realm of private thoughts and inner feelings, a country we can explore but never fully recover. Only occasionally have we encountered other travelers, other observers, along the way. When we move beyond 1920, however, we enter more familiar territory. Our grandparents, parents, we ourselves have made the transition to marriage since 1920; and several generations of social scientists have watched and counted and questioned.

Researchers discovered the world of middle-class courtship in the 1930s and have been mapping it ever since. Nevertheless,

285

in spite of fifty years of systematic study and informal family history, modern courtship remains in some ways less accessible than courtship in the more distant past.* The monographs on "rating and dating" and "going steady," the analyses of "value consensus" in mate selection, the reports on sexual behavior rarely have the resonance of words set down long ago on sheets of letter paper or the pages of a diary.

The written record of middle-class courtship did not disappear overnight in 1920; it ebbed gradually as the telephone and high-speed travel made written communication more of a minor current in the flow of intimate relationships. Certainly during the years of the Second World War, when people were separated from loved ones, ordinary Americans wrote letters by the millions. But little of this correspondence has found its way from attics and closets into public archives and research libraries. Oral histories have been collected, but they tend to stress public accomplishments rather than personal experiences and pay scant attention to the ideas and feelings that surrounded courtship and the transition to marriage.

The student of modern courtship, therefore, must resort to sources that inevitably lack the immediacy of personal documents. Nineteenth-century popular culture abounded with images of love and marriage, and with the rapid spread of mass entertainment after 1900, these images gained new influence. The stories people saw on the screen or read in *True Story*, the songs they heard on the radio or played on the Victrola all had romance as their favorite theme.[2] However, the omnipresent images of courtship in modern American culture present many of the same difficulties of interpretation one faces in sorting out the descriptive from the prescriptive, the imaginative from the realistic elements in nineteenth-century romantic fiction. The social scientists, survey researchers, and commentators who focused on the contemporary scene furnish a more direct route

---

*I am retaining the word *courtship* for the sake of consistency and convenience; but during most of the 1920 to 1980 period, the term was used more by sociologists and antiquarians than by young people themselves. "The term courtship, insofar as their own behavior is concerned, is not part of their vocabulary," sociologist Samuel Lowrie correctly observed in 1951.[1]

to courtship in the recent past. While these accounts shed little light on individual experience, they are useful for charting trends in the behavior and ideas associated with the transition to marriage. And thus it is to them that we turn to assemble a picture of middle-class courtship in our own time.

The result will have the quality of an aerial photograph. I will cover a lot of ground quickly, survey it from a distance, and take note only of the main features of the landscape. Because change provides the landmarks, it appears, from this perspective, more conspicuous than continuity. If we could tell the same story from the individual's point of view, it might be that what seems most significant in the grand design was of only minor importance on the smaller canvas of a single life. Someone who has always lived in the hills might hardly be aware of the vast plain stretching out beyond them, yet from the air it will be the change in terrain that catches our eye.

The census taker gives us our first coordinates: Until the Second World War, Americans continued to marry at the age and rate characteristic of the nineteenth century. The median age at first marriage in 1900 was 21.9 for women and 25.9 for men; after "a slow and measured decline" in the first four decades of the twentieth century, the figure in 1940 was 21.5 for women and 24.3 for men. The rate of marriage dipped in the early 1930s, but by 1939, it had returned to the nineteenth-century level. The 1940s brought a sudden interruption in this remarkable stability. The marriage rate rose and the median age at marriage fell, both dramatically. According to demographer Donald Bogue, during that one decade "the proportion of persons never married and the median age at first marriage declined by as much as they had during the entire preceding half-century." In the late 1940s, more than half of all women were married by the age of twenty-one.[3]

The immediate dislocations of wartime may have accounted for the outbreak of what one commentator called "the war disease," but the epidemic did not subside after V-J Day. Young Americans continued to marry at an age that would, at any other time, have been considered dangerously young. In 1956, the median age at first marriage reached an all-time low (20.1 for women, 22.5 for men); and a year later, the birth rate reached its peak. Beginning about 1960, the median age at first marriage began a gradual rise. By the late 1970s, it had attained its pre-war level. The children of the couples who had participated in the 1940s "marriage marathon" and produced the 1950s "baby boom" returned to patterns of family formation that their parents had broken.[4]*

Thus the twentieth century has been a time of demographic continuity. Except for the 1940s and 1950s, the transition to marriage appears as a steady line on the nation's statistical record. But when we turn from demographic trends to other forms of behavior, a different pattern emerges: a period of rapid change at the beginning (roughly 1910 to 1930); then more gradual, evolutionary change during the middle decades (1930 to about 1965); followed by another period of heightened change since the mid-1960s. The shifts of the last two decades can be gauged, at least indirectly, in the rise of cohabitation and teenage pregnancy; the discontinuity that marked the first quarter of the century is much harder to measure.

The subject of public consternation and celebration at the time, and of literary legend and historical debate ever since, "a first-class revolt against the accepted American order" took place among American youth in the 1920s. The "shock troops of the rebellion," as Frederick Lewis Allen called the fomenters of this "revolution in manners and morals," were not the first to breach the barricades. The assault on "the moral code of the country" had begun well before the battles along the Somme. What happened in the 1920s was that ideas and behavior which had once marked the outermost limits of acceptability moved to the center of middle-class youth culture. The sound of jazz, the smell of cigarette smoke, the discussions of Freud emanated not just from Greenwich Village but from Main Street and Fra-

---

*One important new pattern that appears to be developing in the early 1980s is the increase, among twenty-five- to twenty-nine-year-olds, of those who are single. According to the 1980 census, one fifth of the women in that age group had not yet married, a twofold increase since 1970. There was a 70 percent increase for men, from one fifth in 1970 to one third in 1980. One result of this trend was to raise the median age at first marriage; by 1983, Americans were marrying later than at any time since 1890.

ternity Row. This was not a sudden eruption but rather a series of seismic tremors that occurred with increasing intensity and frequency though the 1910s and 1920s. The automobile, the moving picture, the close dance had all appeared before the First World War; but in the 1920s, they dominated and liberated American youth to an unprecedented extent. By 1930, the terrain through which young Americans passed en route to marriage would be almost unrecognizable to their parents.[5]

The men and women who courted circa 1900 and their children coming of age in the 1920s were separated by as wide a gulf as that between any two American generations. Standards for behavior had undergone change before, of course, but never so radically in such a short time. It was understandable that people who had ridden their wheels around town, danced the two-step at the bandstand, and kissed goodnight on the front porch would be alarmed to see their children go off on joy rides in closed cars, to "petting parties," or to "pictures with hot love-making in them."[6] In 1900, middle-class courtship was more carefully supervised and more formal than it had been at any time since the Revolution; by 1930, the supervision and formality had given way, like a poorly designed dam, and many of the familiar landmarks were swept aside. While the result may have looked like chaos and disarray, a new system, created and regulated by young people themselves, was in place almost as soon as the old one was abandoned. The youths of the 1920s, in the words of historian Paula Fass, "elaborated two basic rituals of social interaction—dating and petting."[7] Separately and together, these two rituals would define the experience of courtship for the next half-century.

The young women and men of the 1920s did not invent paired-off social behavior—couples had been "keeping company" for two hundred years; nor were they the first to discover sexual pleasure.* What they did was to develop a systematic, peer-controlled approach to the social and sexual relationships of late adolescence and early adulthood. The date, one historian

---

*Alfred Kinsey recognized that older generations had engaged in "flirting, flirtage, courting, bundling, spooning, mugging, smooching, larking, sparking, and other activities which were simply petting under another name."[8]

has recently observed, "had a compelling logic quite distinct from that of prior forms: it was a step in an ongoing negotiation with rules defined and deviations punished by age-peers." Dating provided a way to manage the social demands of the peer society. It was an alternative to group activities, on the one hand, and to serious, marriage-oriented courtship, on the other. In a world where "press accounts of high school club dances [were] careful to emphasize the escort of each girl attending," the dating system ensured that a girl need not have a suitor in order to attend a dance.[9] Indeed, the fact that dating could operate independently of mate selection caused some observers to condemn it.

The sociologist Willard Waller, who studied campus life in the 1930s, concluded that dating "is not true courtship, since it is supposed not to eventuate in marriage; it is a sort of dalliance relationship." The decline of "formal modes of courtship" had, in Waller's view, been replaced by a "rating and dating complex" that rewarded "thrill-seeking" and "exploitative" behavior by young men and women. "Whether we approve or not" (and Waller made it clear that he did not), "courtship practices today allow for a great deal of pure thrill-seeking," he wrote in 1937. "Dancing, petting, necking, the automobile, amusement park, and a whole range of institutions and practices permit or facilitate thrill-seeking behavior." In this system, the goal was prestige rather than mate selection, plural rather than exclusive relationships. Men were rated according to the fraternity they belonged to, the clothes they wore, the amount of money they had to spend, and the skill they showed on the dance floor; what mattered was that they were "smooth" and had a "good line." For women, the important criteria were similar: "good clothes, a smooth line, ability to dance well, and popularity as a date."[10]

The pattern Waller described, based on a study conducted at Pennsylvania State University in the 1930s, was neither as novel nor as predominant as he thought.* A system oriented toward

---

*Michael Gordon suggests that Penn State may have been especially well suited to support a "rating and dating complex": it was geographically isolated; it had six males for every female student (as opposed to ratios of three to one at Cornell and two to one at Michigan); and its student body represented the lower rather than the upper reaches of the middle class.[11]

pluralistic, if not competitive, dating had evolved simultaneously among high school and college students well before the Crash.[12] The 1920s campus was above all a social scene, and that scene was designed around dating. Social activities rather than academic pursuits were what demanded time and conferred status. "Study in too enthusiastic a form" was widely considered "bad form. . . . Too constant attendance at the Library is likely to lead to derogatory classification," the *Daily Princetonian* warned in 1926. Such misplaced enthusiasm was rare; at Ohio State that year, the average co-ed went on dates four nights a week. Because selection for fraternity and sorority membership "usually had more to do with superficial attractiveness and personality than rigid socio-economic class," "rating and dating" tended to flourish on campuses where the Greek societies were strong. Even there, however, it functioned alongside a more traditional social system. As one sociologist recently concluded, "rating and dating and less exploitive and pluralistic dating appear to have existed simultaneously."[13]

The social scientists saw good data and the journalists good copy in the collegian; but in 1930, less than 15 percent of the country's eighteen- to twenty-one-year-olds were attending institutions of higher education. And off the campus, "going together" was the norm. The heroine of one 1920s novel described the "thing you called going together":

You went with a boy. He was your fellow then and you were his girl. When you were old enough you got engaged and married. . . . Going together was beautiful. You had fun then; all the fun there was. You were not an odd girl. You were not left out. . . . You could belong to a crowd. You had somebody to walk home with you, pay for your ticket at shows, send you valentines, candy at Christmas.[14]

Whether they were dating many different people or "going together" with one special person (and most young people in and out of college probably experimented with both modes), middle-class youths organized their social lives around dating beginning well before 1930.

One of the chief characteristics—and attractions—of a date was that it took place away from home. In his survey of undergraduate life in the late 1920s, Robert Angell explained, "In seeking means of diversion together there seem to be two principal aims, to have as much privacy and at the same time as much excitement as possible." Angell realized that "the former has probably been present from time immemorial," but he thought that the latter had been "enormously developed in the past years by the automobile and other means of exciting recreation." The middle-class home was, by definition, neither private nor exciting. "Unless couples are engaged, they are rarely content to spend the afternoon or evening conversing in the parlor or even strolling together along shady walks." The same rule applied off the campus as well. In the Indiana town that the sociologists Robert and Helen Lynd called Middletown, in the 1920s, "a 'date' at home [was] 'slow' compared with motoring, a new film, or a dance in a near-by town." Half the boys and girls queried on the subject reported that they were home fewer than four evenings out of the week.[15]*

The most popular pasttime for both high school and college students was dancing. In the early 1920s, many high schools "instituted dances, in an effort of varying success to take the play away from commercial dance halls and road houses."[17] College students could attend dances sponsored by college organizations or patronize local cabarets. By the 1920s, dancing had become an activity for couples rather than groups; it encouraged sensuality rather than sociability. Angell commented on "the slight degree of mingling" at university dances. "Often a man and woman spend practically the whole evening together," he reported. Not only were they together, they were close together. The new dances "fostered an unheard of closeness between partners. . . . Couples often held each other very close." There were rules governing proper behavior on the dance floor, but they were "usually treated in a cavalier fashion."[18] In spite of its sexual potential, however, dancing retained a certain inno-

---

*This distaste for home dates held true when Susan Allen Toth was growing up in Ames, Iowa, in the 1950s. She recalled that young couples rarely spent time in each other's homes. "We might not have been bothered," Toth explained, "but we really wouldn't have been alone. Cars were our private space, a rolling parlor, the only place we could relax and be ourselves. . . . Driving gave us a feeling of freedom."[16]

cent quality. Irene and Vernon Castle, who elevated cabaret dancing to respectability in the 1910s, "took the potentially seductive dance and made it 'fun.'" Irene Castle once explained, "If Vernon had ever looked into my eyes with smoldering passion during the tango, we should have both burst out laughing." Dancing, in the Castle style, offered young people "a means to experience physical closeness and erotic excitement, without the dangers of sexuality."[19]

Like the dance hall, the movie theater was another setting that offered young people privacy and excitement, within limits. As movies became an increasingly legitimate form of middle-class entertainment, they also became increasingly popular. Most collegians in the 1920s regularly attended the movies once a week, and high school students were no less devoted followers of Clara Bow and Rudolph Valentino. In Middletown in 1928, there were nine motion-picture theaters offering over three hundred performances every week of the year. "Go to a motion picture and let yourself go," the readers of the *Saturday Evening Post* were told, and Americans heeded the call by the millions. In a typical week, one third of Middletown's high school students attended the movies once; 20 percent went twice.[20]

Some of their teachers believed that movies were "a powerful factor in bringing about the 'early sophistication' of the young and the relaxing of social taboos," and the Lynds agreed that the "constant public watching of love-making on the screen" had a noticeable effect. The woman who happily sent her daughter "because a girl has to learn the ways of the world somehow and the movies are a good safe way" was not necessarily as naïve as she might have appeared to the Lynds. The movies presented both an opportunity and stimulation for sexual intimacy, but they left conventional boundaries in place. Robert Angell considered the excitement to be found at the movies "much milder" than at the dance hall. As historian Elaine Tyler May explains:

The message of the plot reinforced the need for restraint. Love-struck viewers might hold hands or embrace in the darkened theater; but not much else could happen. They sat in a public place, facing the screen

293

without talking to each other, watching attractive film idols instruct them in the art of gaining allure without losing virtue.[21]

Of all the new influences on the behavior of young women and men, none was more powerful than the automobile. Here, in the closed cars which were fast replacing open ones, anything *could* happen. Of the thirty girls charged with "sex crimes" in Middletown in 1924, nineteen committed the offense in an automobile. In 1923, there were more than six thousand cars in Middletown, two for every three families. Car ownership had reached the point of being an "accepted essential of normal living" for middle-class people.[22]* It had become an "accepted essential of normal" courting for their children as well. The automobile was, however, no less revolutionary for being readily incorporated into normalcy. The Lynds concluded that the automobile had "revolutionized . . . leisure" in general and had specifically caused the "increasing relaxation of some of the traditional prohibitions upon the approaches of boys and girls to each other's persons." Robert Angell concurred. In 1928, he declared:

To this invention must be assigned much responsibility . . . for the change, amounting to almost a revolution, which has come about during the last fifteen years in the conduct of young men and women. The ease with which a couple can secure absolute privacy when in possession of a car and the spirit of reckless abandon which high speed and moonlight drives engender have combined to break down the traditional barriers between the sexes.[24]

Even at slower speeds and in broad daylight, the car allowed a level of intimacy and privacy reminiscent of the early republic. A Rhode Island woman explained in 1923, "You can be so nice and all alone in a machine, just a little one that you can go on crazy roads in and be miles away from anyone but each other."

*As the car became a measure of social status, it also became a source of parent-child conflict. In Middletown, "among the high school set, ownership of a car by one's family has become an important criterion of social fitness; a boy almost never takes a girl to a dance except in a car; there are persistent rumors of the buying of a car by local families to help their children's social standing in high school."[23]

Fifteen years later, when Dorothy Bromley and Florence Britten published their study *Youth and Sex*, it was obvious that the car was "an incredible engine of escape." A boy called for his date, usually just by honking the horn, and the young couple was "off and away, out of reach of parental control. A youth now . . . has a refuge . . . complete privacy. He has taken full advantage of it, not only as a means of going places, but as a place to go where he can take his girl and hold hands, neck, pet, or if it's that kind of an affair, go the limit."[25]

The car provided far more privacy and excitement than either the dance hall or the movie theater, and the result was the spread of petting. In 1928, Robert Angell conceded that "what is vulgarly known as 'petting' is the rule rather than the exception in all classes of society"; and by 1930, Floyd Dell could refer to "the universal convention of petting" with little risk of overstatement.[26] The statistical pattern is clear. A 1924 study of "Certain Aspects of the Sex Life of the Adolescent Girl" found that 92 percent of the respondents (177 college girls) had indulged in "spooning" or "petting." (Spooning was a more old-fashioned term for kissing than petting, which included all forms of erotic behavior short of intercourse.*) This limited data was confirmed in the report on *Sexual Behavior in the Human Female* prepared by Alfred Kinsey and his associates in the early 1950s. About 80 percent of the women born just before 1900—in other words those who courted in the 1910s and 1920s—had engaged in some sort of petting, and the proportion increased with every decade. The story for men was similar. Among the older generation (born between 1895 and 1904), 65 percent had petting experience by age eighteen; while in the younger generation (born between 1917 and 1929), 85 percent had petted by that age.[28]

Much of this petting took place in the quasi-public setting of the "petting party." Petting parties were a regular feature of high school life in the 1920s. When asked if it was true that "nine

---

*According to Kinsey, "distinctions between necking and petting, mild and heavy petting, and still other classifications which are current among American youth, appear to differentiate nothing more than various techniques, or the parts of the body which are involved in the contacts, or the level of arousal which is effected."[27]

out of every ten boys and girls of high school age have 'petting parties,' " 50 percent of the Middletown youths answered yes. Although fewer students themselves admitted to petting, almost half of the boys and more than one third of the girls indicated that they had taken part in a petting party. Such parties were not limited to the high school scene; college students indulged as well. In both cases, the petting party was, as Paula Fass points out, "a self-limiting form of experimentation . . . . Here sexual activity was manifestly regulated by the group . . . a certain aura of intrigue and 'naughtiness' hovered around this semi-illicit behavior in the twenties."[29]

There was nothing *semi*-illicit about premarital coitus. "To maintain one's position with peers," Fass writes, "petting was permitted but intercourse was not." Only a minority violated the prohibition on premarital sexual intercourse, but their action was considered "an indiscretion and not a moral outrage." Virginity had ceased to be an absolute requirement in a bride, even if most men and women still considered it highly desirable. Although most of the young women in a 1936 study conducted by Phyllis Blanchard and Carlyn Manasses "assumed that it would make no difference to the men who wished to marry them if it was known that they had had previous sex experience," the authors concluded that "many girls draw a distinct line between the exploratory activities of the petting party and complete yielding of sexual favors to men." Blanchard and Manasses found a "decidedly tolerant attitude toward pre-marital sex experiences," and a 1936 effort to measure attitudinal change showed that "a consistent liberalizing of opinion" was taking place in the course of young people's college careers.[30]

While attitudes shifted toward greater tolerance for premarital sexual activities, the tie between love and sex remained strong. Indeed, it was, if anything, affirmed by the "rebels" of the 1920s. "I disapprove of promiscuous relations on moral grounds; not, however, between a man and woman in love," one co-ed told Blanchard and Manasses. In Fass's analysis, "it was emotional commitment above all that legitimized eroticism, for the young were true romantics who believed strongly in love."

One college editor described the youth of his generation: "Where the ancient code had touched a vital principle he has hesitated to overstep its bounds." Even as they overthrew the "ancient code," young Americans preserved this principle. The bounds that marked off the sanctity of married love were readjusted, but they were not abandoned. "The revolution in sexual morality went on within the rules of the game," and the rules tied sex securely to love.[31]

Middle-class Americans had long considered love a "necessary condition" for sexual intimacy; what changed now was not the condition but the "point in the courtship process when it is applied." A growing minority of college students "altered the traditional notion of being a virgin when you marry to being a virgin when you reach engagement."[32] The commitment to this new standard is reflected in the fact that the increase in premarital coitus was largely confined to engaged couples. In the Kinsey Report, only a quarter of the women born before 1900 indicated they had had premarital intercourse, while for those born after 1900, the figure was close to 50 percent. However, at least one half of the women in the 1920s who reported engaging in premarital coitus did so only with a future spouse. (Kinsey found a similar trend among his male respondents.)[33]

From data collected in the 1940s, Alfred Kinsey concluded that the greatest increase in premarital sexual activity occurred in the generation that reached adulthood in the late 1910s and early 1920s, and that "later generations appear to have accepted the new pattern and maintained or extended it." Observers in the 1930s agreed. The young no longer seemed to be diverting the mainstream into new directions, perhaps because the turbulence of the 1920s had already made the channel wide enough to accommodate a range of youthful experimentation. Some commentators even detected "a conservative reaction among the young to the 'Scott Fitzgerald wave' " of the early 1920s," but the retreat was more apparent than real. "The innovations of the 1920s," Fass writes, "had been solidified so that by the 30s the sexual mores begun by the college youth of the 20s were already a widespread and casual feature of behavior."[34]

EPILOGUE

When Helen and Robert Lynd returned to Middletown in 1935, they got "a sense of sharp, free behavior between the sexes (patterned on the movies) and of less disguise among the young." The liberalization of attitudes and behavior that had taken place in college in the 1920s now showed up among high school students. One young man, several years out of the Middletown high school, told the Lynds in 1935, "The fellows regard necking as a taken-for-granted part of a date. We fellows used occasionally to get slapped for doing things, but the girls don't do that much any more. . . . Our high school students of both sexes . . . know everything and do everything—openly." The girls of Middletown might read in the local paper's advice columns, "A girl should never kiss a boy unless they are engaged," but few heeded such old-fashioned words.[35]

Petting was less notorious but no less popular than it had been in the 1920s. In their 1938 study of thirteen hundred undergraduates, Bromley and Britten found that, although at some colleges the terms *necking* and *petting* were no longer used, "the custom signified persists . . . on every campus and under many new names." As the novelty of petting wore off, it lost its more extreme, exhibitionistic qualities. Writing in 1937, the sociologist Theodore Newcomb argued that, while there had been "no quantitative decline in premarital sex relations since the alleged excesses" of the 1920s, there had been "changes in manners and morals associated with such behavior." Among the most important changes, Newcomb listed: "more widespread acceptance, particularly by females, of the 'naturalness' of sex intimacies, with or without coitus; less extreme 'petting' on first or early acquaintance; and more 'steady dating' with fewer inhibitions as to sex intimacy following long acquaintance." In June 1936, *Fortune* magazine reported, "As for sex, it is, of course, still with us. But the campus takes it more casually than it did ten years ago. Sex is no longer news."[36]

What was news was the worldwide economic crisis and the mounting threat of war in Europe. As the Depression tightened its grip on America, college enrollments fell, and the size and influence of campus fraternities declined. The Depression cast a long shadow and brought an altogether more somber mood to campus life. For many middle-class youths, college attendance represented a difficult sacrifice. The madcap social whirl of the 1920s was an extravagance few could afford. Academic pursuits and the students who excelled in them were rescued from the margins of college life and given new prestige. At the same time, college students expressed more eagerness for marriage and children than they had in the 1920s. In *Fortune*'s 1936 poll, 60 percent of the women and 50 percent of the men wanted to marry within a year or two of graduation; but when 50 percent to 85 percent of male college graduates were among the thirteen million unemployed, these were dreams to be deferred.[37]

Deferred, but not abandoned. By the time war broke out in Europe, both the marriage rate and the age at marriage had returned to their pre-1930 levels.* With people rushing into marriage in response to the threat of separation and perhaps of death during wartime, symptoms of the "war disease" began to appear in ever younger people. From 1940 to 1948, the median age at first marriage fell by a full year, and three quarters of women born between 1920 and 1924 were married by the age of twenty-four.[39]

The "marriage marathon" was not the only sign of the war's impact on the social life of the middle-class young. At the University of Wisconsin in 1944, there were nine women for every man in the freshman class; and at Ohio State, the ratio was four to one. When a reporter from *Fortune* visited Cornell in 1942, he found Fraternity Row deserted, house parties suspended for the duration, and only meager crowds at the football games. Male students left school early or attended classes year-round and prepared for active duty. Off the campus, most single men over eighteen were in uniform and isolated from normal social life. "In comparison with the civilians, men in the armed forces had less spare time, fewer automobiles, and fewer contacts among the female population. . . . Most servicemen were concentrated by the tens of thousands in one place or another. . . . There were

*The marriage rate fell from 10.14 per 1,000 in 1929 to 7.9 in 1932 and then started up again, reaching its late 1920s level by 1934 and surpassing it by 1940.[38]

just not enough women to go around."[40] With men largely segregated in the armed forces and women in colleges or the war
industries, the normal process and pace of social relationships
were disrupted.

For younger groups, however, the social scene remained
largely unaffected by the war. Petting was as common as ever.
Of the women Kinsey interviewed in the late 1940s, 39 percent
of those under fifteen and 88 percent of those aged sixteen to
twenty were having petting experience. For men in Kinsey's
younger generation, 66 percent had petting experience by the
age of sixteen; 93 percent by the time they were twenty. Kinsey
concluded that the incidence of petting had increased, and that
men were starting to pet at an earlier age. Petting was no longer
restricted to the back seat or the "petting party." "On doorsteps
and on street corners, and on high school and college campuses
. . . [it] may be observed in the daytime as well as in the evening
hours," Kinsey wrote in 1948. Calling it "one of the most significant factors in the sexual lives of high school and college males
and females," Kinsey hailed petting for the education it offered
young people "in making socio-sexual contacts."[41]*

Dating was the context within which most youthful petting
took place, and it too functioned to educate young women and
men about themselves and each other. While some observers
still detected, and decried, a "rating and dating" complex at
work in the "no strings attached" relationships many young
people favored, other commentators recognized that it was precisely the association with freedom that gave dating its appeal.
"Dating is a relationship expressing freedom, lack of commitment or public obligation for any sort of future action," wrote
sociologist Samuel Lowrie in 1951.[43] At the same time, a contra-

---

*While Kinsey recognized the educational value of petting, he had grave doubts
about it on other grounds. He saw petting as the way college groups "attempt to avoid
pre-marital intercourse." He was appalled by "the mixture of scientifically supported
logic, and of utter illogic, which shapes the petting behavior of most of these youths.
. . . They are particularly concerned with the avoidance of genital union. The fact that
petting involved erotic contacts which are as effective as genital union . . . does not dis-
turb the youth so much as actual intercourse would." He suggested that the lower incidence of petting among working-class men reflected their lack of respect for the distinction that was all important to the college group.[42]

dictory pattern was emerging. Far from avoiding commitment, many young Americans were attaching strings with a vengeance. By the end of the Second World War, going steady had taken root, and the result was to impart "a different color to the social life of the youth. It makes it more serious, less frivolous." Writing in *Harper's* in 1957, Amherst College president George Cole expressed regret at what he saw happening to dating:

In the twenties and early thirties, when the social pattern was one of multiple or polygamous dating—on the part of both boys and girls—young people did not think nearly so much about marriage as they do today. . . . They dated each other for the fun of it, because they enjoyed each other's company, because they liked the same things, or merely because in the competitive social life of their time it was a good thing to have dates—the more, the better. Today young people often play with the idea of marriage as early as the second or third date, and they certainly think about it by the fifth or sixth. By the time they have been going steady for a while they are quite apt to be discussing the number and names of their future children.[44]

Indeed, with the marriage age dropping to an all-time low, large numbers of young people were moving through the dating system directly—and immediately—into marriage. Public policy and family values accounted for "the disappearance of the idea that a man should be able to support a wife before he gets married." New resources were available: The government subsidized mortgages and paid veterans a subsistence allowance—sixty dollars if they were single, seventy-five if married—while they were in school. Working wives and parents supplemented that income. "Nowadays," Cole noted in 1957, "one or both sets of parents are expected to help."[45] Another less easily quantifiable factor was at work here, too. In 1958, *Parents Magazine* explained to its readers "Why They Can't Wait to Wed": "Youngsters want to grasp what little security they can in a world gone frighteningly insecure. The youngsters feel they will cultivate the one security that's possible—their own gardens, their own . . . home and families." That they had begun at an early age to "cultivate . . . security" in steady relationships gave "young people the feeling that they really know members of the opposite sex well enough to choose a marriage partner much earlier in life than people . . . would have dared to do . . . in an earlier day," sociologist David Riesman observed a year later.[46]

While public policy directly, and the political climate indirectly, encouraged early marriage, personal experience was the most important ingredient in the equation. By the 1950s, Americans began to acquire dating and petting experience as young teenagers. Winston Ehrmann found that, except for school, dating was the most time-consuming activity in his subjects' lives, beginning in junior high or even elementary school. Doubtless many parents disapproved of their children's early exposure to heterosexual socializing, but other parents clearly promoted it. In the April 1956 issue of *Good Housekeeping*, Phyllis McGinley bemoaned the fact that

abetted, indeed pushed and prodded and egged on by their mothers or the PTA or scoutmasters, sixth-grade children are now making dates on the telephone and ineptly jitterbugging together every weekend evening. . . . They are coaxed and bullied and enticed into "mingling." There are school dances and church dances and scout dances. There are Coke parties and local "assemblies" and what passes for dances at private homes.[47]

It was certainly true that by the time middle-class children entered junior high school, they were full participants in the first stages of dating ritual. Most began with "group dating": "Everything is done in gangs, although pairing off usually occurs sometimes during the evening," reported one student. Another described the process in greater detail:

The boys and girls seldom attend the basketball games together, as couples, but prefer instead to drift in with a crowd of their own gender. When the lights are more discreetly lowered after the games, however, the boys tend to seek out their latest interests and pair off for dancing. At the end of such dances a few boys walk their "girls" home, but the majority of the crowd walks in groups of paired couples "en masse" down to the local hangout for a Coke.

For the clique that "set the pace for the others," there were two rituals of importance: the Saturday night date to the movies and "Coke parlor" afterward, and the more occasional private parties ("minus chaperons") at someone's house. The main attractions there were the games of "Spin the Bottle," "Postoffice," and "Spotlight."[48]

When these students went on to high school, they "began to date with real intent and purpose [and] played the field." Susan Allen Toth, who grew up in Ames, Iowa, in the 1950s, remembered that "high school courtship usually was meticulously slow, progressing through inquiry, phone calls, planned encounters in public places, double or triple dates, hand-holding, and finally a good-night kiss." Dates had a predictable form: "Movie, something to eat, and out to park. Movie, something to eat, come home, and perhaps neck there. Movie, home for something to eat, and then perhaps T.V.," a college student recalled. By senior year, the majority of the class was "going steady with someone." Many of those not going on to college married soon after graduation. College-bound students were less likely to marry their high school steadies than were classmates who went directly into the labor force.[49]

College enrollments rose at a slow rate during the years of Depression and war, but after the passage of the G.I. Bill in 1944, they surged ahead. More than twice as many Americans graduated from college in 1950 as had a decade earlier, and by 1960, 22 percent of the eighteen- to twenty-four-year-old population was in school.[50] College students might not have talked about "going steady," a phrase with more currency in high school than collegiate circles, but "the institution was as strong in the latter as in the former." In a *Harper's* piece titled "American Youth Goes Monogamous," George Cole declared that "the present pre-marital monogamy of youth . . . is one of the most important phenomena of recent times." Nora Johnson, a 1954 graduate of Smith College, reported that when she was on campus in the early 1950s, "everybody [was] doing it." In her view, "the phenomena of pinning, going steady, and being monogamous-minded [were] symptoms of our inclination to play it safe.

. . . What a feeling of safety not to have to worry about a date for months ahead!" Johnson believed that the "male wish for dating security" was as strong as the woman's. "Their fraternity pins are burning holes in their lapels," she wryly observed. Getting "pinned" or "engaged to be engaged" was the ritual—and the symbol—for the college version of monogamy.[51]*

Going steady or being pinned was not merely a source of social security. Sociologist Ira Reiss perceived that one of the great attractions of steady dating for teenagers was that "sex and affection can be quite easily combined"; and that especially for the girl, sexual behavior was "made respectable by going steady." In Nora Johnson's account, the "perpetual twosome" of the college scene was "often based on sex and convenience." Going steady allowed a woman to be respectable and available at the same time. It reconciled the two, often conflicting, principles by which middle-class girls operated: "One is that anything is all right if you're in love . . . and the other is that a girl must be respected, particularly by the man she wants to marry," as Johnson put it in "Sex and the College Girl." The "ideal girl," she suggested, "has done every possible kind of petting without actually having had intercourse. This gives her savoir-faire, while still maintaining her dignity."[53]

The "ideal girl" was also the typical girl: through the 1940s and 1950s, the increases in premarital sexual activity occurred in petting rather than coitus. By the mid-1950s, more than 90 percent of college-age men and women reported engaging in premarital petting. The incidence of premarital intercourse had remained fairly constant since the 1920s: between one third and two thirds of college men and about one third of women reported that they had coitus before marriage. In one 1958 study, 10 percent of the co-eds had had sexual intercourse while in a

*Pinning was "made quite a bit of in the fraternity set" on at least one campus. The couple would announce, after the weekly chapter meeting, that they were about to become pinned; and "then the next weekend the 'fellow' and several of his friends came to the sorority house and there was singing and 'serenading.' After that the pinning was official. Depinning was also a ritual. Both announced after chapter meetings that they were no longer pinned. It was the custom for no one to ask any questions or even to discuss it."[52]

dating relationship, 15 percent while going steady, and twice as many (31 percent) during engagement. The researchers concluded that "engagement was very often the prerequisite to a girl having premarital sexual intercourse." If a girl had coitus, it was likely to be with her fiancé, during the year or two before they were married.[54]

The frequency of this behavior reflects the acceptance among middle-class teenagers of what Ira Reiss has labeled "permissiveness with affection." High school couples "feel it is proper to engage in heavy petting if they are going steady, the justification being that they are in love or at least extremely fond of each other," he explained in 1961. Especially among a slightly older age group, similar reasoning supported the decision to have coitus during the late stages of the transition to marriage. One young man gave a typical rationale for why he and his girl friend "indulged in petting, and at times . . . heavy petting. . . . [It] was the result of a drive that had something beside pure sex as a motivating factor. We didn't believe in petting because of the sex alone, but because we were very much in love and this was a means of expressing our love to each other." They refrained from sleeping together not because they thought it was wrong, but because they "didn't want to take any unnecessary chances."[55]

This young man and his girl friend agreed on where to draw the limits in their sexual relationship; but, in general, "permissiveness with affection" figured more largely in the female than in the male code of sexual ethics. Boys may have been more sexually experienced (more than twice as many boys as girls had coitus in their teens), but they were also more conservative, in the sense that they were more likely to embrace the traditional double standard which sanctioned conduct in men that it condemned in women. However, during the 1950s, young men evinced "increased willingness . . . to accept some coitus on the part of females, especially if it occurs when the girl is in love and/or engaged." An even more egalitarian standard, which made premarital intercourse right for both sexes, gained ground among older teenagers, particularly those in college. By 1959, a majority of the men in Ehrmann's study of college students adhered to a single standard; and for most of them, it was a *liberal* single standard.[56]

Ehrmann concluded that, in spite of these attitudinal changes, women were still the arbiters and enforcers of sexual codes. A survey published in the *Ladies' Home Journal* in January 1962 summarized the sentiments of women sixteen- to twenty-one-years old: "They feel a special responsibility for sex *because* they are women." In their comments, these young women revealed an understanding of the different roles played by men and women in the sexual game. "A woman has much more to lose than a man," one woman said. "Girls especially should have a great deal of self-control, seeing quite a few boys don't," was another's response. One young woman declared, "A man will go as far as a woman will let him," and another agreed, "A girl has to set the standard."[57]*

The standard was based on emotion more than on eroticism. For the women in Ehrmann's study, sexual expression was "primarily and profoundly related to being in love and going steady"; while for the men, "sexuality is more indirectly and less exclusively associated with romanticism and intimate relationships." Ehrmann noticed an even more striking difference in the sexual standards of young men and women: "The degree of physical intimacy actually experienced or considered permissible is among males *inversely* related and among females *directly* related to the intensity of and familiarity and affection in the male-female relation." In other words, the more a young woman loved a man, the more permissive she was likely to be; the more a young man loved a woman, the less permissive he was likely to be. Furthermore, where women rarely went beyond the limits set by their codes, men were often prevented by their partners from going "as far sexually as their codes permit."[59]

By the end of the 1950s, the differences between male and female standards were fading. Men were moving away from the

---

*In spite of the fact that "so few they would hardly count supported greater sexual freedom for men and women than our society condones," George Gallup concluded from this poll that these girls were "unconventional in their attitudes toward sex."[58]

traditional double standard toward permissiveness with affection; while women's attitudes were shifting toward the "transitional double standard—coitus is all right for men under any condition, but it is acceptable for women only if they are in love." Investigators detected signs of a related change in the "steady decrease in the tendency to express different standards for members of one's own sex than for members of the opposite sex." By 1968, the double standard had not disappeared, but its decline was noticeable. It was being eroded by an overall liberalization of sexual attitudes. The new ground broken by the youths of the 1950s was not so much in the incidence of premarital coitus as in the wider acceptance of it.[60]

Reflecting on this convergence of sexual attitudes and behavior, Ira Reiss speculated in 1966, "We may well witness soon an increase in many forms of sexual behavior. . . . The stage is set for another upward cycle of increasing sexual behavior and sexual acceptance." Reiss was soon proved right. After decades of relative stability, the rate of premarital coitus showed a dramatic increase. The most marked change for men occurred among those in college. Half of the college-bound men in a 1972 survey had had premarital intercourse by the age of seventeen, more than twice the rate in the Kinsey Report. (Among males not in college, the increase was substantially lower.)[61] The change for women was even more dramatic. The percentage of women who had first intercourse by the age of seventeen doubled between the 1940–49 and 1950–59 birth cohorts. A range of studies yielded higher premarital coital rates among college women in the late 1960s than in the 1950s and early 1960s. Only two studies showed a nonvirgin rate below 30 percent for college women, and most found between 40 percent and 55 percent.[62]

When Ira Reiss described the teenage girl in 1961 as "the guardian of sexual limits," he observed that "she appears increasingly to be a half-willing guardian who more and more seeks her self-satisfaction and strives to achieve sexual equality." By the late 1960s, she was drawing closer to this goal. It was not just the rate of premarital intercourse that increased dramatically in the 1960s; the context changed as well. In a 1968 replication of a 1958 study, Robert Bell and Jay Chaskes found that, in ten years, the proportion of women having premarital coitus while in dating relationships had gone from 10 percent to 23 percent; for those going steady, the increase was from 15 percent to 28 percent. The rise in the rate of premarital intercourse during engagement was smaller, from 31 percent to 39 percent. The authors concluded that in 1968 women were more likely than a decade before to have their first sexual experience prior to becoming engaged. Furthermore, the young women in the 1968 sample were far more likely than those in the 1958 group to feel comfortable with that decision. The percentage of co-eds who felt they had gone "too far" was cut in half for all three dating levels. Other investigators uncovered a similar pattern: there was a general decline in the proportion of women who reported feeling guilt or remorse after their first coital experience. "What was done by a female in 1925 acting as a rebel and a deviant can be done by a female in 1965 as a conformist," Reiss declared.[63]

While her parents were likely to be more critical than her peers, by the early 1970s older as well as younger Americans were evincing more liberal attitudes toward premarital sex. In a 1969 Gallup Poll, 68 percent of a national sample believed premarital sex was wrong; four years later, only 48 percent agreed. Older respondents remained more conservative than younger ones, but a shift toward permissiveness had taken place among all age groups. "Marriage no longer seemed to occupy its place as the dividing line between socially approved and socially disapproved sexual intimacy," sociologist Robert Sorensen observed. More than half of the teenagers in his 1973 nationwide study thought it was "abnormal or unnatural for a boy not to have sex until he gets married." (That the double standard lingered on is reflected in the fact that only 42 percent of the boys and 27 percent of the girls answered yes when the same question was asked about girls.) The concept of "premarital sex" was fast disappearing. Teenagers assumed "there is nothing wrong with sex without marriage."[64]

Sex without love, on the other hand, was another matter. This generation preserved the rule that had guided their parents: "It's all right for young people to have sex before getting married if they are in love with each other." Behavior patterns suggest that "permissiveness with affection" was still the prevailing standard. In Morton Hunt's 1972 study, twice as many women reported having had premarital coitus as in Kinsey's sample, but the proportion of those whose premarital experience was confined to one partner remained the same. Of the women born between 1948 and 1955 (in other words, those who reached early adulthood in the late 1960s and early 1970s), 53 percent had premarital coitus only with their future husbands. "Today's 'nice' girl is still guiding herself according to romantic and historically rooted values," Hunt concluded in 1974.[65] For the next generation, the teenagers of the 1970s, those values appear to have lost some of their hold. Magazines might remind their young female readers of "Your Right to Say No," but more and more teenage girls were saying yes. In 1979, 50 percent of the teenage girls living in metropolitan areas had had premarital sex, an increase of 20 percent since the start of the decade.[66]*

Young people in the 1970s may have been sexually active at a younger age than earlier generations, but most acquired this sexual experience in settings that would have been familiar to their parents and grandparents.† There was, however, one important addition: a growing minority of young men and women lived together before marriage. Just as the "sexual revolution" of the first quarter of the twentieth century involved the innoculation of mainstream youth with a germ incubated in bohemia, so too the dramatic rise in cohabitation reflects the diffusion of an alternative life style throughout middle-class culture. In the late 1960s, unmarried couples who lived together were described in the pages of the *New York Times* as a "tiny minority" within "the dissident youth subculture—the intellectual, politi-

---

*Virtually all of the growth in coitus between 1976 and 1979 occurred among white teenagers. This increase in teenage sexual activity was accompanied by a steady increase in teenage pregnancy and abortion. In 1979, 16 percent of all teenage women had been premaritally pregnant; 37 percent of these pregnancies were terminated by induced abortion. In spite of "increased and more consistent" use of contraception by teenagers, pregnancy rates were rising, perhaps because many adolescents were substituting withdrawal for more effective methods, such as the pill and the IUD.[67]

†One entirely new setting has recently been introduced to the college social scene. In January 1983, the *New York Times* reported that computer centers were "to some extent replacing libraries as a focus of student life, both academic and social."[68]

cally liberal to radical, from middle- and upper-middle-class backgrounds, anti-materialistic and anti-Establishment." Between 1970 and 1982, the number of cohabiting couples tripled. While some of these couples were older people, a leading demographer concluded that the increase was "accounted for . . . primarily by *young couples without children.*" During the 1970s, the number of cohabiting couples under twenty-five with no children increased eightfold.[69]

In spite of the alarms sounded by parents and the press, cohabitation posed little threat to marriage. An unmarried couple told the *Times* in 1969 that the usual sequence was to "slide from dating into shacking up into marriage." As parents saw their children sliding into marriage rather than into a life in the counter culture, fears subsided. A report on the 1980 census remarked that "young Americans are becoming increasingly attracted to this lifestyle, and their parents are becoming less critical of this behavior." An occasional couple found themselves at odds with the law or a censorious landlord, and many young people continued to conceal their living arrangements from their parents; but by the early 1980s, cohabitation had lost its association with the "dissident youth subculture" that had spawned it. A 1981 research team described it as "part of the courtship process rather than a long-term alternative to marriage."[70]

When couples made the transition from living together to marriage, as so many eventually did, they observed the same rituals as their noncohabiting contemporaries.[71] While a small minority devised "alternative" weddings, most Americans who married in the late 1960s and the 1970s followed a familiar pattern. Three out of four first-time brides received an engagement ring; 85 percent of them wore a formal bridal gown. "We Americans are getting married almost precisely as we did a hundred years ago," Marcia Seligson wrote in 1973:

We are adorning ourselves in long white romantic gowns, going to church or to a hotel or country club, repeating established vows we have heard at other folks' weddings for years, sipping champagne, cutting cake, dancing, tossing the bouquet, posing for pictures, fleeing through a shower of rice as we head for our Caribbean honeymoon.

This list, which would have served as a guide to American wedding ritual any time between 1920 and 1980, explains the growth of the "wedding industry" in the past fifty years. Americans who married in 1979 and their families spent about $12.5 billion dollars on rings, wedding expenses, home furnishings, and honeymoons; and the wedding market seemed immune to hard times. In May of 1982, the *New York Times* reported on a "return to traditionalism," noting that for "bridal merchants, it's a state of bliss."[72]

Were the objects of all this commercial activity equally blissful? Presumably so, yet at a time when one in every two marriages was likely to end in divorce, couples could not help but approach the altar with some sense that they were taking on a challenge at which many of them would fail. Lorenzo Dow's 1833 reflection on matrimony, "If a man have a farm and don't like it, he can pull it down and build another. But this is for life!" had ceased to describe the American experience. Although the annual divorce rate had been rising steadily for well over a century (with the exception of a drop during the Depression and an upsurge after both world wars), it has increased more sharply in the last twenty years than ever before. Between 1966 and 1976, the divorce rate doubled and then, in the late 1970s, showed signs of leveling off. The rate of remarriage declined (along with the rate of first marriage) during the 1970s, but Americans had not lost faith in marriage. Four out of every five divorced persons remarried, half of them within three years, and in 1983, two and a half million marriages were recorded.[73]

When a boyhood friend announced his engagement in the fall of 1905, Walter Price sent his congratulations: "The union of a man and a woman in these days where precedents are disregarded & 'Novelty holds sway' is the one old fashioned thing to which people cling. Without it life's a shipwreck."[74] In the perilous world of the 1980s, Americans are no more willing to let go than their grandparents were.

311

NOTE ON SOURCES

The specific primary sources on which this book is based fall into two major categories: published and unpublished. Each category includes autobiographies, diaries, and letters.

Published Material

The published autobiographies and diaries were selected from Louis Kaplan's *A Bibliography of American Autobiographies* and William Mathew's *American Diaries: An Annotated Bibliography*. Accounts of native-born Protestants, living within the geographical boundaries of the study, who reached adulthood between 1770 and 1920, were identified and surveyed for information relevant to courtship experience.

Although nineteenth-century Americans produced memoirs, reminiscences, and recollections in abundance, they generally dispensed with courtship and marriage in a paragraph or two. Given the didactic or inspirational purpose for which many of these works were written, the struggle to find God assumed far greater proportions than the search for a mate. The fact that most autobiographers were male also helps explain the lack of interest in the most personal of life experiences. Few women were in a position to write, and fewer still to publish, an autobiography. The exceptions tended to be leaders in the women's rights movement who wished to document their "conversion" to the cause.

Some of the richest male autobiographies are those that were never published—and probably never written—as books but appear in the proceedings issued by local and regional historical societies. "The Life or Biography of Silas Felton," printed in the *Proceedings of the American Antiquarian Society* (vol. 69, October 1959), is one of the best of these.

One might expect that the autobiographical record of men and women who came of age in the late nineteenth and early twentieth centuries would be fuller and more revealing than what came before; but except for Henry Canby's indispensable *The Age of Confidence: Life in the Nineties* (New York, Farrar & Rinehart, 1934), and the accounts of the Greenwich Village set, especially Max Eastman and Hutchins Hapgood, the period from 1880 to 1920 remains surprisingly undocumented by autobiographers.

Unlike autobiographies, diaries and journals were rarely written with publication in mind but were the work of men and women who wished to provide themselves, or perhaps their descendants, with a record of the events, accomplishments, and trials of their daily lives. Publication was usually the result of efforts of genealogists, antiquarians, and scholars who saw the value of what ordinary Americans had left behind.

Some diaries and journals were written by individuals who, like the sociologist Lester Frank Ward, achieved distinction later in life. However, diaries kept by obscure people have also been published, both in proceedings and as self-contained volumes. Many of these are revealing of courtship: David Shepard, Jr.'s *Chester and Westfield, Mass. Diaries,* edited by Alexander Rose III (privately printed, Baltimore, 1975); George Cutler's journal, which appears in *Chronicles of a Pioneer School from 1792 to 1833 Being the History of Miss Sarah Pierce and Her Litchfield School,* compiled by Emily Noyes Vanderpoel (Cambridge, Mass., University Press, 1903); and the *Journal of Zadoc Long,* edited by Pierce Long (Caldwell, Idaho, Caxton Printers, 1943) all document courtship. Because women were, if anything, more regular diary writers than men, they are well represented among published diarists. *The Diaries of Sally and Pamela Brown, 1822–1838; Hyde Leslie, 1887, Plymouth, Vermont,* edited by Blanche Brown Bryant and Gertrude Elaine Baker (Springfield, Vt., William L. Bryant Foundation, 1970); Sarah Connell Ayer's *Diary, 1805–1835* (Portland, Me., Lefavor-Towner, 1910); and Maud Rittenhouse Mayne's *Maud,* edited by Richard Lee Strout (New York, Macmillan, 1939)—all provide vivid pictures of courtship.

Published collections of correspondence are both more numerous and generally more revealing than autobiographies or diaries. The correspondence of many public figures has been published as part of their complete works. It is in the early volumes, before the writer has achieved the distinction by which we know him or her, that one finds correspondence reflective of courtship. The papers of such luminaries as William Lloyd Garrison, Ulysses S. Grant, Rutherford B. Hayes, and Daniel Webster all contain accounts of courtship. Men and women less well known than these national leaders, but with reputations in literary, educational, or religious circles, were often honored by volumes devoted to their "life and letters." Although frequently expurgated, many of these are still rich in data on the transition to marriage.

Women who died young were sometimes memorialized by the publication of their letters. *A Girl's Life Eighty Years Ago: The Letters of Eliza Southgate Bowne,* edited by Clarence Cook (New York, Charles Scribner, 1884, reprinted 1974), is among the very best of these. Collections of family correspondence, often published privately but available in research libraries, are another valuable resource. *Chronicles of the Nineteenth-Century: Family Letters of Blanche Butler and*

Note on Sources

Adelbert Ames, compiled by Blanche Butler Ames, and the *Minot Family Letters,* edited by Katherine Minot Channing, are two good examples.

Unpublished Material

Far more extensive than published diaries and correspondence are the letters, diaries, and occasional reminiscences still in manuscript form. Local and state historical societies, state and college archives, and public libraries contain the unpublished papers of a broad spectrum of Americans, from storekeepers and barbers to senators and bankers. Family papers have usually been acquired because of a prominent—and, in most cases, male—individual. However, since most men who had illustrious careers had ordinary courtships, even the papers of famous people can illuminate common experiences. A man's future as college president, scientist, or politician was rarely evident in his courtship.

While most family collections owe their existence to the eminence of one or two members, they often contain the papers of less-noteworthy relatives, including women. The genealogists and antiquarians who were responsible for the collection and preservation of most of these materials recognized that the records of everyday life generated by women were important. While men might note the progress of the harvest, the price of grain, or the rivalries between local office seekers, women were more likely to discuss family concerns—births, illnesses, marriages, visits paid to kinfolk and neighbors. Certain topics turn up with almost equal frequency in men's and women's letters: the state of the family's health, the quality of the local preaching, the weather, and the progress of a courtship were subjects with which both male and female letter writers felt comfortable. During the stage of the life cycle when courtship took place, men were concerned less with the world in which they would later make their mark than with personal relationships, choices, decisions, and conflicts. Correspondence between young people and their families, friends, and prospective mates survives in relative abundance and provides an extensive record of the behavior, ideas, and emotions surrounding the transition to marriage in the American past.

The manuscripts cited here represent the holdings of the major repositories in New England, the mid-Atlantic states, and the Midwest. (See the List of Abbreviations, pages 316–17, for specific names and locations.) With a few exceptions, neither manuscript collections nor published finding aids have been organized to facilitate this kind of research. *Women's History Sources: A Guide to Archives and Manuscript Collections in the United States,* edited by Andrea Hinding and published in 1979, is unique in having a subject index. While *Women's History Sources* is an invaluable tool for the researcher interested in all aspects of family history, it provides a jumping-off place rather than an itinerary for the journey.

In addition to Hinding, I used other published guides, individual collection descriptions and registers, and the archival staff of a library to help identify collections that might contain personal papers of middle-class Americans who reached courting age between 1770 and 1920. Once I established the date of birth of an individual, I examined any journals or letters written during his or her late adolescence and early adulthood. (Obviously, matters were greatly simplified when a marriage date appeared in the catalogue or collection register.) This approach turned up materials that sometimes surprised even the archivists and are the basis of the interpretations in this book.

NOTES

LIST OF ABBREVIATIONS

Manuscript Repositories

AAS	American Antiquarian Society, Worcester, Massachusetts
AIS	Archives of Industrial Society, University of Pittsburgh, Pittsburgh, Pennsylvania
AmC	Department of Special Collections, Amherst College, Amherst, Massachusetts
CHS	Chicago Historical Society, Chicago, Illinois
CL	Countway Library, Harvard Medical School, Boston, Massachusetts
CtHS	Connecticut Historical Society, Hartford, Connecticut
CtSL	Connecticut State Library, Hartford, Connecticut
CU	Columbia University Library, New York, New York
EI	Essex Institute, Salem, Massachusetts
HCL	Harvard College Library, Cambridge, Massachusetts
HL	Huntington Library, Pasadena, California
HSP	Historical Society of Pennsylvania, Philadelphia, Pennsylvania
HSWP	Historical Society of Western Pennsylvania, Pittsburgh, Pennsylvania
HUA	Harvard University Archives, Cambridge, Massachusetts
IHS	Indiana Historical Society, Indianapolis, Indiana
ISL	Indiana State Library, Indianapolis, Indiana
LC	Library of Congress, Washington, D.C.
MeHS	Maine Historical Society, Portland, Maine
MHS	Massachusetts Historical Society, Boston, Massachusetts
MIT	Institute Archives and Special Collections, Massachusetts Institute of Technology Libraries, Cambridge, Massachusetts
MNHS	Minnesota Historical Society, St. Paul, Minnesota
NHHS	New Hampshire Historical Society, Concord, New Hampshire
NL	Newberry Library, Chicago, Illinois
N-YHS	New-York Historical Society, New York, New York
NYPL	Rare Books and Manuscripts Division, Astor, Lenox & Tilden Foundation, New York Public Library, New York, New York
OSV	Old Sturbridge Village Library, Sturbridge, Massachusetts
PC	Private Collection
SDL	Stowe-Day Foundation Library, Hartford, Connecticut
SHSW	State Historical Society of Wisconsin, Madison, Wisconsin
SL	Schlesinger Library, Radcliffe College, Cambridge, Massachusetts
SSC	Sophia Smith Collection, Smith College, Northampton, Massachusetts

UCB   Bancroft Library, University of California, Berkeley, California
UCL   University of Chicago Library, Chicago, Illinois
UWA   University of Wisconsin Archives, Madison, Wisconsin
WCM   Waukesha County Museum, Waukesha, Wisconsin
WRHS   Western Reserve Historical Society, Cleveland, Ohio
YL   Yale University Library, New Haven, Connecticut

Journals Cited

AAAPSS *Annals, American Academy of Political and Social Science*
AHR   *American Historical Review*
AJS   *American Journal of Sociology*
AQ   *American Quarterly*
ASR   *American Sociological Review*
BHM   *Bulletin of the History of Medicine*
EIC   *Essex Institute Collections*
FPP   *Family Planning Perspectives*
FS   *Feminist Studies*
IRSH   *International Review of Social History*
JAH   *Journal of American History*
JAP   *Journal of Abnormal Psychology*
JASP   *Journal of Abnormal and Social Psychology*
JIH   *Journal of Interdisciplinary History*
JMF   *Journal of Marriage and the Family*
JPC   *Journal of Popular Culture*
JSH   *Journal of Social History*
JSI   *Journal of Social Issues*
MFL   *Marriage and Family Living*
N-YHSC *New-York Historical Society Collections*
PAAS   *Proceedings of the American Antiquarian Society*
Signs   *Signs: Journal of Women in Culture and Society*
WMQ   *William and Mary Quarterly*

INTRODUCTION

1. Rutherford B. Hayes, *Diary and Letters,* ed. by Charles Richard Williams (Columbus, Oh., 1922), vol. I, p. 447.
2. Ibid., pp. 447, 444.
3. Ibid., p. 444.
4. Ibid.
5. The regional boundaries of the study shift over time. In the late eighteenth and the early nineteenth centuries, the North was New England and the Middle States (New York, New Jersey, and Pennsylvania). Of the courtships stud-

With the exception of dates, the bracketed figures in a note refer to its original complete citation in a particular chapter.

ied between 1770 and 1830, 85 percent took place in New England. New England-landers predominate in the next decades as well, but to a lesser extent. A quarter of the group courting from 1830 to 1860 lived in the Midwest. From 1860 to 1890, there were as many midwesterners as New Englanders in the data. During the final three decades of the study (1890–1920), New England, the Middle States, and the Midwest each accounted for about 30 percent of the couples, with westerners composing the remaining 10 percent. Because my research was confined to these areas, I cannot make cross-regional comparisons. A similar study has yet to be done on the South. Two recent social histories of the South—Catherine Clinton's *The Plantation Mistress: Woman's World in the Old South* (New York, 1982), and Bertram Wyatt Brown's *Southern Honor: Ethics and Behavior in the Old South* (New York, 1982)—discuss courtship only briefly. Steven M. Stowe's essay, "The *Thing,* Not Its Vision: A Woman's Courtship and Her Sphere in the Southern Planter Class," *FS* 9 (1 [Spring 1983]): 113–30, analyzes one southern courtship in depth.

6. *The Culture of Professionalism: The Middle Class and the Development of Higher Education in America* (New York, 1976), p. 163.

7. *Memories of Martha Seymour Coman* (Boston, 1913), p.26.

8. U.S. Department of the Census, *Historical Statistics of the United States from Colonial Times to the Present,* Bicentennial Edition (Washington, D.C., 1976), pp. 379, 383; Donald J. Bogue, *Population of the U.S.* (Glencoe, Ill., 1959), p. 328.

9. Louisa Jane Trumbull, Diary, 2 April 1835, Trumbull Family Papers, AAS.

10. Simeon Baldwin to Rebecca Sherman, 14 May 1786, Baldwin Family Papers, YL.

11. J. C. Furnas, *The Americans: A Social History of the United States, 1587–1914* (New York, 1969), p. 378; Alvin Harlow, *Old Post Bag: The Story of the Sending of a Letter in Ancient and Modern Times* (New York, 1928), p. 278.

Until the first low-postage act was passed in 1845, rates were based on the number of sheets of paper rather than on weight.

12. Bessie Huntting to Edward Rudd, n.d. [September 1858], Huntting-Rudd Papers, SL.

13. *Life and Letters of John Howard Raymond* (New York, 1881), p. 135.

14. Ibid.

15. Harriet Chamberlain to William H. Mason, 2 November 1866, William H. Mason Correspondence, typescript, SHSW.

Sometimes letters could be a frustrating way for a couple to communicate. Lawrence Chamberlain, for example, found it "vexing . . . this constant harassment & 'uncertainty' . . . I *can't* say any more about these things by letter. I am sick of it—completely," he told his fiancée in 1855 (Lawrence Chamberlain to Fannie Adams, 21 September 1855, Chamberlain Papers, SL).

16. Bessie Huntting to Edward Rudd, n.d. [September 1858] [12].

CHAPTER 1. "A CONNECTION OF HANDS"

1. Ephraim Abbott to Mary Pearson, 1 July and 13 May 1808, Ephraim Abbott Papers, AAS.

2. Ephraim to Mary, 31 December and 30 June 1808.

3. Ephraim to Mary, 26 October and 30 June 1808; Mary to Ephraim, 16 April 1809; Ephraim to Mary, 26 October 1808.

4. Ephraim to Mary, 13 May 1808 and 17 March 1810; Mary to Ephraim, 19 June 1812.

5 Mary to Ephraim, 19 June 1812; Ephraim to Mary, 30 June 1808.

6. Ephraim to Mary, 18 September 1811.

7. Mary to Ephraim, 30 November 1812. This job offer had been relayed to Ephraim through Mary Pearson's family.

8. Ephraim to Mary, 30 September 1811; Mary to Ephraim, 26 May 1813.

9. Ephraim to Mary, August 1811 and 27 October 1813.

10. Mary to Ephraim, 20 December 1813.

11. Mary to Ephraim, 20 December 1813.

12. Mary to Ephraim, 25 October 1812. The great majority of the letters in the Abbott papers were written by Ephraim to Mary. All of her responses during the first four years of the courtship are missing. It is not unusual for the male side of a courtship correspondence to fare better over time: women appear to have preserved letters somewhat more effectively than men did.

13. Mary to Ephraim, 25 October 1812.

14. Ernest Earnest, *The American Eve in Fact and Fiction, 1774–1914* (Champaign-Urbana, Ill., 1974), p. 146; Pamela Brown, Diary, 24 July 1836, in *The Diaries of Sally and Pamela Brown; Hyde Leslie, 1887, Plymouth, Vermont,* ed. by Blanche Brown Bryant and Gertrude Elaine Baker (Springfield, Vt., 1970), p. 47.

In her path-breaking article on female friendship, Carroll Smith-Rosenberg argues that nineteenth-century America was characterized by "severe social restrictions on intimacy between young men and women." I found little evidence of such restrictions in force among middle-class northerners before the Civil War. Smith-Rosenberg's picture of men "as an other or out group, segregated into different schools, supported by their own male network of friends and kin, socialized to different behavior and coached to a proper formality in courtship behavior," may be accurate for the colonial élite and the southern planter class, but it does not describe the middle-class pattern in the ante-bellum North. See "The Female World of Love and Ritual: Relations between Women in Nineteenth-century America," *Signs* 1 (1 [1975]): 9,21.

15. Pamela Brown, Diary, 7 and 8 March and 4 July 1836 [14], p. 36; Christopher Columbus Baldwin, Diary, 22 February 1830, *Diary of Christopher Columbus Baldwin, 1829–1835* (New York, 1901), p. 54.

16. David Shepard, Jr., Diary, 27 May and 27 July 1798, *The Chester and Westfield, Mass. Diaries,* ed. by Alexander G. Rose III (Baltimore, 1975), pp. 159–60. Used by permission. The fact that David Shepard wrote his diary in a Latin-based code may help explain its slightly bawdy tone.

17. Lucy Harris, "My Story," typescript, PC; Mary Guion, Diary, 20 June 1807, N–YHS.

18. Mary Guion, Diary, 20 June 1807 [17].

19. George Elliott Howard, *A History of Matrimonial Institutions,* (Chicago, 1904), vol. II, pp. 164–65.

Most studies of parental control of marriage fail to distinguish adequately between these two different aspects of marriage choice. See, for example, Philip Greven, *Four Generations: Population, Land, and Family in Colonial Andover, Massachusetts* (Ithaca, N.Y., 1970); and Daniel Scott Smith, "Parental Power and Marriage Patterns: An Analysis of Historical Trends in Hingham, Mass." in Michael Gordon, ed. *The American Family in Social-Historical Perspective*, 2nd ed. (New York, 1978), pp. 87–100.

20. Quoted in Edmund Morgan, *The Puritan Family: Religion and Domestic Relations in Seventeenth-Century New England* (New York, 1966), p. 84.

In his intensive demographic analysis of Hingham, Massachusetts, Daniel Scott Smith devised calculations to measure the influence of parental wealth, birth order, and residence on marriage making; all of the indicators point to "the severing of direct property considerations from marriage" and the "decline of parental involvement in marriage formation" during the last quarter of the eighteenth century ("Parental Power" [19], p. 96).

21. The single best work on the experience of young men in this period is Joseph Kett, *Rites of Passage: Adolescence in America, 1790 to the Present* (New York, 1977). The term "semidependence" is his.

22. On young women, see Nancy F. Cott, *The Bonds of Womanhood: Woman's Sphere in New England, 1780–1835* (New Haven, Conn., 1977); and Thomas Dublin, *Women at Work: The Transformation of Work and Community in Lowell, MA., 1826–1960* (New York, 1979).

23. John March to Mrs. Hale, 29 June 1831, John March Correspondence, EI; *A Girl's Life Eighty Years Ago: Selected Letters of Eliza Southgate Bowne*, ed. by Clarence Cook (New York, 1884), pp. 140–41.

24. Hannah Huntington to Samuel Huntington, n.d. [1791], Hannah Huntington Correspondence, WRHS; Lewis Morris, Jr., to his father, 19 December 1782, *N-YHSC* (1875), pp. 509–10.

25. Thomas R. Sullivan to Charlotte Blake, 16 September 1824, Sullivan–Russell Papers, MHS; James Freeman to Daniel Davis, 16 August 1785, in *Minot Family Letters*, ed. by Katherine Channing (Sherborn, Mass., 1957), p. 27; Harriet Porter to Lyman Beecher, 18 September 1817, SDL.

Thomas Sullivan quoted his father's letter in his own letter to Charlotte. Many of the letters cited here include such direct quotations.

26. William Lloyd Garrison to Helen Benson, 5 April 1834, in *Letters*, vol. I, ed. by Walter H. Merrill (Cambridge, Mass., 1971), p. 312.

27. At least one young man deeply resented his family's interference—from afar—in his marriage plans; see Calvin Fletcher to his sister, 27 August 1820, Calvin Fletcher Papers, IHS.

28. Henry Poor to Mary Pierce, 26 January 1840, Poor Family Papers, SL. For three examples of resistance to parental authority, see Eunice Callender to Sarah Ripley, 24 June 1818, Stearns Collection, SL; Marcia [Northy] to Martha Boody, 23 October 1837, Northy Papers, EI; Mary Pierce to Henry Poor, 19 January 1840.

29. Henry Lloyd to James Lloyd, 19 February 1784, HCL; Harriet Atwood, Diary, 16 and 22 April 1811, in *A Sermon Preached at Haverhill (Mass.) in Remembrance of Mrs. Harriet A. Newell, Wife of the Rev. Samuel Newell, Missionary to India to Which Are Added Memoirs of Her Life*, ed. by Leonard Woods (Boston, 1815),

pp. 93–94; Mary Carter to Edmund Hovey, 27 July 1831, Edmund Hovey Papers, ISL.

Mary Beth Norton observes that "girls . . . often deliberately sought the advice of parents and friends as they reached decisions about whom to marry. Far from resenting their elders' interference, they generally welcomed it." Norton fails to comment on the consistency with which parents *declined* to give the advice their daughters sought (*Liberty's Daughters: The Revolutionary Experience of American Women* [Boston, 1980], p. 56).

30. James Freeman to Lois Freeman, 24 December 1782, in *Minot Family Letters* [25], p. 11; Mary Orne Tucker, Diary, 17 April 1802, EI; Susan Kittredge to Eliza Waite, 24 March 1792, Eliza Waite Correspondence, EI.

The "hand and heart" image was a recurrent one, for men as well as women.
31. Herman R. Lantz et al., "Pre-Industrial Patterns in the Colonial Family in America: A Content Analysis of Colonial Magazines," *ASR* 33 (1968): 420; Nancy F. Cott, "Eighteenth-Century Family and Social Life Revealed in Massachusetts Divorce Records," in Nancy F. Cott and Elizabeth Pleck, eds. *A Heritage of Her Own* (New York, 1979), p. 123.

32. Jesse Appleton to Ebenezer Adams, 10 February 1797, Jesse Appleton Letters, AAS.

Ronald Byars points out that the advice books for young men "described how a man might adopt a disciplined, frugal, studied, systematic approach to everything from shaving to choosing a wife"; see Ronald Byars, "The Making of the Self-Made Man: The Development of Masculine Roles and Images in Ante-Bellum America" (unpublished Ph.D. dissertation, Michigan State University, 1979), p. 76.

33. Simeon Baldwin to Rebecca Sherman, 24 December 1786, Baldwin Family Papers, YL; Eliza Southgate to Moses Porter, n.d. [1800], in *Girl's Life* [23], pp. 38, 41; Georgina Amory to John Lowell, Jr., 5 April 1824, John Lowell, Jr., Papers, MHS.

34. Eliza Chaplin to Laura Lovell, 28 July 1820, EI.

35. Ibid.

36. Linda Raymond to Benjamin Ward, 8 February 1822, Gertrude Foster Brown Papers, SL.

See William S. Cruzan to Nancy Tyner, 27 June 1834, Merrick Papers, IHS, for a similar case in the Midwest. Near strangers were not always rejected, however. The itinerant minister Lorenzo Dow proposed to a young woman after only a day's acquaintance and was accepted, at least partly on the strength of his reputation as an evangelist. See Peggy Dow, *Vicissitudes in the Wilderness* (Norwich, Conn., 1833).

37. James Barnard, Diary, June 1826, EI; *Daughter's Own Book* (Philadelphia, 1836), pp. 157–58.

38. Mary Guion, Diary, 12 July 1807 [17]; Eliza Southgate to Moses Porter, n.d. [1800], in *Girl's Life* [23], p. 40.

39. William Lloyd Garrison to Helen Benson, 6 June 1834, in *Letters* [26], vol. I, p. 359.

40. "The Spinning Wheel," in *American Musical Miscellany* (Northampton, Mass., 1798).

41. Zadoc Long to Julia Davis, 1 February 1824, in *The Journal of Zadoc Long*, ed. by Pierce Long (Caldwell, Idaho, 1943), p. 71. Used by permission of Caxton Printers, Inc.

42. Zadoc Long to Thomas Long, 10 July 1822, and to Julia Davis, 6 June 1822, in *Journal* [41], pp. 59, 61–62.

43. Cott, *Bonds*[22], p. 186.

This change in friendship was part of a larger trend which had a powerful effect on same-sex friendship. Cott examines what it meant for women when "ideas about the purpose and content of friendship" broadened and "individuals recognized and dwelled on private feelings, and deemed them worthy of communication to others" (ibid.).

Anthony Rotundo discusses male friendship in this period in "Manhood in America: Middle-Class Masculinity in the Northern United States, 1770–1910" (unpublished Ph. D. dissertation, Brandeis University, 1982), pp. 110–13.

44. Esther D. Berdt to Joseph Reed, 8 Dec. 1764, Joseph Reed Papers, N-YHS; Anonymous, *Reflections on Courtship and Marriage* (London, 1779), p. 22; Eliza Rhodes Fisher to Samuel Fisher, 4 November 1791, Samuel W. Fisher Papers, HSP.

45. Elizabeth Sherman to unknown suitor, n.d. [1786] Baldwin Family Papers, YL.

46. Maria Clinton to Cornelia Clinton, 3 December 1792, Gênet Papers, N-YHS; Mary to Elizabeth Peabody, quoted in Louise Hall Tharp, *Until Victory* (Boston, 1953), p. 127.

47. Dwight Foster, Journal, 7 January 1780, Foster Family Papers, AAS; Wyer Trumbull, Diary, 5 February 1816, EI.

48. Benjamin Ward to Linda Raymond, 21 March and 8 November 1818 [36]; Theodore Dwight to Abigail Alsop, 12 August 1792, Dwight Family Papers, NYPL.

49. Hannah Huntington to Samuel Huntington, n.d. [1791] [24]; Susan Huntington to "Miss L.," 1 January 1810, in Susan Huntington, *Memoirs*, ed. by Benjamin Wisner (Boston, 1826), p. 43; Mary Guion, Diary, n.d. [5 April 1807] [17].

50. Margaret Bayard Smith, Diary, 8 July 1800, LC; Sarah Connell Ayer, Diary, 11 February 1810, in *Diary of Sarah Connell Ayer* (Portland, Me., 1910), p. 43.

In his study of the rural Midwest, John Farragher notes that romantic love appeared in folksongs as "an illness from which no one recovers" (*Women and Men on the Overland Trail* [New Haven, Conn., 1979], p. 155).

51. Daniel White to Mary Wilder, 19 January 1807, in *Memorials of Mary Wilder White*, ed. by Mary Tileston (Boston, 1903), p. 260; John Brace, Journal, 19 February 1814, in *More Chronicles of a Pioneer School, From 1792 to 1833 Being Added History on the Litchfield Female Academy Kept by Miss Sarah Pierce and Her Nephew John Pierce Brace*, ed. by Emily Vanderpeel (New York, 1927), p. 85.

52. Mary Orne Tucker, Diary, 18 April 1802 [30]; Margaret Bayard Smith, Diary, 8 July 1800 [50].

53. Mary Orne Tucker, Diary, 18 April 1802 [30]. Linda Kerber discusses the political implications of women's novel reading in *Women of the Republic:*

Intellect and Ideology in Revolutionary America (Chapel Hill, N.C., 1980), p. 245.

54. Lydia Maria Child, *The American Frugal Housewife* (Boston, 1833), p. 94; Adriel Ely to Aaron Olmstead, 8 August 1836, Olmstead Papers, N-YHS.

55. Aaron Olmstead to Adriel Ely, 31 August 1836 [54]; Lucien Boynton, Journal, 17 August 1839, in "Selections from the Journal of Lucien Boynton, 1835–1853," *PAAS* (New Series) 33 (October 1933): 343.

The classic formulation of the "Cult of True Womanhood" is Barbara Welter's; see her *Dimity Convictions: The American Woman in the Nineteenth Century* (Athens, Oh., 1976), pp. 21–42. For the change in sexual ideology, see Nancy F. Cott, "Passionlessness: An Interpretation of Victorian Sexual Ideology, 1790–1850," *Signs* 4 (2 [1978]): 219–36, and pp. 48–54 in this book.

56. Lucien Boynton, Journal, 4 May 1839, in "Selections" [55], p. 340; Benjamin Ward to Linda Raymond, 13 May 1819 [36]; Calvin Fletcher to his brother, 23 February 1823, *Diary of Calvin Fletcher*, ed. by Gayle Thornbrough (Indianapolis, 1972), vol. I, p. 87; Hannah Huntington to Samuel Huntington, n.d. [1791] [24].

57. Aquila Giles to Elizabeth Shipton, n.d. [1780s], Aquila Giles Papers, N-YHS; Stephen Salisbury to Elizabeth Tuckerman, 13 December 1796, Salisbury Family Papers, AAS; Lewis Morris, Jr., to Nancy Elliott, 1 December 1782, Morris Miscellaneous Papers, N-YHS. Also see Ephraim Abbott to Mary Holyoke Pearson, 16 April and 22 May 1809 and 31 July 1813.

58. John Adams, *Diary and Autobiography*, ed. by Lyman Butterfield, Leonard C. Farber, and Wendell D. Garrett (Cambridge, Mass., 1961), vol. I, p. 109.

59. Margaret Bayard Smith, Diary, n.d. [1800] [50].

60. Mary Wilder to Daniel White, 21 January 1807; Daniel White to Mary Wilder, 23 January and 18 April 1807, in *Memorials* [51], pp. 261, 264, 297.

61. In her discussion of the protective features of the formal courtship style common among genteel Americans in the late eighteenth century, Mary Beth Norton overlooks the fear of insincerity it produced (*Liberty's Daughters* [29], p. 52).

62. Eliza Southgate Bowne to Moses Porter, 18 March 1801, in *Girl's Life* [23], p. 47; Hannah Huntington to Samuel Huntington, Wed. eve. n.d. [1791], and Tues. n.d. [1791] [24].

63. Daniel Scott Smith and Michael Hindus, "Premarital Pregnancy in America, 1640–1971; An Overview and Interpretation," *JIH* 4 (1975): 537–70.

64. Lantz et al., "Pre-Industrial Patterns" [31], p. 423; and Smith and Hindus, "Premarital Pregnancy" [63], p. 547.

65. When Smith and Hindus charted the long-term trends in the premarital pregnancy ratio, they found "troughs" in the seventeenth and mid-nineteenth centuries and "peaks" in the late eighteenth and late nineteenth centuries. ("Premarital Pregnancy" [63], figure 1, p. 538.) Numerous community studies have confirmed this pattern; see, for example, John Demos, "Family in Colonial Bristol, Rhode Island: An Experiment in Historical Demography," *WMQ* 25 (January 1968): 56; Robert Gross, *The Minutemen and Their World* (New York, 1976), p. 235; and Christopher Jedrey, *The World of John Cleaveland: Family and Community in Eighteenth-Century New England* (New York, 1979), p. 152.

66. Henry Stiles, *Bundling, Its Origins, Progress and Decline in America* (n.p., 1871), p. 108. Both Arthur Calhoun's classic *A Social History of the American Family*, vol. I (Cleveland, 1917); and Howard's *History of Matrimonial Institutions* [19] rely, almost to the word, on Stiles's account in their discussions of bundling. Smith and Hindus present the arguments of contemporary scholars ("Premarital Pregnancy" [63], pp. 555–56) and point out that the material explanation for what Stiles called the "progress and decline" of bundling fails to account for the apparent absence of the practice in the seventeenth century, when living conditions were far more primitive than they were by the mid-1700s, or for the seasonal stability in the rate of premarital conceptions. On another point, however, these authors indirectly support Stiles's conclusion, in which Howard concurred, that bundling was "confined to the more humble and less cultivated classes." Smith and Hindus found that the "sexually permissive subculture" in Hingham was drawn from the less wealthy segments of the town's population (ibid., p. 547).

67. Stiles, *Bundling* [66], p. 13; Howard, *Matrimonial* [19], pp. 184–85.

68. Smith and Hindus, "Premarital Pregnancy" [63], p. 556.

69. Quoted in Howard, *Matrimonial* [19], p. 183, and in Stiles, *Bundling* [66], p. 55.

70. The broadside is printed in its entirety in Stiles, *Bundling* [66], pp. 83–89.

71. Ibid., p. 109; Adams, *Diary* [58], vol. I, p. 196.

Laurel Thatcher Ulrich suggests that bundling was "an attempt to preserve traditional parental *protection* of daughters in a marriage system which increasingly emphasized sexual attraction" *(Good Wives: Image and Reality in the Lives of Women in Northern New England, 1650–1750* [New York, 1982], p. 122).

72. Stiles, *Bundling* [66], p. 87.

73. Cott, "Passionlessness" [55], pp. 221, 228.

Stiles's idea was that bundling's decline was due to the French and Indian War: young men who returned "habituated . . . to vice and recklessness stripped bundling of its innocence." Then, he reasoned, after the Revolution, "the improved condition of the people . . . the larger and better warmed houses" brought about its final demise *(Bundling* [66], p. 60).

74. David Shepard, Jr., Diary, 27 May and 17 June 1798, pp. 155–56, 169–70 [16].

One historian has recently argued that because eighteenth-century women who "engaged in premarital sex, or who were merely suspected of having done so, had greatly lessened their chances for a good marriage, . . . many genteel women adhered carefully to strict standards of behavior." My evidence, however, indicates that outside—or even on the fringes—of genteel circles, standards or at least adherence to them may not have been so strict. There are, after all, those pregnant brides to be accounted for. See Norton, *Liberty's Daughters* [29], p. 53.

75. Mary Guion, Diary, 4 September 1807 [17]; Patty Rogers, Diary, 1785, AAS.

76. Cott's "Passionlessness" [55] is the basis for this discussion.

77. Quoted in Cott, "Passionlessness" [55], pp. 226–27; and Cott, *Bonds* [22], p. 148.

78. John Gregory, *A Father's Legacy to His Daughters* (Boston 1791), pp. 20–21;

Charles Rosenberg, "Sexuality, Class, and Role in Nineteenth-Century America," *AQ* 25 (May 1973): 135.

Dallett Hemphill has traced the change in etiquette manuals in her unpublished paper, "Face to Face: Etiquette and Male-Female Relations, 1760–1860."
79. Elias Nason to Mira Bigelow, 23 February 1834, Charles Everett to Elias Nason, 5 May 1833, Elias Nason Papers, AAS; George Cutler, quoted in Earnest, *American Eve* [14], p. 72.
80. Catherine Joss, *Autobiography* (Cleveland, Oh., 1891), p. 82; Charles Everett to Elias Nason, 5 May 1833 [79].
81. Mira Bigelow to Elias Nason, 31 October 1831; Elias to Mira, 19 January 1833 [79].
82. Victorian sexual repression has been widely interpreted as a result of the demands of a nascent capitalist economy; see, especially, Peter T. Cominus, "Late Victorian Sexual Respectability and the Social System," *IRSH* 8 (1963): 18–48, 216–50; and Steven Marcus, *The Other Victorians: A Study of Sexuality and Pornography in Mid-Nineteenth-Century America* (New York, 1966). Carl Degler has pointed out that the analogy between the "movement to limit expenditure" and the "frugal and conserving habits of a nascent capitalist economy" is inappropriate, since "throughout the century the central problem was finding markets for goods, not conserving resources" (*At Odds, Women and the Family in America, 1776–Present* [New York, 1980], p. 293). Nevertheless, for the individual middle-class young man, thrift, frugality, and deferred gratification—although increasingly defined in terms of the consumption they made possible—were still given enough value to make sexual restraint a source of self-esteem.

CHAPTER 2. "THE SCENE IS ABOUT TO BE CHANGED"

1. Timothy Pickering to John Pickering, 9 August 1799, Pickering Family Papers, EI.
2. "The Life or Biography of Silas Felton Written by Himself," *PAAS* 69 (Part 2 [October 1959]): 130–32.
3. Ibid., pp. 136–38, 147.
4. Ibid., pp. 137–38.
5. Ibid., p. 138.
6. Ibid., p. 147.
7. Ibid, p. 137; Mary White Smith to Samuel Francis Smith, 1 September 1834, Samuel Francis Smith Papers, HL; Susan Huntington to "Miss L," 1 January 1810, in Susan Huntington, *Memoirs*, ed. by Benjamin Wisner (Boston, 1826), p. 42; Anna Quincy Thaxter Parsons, Journal, 13 April 1821, *EIC* 87 (4 [October 1951]): 314; Lorenzo Dow, "Reflections on Matrimony," in Peggy Dow, *Vicissitudes in the Wilderness* (Norwich, Conn., 1833), p. 168; Enoch Lincoln to Leonard Parker, 19 May 1814, Leonard Moody Parker Papers, AAS.

8. Theodore Weld, Angelina Grimké Weld, and Sarah M. Grimké, *Letters, 1822–1844*, ed. by Gilbert Barnes and Dwight L. Dumond (New York, 1934), vol. I, pp. 640, 358.

9. William Alcott, *The Young Wife* (Boston, 1837), p. 69; Benjamin Ward to Linda Raymond, 23 May 1818, Gertrude Foster Brown Papers, SL.

10. Daniel Webster to Thomas Merrill, 28 May 1804, in *Writings and Speeches of Daniel Webster*, ed. by Fletcher Webster (Boston, 1913), vol. 17, p. 171; Levi Lockling to Aaron Olmstead, 28 September 1838, Olmstead Papers, N-YHS.

11. Benjamin Ward to Linda Raymond, 14 July 1822 [9]; Jesse Appleton to Ebenezer Adams, 31 May 1797, Jesse Appleton Letters, AAS; Enoch Lincoln to Leonard Parker, 19 May 1814 [7].

12. Daniel Davis to James Freeman, 28 August 1786, in *Minot Family Letters*, ed. by Katherine Channing (Shelburn, Mass., 1957), pp. 47–48; Henry Channing to Simeon Baldwin, 17 August 1787, Baldwin Family Papers, YL.

13. Sarah Chester Williams to Erastus Smith, 2–4 September 1806, Lincoln Clark Papers, HL.

14. Eliza Rotch to her cousin, 2 June 1828, Rotch Family Papers, MHS; Mary L. Ware, *Memoir*, ed. by Edward Brooke Hall (Boston, 1853), p. 183; Catharine Beecher, "Poem" in Emily Noyes Vanderpoel, comp., *Chronicles of a Pioneer School From 1792–1833*, ed. by Elizabeth C. Barney Buel (Cambridge, Mass., 1903), pp. 186–87; Hannah Emery to Mary Carter, 17 October 1791, Cutts Family Ms., EI.

15. William Edmond Curtis, Diary, 28 December 1843, in *Letters and Journals*, ed. by Elizabeth Curtis (New York, 1926), p. 135.

16. Alexis de Tocqueville, *Democracy in America* (New York, 1945), vol. II, p. 213; Mary Orne Tucker, Diary, 13 May 1802, EI; Lydia Maria Child, *The American Frugal Housewife* (Boston, 1832), p. 95.

17. Mary Brown to Eunice Huntington Palmer, 25 September 1808, Ephraim Brown Papers, WRHS; Nancy Flynt to Mercy Flynt Morris, n.d. [1810], Nancy Flynt Morris Diary and Letters, CtHS; Abigail May, Journal, 1796, MeHS.

18. Ware, *Memoir* [14], p. 182; Susan Huntington to her sister-in-law, 30 May 1809, in *Memoirs* [7], p. 34; Hannah Emery to Mary Carter, 17 October 1791 [14]; Harriet Porter to Lyman Beecher, 18 September 1817, SDL; Alcott, *Young Wife* [9], p. 29.

19. Quoted in Barbara Welter, *Dimity Convictions: The American Woman in the Nineteenth Century* (Athens, Oh., 1976), p. 38; Margaret Bayard Smith, Diary, 28 September 1800, Margaret Bayard Smith Papers, LC.

20. De Tocqueville, *Democracy* [16], p. 225; Hannah Huntington to Samuel Huntington, Tues. n.d. [1791], Hannah Huntington Letters, WRHS; Margaret Bayard to Samuel Smith, 19 July 1800 [19]; Ware, *Memoir* [14], p. 183. Samuel Smith's response was to suggest that they "banish the term 'dependence' from [their] language" (Samuel Smith to Margaret Bayard, 22 July 1800 [19]).

21. George Cutler, Journal, 31 August 1820, in Vanderpoel, *Chronicles* [14], p. 196.

22. M. H. Prentiss to Arabella Carter, 13 October 1828, Timothy Carter Papers, MeHS.

23. Susan Lesley, *Recollections of My Mother* (Boston, 1899), p. 68.

24. Catharine Beecher to Louisa Wait, June 1821, Beecher Stowe Collection,

SL; Harriet Coxe to Albert Bledsoe, 6 January 1836 and 17 November 1835, Bledsoe-Herrick Papers, SL.

25. Persis Sibley, Diary, 9 May 1841, MeHS.

On homesickness and separation anxiety among young men, see E. Anthony Rotundo, "Manhood in America: Middle-Class Masculinity in the Northern United States, 1770–1910" (unpublished Ph.D. dissertation, Brandeis University, 1982), pp. 222–28.

26. M. Prentiss to Arabella Carter, 13 October 1828 [22]; Jerusha Brainerd Kellogg to her cousin, 7 June 1823, CtHS; Margaret Bayard to Samuel Smith, 13 September 1800 [19]; Harriet Coxe to Albert Bledsoe, 6 January 1836 [24]; William Lloyd Garrison to Helen Benson, 21 June 1834, in *Letters*, ed. by Walter H. Merrill (Cambridge, Mass., 1971), vol. I, p. 369.

27. For examples, see Garrison-Benson correspondence [26], Grimké-Weld correspondence [8] and the Henry Blackwell–Lucy Stone and Samuel Blackwell–Antoinette Brown letters quoted in Margo Horn, "Family Ties: The Blackwells: A Study in the Dynamics of Family Life in Nineteenth-Century America" (unpublished Ph.D. dissertation, Tufts, 1980), chap. 4, passim.

28. Simeon Baldwin to Rebecca Sherman, 24 September 1786 [12]; Margaret Bayard to Samuel Smith, 13 September 1800 [19].

29. Roger Baldwin to Emily Perkins, 8 May 1820, Baldwin Family Papers, YL.

The usual custom was for the young man to seek the consent of a woman's parents from her father; for one exception, see John March to Mrs. Hale, 29 June 1831, March Correspondence, EI.

30. Morrill Wyman to Elizabeth Pulsifer, 12 June 1839, Robert S. Pulsifer Papers, MHS: John March to Alice Hale, 2 and 6 April 1832 [29].

For Elizabeth Pulsifer's angry response to her fiancé's unseemly patience, see Elizabeth to Morrill, 30 June 1839.

31. John Lowell, Jr., to Georgina Amory, 11 April 1824, John Lowell, Jr., Papers, MHS; Hannah Huntington to Samuel Huntington, n.d. [1791] [20].

32. For examples of couples who struggled with the conflict between male eagerness and female hesitation, see Julia Cowles, Diary, 18 March 1802, in *Diaries of Julia Cowles*, ed. by Laura Hadley Moseley (New Haven, 1931); Mary Pearson to Ephraim Abbott, 20 December 1813, Ephraim Abbott Papers, AAS; John Lowell, Jr., to Georgina Amory, 11 April 1824 and Georgina to John, 16 April 1824 [31]; John March to Alice Hale, 26 March, 2 and 6 April 1832 [29]; Harriet Coxe to Albert Bledsoe, 12 December 1825 [24]; Henry Poor to Mary Pierce, 6 October, 24 November, and 6 December 1839, Mary to Henry, 30 November 1839; Henry to Mary, 10 February, 20 June, and 6 and 20 December 1840, Poor Family Papers, SL.

For examples of externally imposed delays, see *Autobiography of Reverend Enoch Pond* (Boston, 1884), pp. 28–29; Lucy Pierce to Frederick Hedges, n.d. [1830], Poor Family Papers, SL; Edmund O. Hovey to Mary Carter, 16 July 1831 and Mary to Edmund, 27 July 1831, Edmund O. Hovey Papers, ISL; John Shumway to Louisa Russ, 23 March 1858, John Shumway Papers, MNHS.

33. Georgina Amory to John Lowell, Jr., 16 April 1824 [31].

34. Margaret Bayard to Samuel Smith, 13 September 1800 [19]; Anna Rawle to Rebecca Shoemaker, 7 June 1783, Shoemaker Papers, HSP; Hannah Hunting-

ton to Samuel Huntington, n.d. [1791] [20]; Samuel Rowland Fisher, Diary, 25 May 1792, HSP; Mary Holyoke Pearson to Ephraim Abbott, 20 December 1813 [32].

For one man who experienced similar "hopes & fears & anxious thoughts," see Cyrus Farnum to Anne White, 10 December 1843, Hooker Papers, SL.

35. Margaret Bayard to Samuel Smith, 13 September 1800 [19]; Samuel Fisher, Diary, 28 May 1792 [34].

Nancy F. Cott recognized this emotional reaction among middle-class New England women in the 1820s and 1830s and described it as a "marriage trauma." She suggested that it was manifested as a "withdrawal of emotional intensity from the too burdened marriage choice." I would argue that in fact it shows up in the conflicts of women as the wedding day approached and that it was common throughout the 1780–1840 period. See *The Bonds of Womanhood: Woman's Sphere in New England, 1780–1835* (New Haven, 1977), p. 80.

36. Anna Rawle to her mother, 20 July 1783 [34]; Mary Holyoke Pearson to Ephraim Abbott, 20 December 1813 [32]; Georgina Amory to John Lowell, Jr., 5 December 1824 [31].

37. De Tocqueville, *Democracy* [16], pp. 212–13.

38. Alice Morse Earle, *Customs and Fashions in Old New England* (New York, 1894), p. 73.

39. For this formulation of woman's role in early America, see Laurel Thatcher Ulrich, *Good Wives: Image and Reality in the Lives of Women in Northern New England, 1650–1750* (New York, 1982).

40. Hannah Jackson Cabot to Sarah Jackson Russell, 30 May 1844, Almy Family Papers, SL; Harriet Porter to Lyman Beecher, 18 September 1817 [18].

41. Zadoc Long to Julia Davis, 5 July 1824, in *The Journal of Zadoc Long*, ed. by Pierce Long (Caldwell, Idaho, 1943), pp. 72–73.

42. William Andrews to Charles Andrews, 17 June 1895, Charles McLean Andrews Papers, YL. In at least one case, the bride also received help from the groom's mother; see Sarah Chester Williams to Erastus Smith, 15 August 1806 [13].

43. Mary Wilder to Daniel A. White, 9 April 1807, in *Memorials*, ed. by Mary Wilder Tileston (Boston, 1903), p. 295; Sarah Chester Williams to Erastus Smith, 15 August 1806 [13]. For one couple's detailed exchanges on their future living situation, see Caleb Snow to Sarah Drew, 26 January and 5 and 6 February 1827, Caleb Snow Papers, MHS.

44. Mary Guion, Diary, 2 August 1807, N-YHS; Catherine Joss, *Autobiography* (Cleveland, 1891), p. 82.

45. The requirement to post banns two weeks before the wedding persisted in the New England States, but elsewhere in the North, a system of licenses was replacing public notice, see Michael Grossberg, "Law and the Family in Nineteenth-Century America" (unpublished Ph.D. dissertation, Brandeis University, 1980), pp. 82–83.

46. Ira Miltimore to Margaret King, 7 July 1839, Miltimore Papers, CHS.

47. *The Early Days of Thomas Whittemore* (Boston, 1859), p. 281; *The Diary of Sarah Connell Ayer, 1805–1835* (Portland, Me., 1910), p. 174.

48. Eliza Rotch to her cousin, 2 September 1828 [14]; Henry Poor to Mary Pierce, Thanksgiving, 1839 [32].
49. See Henry Poor to Mary Pierce, Thanksgiving, 1839 [32].
50. Roger Baldwin to Ebenezer Baldwin, 11 October 1820, [29]; Harriet Coxe to Albert Bledsoe, 25 February 1836 and Albert to Harriet, 8 March 1836 [24].
51. Mary Guion, Diary, 1, 7, and 8 February 1803 [44].
52. Anna Quincy Thaxter Parsons, Journal, 24 April 1821 [7], pp. 324–25.
53. Lucy Harris, "My Story," typescript, PC.
54. Ibid.; Henry Poor to Mary Pierce, 24 November 1839 [32]; George Moore, Diary, 5 January 1837, AAS.
55. Anna Quincy Thaxter Parsons, Journal, 26 April 1821 [7], pp. 324–25; Eliza Rotch to her cousin, 2 September 1828 [14].
56. Eliza Rotch to her cousin, 2 September 1828 [14]; William Andrews to Charles Andrews, 17 June 1895 [42].
57. Mary Lee to Henry Lee, 17 May 1821, in *Henry and Mary Lee: Letters and Journals*, ed. by Frances Rollins Morse (Boston, 1926), p. 237; Harriet Coxe to Albert Bledsoe, 13 February 1836 [24].
58. Carroll Smith-Rosenberg suggests that this practice "functioned to reassure the young woman herself, and her friends and kin, that though marriage might alter it would not destroy old bonds of intimacy and familiarity"; see "The Female World of Love and Ritual: Relations Between Women in Nineteenth-Century America," *Signs* 1 (1 [1975]): 23.
59. William Lloyd Garrison to George Benson, 12 September 1834, in *Letters*, vol. I, pp. 411–12; Priscilla Webster Page, *Personal Reminiscences* (New York, 1886), p. 106.
60. Sally Howe to Eliza Lee Cabot, 31 October 1813, in Susan Lesley, *Recollections* [23], p. 104; Mary L. Ware to "Nancy," 22 July 1827, in Ware, *Memoir* [14], p. 197.
61. See, for example, Hannah Emery to Mary Carter, 30 December 1791 [14]; Margaret Bayard Smith to her family, 5 October 1800 [19]; Louise Hall Tharp, *Until Victory* (Boston, 1953), p. 90.

CHAPTER 3. *"WE* ARE NOT LIKE MOST PEOPLE"

1. Thomas Woody, *A History of Women's Education in the United States*, (New York, 1929), vol. I., p. 368.
2. Mary Ballard to William Ross, 4 August 1857, Mary P. Ballard Letters, WRHS.
3. William Ross to Mary Ballard, 1 August 1857; Mary to William, n.d. [October 1857].
4. Mary Ballard to William Ross, n.d. [October 1857]; William to Mary, 25 November 1857.
5. William Ross to Mary Ballard, 25 November 1857; Mary to William, 18 December 1857.

There is evidence that in time William did succeed in "influencing" Mary's religious sentiments; see William to Mary, 23 February 1858.

6. William Ross to Mary Ballard, 30 December 1857; Mary to William, 10 March 1858; William to Mary, 17 March 1858; Mary to William, 11 June 1858.

7. Mary Ballard to William Ross, Thursday evening [summer 1858]; William to Mary, 22 August 1858.

8. William Ross to Mary Ballard, 27 September 1858.

9. Woody, *Women's Education* [1], p. 368.

10 Alexis de Tocqueville, *Democracy in America* (New York, 1945), vol. II, p. 223.

11. George Moore, Diary, 26 January 1837 AAS; Emerson quoted by Moore; *The Sphere and Duties of Woman*, quoted in Barbara Welter, *Dimity Convictions: The American Woman in the Nineteenth Century* (Athens, Oh., 1976), p. 28.

12. John Patch to Margaret Poor, 26 April 1848, Patch-Poor Correspondence, EI; Champion S. Chase to Mary Butterfield, 11 July 1845, Champion S. Chase Papers, YL; William Lloyd Garrison II to Ellen Wright, 3 September 1864, Garrison Collection, SSC.

13. Ulysses S. Grant to Julia Dent, 11 July 1845, in Ulysses S. Grant, *Papers*, vol. I, ed. by John Simon (Carbondale, Il., 1967), p. 50. Used by permission of the Ulysses S. Grant Association and the Southern Illinois University Press. Joseph Taylor to Elizabeth Hill, 6 April 1866, Joseph D. Taylor Papers, MNHS.

14. Harry Pierce to Libbie Vinton, n.d. [1875], Pierce-Krull Papers, ISL; *Lecture on Some of the Distinctive Characteristics of the Female*, delivered before Jefferson Medical College, Philadelphia, January 1847, quoted in Welter, "Dimity Convictions" [11], p. 22.

15. George S. Hale, 15 September 1869, Hale Family Papers, MHS.

16. Mary Clarke to Willie Franklin, 11 September 1867 and 26 October 1868, Mary Clarke Letters in Harold Frederic Papers, NYPL; Augusta Anna Elliott to James Alvin Bell, 18 November 1860, James Alvin Bell Papers, HL; Winan Allen to Annie Cox, 20 December 1862, Cox-Allen Papers, NL.

17. Theodore Russell to Charles Russell, 30 May 1838, Charles Russell Papers, MHS.

In his study of the northern middle class, E. Anthony Rotundo finds three standards of manhood—the Manly Achiever, the Christian Gentleman, and the Christian Soldier—all of whom "directed attention to 'the world,'" and argues that, "in the era of the self-made man, men 'made themselves' in the world" ("Manhood in America: Middle-Class Masculinity in the Northern United States, 1770–1910" [unpublished Ph.D. dissertation, Brandeis University, 1982], p. 162).

18. Amelia Lee Jackson to Henry Lee, Jr., 21 September 1838, in Henry and Mary Lee, *Letters and Journals*, ed. by Frances R. Morse (Boston, 1929), p. 270; Mary Clarke to Willie Franklin, 10 September 1868 [16]; Joseph Taylor to Elizabeth Hill, 19 May 1866 [13]; Henry Poor to Mary Pierce, 2 August 1840, Poor Family Papers, SL.

19. Mary Butterfield to Champion Chase, 28 July 1846 [12]; William Ross to Mary Ballard, 20 January 1858 [2].

Rotundo has found that men's attentiveness to work was a conflict in many mid-nineteenth-century marriages; see "Manhood in America" [17], pp. 256–59.

20. Daisy Chamberlain to Horace Allen, 14 March 1880 and n.d. [March 1880], Chamberlain Papers, SL; Harry Pierce to Libbie Vinton, n.d. [1875] [13].

21. Joseph Taylor to Elizabeth Hill, 6 April 1866 [13].

22. George Wright to Serena Ames, 19 June 1859, George B. Wright and Family Papers, MNHS.

23. George Wright to Serena Ames, 26 June 1959 [22].

24. Serena Ames to George Wright, 24 June 1859 [22]; Augusta Hubbard, Diary, 23 May 1860, PC.

25. George Wright to Serena Ames, 12 January 1860 [22]; Serena to George, 26 June 1860.

26. Mary Clarke to Willie Franklin, 5 November 1866 [16].

27. Bessie Huntting to Edward Rudd, 1 October 1858, Huntting-Rudd Papers, SL; Harriet Coxe, private letter, 28 February 1835, Bledsoe-Herrick Papers, SL; Mary Barney to Enos Conkling, 7 August 1858, Enos Conkling Papers, N-YHS; Persis Sibley, Diary, 10 May 1842, MHS.

28. William Ross to Mary Ballard, 25 November 1857 [2]; George Wright to Serena Ames, 24 December 1859 [22]; Winan Allen to Annie Cox, 23 February 1863 [16].

29. Samuel Clayton Kingman to Emily Brooks, September 1853, in Jane Walter, "Pennings from the Past: The Growth of the Nineteenth-Century Relationship: Samuel Clayton Kingman and Emily Eustis Brooks" (Honors Thesis, College of Holy Cross, 1979), p. 189; Joseph Taylor to Elizabeth Hill, 16 November 1865 [13].

30. Jesse Pleck, *The True Woman; or, Life and Happiness at Home and Abroad* (New York, 1857), p. 214; Mary Ann Smith, Diary, March 1871, IHS; Clayton Kingman to Emily Brooks, 20 March 1853, in Walter, "Pennings" [29], p. 154.

31. Joseph Griffin to Abbie Griffin, 5 December 1869, in *Letters of a New England Coaster*, ed. by Ralph Griffin, Jr., (n.p., 1968), p. 72; Annie Cox to Winan Allen, 15 February 1863 [16].

32. Augusta Hubbard, Diary, 21 April 1860 [24].

33. For one exception, see Persis Sibley, Diary, 28 September 1841, MeHS, typescript; this Maine schoolteacher described her friendship with a "Mr. P" as "sweeter than love, for it has no bitter" (p. 101).

34. Will Adkinson to Lu Burlingame, 30 July 1869, Burlingame-Adkinson Papers, SL; Mary Butterfield to Champion Chase, 9 December 1847 [12]; J. M. More to Cornelia Curtis, 24 March 1842, Fayette Brown Papers, WRHS.

35. Winan Allen to Annie Cox, 23 February 1863 [16]; Annie to Winan, n.d. [Nov. 12, 1863]; Will Adkinson to Lu Burlingame, n.d. [Dec. 1869] [34].

36. Mary Ann Smith, Diary, March 1871 [30]; James W. White to Mary E. Thorn, 10 May 1850, James W. White Papers, HSWP; Pleck, *True Woman* [30], p. 214.

37. Mary P. Ryan, *Womanhood in America from Colonial Times to the Present*, 2nd ed. (New York, 1979), p. 95; Mary P. Ryan, "American Society and the Cult of Domesticity, 1830–1860" (unpublished Ph.D. dissertation, University of California, Santa Barbara, 1971), p. 262.

38. Henry Poor to Mary Pierce, 23 February 1840 [18].

See Simeon Baldwin, Journal, 2 June 1865, for a man afflicted with "all the orthodox novel-writer symptoms" (Baldwin Family Papers, YL).

39. For one woman's resistance to romance, see Persis Sibley, Diary, 1 January 1842 [33].

40. Alexander Hamilton Rice to Augusta E. McKim, 2 March 1844, Alexander Hamilton Rice Papers, MHS; Henry Poor to Mary Pierce, 27 February 1841 [18].

41. Elizabeth Prentiss to Anna Prentiss, 24 April 1842, in Elizabeth Prentiss, *Life and Letters, 1818–1878*, ed. by George Prentiss (New York, 1882), p. 79; Winan Allen to Annie Cox, 19 November 1863 [16]; Annie to Winan, n.d. [20 November 1863].

42. Lydia Sigourney quoted in Ryan, *Womanhood* [37], p. 95; Mary Ann Smith, Diary, March 1871 [30].

43. Augusta Hubbard, Diary, 11 August and 2 June 1860 [24].

44. Aurora Koehler, Diary, 19 September 1871, Hutchings-Koehler Papers, IHS; Simeon Baldwin, Journal, 16 February and 2 June 1865.

45. Wilson Carpenter, Journal, 12 February 1868, HSWP.

46. Ibid., 3 June 1868.

47. Ibid., 15 January and 7 November 1872.

48. Alexander Hamilton Rice to Augusta E. McKim, 2 March 1844 [40]; George Wright to Serena Ames, n.d. [26 August 1859] [21]. For a detailed analysis of this literature, see Ryan, "Cult of Domesticity" [37].

49. Champion Chase to Mary Butterfield, 22 March 1848 [12]; Henry Poor to Mary Pierce, 6 October and 14 July 1839 [18]; Eliza Pattee to William Onion, October 1848, in *Vermont History* (Summer 1979), p. 219; Clayton Kingman to Emily Brooks, 25 January and 17 April 1853, in Walter, "Pennings" [29], pp. 144–45; John Morriss to Augusta Griswold, John M. Morriss Papers, CTL.

50. Henry Blackwell to Lucy Stone, 12 February 1854, in *Loving Warriors: Selected Letters of Lucy Stone and Henry B. Blackwell 1853 to 1893*, ed. by Leslie Wheeler (New York, 1981), p. 74; Clayton Kingman to Emily Brooks, 12 September 1852 and 20 March 1853 in Walter, "Pennings" [29], pp. 114, 154.

51. Antoinette Brown to Samuel Blackwell, 14 December 1855, in Margo Horn, "Family Ties: The Blackwells, A Study in the Dynamics of Family Life in Nineteenth-Century America" (unpublished Ph.D. dissertation, Tufts University, 1980), p. 222.

52. Oliver Fuller to Sarah E. Simpson, 15 July 1849, Oliver Fuller Papers, IHS.

53. Lewis Weld to Nellie Browne, 24 May 1864, Browne Family Papers, SL; Katherine Smith to Walter Hill, 10 February and 7 March 1876, Katherine Smith Hill Papers, SL; Mary Butterfield to Champion Chase, 14 January 1847 [12].

54. Katherine Smith to Walter Hill, 2 March 1876 [53].

55. Rotundo, "Manhood in America" [17], p. 146.

Another ideal of manhood, the Christian Gentleman, also "encouraged men to show affection and sensitivity" (p. 155). These two different ideals and "the emotional styles that they fostered" created a tension for men that was similar to, and perhaps reinforced by, the tension between candor and conformity to the male gender ideal.

56. J. M. More to Cornelia Curtis, 29 May 1842 [34]; W. C. Whitridge to Benjamin S. Rotch, 14 February 1841, Benjamin S. Rotch Papers, MHS.

57. Serena Ames to George Wright, 2 March 1860 [22], and George to Serena, 1 April 1860. The middle-class men in Rotundo's study "often had special difficulty in letting down emotional barriers with other men," but he argues that many men succeeded in establishing close friendships with each other, especially during the years just after they left home ("Manhood in America" [17], pp. 243–48). For a contemporary perspective on the difficulties men have in forming close friendships, see Lillian B. Rubin, *Intimate Strangers: Men and Women Together* (New York, 1983), pp. 129–40.

58. George Moore, Diary, 7 August 1838, [11]; Champion Chase to Mary Butterfield, 25 September 1846 [12]; *The Love Life of Byron Caldwell Smith* (New York, 1930), p. 39.

59. George Wright to Serena Ames, 12 January 1860 [21].

60. Katherine Smith to Walter Hill, 23 April [1876] [53]; William Onion to Eliza Pattee, n.d., p. 217 [49]; Pleck, *True Woman* [30], p. 217.

61. Emily Brooks to Clayton Kingman, 30 October 1853 [29]; Blanche Butler to Adelbert Ames, 4 May and 10 June 1870, in Blanche Ames, comp., *Chronicles from the Nineteenth Century: Family Letters of Blanche Butler Ames and Adelbert Ames* (privately printed, 1957), vol. I, pp. 123, 161; Katherine Smith to Walter Hill, 14 February and 29 March 1876 [53].

62. Mary Butterfield to Champion Chase, 10 November 1846 [12]; Mary to Champion, 22 January 1848; Alexander Hamilton Rice to Augusta E. McKim, 19 August 1842 [40]; Emily Smith to Henry O. DuBois, 8 August 1876, Henry O. DuBois Papers, N-YHS.

63. In "The Female World of Love and Ritual," Carroll Smith-Rosenberg asserts that "relations between young women and men frequently lacked the spontaneity and emotional intimacy that characterized the young girls' ties to each other." Without disputing her claim that "young women's relationships with each other were close, often frolicsome, and surprisingly long lasting," I would argue that it is a mistake to present those relationships "in sharp contrast to [young women's] distant relations with boys." Girls may, as Smith-Rosenberg suggests, have regarded boys as "other"; but by the time women reached their late teens and early twenties, the focus of their emotional lives had shifted or at least broadened to include men. Many, perhaps even most, middle-class young women in the North developed closeness with their future mates equal to or greater than that with their female friends. Since this is a study of courtship, which is by definition a time for building bridges between young men and women, I am unable to say whether the intimacy that existed between couples en route to the altar was sustained over the course of married life. See *Signs* 1 (1 [1975]): 21.

64. Mary Pierce to Henry Poor, 9 January 1841 [18]; Serena Ames to George Wright, 26 August 1859 [21]; George to Serena, n.d. [August 1859].

65. Samuel Goodrich, *Fireside Education* (New York, 1838), p. 17.

66. J. S. C. Abbott, *The Mother at Home; or, the Principles of Maternal Duty Famil-*

iarly Illustrated (New York, 1833), p. 152. For the long-term trend in fertility, see Wilson H. Grahill, Clyde V. Kiser, and Pascal K. Whelpton, *The Fertility of American Women* (New York, 1958), pp. 14–15. Nancy F. Cott traces the roots of this emphasis on maternal influence in *The Bonds of Womanhood: Woman's Sphere in New England, 1785–1830* (New Haven, 1977), pp. 84–87.

67. George Rudd to Edward Rudd, 7 October 1858 [27].

Rotundo discusses the distant quality of father-son relationships at length in "Manhood in America" [17], pp. 197–210.

68. Henry Poor to Mary Pierce, 21 June 1840 and 1 August 1841 [18]; Lewis Weld to Nellie Browne, 17 May 1864 [53].

Rotundo documents the emotional dependency that characterized many men's relationships with their mothers ("Manhood in America" [17], pp. 180–97). For another perspective on the same issue, see Bryan Strong, "Towards a History of the Experiential Family: Sex and Incest in the Nineteenth-Century Family," *JMF* 35 (August 1973): 457–66.

69. Adelbert Ames to Blanche Butler, 9 June 1870, in Ames, *Chronicles* [61] p. 159.

70. Joseph Wheelock to Kate French, 12 September 1860, Wheelock Papers, MNHS; Fannie Rudd to Bessie Huntting, 29 May 1859 [27].

71. Blanche Butler to Adelbert Ames, 17 June 1870; Adelbert to Blanche, 31 May 1870, in *Chronicles* Ames, [61], pp. 167, 154.

72. See Mary Pierce to her parents, October 1838–April 1839 [18].

73. Augusta Hubbard, Diary, 10 May 1860 [24]; Martha Osborne Barrett, Diary, 3 June 1849, EI; Augusta Hubbard, Diary, 26 July 1867.

CHAPTER 4. "SUCH A LOVING, JOYOUS TIME"

1. Champion Chase to Mary Butterfield, 12 March 1846, Champion S. Chase Papers, YL; Augusta Hubbard, Diary, 27 July 1960, PC.

2. Augusta Hubbard, Diary [1], 27 July 1860.

3. Ibid., 24 May 1860.

4. Ibid., 30 June and 15 July 1867.

5. Lester Ward, Diary, 6 November 1860, in *Young Ward's Diary*, ed. by Bernhard J. Stern (New York, 1935), p. 19.

6. Ibid., 16 July 1861; 13, 20, and 27 April 1862, pp. 69, 103, 105.

7. Ibid., 24 February 1861, p. 38.

8. Lucy Harris, "My Story," typescript, PC.

9. Alexander Hamilton Rice to Augusta E. McKim, 19 August 1842, Alexander Hamilton Rice Papers, MHS.

10. Lawrence Chamberlain to Fannie Adams, 31 October 1852, Chamberlain Papers, SL.

11. Mary Butterfield to Champion Chase, 27 December 1847 [1]; Elizabeth Prentiss to George Prentiss, 22 February 1843, in Elizabeth Prentiss, *Life and Letters 1818–1878*, ed. by George Prentiss (New York, 1882), p. 89.

12. Ernest Earnest, *The American Eve in Fact and Fiction, 1774–1914* (Champaign-Urbana, Ill., 1974), pp. 72, 74.

13. Mary Ballard to John Ballard, 14 May 1856, Mary P. Ballard Letters, WRHS; Emma Hadley to Miriam Green, 27 December 1863, Miriam Green Letters, IHS.

14. William Ross to Mary Ballard, 22 August 1858 [13]; Charles Everett to Elias Nason, 5 May 1833, Elias Nason Papers, AAS.

15. Albert Green to Miriam Green, 21 May 1866 [13]; Lizzie Parker to Miriam Green, 13 June 1865; Charlotte Willcocks, Diary, 1842, HSP.

16. Stewart Nutting, Diary, 11 August 1853, OSV; Augusta Anna Elliott to James Alvin Bell, 8 March 1861, James Alvin Bell Papers, HL; Annie Cox to Winan Allen, 15 September 1863, Cox-Allen Papers, NL; Mary E. Thorn to James W. White, 22 May 1850; James to Mary, June 1850, James W. White Papers, HSWP.

17. Champion Chase to Mary Butterfield, 3 January 1848 [1]; Mary to Champion, 3 January 1848.

18. Champion Chase to Mary Butterfield, 11 January 1848 [1]; Mary to Champion, 25 March 1848 [1].

19. Champion Chase to Mary Butterfield, 25 March 1848 [1]; Mary to Champion, 17 March 1848.

20. Mary Butterfield to Champion Chase, 1 January 1848 [1]; Lester Ward, Diary, 21 October 1860 [5], p. 15

21. Ward, Diary, 9 February, 18 March, and 25 October 1861 and 14 August 1862 [5], pp. 44, 81, 114.

22. Ibid., 21 October 1860, p. 15.

23. Annie Cox to Winan Allen, 20 October 1863 [16].

This is not the only case where there are significant gaps in correspondence relating to sexual conflict. The survival rate for sexually explicit letters appears to be, not surprisingly, lower than for correspondence on less charged subjects.

24. Annie Cox to Winan Allen, 20 October 1863.

25. Winan Allen to Annie Cox, 1 March 1865 [16].

26. Annie Cox to Winan Allen, 20 October 1863 [16].

27. Nancy F. Cott develops the concept of female passionlessness in "Passionlessness: An Interpretation of Victorian Sexual Ideology, 1790–1850," *Signs* 4 (2 [1978]): 219–36. Samuel Clayton Kingman to Emily Brooks, 25 January 1853, in Jane Walter, "Pennings from the Past: The Growth of the Nineteenth Century Relationship: Samuel Clayton Kingman and Emily Eustis Brooks" (Honors Thesis, College of Holy Cross, 1979), p. 142; Lawrence Chamberlain to Fannie Adams, n.d., [1852] [10].

Carl Degler points out that "the new ideology of sexual control or denial was not something that answered most men's sexual preferences. On the contrary, it usually resulted in limiting sexual satisfaction for men" (*At Odds: Women and the Family in America, 1776-Present* [New York, 1980], p. 257).

28. Lawrence Chamberlain to Fannie Adams, n.d. [1852] [10]; Will Adkinson to Lu Burlingame, 1 July 1871, Burlingame-Adkinson Papers, SL; Cott, "Passionlessness" [27]: 233.

29. Lawrence Chamberlain to Fannie Adams, n.d. [1852] [10]; Fannie to Lawrence, 22 February 1854.

30. Lawrence Chamberlain to Fannie Adams, n.d. [1852] [10].
31. Will Adkinson to Lu Burlingame, 14 December 1869 [28]; Lu to Will, 19 December 1869; 19 December 1870; and 23 February 1871.

For a thorough analysis of this relationship, see Ellen K. Rothman, " 'Intimate Acquaintance': Courtship and the Transition to Marriage in America, 1770–1900" (unpublished Ph.D. dissertation, Brandeis University, 1981), pp. 340–62.

32. Lu Burlingame to Will Adkinson, 22 February 1871; Will to Lu, 13 February 1871; n.d. [December 1869]; and 24 April 1871.
33. Will Adkinson to Lu Burlingame, 1 and 8 July 1871.
34. Will Adkinson to Lu Burlingame, 16 July 1871.
35. Will Adkinson to Lu Burlingame, 16 and 8 July 1871; Lu to Will, 24 July 1871.
36. Lu Burlingame to Will Adkinson, 24 July 1871.
37. Will Adkinson to Lu Burlingame, n.d. [spring 1871]; Lu to Will, 24 July 1871.
38. Lu Burlingame to Will Adkinson, 24 July 1871; 13 August 1871; and 24 October 1871.
39. Lu Burlingame to Will Adkinson, 24 July 1871 and 9 April 1872.
40. Lu Burlingame to Will Adkinson, 9 April 1872; Will to Lu, 1 and 16 July 1871.
41. Cott points out that "the ideology of passionlessness created its own contradictions: on the one hand, by exaggerating sexual propriety so far as to immobilize women; and, on the other, by allowing claims of women's moral influence to obfuscate the need for other sources of power ("Passionlessness" [27], p. 236). These contradictions affected women's personal relationships as well as their role in society.
42. Degler has found "a substantial amount of nineteenth-century writing about women that assumes the existence of strong sexual feelings," and that encourages women to express them; see "What Ought to Be and What Was: Women's Sexuality in the Nineteenth Century," in Michael Gordon, ed., *The American Family in Social Historical Perspective,* 2nd ed. (New York, 1978), p. 406.
43. Alexander Hamilton Rice to Augusta McKim, 2 March 1844 [9]; Oliver Fuller to Sarah Simpson, n.d. [1849], Oliver Fuller Correspondence, IHS.
44. Emily Smith to Henry O. DuBois, 8 August 1876, Henry O. DuBois Papers, N-YHS; Mary Butterfield to Champion Chase, 13 January 1848 [1].
45. Lu Burlingame to Will Adkinson, 18 February 1872 [28]; William Lloyd Garrison II to Ellen Wright, 3 September 1864, Garrison Collection, SSC; Lawrence Chamberlain to Fannie Adams, n.d. [10].
46. Will Adkinson to Lu Burlingame, 28 February 1872 [28]; Lu to Will, 9 April 1872.
47. For a discussion of the content of these treatises on sex, see Degler, *At Odds* [27], chap. 9, passim.
48. Frederick Hollick, *The Marriage Guide: or, Natural History of Generation: A Private Instructor for Married Persons and Those About to Marry Both Male and Female* (New York, 1850), p. 4.
49. Lester Ward, Diary, 18 March 1861 [5], p. 44.
50. Winan Allen to Annie Cox, 1 March 1865 [16]; Annie Cox to Winan Allen,

19 February 1865 [16]; William Lloyd Garrison II to Ellen Wright, 3 September 1864 [45].
51. Will Adkinson to Lu Burlingame, 15 July 1868 [28].

CHAPTER 5. "THIS WAITING & HOPING & PLANNING"

1. Lydia Sigourney, *Whisper to a Bride,* quoted in Barbara Welter, "The Cult of True Womanhood 1820–1860," in *Dimity Convictions: The American Woman in the Nineteenth Century* (Athens, Oh., 1976), p.206, n.34.
2. Alexis de Tocqueville, *Democracy in America* (New York, 1945), vol.II, p.22; Kirk Jeffrey, "Family History: The Middle-Class American Family in the Urban Context, 1830–1870" (unpublished Ph.D. dissertation, Stanford University, 1972), pp. 181, 167; John Patch to Margaret Poor, 26 April 1846, Patch-Poor Correspondence, EI.
3. Annie Cox to Winan Allen, 10 February 1864, Cox-Allen Papers, NL; Mary Ann Smith, Diary, March 1871, IHS.
   For one couple's struggle to believe that practice could conform to theory, see the Henry Blackwell-Lucy Stone correspondence in *Loving Warriors: Selected Letters of Lucy Stone and Henry B. Blackwell, 1853–93,* ed. by Leslie Wheeler (New York, 1981).
4. Georgina Amory to John Lowell, Jr., 16 April 1824, John Lowell, Jr., Papers, MHS.
5. Samuel Clayton Kingman to Emily Brooks, 9 September 1853; Emily to Clayton, 31 August 1853; Clayton to Emily, September 1853, in Jane Walter, "Pennings from the Past: The Growth of the Nineteenth-Century Relationship: Samuel Clayton Kingman and Emily Eustis Brooks" (Honors Thesis, College of Holy Cross, 1979), pp.187–89; Henry Blackwell to Lucy Stone, 24 August 1853, in *Loving Warriors* [3], p.74.
6. *The Love Life of Byron Caldwell Smith* (New York, 1930), p.63.
7. For fuller discussion of these changes, see Nancy F. Cott, *The Bonds of Womanhood: Woman's Sphere in New England, 1785–1830* (New Haven, 1977), chap. 2, passim; and Nancy Osterud, "The New England Family, 1790–1840," Old Sturbridge Village Background Paper, 1978. For a detailed look at how this change played itself out in one community, see Mary P. Ryan, *Cradle of the Middle Class: The Family in Oneida County, New York 1790–1865* (New York, 1981).
8. John Barnard, "Autobiography and Journal," May 1835, EI; "Marriage Service of Edward Allen and Temperance Jerusha Platt, 2 April 1844, Jennings Family Papers, N-YHS.
9. William Lloyd Garrison II to Ellen Wright, 3 September 1864, Garrison Collection, SSC; Katherine Smith to Walter Hill, 24 June 1877, Katherine Smith Hill Papers, SL.
10. Even within these limited channels, women could have profound impact on the life of their community. See Ryan, *Cradle of the Middle Class* [7]; and Carroll Smith-Rosenberg, "Beauty, the Beast and the Militant Woman: A

Case Study in Sex Roles and Social Stress in Jacksonian America," *AQ* 23(4): 562–84.

11. Caroline Barrett White, Diary, 22 June 1851, AAS.

12. Abigail Dodge to James Alvin Dodge, 4 January 1848, in H. Augusta Dodge, ed., *Gail Hamilton's Life in Letters* (Boston, 1901), p.20; Mary Butterfield to Champion Chase, 19 January 1848, Champion S. Chase Papers, YL.

13. Will Adkinson to Lu Burlingame, 2 June 1872, Adkinson-Burlingame Papers, SL; Carrie Ingersoll to George Hale, 15 October 1868, Hale Family Papers; MHS; Lu Burlingame to Will Adkinson, 9 June 1872.

14. Henry Poor to Mary Pierce, 27 February 1841, Poor Family Papers, SL; Winan Allen to Annie Cox, 26 April 1865 [3].

15. Kate French to Joseph Wheelock, 9 September 1860, Wheelock Papers, MNHS.

On the reformers' critique of individual housekeeping, see Margo Horn, "Family Ties: The Blackwells, A Study in the Dynamics of Family Life in Nineteenth-Century America (unpublished Ph.D. dissertation, Tufts University, 1980), chap. 4, passim.

16. George P. Rudd to Edward Rudd, 7 October 1858, Huntting-Rudd Papers, SL; Charles R. VanHise to Alice Ring, 8 March 1879, Charles R. VanHise Papers, UWA; Alexander Hamilton Rice to Augusta E. McKim, 2 March 1844, Alexander Hamilton Rice Papers, MHS.

17. Joseph Taylor to Elizabeth Hill, 6 April 1866, Joseph Taylor Papers, SHSW; Will Adkinson to Lu Burlingame, n.d.[spring 1871] [13].

18. George P. Rudd to Edward Rudd, 7 October 1858 [16].

19. Serena Ames to George Wright, 6 February 1869, George B. Wright and Family Papers, SHSW.

20. Winan Allen to Annie Cox, 26 April 1865 [3]; Clayton Kingman to Emily Brooks, 12 September 1858, in Walter, "Pennings" [5] pp.112–13; Charles VanHise to Alice Ring, 11 September 1881 and 6 October 1878 [16].

21. Alexander Rice to Augusta E. McKim, 2 March 1844 [16].

22. Charles VanHise to Alice Ring, 5 May 1879 [16]; Albert Hart to Mary Hornell, 5 September 1842, in Albert G. Hart Papers, WRHS.

23. Mary Butterfield to Champion Chase, 7 April 1846 [12]; T. S. Arthur, quoted in Welter, *Dimity Convictions* [1], p.31.

24. Augusta Hubbard, Diary, 9 August 1860, PC.

25. Champion Chase to Mary Butterfield, 12 March 1848 [12]; Mary to Champion, 7 April 1846.

26. Annie Cox to Winan Allen, 5 October 1862 [3].

27. Annie Cox to Winan Allen, 1 and 18 February and 19 December 1863 [3].

28. Annie Cox to Winan Allen, 5 October 1862; *Woman in Her Social and Domestic Character* (1842), quoted in Welter, *Dimity Convictions* [1], p. 31; Blanche Butler to Adelbert Ames, 18 May 1870, in Blanche Butler, comp., *Chronicles of the Nineteenth Century: Family Letters of Blanche Butler and Adelbert Ames* (privately printed, 1957), vol.I, p.130.

29. "Sallie" to Tom McFarland, 5 October 1861, McFarland Hall Beck Papers, AIS; Ada Jefferson to George Wright, May [1860] [19]. Both Sallie and Ada Jefferson were writing to men. The effect of marriage on friendships between

women and men was obviously clearer, and probably easier to accept, than the effect on female friendships.

30. Emily Blackwell, Diary, 26 August 1850, quoted in Horn, "Family Ties" [15], p. 187; Mary Clarke to Willie Franklin, 5 November 1866, Harold Frederic Papers, NYPL.

Carroll Smith-Rosenberg argues that female friendship "lasted with undiminished, indeed often increased intensity throughout the women's lives"; see "The Female World of Love and Ritual: Relations between Women in Nineteenth-Century America," *Signs*, 1 (1 [1975]):26. My evidence suggests that many women expected marriage to disrupt their female friendships and that in many cases, including some of those in Smith-Rosenberg's sample, the disruption lasted several years or longer. For example, while asserting that Eleanor Custis Lewis's "love for and dependence on Elizabeth Bordley Gibson only increased after her marriage," Smith-Rosenberg does not account for the six-year hiatus in their correspondence after Eleanor's marriage. It is no accident that so many of the relationships in Smith-Rosenberg's study involve a woman who remained single for at least a few years after her friend married. During courtship and the early years of marriage, women had less time— and less need—for the friendships that may have been important to them during girlhood and late adolescence. Even then, the "sisterly bonds" Smith-Rosenberg sees as the basis of the "female world of love and ritual" were strongest among élite women, southerners, and women who attended girls' schools or academies.

31. Annie Wilson to James Wilson, Jr., 18 November 1858, James Wilson, Jr., Papers, NHHS.

32. James White to Mary E. Thorn, 8 March 1850, James W. White Papers, HSWP; Joseph Taylor to Elizabeth Hill, 6 and 29 April 1866 [17].

33. Annie Cox to Winan Allen, 23 December 1863 [3].

34. Annie Cox to Winan Allen, 7 November 1863.

35. Fannie Adams to Lawrence Chamberlain, 22 February 1854, Chamberlain Papers, SL; Lucy Harris, "My Story," typescript, PC.

36. Elizabeth Blackwell, Diary, 29 January 1839, quoted in Horn, "Family Ties" [15], p. 180; Mary Butterfield to Champion Chase, 27 December 1847 [12].

37. Katherine Smith to Walter Hill, 3 September 1877, [9].

38. Annie Cox to Winan Allen, 19 February 1865 [3]; Lizzie Smith to John Ross, 16 July 1866, WCM.

39. Robert Koehler to his mother, 29 November 1868, Hutchings-Koehler Papers, IHS.

40. William Ross to Mary Ballard, 17 March 1858; Katherine Smith to Walter Hill, 17 September 1877 [9].

41. Lu Burlingame to Will Adkinson, 21 May 1872 [13].

42. Mary E. Thorn to James White, n.d. [27 February 1850] [32]; Persis Sibley, Diary, 27 March 1842, MHS.

43. Persis Sibley, Diary, 23 March 1842 [42].

44. Mary Pierce to Henry Poor, 21 June 1841 [14]; Ruth Huntington Sessions, *Sixty Odd: A Personal History* (Brattleboro, Vt., 1936), p. 263.

45. Blanche Butler to Adelbert Ames, 2 May 1870 [26].

46. Lizzie Smith to John Ross, 3 May 1866 [38]; George E. Tucker to Anna Sitwell, 31 December 1842, George E. Tucker Papers, MHS; William H. Mason to Harriet Chamberlain, 19 July 1866, William H. Mason Letters, SHSW.

47. Mary Butterfield to Champion Chase, 31 October 1846 and 18 December 1847 [12].

48. Mary Butterfield to Champion Chase, 31 October 1846.

49. Emily Smith to Henry O. DuBois, 26 May 1876, Henry O. DuBois Papers, N-YHS.

50. Annie Cox to Winan Allen, 25 January 1864 [3]; Anna Webb to Thomas Farris, 11 August 1844, Shaw-Webb Papers, AAS.

51. Elizabeth Cady Stanton, *Eighty Years or More: Reminiscences 1815–1897* (New York, 1971; first published 1898), p.71.

52. William Edmond Curtis, Diary, 26 August 1851, in Elizabeth Curtis, *Letters and Journals* (New York, 1926), p.232; Annie Wilson to James Wilson, Jr., 18 November 1858 [31]; Joseph Taylor to Elizabeth Hill, 6 April 1866 [17].

53. Katherine Smith to Walter Hill, 3 September 1877 [9].

54. Annie Cox to Winan Allen, 4 February 1865 [3]; Emily Brooks to Clayton Kingman, 20 October 1853, in Walter, "Pennings" [5], pp. 197–98.

55. Caroline Barrett White, Diary, 30 August 1849 [11]; Lucy Harris, "My Story" [35]; Aurelia Porter to Helen Porter, 4 October 1871, Porter-Griffin Papers, ISL.

56. Mary Roberts Coolidge, *Why Women Are So,* (New York, 1912), p. 26.

57. Mary Roberts Coolidge deplored the fact that "the friends of both families vied with each other in expressing not so much their affection as their social status by the elegance of their contribution to the display" (*Why Women Are So* [56], p. 27).

58. Thorstein Veblen, *Theory of the Leisure Class* (New York, 1934), p. 83. Coolidge saw women as the perpetrators as well as the beneficiaries of this gift giving. In her analysis, "after the [Civil] War, the increase of wealth and the growth of urban communities gave women, particularly, leisure and excuse for excessive emphasis on the ornamental side of life" (*Why Women Are So* [56], p. 27). For one man who expected to receive presents on his wedding, see Wilson Carpenter, Journal, January 1875, HSWP.

59. See Harvey Green, *The Light of the Home: An Intimate View of the Lives of Women in Victorian America* (New York, 1983), pp. 23–24.

60 See, for example, Elizabeth Wilson to James Wilson, Jr., 9 November 1851 [31]; Adelbert Ames to Blanche Butler, 24 May 1870, in *Chronicles* [28], p. 138.

61. Bessie Huntting to Edward Rudd, 31 May 1859 [16]; Charles R. VanHise to J. G. Conway, 14 December 1881 [16].

62. Mary Pierce to Henry Poor, 11 September 1840 [14].

63. *The Art of Good Behavior & Letter Writer on Love Courtship & Marriage: A Complete Guide for Ladies & Gentlemen Particularly Those Who Have Not Enjoyed the Advantages of Fashionable Life* (New York, 1846), p. 48. Green concludes that Victorian men did not commonly wear wedding bands. See *Light of the Home,* p. 19.

64. George Chapman, Journal, 13 September 1842, SHSW.

65. *The Art of Good Behavior* [63], pp. 47–50; Henry Poor to Mary Pierce, 24 No-

vember 1839 [14]; Addie Hibbard Gregory, *A Great Grandmother Remembers* (Chicago, 1940), p. 18. For other examples of the etiquette and advice literature on the subject, see George W. Hervey, *The Principles of Courtesy* (New York, 1852), pp. 145–48; *How to Behave: A Pocket Manual of Republican Etiquette & Guide to Correct Personal Habits* (New York, 1872), pp. 96–99; Florence Hartley, *The Ladies Book of Etiquette & Manual of Politeness* (Boston, 1873), pp. 259–63; Mrs. H. O. Ward, *Sensible Etiquette of the Best Society* (Philadelphia, 1878), pp. 337–39; W. R. Andrews, *The American Code of Manners* (New York, 1880), pp. 121–29; Alice E. Ives, *The Social Mirror* (Detroit, 1886), pp. 192–204; S. J. Hale, *Manners, Happy Homes & Good Society* (Boston, 1889), pp. 121–28; *American Etiquette & Rules of Politeness* (Chicago, 1890), pp. 195–203; Daphne Dale, *Our Manners & Social Customs* (Chicago, 1892), pp. 94–108.

66. This formulation is Barbara Welter's; see "The Cult of True Womanhood," in *Dimity Convictions* [1], pp. 21–41.

67. For a discussion of these trends, see Richard Brown, "Modernization and the Modern Personality in Early America, 1660–1865: A Sketch of a Synthesis," *JIH* 2 (1972): 218–19; Stuart Blumin, *The Urban Threshold: Growth and Change in a Nineteenth-Century American Community* (Chicago, 1976); Clifford E. Clark, Jr., "Domestic Architecture as an Index to Social History: The Romantic Revival and the Cult of Domesticity in America, 1840–1870," *JIH* 7 (1976): 49–52.

68. Wilson Carpenter, Journal, January 1875 [58].

69. Ibid.

70. Champion Chase to Mary Butterfield, 11 May 1846 [12]; Anna Webb to Thomas Farris, n.d. [24 September 1845] [50]; Sarah Park Gray to Cornelia Curtis, 6 June 1847, Fayette Brown Papers, WRHS; Augusta Hubbard, Diary, 24 July 1867 [24]; Joseph Taylor to Elizabeth Hill, 6 November 1866 [17].

71. Persis Sibley, Diary, 12 June 1842; [42]; Lizzie Waller to Bessie Huntting, 7 November 1854 [16]; Caroline Barrett White, Diary, 26 June 1851 [11]; Mary Pierce to her parents, 15 September 1841 [14].

72. Elizabeth Ann Jennison, Diary, April 1849, AAS; Caroline Barrett White, Diary, 24 June and 25 May 1851 [11]; Emily Brooks to Clayton Kingman, 31 August 1853, in Walter, "Pennings" [5], p. 184.

73. "Hattie" to Harry Pierce, 12 December 1873, Pierce-Krull Papers, ISL.

74. James White to Mary E. Thorn, 1 June 1850 [42]; Lucy Smith Rogers, Diary, August 1855, CtHS; Elizabeth to Charles Andrews, 24 June 1895, Charles McLean Andrews Papers, YL.

75. Ward, *Sensible Etiquette* [65], p. 344.

CHAPTER 6. "THIS STRONG FASCINATION FOR EACH OTHER"

1. John Franklin Jameson to Sara Elwell, 28 and 11 September 1892, J. Franklin Jameson Papers, LC.

2. J. Franklin Jameson to Sara Elwell, 28 and 11 September and 19 June 1892.

3. J. Franklin Jameson to Sara Elwell, 20 and 7 June 1892.

4. J. Franklin Jameson to Sara Elwell, 20 June 1892; Sara to Franklin, 28 June 1892.

5. J. Franklin Jameson to Sara Elwell, 20 June 1892; Sara to Franklin, 29 June 1892.

6. J. Franklin Jameson to Sara Elwell, 5 February 1893.

7. J. Franklin Jameson to Sara Elwell, 13 March 1893.

8. J. Franklin Jameson to Sara Elwell, 11 September 1892.

9. J. Franklin Jameson to Sara Elwell, 1 and 2 April 1893; Sara to Franklin, 9 March and 6 and 7 April 1893.

10. Sara Elwell to J. Franklin Jameson, 28 June 1892.

11. Kate Gannett Wells, "Why More Girls Do Not Marry," *North American Review*, January 1891, p. 177.

12. Carroll Smith-Rosenberg, "Beauty, the Beast, and the Militant Woman: A Case Study in Sex Roles and Social Stress in Jacksonian America," *AQ* 23, (4): 562–84, is a classic study of the early period in female agitation against male vice. Ruth Rosen's, *The Lost Sisterhood: Prostitution in America* (Baltimore, 1982) discusses the Progressive response to the social evil.

13. Annie Winsor, Notebook, May 1886 and 24 March 1885, Annie Winsor Allen Papers, SL; Maud Rittenhouse, Diary, 28 August 1892, in Isabelle Rittenhouse Mayne, *Maud,* ed. by Richard Lee Strout (New York, 1939), p. 554.

14. Wells, "Why More Girls Do Not Marry" [11], p. 176.

15. Eleanor Abbott, *Being Little in Cambridge When Everyone Else Was Big* (New York, 1936), p. 104; Maud Rittenhouse, Diary, June 1882, in *Maud* [13], p. 108.

16. Helen Swett to Charles Ernest Schwartz, 18 and 22 October 1899, Charles Ernest Schwartz Papers, UCB.

17. Helen Haskell to Stephen Thomas, March 1892, Haskell Papers, UCB; Annie Winsor, Notebook, 24 March 1885 [13]; Abbott, *Being Little* [15], p. 103.

On the male idea that a woman was "all that makes a man a man," see E. Anthony Rotundo, "Manhood in America: Middle-Class Masculinity in the Northern United States, 1770–1910" (unpublished Ph.D. dissertation, Brandeis University, 1981), pp. 366–67.

18. Cass Gilbert to Julia Finch, 29 March 1887, Cass Gilbert Papers, LC; Frank Lillie to Frances Crane, 24 September 1894, Crane Papers, CHS, typescript.

19. Henry S. Canby, *The Age of Confidence: Life in the Nineties* (New York, 1934), p. 162.

20. Christina Simmons, "Marriage in the Modern Manner: Sexual Radicalism and Reform in America, 1914–1941" (unpublished Ph.D. dissertation, Brown University, 1982), p. 31.

21. Cass Gilbert to Julia Finch, 29 March 1887 [18]; J. Franklin Jameson to Sara Elwell, 11 September 1892 [1]; Raymond Brown to Gertrude Foster, n.d. [summer 1892], Gertrude Foster Brown Papers, SL; Richard Cabot to Ella Lyman, n.d. [18 March 1894], Ella Lyman Cabot Papers, SL.

22. Mary Roberts Coolidge, *Why Women Are So* (New York, 1912), p. 32.

23. See Mary Ryan, *Womanhood in America from Colonial Times to the Present* (New York, 1979), p. 148; and Peter Filene, *Him/Herself: Sex Roles in Modern America* (New York, 1974), p. 35 for more on the connection between woman's moral superiority and the movement for women's suffrage.

24. Coolidge, *Why Women Are So* [22], p. 332; Annie Winsor, Notebook, 8 June 1884 [13]; "At Home with the Editor," *Ladies' Home Journal,* April 1892, p. 12; Annie Winsor, Notebook, n.d. [1888]; Madeleine Wallin to George Sykes, 31 July 1891, Madeleine Wallin Papers, UCL.

25. Madeleine Wallin to George Sykes, 31 July 1891 [24].

26. On developments in education in this period, see Burton Bledstein, *The Culture of Professionalism: The Middle Class and the Development of Higher Education in America* (New York, 1976); Michael Katz, *The Irony of Early School Reform: Educational Innovation in Mid-Nineteenth-Century Massachusetts* (Boston, 1968); George Peterson, *The New England College in the Age of the University* (Amherst, Mass., 1964); and Lawrence Veysey, *The Emergence of the American University* (Chicago, 1965).

27. On changes in women's employment patterns, see W. Elliot Brownlee and Mary M. Brownlee, *Women in the American Economy: A Documentary History, 1675–1929* (New Haven, 1976); Carl Degler, *At Odds: Women and the Family in America, 1776–Present* (New York, 1980); and Alice Kessler-Harris, *Out to Work: A History of Wage-Earning Women in the United States* (New York, 1982).

28. Annie Winsor, Notebook, n.d. [1888] [13].

29. "At Home with the Editor," *Ladies' Home Journal,* April 1892, p. 12; William A. Brown to Helen Gilman Noyes, 1 June 1891, William A. Brown Papers, NYPL.

30. Maud Rittenhouse, Diary, 28 August 1892, in *Maud* [13], p. 554; Annie Winsor, Notebook, 24 March 1885 [13]; Richard Cabot to Francis Curtis, n.d. [1886], Richard C. Cabot Papers, HUA.

31. Richard Cabot to Francis Curtis, n.d. [30]; Wilson Carpenter, Journal, 8 January 1868, HSWP. For more on male friendship, see Rotundo, "Manhood in America" [17], pp. 361–65.

32. Frances Crane to Frank Lillie, 16 December 1894 [18].

Frances and her friends were in the habit of getting together for what she called "kitten times"; see Frances to Frank, 8, 12, and 14 December 1894. In the late nineteenth and early twentieth centuries, the power of female friendship diminished as heterosexual love became the exclusive instrument of intimacy; see Simmons, "Marriage in the Modern Manner" [20], p. 110.

33. Charles R. VanHise to Alice Ring, 5 June 1879, Charles R. VanHise Papers, UWA.

34. "At Home with the Editor," [29]; Annie Winsor, Notebook, n.d. [May 1886] [13]; Madeleine Wallin to George Sykes, 31 July 1891 [24].

35. Maud Rittenhouse, Diary, 19 March 1882, *Maud* [13], p. 70; Caroline Drayton (Phillips), Diary, 11 January 1908, SL.

36. "Ray" to Edna Rankin, n.d. [1916], Edna Rankin McKinnon Papers, SL.

37. Helen Haskell to Stephen Thomas, 17 March 1892 [17]; Caroline Drayton, Diary, n.d. [30 January 1908] [35].

38. Maud Rittenhouse, Diary, 3 February and October 1883, in *Maud* [13], pp. 163, 229; Florence Hemsley to William H. Wood, 17 June 1889, William H. Wood Papers, N-YHS; Caroline Drayton, Diary, 8 May 1908 [35]; LaRue Brown to Dorothy Kirchwey, n.d. [spring 1915], Dorothy Kirchwey Brown Papers, SL.

39. Evangeline Walker to Charles Andrews, 28 May 1895, Charles McLean An-

drews Papers, YL; Maud Rittenhouse, Diary, 30 June 1888, in *Maud* [13], p. 453; Eugenie Homer to Oliver Emerson, 8 December 1894, Emerson-Nichols Papers, SL.

40. Caroline Drayton, Diary, 22 January 1908 [35]; Nella Hubbard, Diary, 3 July 1872, PC.

41. Elizabeth Sherman to an unknown correspondent, n.d. [c.1786], Baldwin Family Papers, YL; Nella Hubbard, Diary, 3 July 1872 [40]; Dorothy Kirchwey to LaRue Brown, 4 October 1915 [38]; Margaret Lesley to Henry Bush-Brown, 29 March 1885, Henry Bush-Brown Papers, SSC.

42. Caroline Drayton, Diary, 30 January 1908 [35]; Eugenie Homer to Oliver Emerson, 13 January 1895 [39].

43. Mary Bulkley, "Mother, Grandmother, and Me," typescript, pp. 61, 63, SL; Emily Smith to Henry O. DuBois, 1878, Henry O. DuBois Papers, N-YHS; Caroline Drayton, Diary, 27 May 1908 [35].

44. Lucy Sprague to Wesley Clair Mitchell, 26 October 1911, in Lucy Sprague Mitchell, *Two Lives: The Story of Wesley Clair Mitchell and Myself* (New York, 1953), p. 224; Caroline Drayton, Diary, 22 January 1908 [35]; Lucy Tufts Harris, *The Younger Sister* (n.p., 1929), pp. 245, 284; Marion Watrous to James Angell, 14 February 1892, James Angell Papers, YL.

45. Madeleine Wallin to George Sykes, 27 October 1895 [24].

46. These terms are borrowed from Rotundo, who examines the contradictions imbedded in middle-class ideals of masculinity, in "Manhood in America" [17], pp. 302–25.

47. Dorothy Kirchwey to LaRue Brown, 4 October 1915 [38]; Marion Watrous to James Angell, 14 February 1892 [44].

48. Marion Watrous to James Angell, 14 February 1892 [44]; Bulkley, "Mother" [43], p.61.

49. Alice Stockham, *Tokology: A Book for Every Woman* (Chicago, 1887), p.153.

50. Sydney Smith, quoted in Rotundo, "Manhood in America" [17], p. 307; Howard Taylor Ricketts to Myra Tubbs, 20 January 1900, Howard Taylor Ricketts Papers, UCL.

51. William Zorach to Marguerite Thompson, 29 April 1911, William Zorach Papers, LC; LaRue Brown to Dorothy Kirchwey, n.d. [spring 1915] [38].

52. LaRue Brown to Dorothy Kirchwey, n.d. [spring 1915] [38].

CHAPTER 7. "GOING SOMEWHERE"

1. Alexander Black, *The American Husband and Other Alternatives* (New York, 1925), pp. 34–36.
2. Ibid., p.36.
3. Ina Smith, Diary, 4 and 18 July 1899. The diary of Ina Smith belongs to Dorothy and Leigh Ames of Maine, New York. I am grateful to Nancy Grey Osterud for making her analysis of the diary available to me and for sharing with me her work on the Nanticoke Valley.
4. The increasing cost of courtship was born largely by men, although one

study of Ohio women found that those who courted around 1900 had subtle ways of easing the financial burdens on their suitors; see Marvin Koller, "Some Changes in Courtship Behavior in Three Generations of Ohio Women," *ASR* 16 (1951):368.

5. Ina Smith, Diary, 5 July 1899 [3].

6. Linda Gordon, *Woman's Body, Woman's Right: Birth Control in America* (New York, 1977), p. 204.

7. Lewis Erenberg discusses the new amusements in *Steppin' Out: New York Nightlife and the Transformation of American Culture, 1890–1930* (Westport, Conn., 1981), pp. 65–77.

8. Henry S. Canby, *The Age of Confidence: Life in the Nineties* (New York, 1934), p. 52; Otto Follin to Madeleine Wallin, 10 and 13 October 1895, Madeleine Wallin Papers, UCL.

9. Canby, *Age of Confidence* [8], p. 159; Theodore Dreiser, *Dawn: A History of Myself* (New York, 1931), pp. 264, 266.

One must keep in mind the problems inherent in using autobiography as a source for re-creating the sexual climate of a time and place. Did Dreiser, who felt "doomed to sex loneliness," exaggerate the amount of physical contact among young people in Warsaw? Did Canby, who wanted to rescue his generation from the stigma of Victorianism, overestimate the freedom of relations between young men and women?

10. Quoted in Gilman M. Ostrander, *American Civilization in the First Machine Age, 1890–1940* (New York, 1970), pp. 71–72.

11. Robert Lynd and Helen Merrell Lynd, *Middletown: A Study in Modern American Culture* (New York, 1929), pp. 137–38.

12. Mrs. Burton Harrison, *The Well-Bred Girl in Society*, quoted in Ostrander, *American Civilization* [10], p. 72.

13. Frances Parkinson Keyes, *All Flags Flying: Reminiscences* (New York, 1970), p. 5.

14. Raymond Brown to Gertrude Foster, n.d. [16 March 1892], Gertrude Foster Brown Papers, SL; Hutchins Hapgood, *A Victorian in the Modern World* (New York, 1939), p. 160.

15. Emily Hemsley to William Halsey Wood, 16 June 1889, William Halsey Wood Papers, N-YHS; Koller, "Changes in Courtship Behavior" [4]: 368.

Women in the Koller study reported that "since many of their dates centered around the church, home, and community, they felt they were not chaperoned in the formal sense of the word." While the percentage of women whose social activities were chaperoned declined for these women's daughters and granddaughters, formal chaperonage did not disappear. Indeed, it is still with us today in the form of adults who oversee dances, outings, ski trips, etc., for junior high and high school-age students.

16. Thomas Arkle Clark, "The Passing of the Chaperon," *Atlantic Monthly* 129 (1922): 516–17.

17. United States Bureau of Education Bulletin, 1929, no. 38, "Statistics of Universities, Colleges and Professional Schools," by Frank M. Phillips, table 1, p. 8; Mabel Newcomer, *A Century of Higher Education for American Women* (New York, 1959), table 3, p. 49.

The surge in high-school enrollments was even greater. In 1900, there were more than 600,000 students in secondary schools; by 1910, there were nearly 1,000,000, and the biggest leap was yet to come: in 1920, there were close to 4,475,000—almost a five-fold increase in ten years. See Paula Fass, *The Damned and the Beautiful: American Youth in the 1920s* (New York, 1978), p. 408.

18. Louise Sheffield Brownell Saunders, "Government of Women Students in Colleges and Universities," *Educational Review* 20 (December 1900): 481, 498.

19. Rosalind Rosenberg, *Beyond Separate Spheres: The Intellectual Roots of Modern Feminism* (New Haven, 1982), p. 191, n. 29.

20. Madeleine Wallin to George Sykes, 28 February 1896 [8].

Rosenberg suggests that there was an "antipathy" between men and women on campuses before 1900. She argues that "male college students, feeling devalued by the post-Civil War surge in female enrollment, pointedly shunned women students; while women students, trying to prove their academic seriousness, adopted a self-consciously stiff manner in their relations with men" (*Beyond Separate Spheres* [19], p. 189). This is an intriguing idea, but it needs more documentation than Rosenberg provides.

21. Helen R. Olin, *The Women of the State University: An Illustration of the Working of Coeducation in the Middle West* (New York, 1909), p. 232; Fass, *The Damned* [17], pp. 141–45; Erenberg, *Steppin' Out* [7], pp. 150–55.

22. Quoted in Fass, *The Damned* [17], p. 139.

23. Everett Baker to his mother, [spring 1923], Everett Baker Papers, MIT.

24. Even in 1920, less than 10 percent of all nineteen-, twenty-, and twenty-one-year-olds were enrolled in colleges and universities; see Phillips, "Statistics" [17], p. 8.

25. Marian Curtis, Journal, 13 and 22 September, 5 and 6 November 1916. Marian Curtis Gerritson's diary belongs to her grandson Steve Gerritson who was kind enough to share it with me.

26. Myrtle Reed, *The Spinster's Book* (New York, 1901), pp. 86–87; Lois Fay Powell, "Biography of Anna C. Harthan Fay," typescript, p. 14, AAS.

27. Annie Winsor, Notebook, January 1884, Annie Winsor Allen Papers, SL.

28. Marion Watrous to James R. Angell, 28 April 1892, James R. Angell Papers, YL; Marguerite Thompson to William Zorach, 6 June and 26 September 1912, William Zorach Papers, LC.

29. See, for example, Hannah Leland to Minerva Leland, 14 March and 13 June 1880, Minerva E. Leland Papers, SL, and unknown correspondent to Douglas Vanderhoof, 4 February 1914, Carl Ackerman Papers, LC.

30. Leander McCormick to Constance Plummer, 15 November and 9 December 1886, Leander H. McCormick Papers, CHS.

31. George Sykes to Madeleine Wallin, 25 May 1896 [8].

32. Daisy Chamberlain to Horace Allen, 22 March 1880, Chamberlain Papers, SL.

33. Raymond Brown to Gertrude Foster, 20 July 1892 [14].

34. Maud Rittenhouse, Diary, 25 September 1885 in Isabelle Rittenhouse Mayne, *Maud*, ed. by Richard Lee Strout (New York, 1939), p. 358; William Allen White, *Autobiography* (New York, 1946), p. 242.

35. White, *Autobiography* [34], p. 242.

36. Ruth Huntington Sessions, *Sixty Odd: A Personal History*, (Brattleboro, Vt., 1936), pp. 262–63.

37. Maud Rittenhouse, Diary, June 1882 in *Maud* [34], p. 110.

38. Ella Lyman to her mother, 18 August 1892 and 28 February 1894, Ella Lyman Cabot Papers, SL.

Although the evidence is fragmentary, it seems as though confidential mother-daughter relationships tended to be found in families with only one daughter. For other close mother-daughter dyads, see Frederick Koehler to Florence Cary, 1 and 3 June 1881, Florence Koehler Papers, SL; Sadie Treat to George Child, 10 November 1889; George Child Papers, UCB; and Helen Gilman Noyes to William A. Brown, 9 May and 7 July 1891, William A. Brown Papers, NYPL.

39. G. L. Locke to Ellen Hale, 25 February 1903, Richard Hale Papers, MHS; White, *Autobiography* [34], p. 236; Waldo Leland to his mother, 18 April 1904, Waldo Leland Papers, LC. Waldo's letter was addressed to both Nellie Leland and his sister Minnie; it was not uncommon for men to include their sisters when they reassured their mothers of their unchanging love.

40. Nellie Leland to Waldo Leland, 18 November 1903 [39]; Charles Andrews to Elizabeth Andrews, 26 and 29 November 1893, Charles McLean Andrews Papers, YL.

41. Elizabeth Andrews to Charles Andrews, 30 November 1893; Charles to Elizabeth, 3 December 1893; Elizabeth to Charles, 8 December 1893; Charles to Elizabeth, 10 December 1893.

42. Cass Gilbert to Julia Finch, 10 November 1887, Cass Gilbert Papers, LC.

Not all men with close ties to their mothers went through Cass Gilbert's painful experience. Frank Lillie told Frances Crane, "Whenever [Mother] felt badly she used to come to me and I would hold her and pet her and let her cry a little and then she would feel some better"; but he was "quite *sure*" that his mother would love Frances, and, apparently, she did (Frank Lillie to Frances Crane, 16 December 1894, Crane Family Papers, typescript CHS).

43. James Laidlaw to Harriet Burton, n.d. [summer 1905], Harriet Burton Laidlaw Papers, SL.

44. Dorothy Dix, "The Girl and Her Mother," *Boston American*, 18 July 1913; Frances Dummer to Ethel Dummer, 2 March 1919, Dummer Family Papers, SL; Mary Elliott to John Harold Foster, 16 October 1914, John Harold Foster Papers, NHHS.

45. Marian Curtis, Diary [25]. See, for example, 22 June, 14 September, 8 and 22 November 1916.

46. John Lewis to Sophie Borel, 14 July 1898, Lewis Family Papers, UCB.

47. John Lewis to Sophie Borel, 10 August 1900.

48. Katharine Dummer to Walter Fisher, 1 December 1914, and 15 March and 17 June 1915, Dummer Family Papers, SL.

49. Duncan Aikman, "Amazons of Freedom," *Harper's* (June 1926) pp. 26–33.

50. Everett Baker to his mother, n.d. [spring 1920] [23]; quoted in Lynd and Lynd, *Middletown* [11], p. 120. For a thoughtful discussion of this new style of romance, see Elaine Tyler May, *Great Expectations: Marriage and Divorce in Post-Victorian America* (Chicago, 1980), pp. 68–71.

51. Lucy Sprague Mitchell, *Two Lives: The Story of Wesley Clair Mitchell and Myself* (New York, 1953), p. 225; LaRue Brown to Dorothy Kirchwey, n.d. [June 1915], Dorothy Kirchwey Brown Papers, SL; Dorothy Dix, quoted in Lynd and Lynd, *Middletown* [11], p. 120.

52. Daisy Chamberlain to Horace Allen, 14 March 1880 [32]; Howard Taylor Ricketts to Myra Tubbs, 22 October 1894, Howard Taylor Ricketts Papers, UCL; Henry Bush-Brown to Margaret Lesley, 16 July 1885, Henry Bush-Brown Papers, SSC.

For one dissent from this view, see George Child to Sadie Treat, 6 July 1889 [38].

53. Henry Bush-Brown to Margaret Lesley, n.d. [11 July 1885] [52]; Gertrude Foster to Raymond Brown, 5 August 1892 [14]; Julia Finch to Cass Gilbert, 27 May 1887 [42].

54. Vernon Wright to Grace Clarke, 25 February 1899, George B. Wright & Family Papers, SHSW.

Rosalind Rosenberg suggests another dimension to this problem. She observes that men and women in college in the early 1900s were likely to experience a "tension between . . . competing academic ideals of self-control and self-expression." Rosenberg sees the source of this tension in the emphasis universities placed on "the cultivation of mental faculties," while at the same time they encouraged "a critical attitude toward all received wisdom—including, inevitably, the idea that the life of the mind was in conflict with the life of the body" (*Beyond Separate Spheres*, [19] p. 194). Rosenberg is primarily concerned with how this tension affected the development of sexual identity, but it has implications for other aspects of personality as well.

55. Howard Taylor Ricketts to Myra Tubbs, 22 October 1894 and 28 August 1895 [52].

56. Howard Taylor Rickets to Myra Tubbs, 17 March 1895 and 1 November 1898.

57. Charles R. VanHise to Alice Ring, 2 December 1881, Charles R. VanHise Papers, UWA; LaRue Brown to Dorothy Kirchwey, n.d. [September 1915] [51].

There is some evidence to suggest that mothers were troubled by their sons' emotional coolness; see, for example, Everett Baker to his mother, 16 January 1920.

58. Marguerite Thompson to William Zorach, n.d. [1911] and 20 July 1900 [28]; Katharine Dummer to Walter Fisher, 17 June 1915 [48].

59. Walter Fisher to Katharine Dummer, 1 December 1914 [48]; Katharine to Walter, 17 June 1915.

60. Katharine Dummer to Walter Fisher, 13 July, 12 June, and 17 July 1915.

Katharine's mother, Ethel, recognized "the danger of thwarting and suppressing nature" and thought it a reason to encourage the early marriage of her daughter and Walter Fisher; see Ethel Dummer's un-sent letter to Mrs. Fisher, 28 June 1915 [48].

61. Quoted in E. Anthony Rotundo, "Manhood in America: Men and Masculinity in the Northern United States, 1790–1910" (unpublished Ph.D. dissertation, Brandeis University, 1981), p. 187.

62. Manus McCloskey to Sara Munro, 6 April and 25 December 1900, Manus McCloskey Papers, AIS.
63. Theodore Dreiser, *Book about Myself* (New York, 1922), p. 85; Max Eastman, *Enjoyment of Living* (New York, 1948), p. 302.
64. Maud Rittenhouse, Diary, 10 June 1882 in *Maud* [34], p. 106; Florence Hemsley to William Halsey Wood, 10 July 1889 [15].
65. Mary Bulkley, "Mother, Grandmother and Me," typescript., p. 64, SL; Emma Lou Story to George W. Bellows, 1 June 1906, George W. Bellows Papers, AmC.
66. Sadie Treat to George Child, 6 June 1890 [38]; Canby, *Age of Confidence* [8], p. 163. See George to Sadie, 31 August 1887, 9 April 1888, 6 July 1889, and 29 June 1890, for the fragmentary history of this couple's sexual relationship.
67. Beatrice Fairfax, "The School of Love," *Boston American*, 8 February 1917.
68. Frances Dummer to Ethel Dummer, 2 March 1919 [48].
69. Howard Taylor Ricketts to Myra Tubbs, 5 August 1895 and 6 July 1898 [52].
70. Eastman, *Enjoyment of Living* [63], p. 219.
71. John Ripley Freeman, Diary, 12–13 June 1886, 6–15 March and 29 May–2 June 1887, MIT.
72. Raymond Brown to Gertrude Foster, 12 July, 22 August, and 1 February 1892 [14].
73. Raymond Brown to Gertrude Foster, 1 February and 16 March 1892, and 16 July 1893; Gertrude to Raymond, n.d. [July 1893].
74. Gertrude Foster to Raymond Brown, n.d. [July 1893].
75. Raymond Brown to Gertrude Foster, 22 August 1892.
In her book *Why Women Are So* (New York, 1912), Mary Roberts Coolidge complained that "men still associate sex-vigor with manliness" (p. 330).
76. Frances Crane to Frank Lillie, 16 November 1894 [42]; Frank to Frances, 18 December 1894; Frances to Frank, 7 December 1894; Frank to Frances, 6 December 1894.
77. Frank Lillie to Frances Crane, 6 December 1894; Frances to Frank, 4 December 1894.
78. Frances Crane to Frank Lillie, 4 December 1894; Frances to Frank, 4 and 18 October 1894.
79. Frank Lillie to Frances Crane, 6 December 1894; Frances to Frank, 6 December 1894.
80. Delbert Boston to Ella Furley, 7 October 1889; Ella to Delbert, 18 October 1889; Delbert to Ella, 23 April 1889, Delbert Boston Papers, IHS.
Charles Rosenberg's sensible observation that "many Americans paid no attention to the pious injunctions" of the experts seems to apply to Delbert Boston; however, Boston appears to contradict Rosenberg's hypothesis that "individuals of marginal social status"—such as a barber from Harlan, Indiana—might seek "security and dignity" through "the process of deferring pleasure" and showing sexual self-control. See Rosenberg, "Sexuality, Class and Role in Nineteenth-Century America," *AQ* 25 (2 [1973]): 149–50.
81. Blanche Ames, Diary, 1 January 1900, Ames Family Papers, SSC.
82. Oakes Ames to Blanche Ames, 5 February 1900 [81]; Blanche Ames, Diary, 19 January 1900; Oakes to Blanche, 12 March and 28 February 1900.

83. Rosalind Rosenberg discusses the development of American sex research in *Beyond Separate Spheres* [19], chap. 7, passim.
84. Madeline Z. Doty, "Autobiography," typescript, SSC.
85. Bernardine Kielty Scherman, *Girl from Fitchburg* (New York, 1964), p. 88. For more on Greenwich Village, see Allen Churchill, *Improper Bohemians A Re-creation of Greenwich Village in Its Heyday* (New York, 1959); Leslie Fishbein, *Rebels in Bohemia: The Radicals of the Masses, 1911–1917* (Chapel Hill, N.C., 1982).
86. Scherman, *Fitchburg* [85], p. 88; Eastman, *Enjoyment* [63], p. 264.
87. For the statistical trend in premarital coitus among engaged couples, see Fass, *The Damned* [17], pp. 275–76, 455. On the implications of this increase in "indulgence" for the decline of prostitution, see Gordon, *Woman's Body* [6], p. 192.
88. LaRue Brown to Dorothy Kirchway, n.d. [September 1915] [51].
89. Rosenberg, *Beyond Separate Spheres* [19], p. 192. For the rates of premarital intercourse in women born after 1890, see Alfred Kinsey et al., *Sexual Behavior in the Human Female* (Philadelphia, 1953), pp. 298–99. For a discussion of the search for a "turning point" in female sexual behavior, see Fass, *The Damned* [17], p. 448, n.2.
90. The timing of the "sexual revolution" is the subject of an extensive historical debate. For the main lines of argument, see James McGovern, "Women's Manners and Morals before World War I," *JAH*, 55 (3 [1918]): 315–33; and Daniel Scott Smith, "The Dating of the American Sexual Revolution: Evidence and Interpretation," in *The American Family in Social Historical Perspective*, ed. by Michael Gordon, 2nd ed. (New York, 1978), pp. 426–38. Smith argues that college-educated women "maintained conservative sexual standards longer than the remainder of the population." He concludes, from the upward trend in the premarital pregnancy ratio, that in the general population, "important changes in premarital sexual behavior already were under way during the late nineteenth century" (p. 329).
91. Quoted in Peter Filene, *Him/Herself: Sex Roles in Modern America* (New York, 1974), p. 118; Phyllis Blanchard, *The Adolescent Girl: A Study from the Psychoanalytic Viewpoint* (New York, 1920, rev. 1930), p. 214.

CHAPTER 8. "A SEASON FOR SHOW"

1. Madeleine Wallin to George Sykes, 24 February 1895, 24 March 1894, and 15 January 1893; Madeleine to her mother; 28 March 1894; Madeleine Wallin Papers, UCL; George Child to Sadie Treat, 27 November 1887, George Child Papers, UCB.
2. See, for example, "Are Women to Blame?" *North American Review*, May 1889, pp. 624–35 and "Making Marriage a Problem," *Ladies' Home Journal*, April 1895, p. 14.
3. "Making Marriage a Problem" [2], p. 14.
4. Eugenie Homer to Oliver Emerson, 24 January 1895, Emerson–Nichols Papers, SL; Charles E. Garman to Eliza Miner, 11 April 1880, Charles Garman

Papers, AmC; Helen Gilman Noyes to William A. Brown, 5 July 1891, William A. Brown Papers, NYPL; Madeleine Wallin to George Sykes, 26 August 1882.

5. Madeleine Wallin to George Sykes, 26 August 1892 [1].

6. Henry O. DuBois to "John," 30 May 1892, Henry O. DuBois Papers, N-YHS.

7. Sadie Treat to George Child, 19 June 1890 and n.d. [1891]; George to Sadie, 5 October 1890; Sadie to George, 6 June 1890 [1].

8. Paula Fass, *The Damned and the Beautiful: American Youth in the 1920s* (New York, 1978), p. 68; Peter Filene, *Him/Herself: Sex Roles in Modern America* (New York, 1974), p. 27.

Willystine Goodsell, *The Education of Women: Its Social Background and Its Problems* (New York, 1923), devotes a chapter to the controversy surrounding the marriage rate of college women (pp. 34–49).

9. Louise Arthur to Harriet Burton, 23 October 1905, Harriet Burton Laidlaw Papers, SL; Raymond Brown to Gertrude Foster, 18 July 1892, Gertrude Foster Brown Papers, SL.

10. Helen Gilman Noyes to William A. Brown, 26 July 1891 [4]; Marion Watrous to James Angell, 7 April 1892, James Angell Papers, YL; Florence Kelly, *Flowing Stream* (New York, 1939), p. 225.

11. Josephine Preston Peabody, Diary, January 1893, in *Diary and Letters,* ed. by Christina Baker (Boston, 1925), p. 12; Henry Bush-Brown to Margaret Lesley, 14 May 1885, Henry Bush-Brown Papers, SSC; Frances Crane to Frank Lillie, 26 August 1894, and Frank to Frances, 20 December 1894, Crane Family Papers, typescript, CHS.

12. Annie Winsor, Notebook, March 1888 and 13 December 1883, Annie Winsor Allen Papers, SL.

13. Ruth Huntington Sessions, *Sixty Odd: A Personal History* (Brattleboro, Vt., 1936), p. 180; Lu Burlingame to Will Adkinson, 8 November 1871, Burlingame–Adkinson Papers, SL; Louisa May Alcott, "Early Marriages," *Ladies' Home Journal,* September 1887, p. 3.

14. Marion Harland, "Are Women to Blame?" [2]p. 630; "Annie" to Harriet Burton, 24 September 1905 [9]; Harry Judson to Madeleine Wallin, 22 May 1896 [1]; Charlotte Perkins Gilman, *The Home* (New York, 1910), p. 270; Richard Cabot to Ella Lyman, 10 February 1892, Ella Lyman Cabot Papers, SL.

15. "Amy" to Harriet Burton, 11 October 1905 [9]; Harriet Forbes to Harriet Burton, n.d. [1905].

16. Poem composed (or copied) by Emily Andrews, c. 1895, Charles McLean Andrews Papers, YL; Lucy Sprague, poem, in Lucy Sprague Mitchell, *Two Lives: The Story of Wesley Clair Mitchell and Myself* (New York, 1953), p. 211.

17. Caroline Drayton, Diary, 29 February 1909, and 30 January and 8 and 9 March 1908, Caroline Drayton Phillips Papers, SL.

An occasional man expressed his desire for a child: see Walter Fisher to Katharine Dummer, 4 August 1915, Dummer Family Papers, SL; and Chester Alan Arthur III to Charlotte Wilson, 19 December 1920, Chester Alan Arthur Papers, LC.

18. Caroline Drayton, Diary, 18 June 1908 and 27 May 1906 [17]; Mary Bulkley, "Mother, Grandmother, and Me," typescript, SL.

There is some controversy among historians about whether the risks of childbirth were in fact declining in the late nineteenth century. Joyce Antler and Daniel M. Fox argue that, in spite of "spectacular improvements in medical science and technology" between 1890 and 1915, the death rate from "causes incidental to bearing children . . . showed no improvement" ("The Movement toward a Safe Maternity: Physician Accountability in New York City, 1915–1940," *BHM* 50 [1976]: 570). Edward Shorter has recently claimed that because the statistics "were crammed with abortion deaths, they gave a false picture of full-term sepsis mortality," and that the rate of infection and with it the rate of sepsis mortality was dramatically reduced in both home births and hospitals around 1900 (*A History of Women's Bodies* [New York, 1982], pp. 130–35).
19. Dr. William Acton, quoted in Carl Degler, *At Odds: Women and the Family from the Revolution to the Present* (New York, 1980), p. 250.

For an analysis of the marital education literature, see Michael Gordon, "From an Unfortunate Necessity to a Cult of Mutual Orgasm: Sex in American Marital Education Literature," in James Henslin, ed. *Studies in the Sociology of Sex* (New York, 1971), pp. 53–77.
20. Alice Stockham, *Tokology: A Book for Every Woman* (Chicago, 1887), pp. 151–52.
21. *The Mosher Survey: Sexual Attitudes of 45 Victorian Women*, ed. by James Ma-Hood and Kristine Wenburg (New York, 1980). Mosher's respondents were an unusually well-educated group (thirty-four attended college or normal school); but Degler believes that, from a demographic point of view, they are a representative sample (*At Odds* [19], p. 262). At least one historian has drawn inferences about the husbands of the women surveyed by Clelia Mosher: see Rosalind Rosenberg, *Beyond Separate Spheres: Intellectual Roots of Modern Feminism* (New Haven, 1982), p. 185.
22. These figures differ slightly from Degler's. The way the questions are phrased and the lack of clarity in the answers make it difficult to quantify the results with any precision. Different interpretations can be supported. Degler's analysis of the Mosher Survey concludes that "sexual expression was a part of healthy living and frequently a joy" for the middle-class married women who responded to the questionnaire; see "What Ought to Be and What Was: Women's Sexuality in the Nineteenth Century," in Michael Gordon, ed. *The American Family in Social Historical Perspective*, 2nd ed. (New York, 1978), p. 419. For a less sanguine interpretation, see Rosenberg, *Beyond Separate Spheres* [21], pp. 184–87.
23. Mosher Survey [21], no. 22; Frances Parkinson Keyes, *All Flags Flying: Reminiscences* (New York, 1970), p. 7.
24. Keyes, *All Flags* [23], p. 7.
25. *Mosher Survey* [21], nos. 22, 35, 18, 33; Mary Bulkley, "Mother" [18], p. 67.
26. Sylvanus Stall, *What a Young Husband Ought to Know* (Philadelphia, 1907), p. 126; Mosher Survey [21], nos. 18, 33.
27. *Mosher Survey* [21]; see, for example, nos. 11, 26, and 28.
28. On the explicit quality of the early nineteenth century works, see Degler, *At Odds* [19], p. 252. Eliza Bisbee Duffey, *What Women Should Know: A Woman's Book About Women* (Philadelphia, 1873); Henry Chavasse, *Advice to a Wife on the*

Management of Her Own Health (Toronto, 1879); Mrs. P.B. Sarr, M.D. *Maternity: A Book for Every Wife and Mother* (Chicago, 1891); Stockham's *Tokology* [20]; and Hayden Brown's *Advice to Single Women* (London, 1907), all treat intercourse obliquely—or not at all. G. L. Austin, *Perils of American Women or a Doctor's Talk with Maiden, Wife and Mother* (Boston, 1883) is a notable exception. For a systematic discussion of this literature, see John S. Haller, Jr., "From Maidenhood to Menopause: Sex Education for Women in Victorian America," *JPC* 6 (1 [summer 1972]): 49–70. There is, unfortunately, no comparative analysis of what *men* were taught about sexuality in the nineteenth century.
29. *Mosher Survey* [21], nos. 22, 36.

For examples of explicit discussion of contraception and menstruation, see Helen Swett to Charles Ernest Schwartz, 30 July 1899, Charles Ernest Schwartz Papers, UCB; Oakes Ames to Blanche Ames, 2 May 1900, Ames Family Papers, SSC; Dorothy Kirchwey to LaRue Brown, 27 October 1915, and LaRue to Dorothy, 27 October 1915, Dorothy Kirchwey Brown Papers, SL.
30. Mary Wood-Allen, *Ideal Married Life: A Book for all Husbands and Wives* (New York, 1901), p. 213; Helen Swett to Charles Ernest Schwartz, 2 July 1899 [29].
31. Maud Rittenhouse, Diary, 25 November 1894, in Isabelle Rittenhouse Mayne, *Maud*, ed. by Richard Lee Strout (New York, 1939), p. 583.
32. Helen Swett to Charles Ernest Schwartz, 2 July 1899 [29].
33. Helen Swett to Charles Ernest Schwartz, 16 June and 18 and 22 October 1899.
34. Helen Swett to Charles Ernest Schwartz, 16 June and 2 July 1899.
35. Linda Gordon analyzes the early twentieth century race-suicide controversy at length in *Woman's Body, Woman's Right: Birth Control in America* (New York, 1977), chap. 7, passim.
36. Barbara Strachey, *Remarkable Relations: The Story of The Pearsall Smith Women* (New York, 1982), p. 103.
37. Fass, *The Damned* [8] pp. 69–71; L. Gordon, *Woman's Body* [35], pp. 60, 68, 171; M. Gordon, "Marital Education Literature" [19], pp. 60–64; Christina Simmons, "Purity Rejected: The New Sexual Freedom of the Twenties," unpublished paper, Berkshire Conference, 1976, p. 8.
38. Ethel Sturges Dummer to Mrs. Fisher, 28 June 1915 [probably never sent], Dummer Family Papers, SL; Simmons, "Purity" [37], p. 9; William Lee Howard, *Facts for the Married* (New York, 1912), and William J. Robinson, *Woman and Her Sex and Love Life* (New York, 1917), both quoted in M. Gordon, "Marital Education Literature" [19], pp. 60–61.
39. John Burnham, "The Progressive Era Revolution in American Attitudes toward Sex," *JAH* 59 (4 [1973]): 907; James R. McGovern, "Women's Manners and Morals Before World War I," *JAH*, 55 (3 [1968]): p. 316.
40. Agnes Repplier, "The Repeal of Reticence," *Atlantic Monthly* 113, March 1914, pp. 301, 298.
41. Robert Latou Dickinson, *A Thousand Marriages: A Medical Study of Sex Adjustment* (Baltimore, 1931), p. 13.
42. *Sherwood Anderson's Memoirs*, ed. by Ray Lewis White (Chapel Hill, N.C., 1969), p. 343.

43. LaRue Brown to Dorothy Kirchwey, 16 October 1915 [29].

44. Dorothy Kirchwey to LaRue Brown, 4 and 17 October 1915 [29].

45. Alice Preston, "The Things of Girls," *Ladies' Home Journal*, March 1905, p. 26; Howard Taylor Ricketts to Myra Tubbs, 8 November 1897, Howard Taylor Ricketts Papers, UCL.

46. Frances Crane to Frank Lillie, 30 October 1894 [11]; Katharine Dummer to Walter Fisher, 7 May 1915 [17].

47. Richard Cabot to Francis Curtis, n.d. [1886], Richard Cabot Papers, HUA.

48. On the trend toward more paternal involvement in child rearing, see Fass, *The Damned* [8], pp. 86–87; and E. Anthony Rotundo, "Manhood in America: Middle-Class Masculinity in America" (unpublished Ph.D. dissertation, Brandeis University, 1982), pp. 338–47.

49. Susan Strassen's *Never Done: A History of American Housework* (New York, 1982) and Ruth Schwartz Cowan's *More Work for Mother* (New York, 1983) are the best studies of these changes in domestic technology and routine.

50. Daniel Scott Smith, "Family Limitation, Sexual Control, and Domestic Feminism in Victorian America," in *Clio's Consciousness Raised*, ed. by Mary Hartman and Lois Banner (New York, 1974), p. 122; Fass, *The Damned* [8], pp. 60–63, 389 [table C].

51. Henry Canby, *The Age of Confidence: Life in the Nineties* (New York, 1934), p. 51.

52. Mary Elliott to John Harold Foster, 29 March 1915, John Harold Foster Papers, NHHS; Marguerite Thompson to William Zorach, 6 June 1912, William Zorach Papers, LC.

53. Marguerite Thompson to William Zorach, 6 June 1912; Mary Elliott to John Harold Foster, 14 April 1915 [52]; Katharine Dummer to Walter Fisher, 5 May 1915 [17].

54. Keyes, *Flags Flying* [23], p. 5.

55. Christina Simmons has insightfully analyzed the process whereby "sexuality became the new basis of the conjugal bond" ("Purity Rejected" [37], p. 21).

56. J. Franklin Jameson to Sara Elwell, 12 March 1893, J. Franklin Jameson Papers, LC; William McCormick to Katharine Merrill [25 August 1925], PC.

57. Helen Swett to Charles Ernest Schwartz, 9 October 1899 [29].

58. Walter Fisher to Katharine Dummer, 4 August 1915 [17]; Oakes Ames to Blanche Ames, 5 February 1900 [29]; Blanche Ames, Diary, 16 January 1900; Oakes to Blanche, 6 and 5 February 1900.

59. Oakes Ames to Blanche Ames, 5 February 1900 [29].

60. Helen Gilman Noyes to William A. Brown, 7 July 1891 [4]; Oakes Ames to Blanche Ames, 28 February 1900 [29]; Harry Pierce to Libbie Vinton, n.d. [1875], Pierce–Krull Papers, ISL.

61. Helen Gilman Noyes to William A. Brown, 31 July 1891 [4]; Marion Watrous to James R. Angell, 14 February 1892 [10].

62. Blanche Ames, Diary, 3 January 1900 [29]; Dorothy Kirchwey to LaRue Brown, 2 November 1915 [29].

63. Helen Gilman Noyes to William A. Brown, 21 July 1891 [4]; Blanche Ames, Diary, 3 January 1900 [29].

64. Maud Rittenhouse, Diary, 25 September 1885 in *Maud* [31], p. 359.

65. For two examples of this pattern, see Ella Lyman to her mother, 28 February 1894 [14]; and Eugenie Homer to Oliver Emerson, 9 November 1895 [4].
66. See Thora Claney to Sophie Claney, 8 February 1892, CHS.
67. William Allen White, *Autobiography* (New York, 1946), p. 241; Florence Hemsley to William Halsey Wood, 10 July 1889, William Halsey Wood Papers, N-YHS.
68. Julia Finch to Cass Gilbert, 24 April 1887, Cass Gilbert Papers, LC; Oakes Ames to Blanche Ames, 28 February 21 April, and 21, 9, and 7 May 1900 [29].
69. Oakes Ames to Blanche Ames, 7 May 1900 [29].
70. Mary Elliott to John Harold Foster, 18 March 1915 [52].
71. Mary Elliott to John Harold Foster, 8 May 1915 [52]; LaRue Brown to Dorothy Kirchwey, 25 October 1915 [29].
72. Mary Elliott to John Harold Foster, 16 February 1915 [52]; Florence Hemsley to William Halsey Wood, 1 November 1889 [67]; "Maggie" to her sister, 5 June 1895, Porter-Griffin Papers, ISL; Hutchins Hapgood, *A Victorian in the Modern World* (New York, 1939), p. 161.
73. Howard Taylor Ricketts to Myra Tubbs, 13 November 1899 [45]; Helen Swett to Charles Ernest Schwartz, 30 July 1899 [29].
74. For an insightful discussion of how middle-class husbands and wives dealt with the process of home furnishing between 1880 and 1920, see Joan M. Seidl, "Consumers' Choices: Furnishing Middle-Class Homes," *Minnesota History* 48 (5 [Spring 1983]): 182–97.
75. Mary Elliott to John Harold Foster, 12 May and 28 April 1915 [52].
76. Helen James Sommers to Cornelia James Cannon, 17 May and 6 September 1919, Frances Haynes James and Family Papers, MNHS.
77. Walter Teller Post to his father, 20 July 1894, Walter Teller Post Papers, MNHS. I am grateful to Joan M. Seidl for bringing this collection and the James Papers to my attention.
78. Charles Andrews to Elizabeth Andrews, 24 June 1895[16].
79. George Napheys, *The Physical Life of Woman: Advice to the Maiden, Wife and Mother* (Philadelphia, 1871), p. 70.
80. For examples of couples who took menstruation into account in making wedding plans, see Dorothy Kirchwey to LaRue Brown, 27 October 1915 [29]; Charlotte Wilson to Chester A. Arthur III, 15 May 1922 [17]; and Rebekah Van Waters to her mother, 14 January 1923, Miriam Van Waters Papers, SL.
81. Wood-Allen, *Ideal Married Life*, [30], p. 47. Her solution was for newlyweds to return to work immediately after the wedding.
82. Napheys, *Physical Life* [79], p. 69; Duffey, *What Women Should Know* [28], p. 101; Stall, *Young Husband* [26], p. 135; Charles Rosenberg, "Sexuality, Class, and Role in Nineteenth-Century America," *AQ* 25 (2 [1973]): 140.

Rosenberg asserts that the marriage night was "an institutionalized trauma for the pure of both sexes." There is no doubt that it appeared that way in the prescriptive literature, right through the nineteenth century; but whether in fact most couples' experience was traumatic is another matter and one for which there is, understandably, little evidence.
83. Waldo Leland to Gertrude Dennis, 1 March 1904, Waldo Leland Papers, LC; Wood-Allen, *Ideal Married Life* [30], p. 43.

84. Gertrude Foster to Raymond Brown, n.d. [1 August 1893] [9]; Raymond to Gertrude, n.d. [3 August 1893]; Waldo Leland to Gertrude Dennis, 7 and 18 April 1904 [83].
85. Gordon, *Woman's Body* [35], p. 137.
86. Ibid., p. 179.
87. Rotundo found that middle-class marriages in the late nineteenth and twentieth centuries were more intimate: "A close, engaging relationship with a wife took on greater and greater importance in men's descriptions of their marriages" ("Manhood in America" [48], pp. 277–79).
88. Mary Hallock Foote to Helena Gilder, 18 June 1876, Hague Collection, HL.

CHAPTER 9. "ALMOST A REVOLUTION"

1. Samuel Harman Lowrie, "Dating Theories and Student Responses," *ASR* 16 (3 [June 1951]): 340.
2. For two examples of content analysis of the popular song as a measure of changes in courtship, see Donald Horton, "The Dialogue of Courtship in Popular Songs," *AJS* 62 (May 1957): 569–78; and James T. Carey, "Changing Courtship Patterns in the Popular Song," *AJS* 74 (1969): 720–31. The Lynds suggested that there was a relationship between popular songs and courtship habits in Middletown in the 1920s; see Robert S. and Helen Merrell Lynd, *Middletown: A Study in Modern American Culture* (New York, 1929), p. 138, n. 14.
3. U. S. Census, Current Population Reports, "Marital Status and Living Arrangements," series P-20, no. 365, March 1980, pp. 1–2; Andrew J. Cherlin, *Marriage Divorce Remarriage* (Cambridge, Mass., 1981), Figures 1.1, 1.2; Donald J. Bogue, *The Population of the United States* (Glencoe, Ill. 1959), p. 215.
   Related changes that occurred in the 1940s were the increasing independence of the transition to marriage from the transition to labor force participation and from parenthood; and the sharp reduction in the spread of ages at which Americans married. For a detailed examination of these phenomena, see John Modell, Frank Furstenberg, Jr., and Douglas Strong, "The Timing of Marriage in the Transition to Adulthood: Continuity and Change, 1860–1975," in John Demos and Sarane Spence Boocock, eds. *Turning Points*, supplement to *AJS* 84 (1978): S122–47. Here, and elsewhere in this chapter, the figures apply only to whites. Cherlin discusses the similarities and differences in the demographic patterns of the black and white populations (*Marriage*, chap. 4, passim).
4. Cherlin, *Marriage* [3], chap. 1, passim.
5. Frederick Lewis Allen, *Only Yesterday: An Informal History of the 1920s* (New York, 1931; Perennial Library ed. 1964), p. 73. For the classic statement of the changes under way in American life before the First World War, see Henry F. May, *The End of American Innocence* (New York, 1959), pp. 138–39, 266–67.
6. Lynd and Lynd, *Middletown* [2], p. 139
7. Paula Fass, *The Damned and the Beautiful: American Youth in the 1920s* (New York, 1977), p. 262. While Fass has a tendency to overgeneralize from the college

youth who are the focus of her book, *The Damned and the Beautiful* is an indispensable resource to anyone interested in the experience of young Americans during the 1920s.

8. Alfred C. Kinsey, et al., *Sexual Behavior in the Human Female* [hereafter cited as *SBHF*] (Philadelphia, 1953), p. 231.

9. John Modell, "Dating Becomes the Way of American Youth," in *Essays on the Family and Historical Change*, ed. by Leslie Page Moch and Gary D. Stark (College Station, Tex., 1983), p.102; Lynd and Lynd, *Middletown* [2], p. 138. I am grateful to Professor Modell for sharing this essay with me before publication.

10. Willard Waller, "The Rating and Dating Complex," *ASR* 2 (1937): 729, 728, 730. Christopher Lasch discusses the challenge Waller presented to sociological orthodoxy in the 1920s and 1930s; see *Haven in a Heartless World* (New York, 1977), pp. 50–55.

11. Michael Gordon, "Was Waller Ever Right? The Rating and Dating Complex Reconsidered," *JMF* 43 (1 [February 1981]): 69, n. 3.

12. Modell argues persuasively that Fass's account of the development of dating needs to be revised to take into account the importance of peer-group activities, especially dating, on the high school level. He points out that "high schools had almost even sex ratios—a demography far more conducive to widespread dating than that in college" ("Dating" [9], p. 104).

13. Fass, *The Damned* [7], pp. 175, 200, 153; Gordon, "Was Waller Ever Right" [11]: 73.

14. Louise Dutton, *Going Together* (Indianapolis, Ind., 1923), pp. 20–21.

15. Robert Angell, *The Campus: A Study of Contemporary Undergraduate Life in the American University* (New York, 1928), pp. 165–69; Lynd and Lynd, *Middletown* [2], p. 134.

16. Susan Allen Toth, *Blooming: A Small Town Girlhood* (Boston, 1981), p. 52.

17. Modell, "Dating" [9], p. 106.

18. Lewis Erenberg, *Steppin' Out: New York Nightlife and the Transformation of American Culture, 1890–1930* (Westport, Conn., 1981), pp. 154–55; Angell, *Campus* [15], p. 169; Fass, *The Damned* [7], p. 196.

19. Elaine Tyler May, *Great Expectations: Marriage and Divorce in Post-Victorian America* (Chicago, 1980), p. 69. Erenberg examines the Castle phenomenon at length in *Steppin' Out* [18], pp. 146–76.

20. Fass, *The Damned* [7], p. 206; Lynd and Lynd, *Middletown* [2], pp. 263–64.

Children unaccompanied by a parent accounted for the largest share of the movie audience in Middletown, prompting the Lynds to wonder about the "decentralizing tendency of the movies upon the family" (p. 265).

21. Lynd and Lynd, *Middletown* [2], pp. 267, 139, 268; Angell, *Campus* [15], p. 169; May, *Great Expectations* [19], p. 69.

The Lynds suggested that the "sex adventure" magazines which were widely read in Middletown had some of the same effects as the movies (pp. 241–42). For a discussion of the evolution of movies as a reflection of and stimulus to middle-class values, see Lary May, *Screening Out the Past: The Birth of Mass Culture and the Motion Picture Industry, 1896–1929* (New York, 1980).

22. Lynd and Lynd, *Middletown* [2], pp. 258, 253.

23. Ibid., p. 137.

24. Ibid., p. 137; Angell, *Campus* [15], p. 169.

25. Katharine Merrill to William McCormick, 25 August, 1923, PC; Dorothy Dunbar Bromley and Florence Haxton Britten, *Youth and Sex: A Study of 1300 College Students* (New York, 1938), p. 11.

26. Angell, *Campus* [15], p. 169; Floyd Dell, *Love in the Machine Age* (New York, 1930), p. 166. According to Modell, petting in the 1920s "was almost universal, in the sense that all daters petted at some time, but not in the sense that all couples petted." ("Dating" [9], p. 100).

27. Alfred Kinsey, Wardell B. Pomeroy, and Clyde E. Martin, *Sexual Behavior in the Human Male* [hereafter cited as *SBHM*] (Philadelphia, 1948), p. 228.

28. Geraldine Frances Smith, "Certain Aspects of the Sex Life of the Adolescent Girl," *JAP* (September 1924) 348–49; *SBHF* [8], pp. 298–301; *SBHM* [27], p. 406.

29. Lynd and Lynd, *Middletown* [2], pp. 138–39; Fass, *The Damned* [7], pp. 266–69.

30. Fass, *The Damned* [7], pp. 266, 278, 268; Phyllis Blanchard and Carlyn Manasses, *New Girls for Old* (New York, 1930), pp. 69, 73, 75; Walter Buck, "A Measurement of Changes in Attitudes and Interests of University Students over a Ten-Year Period," *JASP* 31 (1936): 14.

31. Blanchard and Manasses, *New Girls* [30], p. 71; Fass, *The Damned* [7], pp. 273, 274, 276.

32. Robert R. Bell and Jack V. Buerkle, "Mother and Daughter Attitudes to Premarital Sexual Behavior," *MFL* 23 (1961): 391. This statement was written about the 1950s, but it is an accurate description of a process that began in the 1920s and 1930s.

33. *SBHF* [8], table 83, figure 50, p. 339; Fass, *The Damned* [7], p. 455, n. 28; SBHM [27], pp. 410–13.

34. SBHF [8], p. 299; Robert S. Lynd and Helen Merrell Lynd, *Middletown in Transition: A Study in Cultural Conflicts* (New York, 1937), p. 170; Fass, *The Damned* [7], p. 271.

35. Lynd and Lynd, *Middletown in Transition* [34], p. 170.

36. Bromley and Britten, *Youth and Sex*, [25], pp. 15–16; Theodore Newcomb, "Recent Changes in Attitudes toward Sex and Marriage," *ASR* 2 (1937): 667, 662; "Youth in College," *Fortune* 13, 3 June 1936, p. 101.

Michael Gordon has tried to explain the apparent contradictions between the views of 1930s campus life offered by Waller and Newcomb; see "Was Waller Ever Right?" [11]: 68–69.

37. Fass, *The Damned* [7], p. 180; "Youth in College" [36], p. 101; Calvin B. Lee, *Campus USA 1900–1970: Changing Styles in Undergraduate Life* (New York, 1970), p. 48.

38. Paul Glick and Hugh Carter, *Marriage and Divorce: A Social and Economic Study* (Cambridge, Mass., 1970), p. 41.

39. U.S. Census, Current Population Reports, "Statistical Portrait of Women in the United States: 1978," series P–23, no. 100, p. 24; Cherlin, *Marriage* [3], p. 9.

40. Lee, *Campus USA* [37], p. 76; "Education for War," *Fortune*, December 1942, p. 146; Winston Ehrmann, *Premarital Dating Behavior* (New York, 1959), p. 76.

41. *SBHF* [8], p. 234; *SBHM* [27], pp. 406, 539, 541.

42. *SBHM* [27], pp. 541, 543–44.
43. Lowrie, "Dating Theories" [1]: 337. Lowrie takes a pro-dating position. He attacks the negative view of dating offered by Waller and others by showing that students themselves emphasized the learning rather than the thrill-seeking aspects of dating behavior.
44. Ira Reiss, "Sexual Codes in Teen-Age Culture," *AAAPSS* (November 1961): 54; Charles W. Cole, "American Youth Goes Monogamous," *Harper's Magazine*, March 1957, p. 32. What Cole missed in the 1950s approach to dating are precisely those elements that Willard Waller found so disturbing in the 1930s.
45. Cole, "American Youth," p. 32.
Co-residence with parents was, however, not a popular strategy. After 1947, the "prevalence of family extension declined abruptly" (Modell, Furstenberg, and Strong, "Timing of Marriage" [3], pp. S136–37).
46. Mildred Gilman, "Why They Can't Wait to Wed," *Parents Magazine*, November 1958, p. 46; David Riesman, "Permissiveness and Sex Roles," *MFL* (August 1959): 21.
Elaine Tyler May has recently suggested that one of the attractions of early marriage in the 1950s was the containment of sexuality which, like communism and atomic war, threatened American stability and order ("Explosive Issues: Sex, Women, and the Bomb in Post-War America," unpublished paper, American Historical Association, December 1982). The couples who married during this period were the "only cohorts in the last hundred years to show a substantial, sustained shortfall in their lifetime levels of divorce": that is, they had a lower rate of divorce than one would expect from the long-term trends (see Cherlin, *Marriage* [3], p. 25).
47. Ehrmann, *Premarital Dating* [40], p. 268; Phyllis McGinley, "The Fearful Aspect of Too-Early Dating," *Good Housekeeping*, April 1956, pp. 60–61, 287–88.
Ira Reiss attributed this early socialization to the spread of junior high schools: "The anticipatory socialization of sex games like 'spin the bottle, . . . begins prior to junior high levels and thus prepares students for dating in junior high" ("Sexual Codes" [44], p. 54, n. 3).
48. Jesse Bernard, Helen E. Buchanan, and William M. Smith, Jr., *Dating, Mating and Marriage* (Cleveland, Oh. 1958), pp. 34, 25–28. The Bernard book is unusual among marriage and family texts in that it takes a "documentary case approach." The "informants" are unidentified college students, presumably enrolled in the authors' courses.
49. Ibid., pp. 27–28; Toth, *Blooming* [15], p. 49.
50. Godfrey Hodgson, *America in Our Time* (New York, 1978), pp. 53–54; *Historical Statistics of the United States from Colonial Times to 1970*, Bicentennial Edition (Washington, D.C., 1975), part I, p. 383.
51. Cole, "American Youth" [44], pp. 30, 33; Nora Johnson, "Sex and the College Girl," *Atlantic*, November 1959, pp. 57–58.
52. Bernard, Buchanan, and Smith, *Dating,* [48], p. 43.
53. Reiss, "Sexual Codes" [44], pp. 55, 59; Johnson, "College Girl" [51], pp. 57, 59, 60.
54. Ehrmann, *Premarital Dating* [40], p. 36, tables 1.6, 1.7; Robert R. Bell and

Jay B. Chaskes, "Premarital Sexual Experience among Coeds, 1958–1968," *JMF* 32 (1 [February 1970]): 83.

Ehrmann pointed out the "curious fact [that] there exist more quantitative data about the incidence rates of coitus, the most taboo of premarital heterosexual activities, than about kissing and hugging, the most socially acceptable" (p. 32).

55. Reiss, "Sexual Codes" [44], 55; Bernard, Buchanan, and Smith, *Dating* [48], p. 58. Reiss's *Premarital Sexual Standards in America* (Glencoe, Ill., 1961) is a detailed inquiry into the values underlying sexual standards in America.

56. Reiss, "Sexual Codes" [44], 59; Ehrmann, *Premarital Dating* [40], p. 270.

57. "Shaping the 60s . . . Foreshadowing the 70s," *Ladies' Home Journal,* January 1962, pp. 30, 73.

58. Ibid., p. 30.

59. Ehrmann, *Premarital Dating* [40], p. 269. All of these distinctions prompted Ehrmann to suggest that there were "distinct male and female subcultures" in the world of American youth; see pp. 270–77, for his discussion of this idea.

60. Edwin O. Smigel and Rita Seiden, "Decline and Fall of the Double Standard," *AAAPSS* 376 (March 1968): 12; Gilbert R. Kaats and Keith E. Davis, "The Dynamics of Sexual Behavior of College Students," *JMF* 32 (3 [August 1970]: 391; Ira Reiss, "The Sexual Renaissance: A Summary and Analysis," *JSI* 22 (1966): 126.

61. Reiss, "Sexual Renaissance" [60]: 126; Morton Hunt, *Sex in the 70s* (Chicago, 1974), p. 149.

62. J. Richard Udry, Karl E. Bauman, and Naomi M. Morris, "Changes in Premarital Coital Experience of Recent Decade-of-Birth Cohorts of American Women," *JMF* 37 (4 [November 1975]): 784; Kenneth L. Cannon and Richard Long, "Premarital Sexual Behavior in the 60s," *JMF* 33 (1 [February 1971]): 40; Kaats and Davis, "Dynamics" [60], 391.

63. Reiss, "Sexual Codes" [44]: 58–59; Bell and Chaskes, "Premarital Sexual Experience" [54]: 82–83; Cannon and Long, "Premarital Sexual Behavior" [62]: 41; Reiss, "Sexual Rennaissance" [60]: 126.

64. Hunt, *Sex in the 70s* [61], p. 21; Smigel and Seiden, "Decline and Fall" [60]: 14; Robert C. Sorensen, *Adolescent Sexuality in Contemporary America* (New York, 1973), pp. 341, 242, 100.

Sorensen suggests that his subjects' lack of interest in marriage was a reflection of the developmental nature of adolescence. Adolescents do not "seek lifelong companionship and financial security in their immediate post-adolescent life. They are moving away from their own family ties, and few seek to replace them with new ones. . . . Commitment to the future is not to their liking, and when most adolescents think of marriage, they think of commitment" (p. 345). While this argument is sensible, it fails to explain the phenomenon of teenage pregnancy—and parenthood.

65. Sorenson, *Adolescent Sexuality* [64], p. 100; Hunt, *Sex in the 70s* [61], pp. 151–53.

66. Sally Helgesen, "Your Right to Say No," *Seventeen*, August 1981, pp. 284–85; Melvin Zelnik and Jon F. Kantner, "Sexual Activity, Contraceptive Use and Pregnancy among Metropolitan-Area Teenagers," *FPP* 12 (5 [September/October 1980]): 230–31.

67. See Zelnik and Kantner, "Sexual Activity" [66], p. 237.

68. *New York Times*, 2 January 1983, p. A:1.

69. Arno Karlen, "Unmarried Marrieds on Campus," *New York Times Magazine*, 26 January 1969, p. 77; U.S. Census, "Marital Status" [3], p. 1; Paul Glick and Graham B. Spanier, "Married and Unmarried Cohabition in the United States," *JMF* 42 (1 [February 1980]): 20–21.

Some of this increase is the result of the absolute increase in the numbers of young adults in the population and of greater frankness in reporting; but all analysts agree that while it may be exaggerated by the statistics, the real magnitude of the change is very great.

70. Karlen, "Unmarrieds" [69], p. 78; Glick and Spanier, "Married and Unmarried Cohabitation" [69], 21; Barbara J. Risman et al., "Living Together in College: Implications for Courtship," *JMF* 43 (1 [February 1981]): 82.

71. Risman et al., found some evidence that cohabiting couples were more likely to have smaller and, presumably, less formal weddings than their non-cohabiting counterparts ("Living Together" [70], p. 82).

72. "Big Weddings Are Back," *McCall's*, April 1981, pp. 124–34; Marcia Seligson, *The Eternal Bliss Machine: America's Way of Wedding* (New York, 1973), p. 4; *New York Times*, 26 October 1980, p. C:19; *New York Times*, 18 May 1982, p. B:2.

73. Lorenzo Dow, "Reflections on Matrimony," in Peggy Dow, *Vicissitudes in the Wilderness* (Norwich, Conn., 1833), p. 156; Cherlin, *Marriage* [3], pp. 22–23; Arthur J. Norton and Paul C. Glick, "Marital Instability in America: Past, Present, and Future," in *Divorce and Separation*, ed. by George Levinger and Oliver C. Moles (New York, 1979), p. 13.

74. Walter W. Price to James Lee Laidlaw, 8 September 1905, Harriet Burton Laidlaw Papers, SL.

INDEX

363

Index

Index

Index

Index

Index

Index

Riesman, David, 302
Ring: engagement, 161–62, 269, 310; wedding, 170, 170n, 340n63
Ring, Alice, 154
Rittenhouse, Laura, 218
Rittenhouse, Maud: views of men, 185–86, 192–93; courtship, 195, 196, 197; relationship with mother, 217–18, 258n; engagement, 272
Rittenhouse, Wood, 216
Robbins, Anne, 67n
Rogers, Patty, 49, 50
Romantic love: as condition for marriage, 30, 35; in colonial divorce cases, 31; in colonial magazines, 31; preferred to friendship, 37–38; distrust of, 39–40, 322n43; domination of, 103–10; see also "Falling in love"
Ross, William, 87–90, 99, 124–25, 160
Rotch, Eliza, 81

Saturday Evening Post, 293
Savage, Ellen, 25, 49, 120
Schwartz, Charles Ernest, 186, 258–59, 261, 269
Self-doubt: in women, 65, 67, 70–73, 76, 197–98, 200, 282, 284; in men, 70, 282
"Semidependence": of young men, 27, 68–69; of young women, 27–28, 69
Separation from home: as result of marriage, 56, 67–68, 69–71, 83, 117, 156, 160, 283; difficult for men, 69, 327n25
Separate "spheres": development of, 74, 172; as result of marriage, 75, 94, 148, 172; effect on courtship, 91, 95–96, 107, 110, 114, 194; definition of, 92, 184, 194
Setting up house, 76, 77, 81, 277–80
Sessions, Archie, 217
Sex education, 188n, 256–58
Sex research, 240
Sex roles, 50–51, 91–92, 95–96, 98, 104, 110–13, 183–89; see also Ideals, Images of women
Sexual behavior: evidence of, 45; in early republic, 49, 51–54; at mid-century, 123–30, 134–36; in late nineteenth century, 231–41, 350n90; after 1900, 242–43; among college students, 298, 304–5, 308; see also Bundling, Sexual conflict
Sexual Behavior of the Human Female, 295
Sexual conflict, 52–53, 130, 135–37, 230, 233–41

Sexual fantasy, 122–23, 231, 237
"Sexual revolution," 243, 288, 309, 350n90
Shepard, David, Jr., 24, 49, 120, 319n16
Sherman, Elizabeth, 37, 197
Sibley, Persis, 69, 98, 160, 173, 331n33
Sigourney, Lydia, 104, 144
Simmons, Christina, 188n
Sincerity, 42–43
Single women, 32–33, 251–53, 283
Sitwell, Anna 162
Smith, Abigail, 43n, 48
Smith, Emily, 140, 163, 198
Smith, Erastus, 63
Smith, Ina, 204–5, 208, 209
Smith, John Henry, 124, 125
Smith, Katherine, 109, 110, 113, 159, 160, 164
Smith, Margaret. *See* Bayard, Margaret
Smith, Mary, 259n
Smith, Mary Ann, 105, 145, 146, 247
Smith, Samuel, 67, 69, 70
Smith-Rosenberg, Carroll, 319n14, 329n58, 333n63, 339n30, 342n12
Somers, Harry, 278–79
Songs, 34, 47–48, 286
Sorensen, Robert, 308, 360n64
Sororities: growth of, 211; membership in, 291; and "pinning" ritual, 304n; mentioned, 223
Southern courtship, 318n5, 319n14
Southgate, Eliza, 28, 32, 34, 44
Spooning, 233n, 235, 244, 289n, 295; see also Petting, Sexual behavior
Sprague, Lucy, 199, 225–26, 254
Stall, Sylvanus, 281
Stanton, Elizabeth Cady, 163
Stiles, Henry, 46, 324n66, 324n73
Stockham, Alice, 200, 255
Story, Emma Lou, 232
Swett, Helen, 186, 258–59, 261, 269, 277
Sykes, George, 211, 215, 247
Sympathy, 107, 108, 247

Taylor, Joseph, 99, 151–52, 157, 164, 173
Teaching: men in, 7; women in, 8, 28, 158, 191, 249
Telephone, 181, 209, 223–24
Thompson, Marguerite, 201, 215, 215n, 229, 267
Thorn, Mary, 125, 160

369

Index

Timing of marriage: parents' influence on, 27, 160; as source of conflict, 56, 70–72, 157, 327*n*32; economics of, 57–59; and conception, 71*n*; issue for men, 150–52; effect of family on, 159–60; and sex, 348*n*60

Tocqueville, Alexis, de, 64, 66, 73–74, 91, 145, 146

Tokology, 200, 255

Toth, Susan Allen, 292*n*, 303

Trall, R.T., 141*n*, 142

"Transportation revolution," 10, 82

Treat, Sadie, 233, 248, 249

Trousseau, 166, 166*n*

"True Womanhood": as new ideal, 41, 51, 66, 74; moral superiority of, 42; expectations of, 67, 68, 93, 113, 202; and marriage, 73, 75

Tubbs, Myra, 201, 227–28, 234

Tucker, George, 162

Twin beds, 278*n*

VanHise, Charles, 154, 228

Veblen, Thorstein, 167–68

Vinton, Libbie, 93

Virginity: rate of, 243; importance of, 296, 297

Vought, Lizzie, 121–22, 128–29, 131, 141

Wallin, Madeleine, 190, 194, 211, 246, 247, 248

Ward, Benjamin, 16, 61, 62

Ward, Lester, 120–22, 128–29, 141

Ware, Henry, 65, 67

Waring, Ed, 172, 173

Walker, Evangeline, 196, 219

Waller, Willard, 290, 358*n*36, 359*n*44

Watrous, Marion, 214, 271

Webb, Anna, 163

Webb, Lucy. *See* Hayes, Lucy Webb

Webster, Daniel, 61

Wedding: preparation for, 76, 79, 165, 168, 182, 275; presents, 76, 167–68, 168*n*, 172, 182, 276–77, 340*n*57, 340*n*58; guests, 77–78, 169, 172, 183, 273, 277; ceremony, 78, 79–80, 169, 170, 172, 273; reception, 80, 169, 172, 310; dress, 80, 166, 171, 172, 273, 275–76, 310; scheduling of, 80*n*; trousseau, 166; ring, 170, 340*n*63; veils, 171; conflict with parents about, 274–75; man's role in, 274–75; controlled by mother of the bride, 276

Weld, Theodore, 60

Wells, Kate Gannett, 184, 185

Wheeler, Frances. *See* Keyes, Frances Parkinson

White, Caroline. *See* Barrett, Caroline

White, Daniel, 40, 43

White, William Allen, 216, 216*n*, 219, 273

White, James, 125, 157, 160

Whitridge, W.C., 111

Whittemore, Thomas, 79

Wilder, Mary, 43

Willcocks, Charlotte, 125, 161

Williams, Sarah Chester, 63, 76

Wilson, Annie, 157

Winchester, Susan, 106

Winsor, Annie, 184, 186, 190–94 *passim*, 214

Winsor, Mary, 65, 67

Wood-Allen, Mary, 258, 280, 282

Woman suffrage, 187, 189, 266, 342*n*23

Women's Christian Temperance Union, 184

Women's education, 7, 90–91, 165, 191, 249

Women's Rights, 96–97

World War I, 241, 243, 244, 289

World War II, 286, 299–300, 301

Wright, Ellen, 140

Wright, George, 96–98, 107, 112, 114, 152

Youth and Sex, 295

Zorach, William, 201, 202, 215*n*

170-2 n.c. stuff on wedding rituals &
        domesticity